THE SOCIAL REALITY
OF DEATH

D1261884

THE
SOCIAL REALITY
OF DEATH
DEATH IN
CONTEMPORARY AMERICA

KATHY CHARMAZ
Sonoma State University

 ADDISON-WESLEY PUBLISHING COMPANY

Reading, Massachusetts • Menlo Park, California
London • Amsterdam • Don Mills, Ontario • Sydney

Library of Congress Cataloging in Publication Data

Charmaz, Kathy, 1939-
   The social reality of death.

   Includes index.
   1. Death--Social aspects--United States.
2. Symbolic interactionism. 3. Social interaction.
4. Grief. I. Title.
HQ1073.5.U6C48   301.11   79-21838
ISBN 0-201-01033-X

ISBN 0-201-01033-X
ABCDEFGHIJ-AL-8987654321

PREFACE

In the four years I have been working on this project, social scientists have increasingly shifted their view of death in American society. As death has been brought into the public arena, their view has changed from a taboo topic to one that is infused with new meanings. Certainly the American rediscovery of death in the past decade has fostered discussion of new ways to view and handle it. Yet, while research and theorizing on the topic has proliferated, the major theoretical stance toward death continues to be fundamentally dominated by psychological and medical points of view. I believe that a theoretical perspective founded in sociological thought raises new questions and challenges earlier assumptions about death.

In this book, I aim to take a fresh look from a sociological perspective at both earlier assumptions and current issues about death and dying. Specifically, the major source of my theoretical perspective is symbolic interactionism. By examining the thoughts, feelings, and actions of the dying and those affected by death from this perspective, we can gain greater insight into the subtle relationships these actors have with each other and, moreover, with death.

Although symbolic interactionism is the approach stressed in this book, it is neither the only intellectual source of ideas nor is it the only viewpoint considered. I have also been influenced by developments in sociological theory over the past decade that question the objectivist stance taken by much of the discipline. In that respect, the phenomenological critique of scientism in traditional social scientific methods has influenced my thinking. Since I aim to take a critical view of society, I have found the recent developments in the Marxist critique of capitalist society to be compelling. More specifically in relation to death, some central assumptions of existentialism have influenced my thinking, particularly the prescription to face death subjectively in order to create meaning in one's life and assume responsibility for one's actions. With these sources of intellectual influence comes a strong moral bias toward a humanistic concern for the individual. I mention these influences because I believe that any analysis rests on a set of assumptions. If readers are aware of the kinds of assumptions made, then they are better able to assess that analysis and put it into perspective.

Consistent with the traditional symbolic interactionist approach, the book's decided emphasis is on self and social interaction. In addition, the analysis reflects the other influences on my thinking as well as the current concern of some interactionists to establish more links between the individual and the social structure.

Throughout the book I have attempted to demonstrate relationships between wider cultural values on which the social structure rests and thoughts and actions of individuals who confront death in their daily lives. In that way, I aim to show the dialectical relationship between individual consciousness and the wider society. Specifically, I argue that in subtle, although pervasive, ways, the values of individualism, independence, and achievement of the Protestant Ethos still play a significant role as individuals grapple with the issues posed by death.

During my study of death and dying, I came to believe that the problems and dilemmas facing those who confront death (including the dying, suicidal, or bereaved) are not so different in kind from those experienced in more ordinary circumstances. Making sense of one's life and one's world, taking control over them, and maintaining meaningful human relations are all problematic in everyday American life. Therefore, the situations of the dying, suicidal, bereaved, and others affected by death are amplifications of the problematic features of everyday life.

Because this work represents a sociological interpretation of topics in the field of death and dying, I have attempted to cover the topics that have raised most concern, particularly in everyday life. While the coverage is not exhaustive, many issues affecting individuals are dealt with, particularly those that have captured the interest of death researchers who analyze direct experience. In some ways this work reflects the current concerns and consciousness of the public and death researchers alike in its coverage. Hence, it covers aspects of the dying process, suicide, and grief in detail, but does not explore in depth meanings and implications of the potential apocalypse of our time, the proliferation of arms and nuclear weapons. In addition, it does not cover the hospice movement thoroughly. While there is much current interest in organizing hospice care at the community level, very little systematic research has been conducted on it to date.

Basically, this work seeks to review, synthesize, and extend current thought on death and dying. Rather than simply summarizing earlier research on death and dying, I develop a sociological analysis of it. Much of the material drawn upon consists of psychological or psychiatric studies; however, I make sociological interpretations of them in order to examine them in a new light. By using these materials, I intend to take a close look at death and dying in everyday worlds to see how these worlds are constructed in social interaction. Hence, questions like these will be raised: What role do wider social values play in the construction of thought, feeling, and action among individuals who confront death? What kinds of death conceptions support common practices for handling it? What do dying, suicide, and bereavement mean to those who are centrally involved? In what ways are the self-images of individuals affected by their experiences with death? What kind of interaction shapes the dying process? How do institutional values affect the thoughts and actions of various participants? In what ways do assumptions about death affect interaction?

Much of what follows is a qualitative description of the ways in which the underlying structure of social life is created and maintained as people with diverse interests interact as they face and handle death. Although the book addresses direct experience, it is not experiential in nature, nor was it intended to be. Instead, it contains analyses of experience. While most of the material consists of analytic description, on occasion I use the material to make theoretical statements on topics of interest to sociologists and other professionals (such as about the self). As a result, the book may be of interest as a resource to the instructors and researchers who use it. But the major audience for whom the book is intended consists of upper-division undergraduate and graduate students. Because my objective is to treat the topic analytically, I have included a chapter on theoretical perspectives. This chapter provides students with background in ways to study and understand death. It should give instructors substance for amplification, application, and debate. Introducing theoretical issues in a course such as death and dying gives the instructor the opportunity to integrate abstract ideas with actual experience. In this way, diverse audiences, who might otherwise remain unexposed to the kinds of questions raised from these perspectives, are further informed of the interplay between theory and experience.

I have grounded the abstract analysis with experience by using materials collected about death in everyday life. Among these materials are vignettes, cases, and actual statements persons made about their experiences. These materials are used to illustrate points rather than to represent any statistically general case. They are taken from the literature, unpublished papers, and data that I have collected over the years from several related studies. Where possible, I have identified the sources. Unidentified material, including examples, is from a personal repertoire of sources which must remain anonymous. Hypothetical examples are pointed out to the reader.

The book is organized as follows: Chapter 1 examines the growing interest in death and relates it to current practices and wider social values.

Chapter 2 explicates major theoretical and philosophical perspectives for studying death. Chapter 3 illuminates conceptions of death held by people in everyday life. Chapter 4 explores the ethical issues born out of the techno-logical prolongation of life. Chapter 5 focuses on dying individuals, with special emphasis given to their role as patients. In contrast, Chapter 6 focuses on workers who are involved with dying and bereaved. Chapter 7 also emphasizes the worker, but addresses those whose work with death is of an extraordinary nature, such as the combat soldier. Chapter 8 deals with the issue of suicide, primarily from the vantagepoint of the experiencing self. Chapter 9 also concentrates on the self but does so in the context of experiencing grief. The final chapter raises questions and offers ideas about the future of death.

Because both my ideas and mode of analysis reflect my intellectual heritage, I owe an obvious debt to Anselm L. Strauss and Barney G. Glaser. Specifically, I wish to express my appreciation to Patrick L. Biernacki, Noel Byrne, Loraine P. Calkins, Daniel L. Haytin, Maxine J. Haytin, Michael P. Lerner, Lyn H. Lofland, A. Richard Rizzo, Lynn Roberts, and Harvey Segal for reading drafts of specific chapters. I have especially benefited from conver-sations about the topic with Patrick L. Biernacki and Lyn H. Lofland, whose insightful reflections always stimulated my thinking. Also, I am grateful to Celeste Durrum, Leslie Hoffman, and Julia Winters for their help in preparing the manuscript. Last, I wish to give George Abbott, Robert Drake, and Stanley Evans from the Addison-Wesley Publishing Company a note of thanks.

Rohnert Park, California   K.C.
February 1979

CONTENTS

CHAPTER ONE

THE REALITY OF DEATH

She was still living with my sister and she had a convulsion and my sister said that it was just horrible in the car and she had to rush my mother to the hospital. And I said, "Susan, why didn't you just put her to bed and just let her die?" And my sister said, [with shock] "Oh, Alice! I couldn't do that; I have to—for my own conscience—I have to do everything I can to save her." And I thought, "Susan, she's dying, let her die, why put this woman through all this?" She didn't know what was happening to her by that time. Why not just let her die? But I knew my sister had to do it.

In an interview I conducted with her, a 40-year-old woman recounted this experience about the death of her mother. The dilemma of extending an already lengthy dying process or choosing to allow death to occur earlier is common. The reality of death poses many such dilemmas to those who confront it. Although the face of death takes many forms in contemporary society, and responses to it are varied, common problems and patterned responses to them are discernible. A more thorough discussion of this woman's story will illuminate some of these problems and responses.

In this case, both of the woman's parents were dying almost simultaneously, as they succumbed within four months of each other. Because of earlier severe heart disease, her father, formerly a truckdriver, had been forced to retire early. Her mother, a shy, passive, and dependent woman who married at 17, had devoted her life to caring for her husband and daughters. This working-class couple had led a quiet, insular life, although Alice describes her father as a difficult person to get along with despite her mother's lifelong efforts to avoid any unpleasantness or argument with him. Her mother's condition gradually deteriorated as her lung cancer spread to the brain and throughout her body. Alice portrayed her parents' responses to their respective illnesses in this way:

1

After the heart attack I think he was resigned to the fact that he was going to die of a heart attack soon. He was doing everything that he was supposed to do. The doctors told him that if he lost weight, if he watched his diet, if he exercised mildly, if he did all the right things, he could prolong his life. And I think he knew that. But it wasn't going to save him. He was more of a realist than my mother was.

. . . Her response was that she believed in the doctors when they said that there might be a cure for cancer. My father always knew that he was going to die, but my mother always knew it but never talked about it.

Alice surmised that her father's death would precede her mother's and she became more involved with him in his final months after a lifetime of animosity. She related:

My father and I had conversations the last two years before my mother died and before he died; he, too, didn't like to talk about things but not for the same reasons my mother didn't. My father was just a private person. He handled what he had to do privately until I'd say the last three years. . . . [Once] we were picking beans and he said, "Do you know how hard it is for me to sleep in the same bed with your mother dying, listening to her dying?" And I thought—we talked for quite a while about that— and I thought then and there, "When the chips are down, I have a feeling that my father is going to die first." This was because my mother took care of my father all of his life. She met all of his physical, emotional needs—all of them were met by this woman.

Despite her increasing deterioration, Alice's mother took care of her father until three months before he died. Because her father was a disabled Teamster, her mother was eligible for some nursing assistance for herself while he was alive. Alice appreciatively described the emotional support the nurses gave her mother. She said, "They sat down and talked to her and, you know, they had a relationship with her which was probably the first time in her life that she had any relationship outside the home other than family." Because Alice lived 89 miles away from her parents and had to work, her sister, Susan, shifted from giving assistance to their mother to becoming a major provider of care. After her father died, they tried to get a home health aide twice a day to cook and clean house for her mother, but the cost was larger than her mother's income. Since her mother did not wish to move so far away from her home to live with Alice, she agreed to move in with Susan and her family. Before losing consciousness, she suffered greatly from pain caused by the cancer and the discomfort caused by massive amounts of radiation and chemotherapy.

Although Alice had already told her sister that there wasn't anything the physicians could do at this point except make their mother comfortable, her sister asked the doctor if something couldn't be done to keep her alive. Alice reported:

The doctor said, "Well you know she's terminal, don't you?" And, of course, this was the first time the doctor had ever said to any of us recognizing or admitting that my mother was terminal. . . . I said of course I knew and my sister said, "I just didn't realize it until then."

Alice had long-established views on what exactly her obligations were to each parent. Because of the years of animosity and her feeling that her father had never loved or supported her, she stated that she would not have been willing to care for him in her home or give him the attention she gave her mother. Initially, she was angry with him for dying first, since she felt it was a conscious choice to avoid watching her mother die. Besides, she felt angry towards him for never giving psychological support to anyone. By dying first, he ultimately gave up the opportunity to do so. Yet Alice later felt relieved that his death preceded her mother's because, "I was spared of having to reject him if he had been the living spouse."

Though the exigencies surrounding these situations might seem all-consuming in themselves, Alice simultaneously experienced a personal crisis, a divorce. I asked her if she felt that she was experiencing multiple losses. She stated:

Yes, at times I really felt that I wasn't going to make it. I had a really good counselor, a woman who really saw a lot of my strengths, and she really pulled me through. By pulling me through what I really mean is that she pushed me through. [laughs]. She was very supportive of my strengths, and my assertiveness and even my aggressiveness. . . . She was very supportive of my being aggressive too; she wanted me to get out there and fight.

When I asked her if she could give me some examples of what she was fighting, she said slowly:

Okay. There were times when I was thinking about suicide . . . as a response to the relationship breaking up, my marriage, and also, as a response to what I saw was no possibilities for me to make it, but I didn't want to be dependent anymore. I didn't see options, alternatives. And she saw this [her suicidal feelings] because I didn't talk about it to a whole lot of people, but it was there and it was pretty obvious to her. A couple of times when I came very very near to it [committing suicide] she made it very clear to me that a lot of people choose that as an option, and if that is the option you choose, then you go ahead and do it, but how can you do anything like that without investigating your other options?

In another interview I conducted several weeks after his mother's death, Clark, a retired Air Force pilot, described the circumstances surrounding her terminal illness. Close to his mother all his life and now twice divorced, he felt himself to be more available to help his father with her care than his two sisters, who each lived within a hundred miles but had families. He moved half-way across the country to help out. With an easy smile, he remarked, "You don't buy a lot of mothers, but you can get a lot of wives and husbands."

Because they had always been a private, self-sufficient unit, the family members wished to handle her illness and dying themselves. His father planned to avoid a nursing home placement at all costs. Clark observed, "His whole life was donated to accomplishing and making enough so that my mother would never have to go to a rest home or rely on anyone; my mother could have nurses at her house, anything she needed."

As she became bedridden, her arduous care demanded the full attention of the immediate family. They discovered that her impending death elicited other problems as well. Foremost among them was the unwelcome descent of relatives who dutifully felt compelled to pay their respects to the dying woman in lengthy visits, despite the inconvenience to the family of their extended stays. Clark described the visit of his mother's sister, who managed to anger the nurses, disrupt care, and inconvenience family members in the following way:

> There were problems taking care of them. We were concerned about my mother, not company. We didn't need them, and they were doing us no good, no help. She would do the wrong thing; she would give my mother the wrong thing; she would be in the way is what I am trying to say.

The issues raised by death and dying do not end with biological death. After giving months of devoted care, Clark expressed some feelings about not having done enough. He disclosed:

> I always was kind of protective of my mother. Usually, when I'd go to Vietnam, I'd kind of delay until it was almost time to come back from Vietnam to tell her. Then I'd tell her, "Mom, I'm on my way back from Vietnam," so she wouldn't have to worry. I've done many things for my mother as we all have, but there's always more that you could have done.

Now Clark is concerned about his father's isolation and withdrawal into his grief. After fifty years of marriage, he seems lost without his wife and without even the round of activities that her illness necessitated. Clark remarked:

> I asked him the other night, I said that I'll come down and take you to dinner or you come up and I'll cook. He says, "I want to be alone," and then when I do go down there he says, "You're not going to leave, are you?" . . . He's very hardheaded; he says, "Dammit, I don't need you." He's doing what he wants. He won't touch anything that belonged to my mother. He says nothing will be touched in this house for six months, and he is very capable of taking care of himself, but I don't think he has purpose or reason to hang on, and I'm really concerned about that. He did finally go to a doctor, and he's going back twice a week for his blood pressure. I think it's the stress.

These two cases illuminate some common concerns, crises, and dilemmas precipitated by death and dying. In both cases, someone was available to give emotional support as well as undertake the necessary physical care. But in both cases, problems escalated, thereby necessitating professional assistance and, ultimately, hospitalization in the last days of dying. Although delegation of responsibility was not an issue in either of these cases, it often is. But what kind of responsibility should be taken? While Alice believed responsibility to be symbolized by not prolonging the torment of dying, her sister believed responsibility was demonstrated by preserving the last thread of her mother's life. Another concern of Alice's was her mother's seeming denial of death and her sister's lack of awareness of her dying. Whether terminal patients accurately read and confront their developing signs of impending death and whether they are directly told that they are dying affects the character of communication and, often, relationships with others. Further, as seen in Alice's interview, crises may be experienced in other relationships besides ones precipitated by a terminal illness. The last point to note from these cases suggests a common dilemma of intimates of the bereaved: to act to involve the bereaved is to be intrusive; yet not to act is to foster their further withdrawal and isolation.

Such concerns, predicaments, and dilemmas shape the reality of death, a reality constructed from social meanings and actions. Although death is a biological universal, everything human about it—meanings, rituals, customs, and institutions—consists of social realities defined and made real through thought and action.

Because of the special concerns and dilemmas posed by the reality of death, it may seem to be outside the realm of everyday life. But similar themes may be discovered in routine existence. Examples are numerous: The dominant values of the work ethic affect individuals' conceptions of success and failure. The relationship of individuals to their social world shapes ideas and actions. Developing intimacy and reducing isolation are, for many, problematic features of ordinary existence. Maintaining self-esteem depends upon social supports. Information gathering and information control, about one's self as well as others, is a common part of everyday life. Similarly, control over decision making is a problematic feature of everyday life. And the institutionalization of science and technology has consequences for the structure of everyday worlds.

In many ways, then, the situations of the dying, suicidal, bereaved, and others discussed throughout the book *symbolize* in *bold relief* the kind of problematic issues confronted in everyday life among those not immediately face-to-face with death. Nevertheless, in both circumstances, problematic issues such as awareness of impending events, choice about future actions, and responsibility for them are sometimes avoided or glossed over, and hence remain unacknowledged. But when death of oneself or an intimate directly confronts one, problematic issues become much more visible, are more difficult to ignore, and attempts to gloss over them are considerably less successful. Importantly, in the study of death and dying, fundamental issues and questions regarding life in contemporary American society are raised. In essence, the drama so frequently visible in the situations of the dying, suicidal, and bereaved resembles a spotlighted and intensified version of what happens in ordinary existence.

What is the nature of the issues faced in death and dying, and how do they reflect more fundamental issues in everyday life? Although there are many, several major ones stand out. To experience losses of self raises the issue of possessing crucial information about oneself. To control treatment raises the issue of individual autonomy and social responsibility. To make choices about handling the dying process raises the issue of action by decision or default. To elect death raises the issue of individual choice and social coercion. To desire emotional support raises the issue of intimacy or isolation. To plan new modes of terminal care raises the issue of innovation and routinization. By looking at these and related issues, we gain insight, not only into the plight of the dying, suicidal, and bereaved, but also into our own.

Throughout the book I argue that values consistent with the Protestant Ethos, such as individualism, independence, and achievement, although reinterpreted by individuals, still affect our beliefs and practices about death. But, importantly, values and practices are not always blindly accepted by individuals. Instead, they are acted upon, reinterpreted, and sometimes transformed through thought and action. The ways in which wider values and practices correspond with the social world and views of individuals shape their specific actions. The individual is, therefore, an active participant in whatever scenes unfold.

In the following chapters, the meanings and actions of individuals affected by death are viewed in relation to the social worlds in which they occur. *What* death means and *how* it is handled in everyday life reflect the larger society. My treatment of the subjective dimension of death reveals the influence of society as individuals construct meanings of death and death-related actions. The seemingly disparate topics covered in various chapters are linked by similarities in the issues individuals face. In addition, these individuals draw upon wider social values in similar ways in their attempts to understand and act upon their diverse situations.

This book, then, offers a sociological interpretation of the relationship between society and death and dying, particularly as they affect the selves and situations of those most centrally involved. First, in order to further understand their situations, I outline major conceptual frameworks. Second, I link everyday death conceptions and concerns to these conceptual frameworks, the medical conception of death, and technologized dying. Third, in the analysis of the social process of dying I emphasize the implications of institutionalized dying for the patient's self-image. Fourth, I view death and dying from the different contexts of ordinary and extraordinary death work that process the dying and dead into routine objects of work. These topics lead to discussions of the routinization and legitimation of death. Fifth, I analyze suicide as a crisis of self-worth. Suicide is perhaps the most common form of extraordinary death and one of the most difficult to legitimize. Sixth, I describe a similar crisis of self experienced in the isolation and loneliness of intense grief. Finally, I examine the diverse ways in which individuals face death from their respective situations and comment on the future of death.

Before moving to these topics, I will provide some remarks to put the subsequent analysis into perspective. To begin, I will offer some ideas why death conceptions and practices are currently being questioned. Then, I will introduce a discussion of social values because they form the backdrop of a number of concerns raised in later chapters.

WHY DEATH NOW?

In view of institutionalized care, prolonged dying, and potential nuclear devastation, the many dilemmas posed by death take new dimensions in our time, thus forcing new questions about them. Recent awareness that death causes human dilemmas has been transformed into a vision of death as the new social problem of our time. To define death as a problem suggests that there are solutions to it, typically of a technical nature whether they might consist of medical or psychotherapeutic techniques (cf. Steinfels 1973). As Feifel (1977) implies, in times of uncertainty, previous recipes for handling the dilemmas that death poses are called into question. In some arenas concerned with death, they are explicitly being called into question already; but often, new trends and old ones currently co-exist, sometimes in uneasy tension. Thus, while some crusade for changes to permit a greater openness in attitudes toward death, others seek to hide, evade, and conceal it.

In view of the kinds of concerns shaping the face of death today, I explore the following four themes: (1) the implications of the nuclear age, (2) a disillusionment with the institution of science, (3) trends in the nature of dying, and (4) the development of a death and dying movement. The ideas presented are not put forth as a definitive explanation of the source of the interest in death, but are simply offered as possibilities.

The awesome possibility of a nuclear holocaust underlines the *uncertainty* of the present age. The unrelenting growth of technology alone has been thought by some to give rise to uncertainty and meaninglessness in Western society (see for example Feifel 1977; Fromm 1962). But some think the potential of the nuclear age greatly surpasses the uncertainty of previous historical periods. In their discussion of the implications of the nuclear age, Lifton and Olson (1974) argue that a crucial dimension of meaninglessness they see as characterizing the twentieth century is the anxiety caused by the uncertainty about the irrational use of nuclear power. For them, awareness that actual and symbolic worlds may suddenly disappear makes human relationships as well as human creation problematic or even pointless. They argue that in the face of possible nuclear or ecological devastation basic aspects of human life become absurd. The extent to which the nuclear age shapes our consciousness, if it does, and if so, precisely how it does is as yet unknown. Some, like Lifton and Olson, believe that people deny the actual threat of nuclearism since they are unwilling to confront the possibility of such great destruction. Others believe that we are aware of nuclear devastation but the anxiety elicited by it is repressed. If so, average people are more likely to be affected by the potential threat of nuclearism than they realize. Lifton and Olson (1974) argue that the twentiety century holocaust and dislocation have combined in ways to create what they call a "symbolic gap." This gap reflects the difference between the human capacity to interpret experience symbolically and actual historical change. If they are correct, the meanings of nuclearism may only be dimly recognized. Thus a contradictory attitude toward nuclearism may be discerned. At times, awareness of its potential devastation may be heightened. But in everyday affairs it may be quite forgotten.

The threat of a limited war may evoke similar responses. The echoes of the Vietnam War still reverberate in our society since it is widely suspected that the deaths sustained there were meaningless, absurd deaths. When war is not justified symbolically with purpose and honor, death becomes absurd. The possibility of experiencing what is felt to be a meaningless death or having an intimate confront this possibility may then make death itself a more immediate reality.

The problem of making sense of the possibility of destruction is also, conceivably, altering our understanding of *scientific progress*. Basically, there has been some disillusionment with certain sectors of the institution of science. Earlier in the twentieth century, most adults were well socialized to believe in the progress of science, in its capacity to ameliorate human problems and enhance the quality of life. But science itself has generated grave problems for humankind. Foremost among them is the depletion of natural resources now beginning to be understood as finite. Again, the possibility of worldwide devastation through hunger, lack of water, and diseases spawned by industrial living cast a shadow upon our view of life and death. The contradictions born of science are apparent. The technology born out of modern industrialism contains both threat and promise: massive death and destruction on the one hand and an end to the degenerative processes associated with aging on the other.

Not only views of science but also views of nature are undergoing transformation. That transformation consists of a changing view of nature from one of *unlimited abundance* to one of circumscribed and sometimes foreseeable *limits*. Additionally, the wider public is becoming more aware of the complex consequences of intervention upon the natural environment. With this awareness comes the realization that demands placed upon nature can well become greater than available resources. Consequently, not only a way of life may die but also large sectors of the world's population as well. Due to the depletion of natural resources, the possibility of death may be a realization that more persons will share.

Turning to more specific influences on the current interest in death, we see two important trends in the nature of dying (see Crane 1975; Cutter 1974; Lerner 1970; L. Lofland 1977). These include (1) *prolonged dying* and (2) the *shift* to an *institutionalized milieu*. Both of these trends promote contemporary responses to death.

Prolonged dying is, in part, a result of changes in the causes of death in this century. In the past, death was commonly caused by acute illnesses and affected people of all ages. Now people suffer from chronic illnesses, and the dying process is greatly extended as more people die in old age. Some medical conditions, such as types of heart disease, progress over such a long period that it is difficult to distinguish precisely when the point of chronic illness ends and the terminal phase of illness begins. With other conditions, such as cancer, the terminal phase sometimes is rightly or (more often) wrongly defined at the time the diagnosis is made. At any rate, the dying process becomes a lengthy one punctuated by many hospitalizations and often followed by a later admission to a nursing home as the final stages of dying approach.

Due to the conquest of the major causes of death from acute illnesses, the age when dying occurs is likely to be after retirement. Lerner (1970) points out that the category, "diseases of the heart," was fourth on the list of causes of death in 1900; by 1966 it was the leading cause of death. Paradoxically, some individuals may be saved from an acute illness only to live with chronic and terminal illnesses. Thus, with greater life expectancy comes the increased possibility of suffering a lengthy dying process.

The dying process is subject to continual scrutiny by the medical profession. Medical efforts are now being made to effect the type of radical intervention with chronic conditions successfully accomplished earlier with acute illnesses. But this effort occurs within a context in which scientism still reigns and technological innovation continues to be worshipped. Hence, the gains to be made from scientific discovery and explanation through the advancement of new techniques and procedures often take precedence and dominate other concerns. The feelings, preferences, and experiences of the individual patient sometimes are ignored or negated. The values on which medicine is based foster a stance of fighting death by using all the technical knowledge that is possible. When "failure" is impending since death is certain, patients may be left bereft of the attention they received when their conditions were more interesting and some possibility existed for successful intervention of the disease process. (This will be further discussed in Chapter 4.) Dying patients may be literally removed from the scene since the "hopeless" are segregated from the potentially "salvageable" in the medical care system.

Quite clearly, efforts to prolong life must be viewed in the kind of setting in which they occur, an *institutionalized setting*. Medical institutions are formal organizations presumably set up to accomplish their major goal of patient care. Yet, in these settings, three other goals may take precedence over this care: (1) the educational goals of teaching and research, (2) protection of the institution and practitioner, and (3) profit. All, of course, have consequences for what it means to die.

Further, relationships in the bureaucratic medical institution also shape the dying process. They typically are characterized by their impersonal content. Since the setting is organized for the formation of formalized, task-oriented relationships, the patient may come to feel anonymous and alone without human contact. Because daily life on a ward is organized around work, other needs the patient has may be unrecognized, ignored, or subordinated to daily work routines. Dying may become an almost unacknowledged process for the patient to handle alone.

Death is being brought to the public attention by groups of individuals who are interested in changing the above practices. These groups sometimes overlap although there have been some distinct, independent sources of interest. Crane (1975) points out that social and technological changes in the medical arena where dying occurs have provided the context for a diffuse social movement that concerns itself with the issues posed by dying. There are three somewhat overlapping dimensions of this death and dying movement. The first dimension concerns the relative value of opting for the *quantity* of life through prolonging the dying process. The second concerns the *quality* of the dying process. The third concerns the emergence of a *secular spiritualism*.

The first dimension of the death and dying movement raises questions about the quantity of life. Organizational advocates of voluntary euthanasia and "natural" death have attempted to increase public awareness of prolonged dying through "life-sustaining" techniques. In their efforts, they have also questioned the lack of participation of the patient and family in the decision-making processes for handling dying. Their combined efforts have increased public awareness of death and dying as they challenged the public's image of a quick and easy dying process. They have shown, on the contrary, that dying is often lengthy and fraught with ethical dilemmas.

The second dimension concerns the growing interest in the quality of the dying process. Though spurred by psychologically oriented practitioners, members of the public show increasing interest in the quality of the individual's psychological response to dying. In contrast to those above, movement proponents who emphasize the psychological response to dying are typically less questioning about the decisionmaking processes with dying except as they impinge upon the patient's feelings. Practitioners with an initial interest in the psychological response to dying have gone on to raise more general questions about the meaning of death and the emotions elicited by it. Foremost among them is Elisabeth Kübler-Ross, whose works (1969, 1974) gained widespread public appeal. Because this dimension of the death and dying movement has had perhaps the greatest influence on the general public, I shall outline its development in greater detail.

This dimension of the death and dying movement has its origins in a stance combining general psychiatric conceptions with views and techniques from the human potential movement, a direct predecessor in the field of popular psychology. The psychiatric influence emphasizes the fear and denial of death, anxiety, and the patient's motivation. The human potential movement influence is shown in the priority of feeling over thinking about death. With its emphasis on spontaneous, immediate expression of feeling, proponents of this perspective view the confrontation of death as a prerequisite to realizing human potential. The sector of the movement that most directly reflects the human potential orientation gives it the trendy character mentioned above and noted by several observers (see Gutmann 1977; L. Lofland 1977).

Though the initial impetus of many movement proponents was to advocate expression of personal concerns about death, increased emphasis may be seen now on creating organizational forms to deal with death. The emergence of a hospice movement is one example. The development of community volunteer organizations to help the dying is another. However, some of these forms are primarily designed to provide an organizational setting for expressing personal concerns. Others are designed to fundamentally change the form of the dying or grieving process. Thus, from the perspective of these psychologists, the "problem" of death is currently defined as largely psychological in nature. That is, facing up to death, remaining aware of it, and accepting it are thought to be key issues. Death attitudes and behaviors are held to be amenable to change through such trendy techniques as encounter group exercises, self-explorations, and controlled mind-altering drug experiences of "death" and "rebirth." As Gutmann (1977) suggests, death has become the latest (but undoubtedly not the last) arena in which lay psychologists wage the struggle for "inner liberation." In this case, they struggle against the fear and denial of death. Thus, the confrontation of self with death has become a necessary part of human development for seekers of "personal growth."

The third dimension of the death and dying movement concerns what I call the emergence of a *secular spiritualism*. In recent years, especially since medical specialists like Kübler-Ross affirmed beliefs in some type of continued existence in a spirit world, there has been a growing, widespread interest in the possibility of an afterlife. The intriguing aspect of this interest is the new support given to these beliefs by the accounts of persons who were clinically "dead" but who were revived through emergency medical intervention. Moody's account (1975) of the out-of-the-body experiences of the persons he interviewed has been an important source of the new interest in the possibility of spiritual survival. Granted that American interest in the occult and spiritualism has existed for decades, it appears that there is a new surge of interest in the field with a wider popular following than ever before. The appeal of the possibility of spiritual survival may be directly linked to the special social-historical circumstances currently faced by Americans. The fact that the type of spiritualism associated with the current dying movement has a secular cast, rather than a specific alignment with a religious doctrine, also attests to shifting conceptions of death.

These trends are often taken as sure indicators of a fundamental reconstruction of our cultural stance toward death. Has this occurred? I think not. For such a reconstruction to occur, I believe that the institutions that deal with death must also show fundamental changes in social structure. Thus far, the social structure of these institutions remains relatively unchanged, although professional and public interest in developing alternative organizational forms, such as the hospice, is growing. In addition, in order to claim that a fundamental reconstruction of our cultural stance toward death has taken place, evidence of it must be general throughout the society. Currently, many people still avoid, ignore, or hide death despite its currency among some increasingly visible sectors of the society. Although we may be experiencing the birth of such a change, I see it as only a beginning, though perhaps the beginning of a major transformation (see L. Lofland 1977). And if such a transformation takes place, it will occur in conjunction with other cultural changes.

Even though they may not reflect fundamental changes in the American stance toward death, all of the trends discussed above have clearly contributed to the current interest in death. And many of them have arisen as a direct response to the ordinary treatment of death by silence, pretense, and concealment. At this point one might ask: On which underlying social values do old and new trends toward death rest?

DEATH AND SOCIAL VALUES

Any sociological exploration into the social reality of death must come to grips with values. Whether values are fixed and stable within a group or are open to reinterpretation, they give rise to the construction of the reality of death. Put simply, death does not occur in a vacuum. Rather, it is a dimension of human existence shaped by values. In particular, I submit that values built on the Protestant Ethos still have a pervasive but subtle effect on death and dying although cultural diversity and biographical experience may give rise to other effects. In that sense, values not only give rise to meanings of death but also to the everyday *practices* through which death is handled.

In any event, values shape and are shaped by experience. The character of American experience contributes to our views on death. For the most part, massive death has not been part of conventional American experience; hence, it may be difficult for Americans to conceive of collective death. Also, our values typically do not focus on the collective, and American views of death are, for the most part, constructed around the *individual* in a manner consistent with other American traditions.

Because we value individualism, the self is integral to the American consciousness. Further, there is a tendency to see individuals as *separate* and *unique*, that is, apart from their collective origins. Thus, the view of each death both as unique and uniquely the dying individual's problem is consistent with wider values, although interpretations of that uniqueness may vary considerably. A common interpretation of death is that it is the individual's unique *possession* and *responsibility*. Adherents of the death and dying movement such as Keleman (1974) stress living while dying in order that uniqueness may be rediscovered and possessed by the dying individual.

The relation of the individual's death to his or her uniqueness and separateness is, of course, consistent with values of the Protestant Ethos. Like Aries (1974) and Gorer (1965), I maintain that dominant views of death in Western society are built on the vestiges of the Protestant Ethos, in which the individual is paramount. Values such as *privatism, independence, hard work*, and *individual achievement* are part and parcel of the Protestant Ethos; furthermore, they become evident in a critical analysis of American views and practices of death.

Except for those proponents of the death and dying movement who "go public," death is typically a private affair. That someone is dying is often treated as a carefully guarded secret, like pregnancy, even when it is obvious and everyone talks about it. Actions of friends and relatives serve to construct an aura of mystery around the dying process. Commonly, the mystifications that follow extend to the dying person.

Further, the cultural emphasis on privacy leads to all kinds of secrets and private dealings between family members and sometimes friends when someone is dying or has recently died. At this time, prior secrets and present negotiations are apt to be both revealed and intensified. Secrets about relationships become more visible or more difficult to hide. For example, a dying young man may insist upon maintaining his current living arrangement with his male lover to the surprise of his parents, who never knew he was homosexual. Old concealed tensions between family members may erupt during the pressures of their crisis. And as tensions develop, they may in turn result in more factions and private dealings, giving rise to yet more secrets.

All these interactions may be going on around the dying person, but they do not always include him or her. Particularly with certain individuals, like the elderly, dying is something one does alone in this society; one is an individual unto death. In turn, being able to handle it demonstrates another social value, *independence*. Handling feelings, concerns, and plans independently tends to be subtly encouraged or blatantly insisted upon by friends and practitioners alike. Consequently, as individuals handle their situations, independence may be achieved at the cost of loneliness, fear, and despair. Those without a spouse, friend, or adult offspring who can tolerate giving support may be left without any human contact, yet still be expected by practitioners to accept stoically the burden of their concerns and the fate of impending death. Often, however, dying patients do have the humane concern of another, coupled with the tacit agreement that their deaths will not be openly discussed. Proponents of the death and dying movement explicitly attempt to break down the silence and self-sufficiency that characterize dying. As a result, their normative demand for immediate expression of feeling prompts disclosures of a more public nature and simultaneously pulls others into the interactional arena.

Self-sufficiency continues, however, to be a common way of dealing with death, and it is not limited to the dying person. It is also expected of whomever else is involved. They too are likely to carry alone the burden of uncertainty, sorrow, fear, anger, remorse, or whatever they are feeling. Moreover, those who have internalized the values of the Protestant Ethos believe it is their responsibility and socially prescribed obligation to carry this burden. And, even if they don't believe it, given the structure of contemporary social relationships, they may find that they have no alternative but to handle their grief alone.

The privatization of dying is consistent with other, related cultural practices. Health and illness are also viewed as private affairs if one has a sufficient amount of money to keep them private. Certainly, paying for terminal care is construed as, essentially, the responsibility of the individual and/or family. How they wish to handle their responsibility is their own affair, but it deemed able to handle it at all, handle it they must.

At this point, one might ask how values such as achievement and hard work enter in. As I will elaborate in a later section, achievement is seen, in one stance frequently taken to dying, as the ability to *overcome* it. One attempts to achieve a victory over death. Along this line of logic, death becomes the ultimate *failure*. Achievement values may also be seen in a more subtle context. A "good" death becomes something to be achieved, worked at. An "appropriate death" (Weisman 1972) becomes something that both practitioners and patients strive for. Other areas of work and achievement include confronting death and overcoming the fear of death.

Taking these values in a larger sense, let us now look at the situation of the dying person. Since values of independence, hard work, and achievement are impressed upon the consciousness of most persons in the society, where does that leave the dying? They are reduced in value and left out. They are no longer productive; they are dependent. The unproductive in this society tend to be relegated to a separate and unequal existence from others. Thus the dying become systematically separated from the rest of society.

As dying becomes prolonged, some dying individuals make concerted attempts to extend their stay among the productive, if not to entirely reverse the process of becoming separated. By doing so, they also alter the concept of dying as personal failure by putting forth new notions of what it is to achieve a "successful" dying (such as by "working" through and resolving old fears and anxieties completely).

In summary, unique socio-historical conditions emerging during the latter half of the twentieth century create a situation in which death takes on new, problematic dimensions. Western values give rise to the scientific institutions that manage death in contemporary American society; moreover, these values lead to the problematic situations confronting individuals who face the imminence of death.

Both old and new stances toward dying are constructed out of social values. This construction is an active process developed out of interpretations of experience, and interpreting experience in various contexts will be a central concern in this book.

In this chapter, I outlined possible reasons for the current interest in death and discussed the relationship between death and social values. In the next chapter, I will introduce conceptual approaches through which death and the values it reveals may be analyzed.

REFERENCES

Aries, Philippe (1974). *Western Attitudes toward Death.* Baltimore: John Hopkins University Press.

Crane, Diana (1975). *The Sanctity of Social Life.* New York: Russell Sage Foundation.

Cutter, Fred (1974). *Coming to Terms with Death.* Chicago: Nelson-Hall.

Feifel, Herman (1977). Death in contemporary America. In Herman Feifel (ed.), *New Meanings of Death.* New York: McGraw-Hill.

Fromm, Erich (1962). *Marx's Concept of Man.* New York: Frederick Ungar.

Gorer, Geoffrey (1965). *Death, Grief and Mourning.* Garden City, N.Y.: Doubleday, Anchor Books.

Gutmann, David (1977). Dying to power: death and the search for self esteem. In Herman Feifel (ed.), *New Meanings of Death.* New York: McGraw-Hill.

Keleman, Stanley (1974). *Living Your Dying.* New York: Random House.

Kübler-Ross, Elisabeth (1969). *On Death and Dying.* New York: Macmillan.

_____ (1974). *Death, The Final Stage of Growth.* Englewood Cliffs, N.J.: Prentice-Hall.

Lerner, Monroe (1970). When, why and where people die. In Orville G. Brim, Jr., Howard E. Freeman, Sol Levine, and Norman A. Scotch (eds.), *The Dying Patient.* New York: Russell Sage Foundation.

Lifton, Robert Jay, and Eric Olson (1974). *Living and Dying.* New York: Bantam Books.

Lofland, Lyn H. (1977). The face of death and the craft of dying: individual and collective constructions. Unpublished manuscript, University of California, Davis.

Moody, Raymond A. (1975). *Life After Life.* New York: Bantam Books.

Shneidman, Edwin S. (1973). "Death, the Enemy," Tape 19, produced by *Psychology Today.* Del Mar, Calif.: Ziff-Davis.

Steinfels, Peter (1973). Introduction. In Peter Steinfels and Robert M. Veatch (eds.), *Death Inside Out.* New York: Harper and Row.

Weisman, Avery D. (1972). *On Dying and Denying.* New York: Behavioral Publications.

CHAPTER TWO

CONCEPTUAL APPROACHES TO THE STUDY OF DEATH

In the area of death and dying, as in any study of the human condition, concrete circumstances are known and understood by conceptualizing them into a coherent body of ideas. Whatever perspectives are brought to bear on death, whether they are scientific theorizing, philosophical interpretation, or common-sense reasoning, they give shape and meaning to the reality of it. It can readily be discerned that each perspective suggests particular kinds of questions and therefore has its own particular limitations since questions derived from other perspectives are usually omitted.

In the following pages, analyses of major perspectives that inform sociological and intellectual thought concerning death will be presented. Those perspectives are stressed that either offer the possibility of new questions or that have been central in previous analyses of death. All of the perspectives included influence sociological thinking on the topic to a greater or lesser degree. The chapter is divided into two basic sections: (1) *major sociological perspectives* and (2) *philosophical and psychoanalytic perspectives*. The first section includes discussions of symbolic interactionist, structural-functionalist, and Marxist approaches. The second includes discussions of existentialist, phenomenological, and psychoanalytic perspectives.

MAJOR SOCIOLOGICAL PERSPECTIVES

In this section, three perspectives are introduced and analyzed in relation to death. Since symbolic interactionism is the perspective stressed throughout the book, it will be given most emphasis. Special emphasis will then be given to explicating the assumptions on which symbolic interactionism rests. That discussion will be followed by a presentation of one of its subtypes, the dramaturgical approach. This approach holds much potential for new research about death through the application of the analogy of the theatre to social relations. The structural-functional perspective discussed next is explicated to show the complex institutional relationships that need to be addressed in a study of death. Finally, a Marxist perspective is introduced to raise, primarily, a set of provocative issues largely ignored in the past.

Symbolic Interactionist Perspective

The symbolic interactionist position postulates that selves and social structures are constructed through continuous interaction over time. This general perspective and how it relates to the study of death will be explored in the first part of this section. This will be followed by a synthesis of the perspective's basic premises in order to explicate the fundamental assumptions on which it rests. Last, the dramaturgical method will be introduced.

Statement of the position Symbolic interactionism is a theoretical perspective in sociology which assumes that society, reality, and selves are *socially created* through interaction processes (see Blumer 1969; Lindesmith, Strauss, and Denzin 1975; and Strauss 1964). Hence, what we know, how we define situations in the world, and who we are are all built through interaction. In the area of death, then, the symbolic interactionist perspective informs us that our conceptions of death, our images of the social worlds where death takes place, as well as the everyday actions that constitute the process of "dying," are socially constructed. Although death is a biological fact, what it *means* to us results from our socially shaped ideas and assumptions. In short, from this perspective we can understand "death" only in the context of the definitions and assumptions we have attributed to it. For example, death has varied definitions such as loss, transition, or peace depending on the assumptions one has about it. To illustrate, a young woman confided:

> *To me, death is loss. It is more than loss of another person, or a relationship; it is loss of a part of my life. I know a lot of people my age believe in reincarnation and see death as some kind of new beginning, but to me death is a loss.*

Meanings of death in the symbolic interactionist perspective are assumed to arise out of the individual's experience. In turn, that experience is grounded in interaction. Furthermore, interaction itself is a *symbolic process*. In order to interact with another, a reasonably similar set of symbols from which meanings develop must be shared. In everyday life, our use of symbols emerges out of language and cultural understandings shared between members of a group. The kinds of symbolic meanings created can be exceedingly diverse, since specific meanings arise in different groups. In turn, these meanings shape the experiences shared by members. Such diversity may be observed in the responses of members of different ethnic groups. From Kalish and Reynolds's study of death and ethnicity (1976), one concludes that Mexican Americans hold significant meanings of the family as the major source of emotional support and warmth in the face of dying and death. In contrast, Japanese-Americans develop meanings of the family as the "locus of control of shame and pride and of self-identity" (Kalish and Reynolds 1976, p. 170). As a consequence, one's responsibility to one's family and self emphasizes the importance of emotional control in the face of death by members of this group.

Diverse meanings also may be discerned among others who are not linked by ethnicity. For that matter, group members who share certain practices regarding death may hold rather diverse meanings about other aspects of it. For example, members of a memorial society share similar views about keeping funeral expenses low; however, they may hold rather diverse conceptions of death.

Through experience, interpretations may be changed or reaffirmed. For example, some people who until recently did not have any direct interaction with members of the funeral industry held positive views of it. They now avow that they will set up their own plans outlining their personal preferences for their funerals after their initial experience with representatives of the trade since they felt pressured to purchase unwanted services.

Here, the initial encounter causes them to reassess their views and construct a different course of action in light of the experience. In contrast, others become notably more sympathetic toward the funeral industry after their initial encounter with it. Hence, in the symbolic interactionist perspective, it is assumed that persons reinterpret previously accepted views and construct new meanings as they have new experiences that are not accommodated by their former views.

Since the symbolic interactionist position is predicated upon the premise that interaction consists of an interpretative process, it follows that the interactionist viewpoint heavily stresses the human capacity for reflection. This stress on reflection suggests an image of human nature viewing human beings as reflective, creative, and active. This view of human nature becomes clearer if it is juxtaposed with views of human beings as passive objects who are pushed and pulled by larger social forces over which they have no control (Lindesmith, Strauss, and Denzin 1975). One who adheres to the symbolic interactionist perspective expects conscious, dying persons to be capable of interpreting their worlds and of participating actively in whatever decisions are made regarding them. Essentially then from this perspective, meaning shapes experience and experience shapes meaning.

Taken to its logical extension, the symbolic interactionist viewpoint emphasizes the *freedom* of the individual to construct reality since reality is not a given, but rather is a social construction. Thus, implicit in the perspective is the notion that, to a degree, we shape our own destinies. Worlds of death are then created through the interpretations, choices, and actions of interactants. To illustrate, simply because some medical practitioners assume that patients do not wish to be informed of the life-threatening nature of their illnesses does not mean that this is necessarily true. Rather, their assumption is a social construction serving to affirm the validity of their choice not to inform the patient. It is an assumption that bears a closer relationship to the practitioner's comfort than to the patient's. Anxiety and stress exhibited by the patient also affirm the practitioner's belief that "bad news" will result in further psychological distress for the patient. Consequently, the practitioner chooses to avoid the topic.

The emphasis on the range of human *choice*, which is derived from the individual's interpretation of a given situation, leads the symbolic interactionist to assume a certain amount of *indeterminacy* in interaction and events. From this perspective, it is assumed that people may choose to create new modes of action instead of merely following the dictates of the wider culture. Consequently, the ways in which we treat death in this society represent certain types of choices that have become part of institutionalized patterns of handling death. As new meanings about death emerge, new means of handling death will be developed.

As Blumer (1969) repeatedly emphasized, the symbolic interactionist perspective is predicated on the assumption that human beings can think and have minds and thus do not respond automatically to our environment as in a stimulus-response reaction. Through our capacity for reflective thought, we can take into account and attempt to understand the different perspectives of others. For example, when a young man told his work supervisor that he would need to be absent on the following day, she reflected upon his tone of voice and facial expression rather than simply responding to his statement. By gently inquiring, she discovered that he was scheduled for a biopsy for a particularly lethal type of cancer and was very frightened. Through taking his tone and demeanor into account, she was able to gain insight into his perspective and concerns.

The process of taking into account the perspective of another person is a symbolic process rooted in the meanings that participants attribute to ongoing interaction. Specifically, within the content of interaction, we are able to attribute meanings to what the other person is saying and doing. Unfortunately, much research about death and dying consists of imputing meanings and therefore motivations to other persons on the assumption that these meanings and motivations represent what these persons actually think and feel. Hence, in fundamental ways, meanings about death and dying have unfortunately been *imposed* upon those who are studied instead of elicited from them.

In the symbolic interactionist perspective, consciousness is linked to the possession of a self. Having a self means that we can act toward ourselves as we act toward others. People who are dying may act toward themselves as devalued objects in the same way that they have treated others who were dying in the past. For example, a dying old man instructed an attentive young nursing assistant:

> Oh, don't bother 'bout me. Spend your time with those who need it. There's some here who can use the help and get out of here. I know I ain't goin' no place. . . . I never bothered much with people in the shape I'm in and I don't see why anyone should bother with me.

In this case, the old man viewed himself as someone who no longer merits help. Importantly, he assessed himself and evaluated his situation. Speaking generally, because we have selves and minds we can carry on conversations with ourselves as we assess ourselves and our situations. Through the conscious activity of the thinking self, a person differentiates objects and events in the world and gives them meanings, usually in direct relationship to his or her construction of action.

Similarly, because we can take ourselves as objects to assess, we can place valuations on ourselves that differ from the definitions that are socially placed upon us by others. Some dying patients, for example, define themselves as quite different kinds of "objects" than those around them define them as being. Under these circumstances, dying patients view themselves as having an identity that supersedes the negative identities currently placed upon them by others.

With the emphasis on the dialectical relationship between interpretation and action, one might question how this perspective accounts for the stable relationships that are so often observed. To answer this question, the symbolic interactionist would ask another: How do members *themselves* voluntarily construct their everyday actions in such a way that they are habitualized? Thus, the stability of social structures is not assumed in advance, but is seen as a product of people acting concertedly to produce this stability. Therefore, if a particular social structure appears to be fixed and stable, one must question how the everyday actions of the members are defined, interpreted, and acted upon to construct the observed stability. To illustrate, by taking for granted that others consider old men like himself of doubtful value, the views and actions of the old man cited above contribute to the tendency of staff in that institution to ignore dying patients.

More generally, routine ways of handling dying in the hospital are stable only as long as (1) people actively and continually recreate the actions constituting that "stability" and (2) take for granted views legitimizing it. From the interactionist standpoint, one cannot have fixed and stable social relationships, scenes, organizations, societies, or selves without full, or at least tacit, cooperation of members who create and recreate those stable situations. The actions upon which stability is founded are *constructed actions;* that is, they are performed consciously by human beings. Everyday processes take on stability when they eventually become *routinized* and *unquestioned.* To underscore the point, since the nature of existence is processual, social stability is contingent upon routinized everyday processes constructed by human beings to support that stability.

When actions become *habitualized*, the problematic aspects of everyday actions and events become minimized as they are fit into routines. Consequently, little strain is placed upon people as they interpret their realities and construct their actions (Blumer 1969). Also, when actions become habitualized, the range of interpretations made about them tends to remain limited by members of the group; in fact, "tunnel vision" may set in. But, to make the point again, actions emerge, nevertheless, out of the choices of individuals. If what is happening is reinterpreted, then new courses of action may be entertained and organized as the individual ceases to take for granted what had been previously assumed. When someone raises questions about the accepted ways of doing things, then that person is opening up the possibility of examining ways in which the group can change their ideas and actions. For example, institutionalized ways of handling dying are currently being questioned. Consequently, more ideas about ways to handle the dying process are emerging. From this, new organizational modes can be experimented with and thus conceivably lead to the evolution of new institutional forms of dealing with death.

Assumptions underlying the perspective A clarification of the assumptions underlying the symbolic interactionist perspective is provided to sharpen the discussion. An underlying assumption of this perspective is that social reality consists of *process* and *change*. But processes and change occur within a context; it is assumed that changes emerge out of present interaction as the future unfolds. Hence, the present gives shape to the future but does not determine it. Within the symbolic interactionist perspective, a certain flexibility or latitude for change is assumed. But even those changes are predicated upon the shared understandings that come with a common language and culture. In the past, perhaps, symbolic interactionists have emphasized the underpinnings of their perspective which emphasize *consensus*, that is, agreement, more than those who deal with the development of conflicting definitions of the situation. But in the study of dying, conflicting definitions, with their implied conflicting directions of action, become especially important to consider.

Yet shared meanings about death and dying also need to be analyzed. Some of these shared meanings may lead to actions contradicting the "objective" interests of those who hold them. For example, some lonely elderly persons accept the notion that death is something one ultimately handles alone even though they themselves would prefer social support. One elderly widow encouraged her son to send her to a nursing home. Although frightened by the unfamiliar setting and unfamiliar routines, she believed that she had no other alternative but to endure being there until she died. Not only did she think it improper to discuss death, but also she did not wish to burden either staff or relatives with her concerns. She felt that handling her death alone was her one last task in life. Although she occasionally hinted to staff that she was not as "strong" as she seemed, she did not disclose her feelings when given the rare occasion to do so. Members of the staff felt that her last days were spent in great loneliness and that she had wanted more support, but she could not accept what little they were able to offer her since she saw this as burdening them.

Under this kind of circumstance, individuals set beliefs and actions into motion that are not in their own interests. By accepting the general conceptions of what has to be done, they in effect perpetuate situations that adversely affect them.

The basic premises supporting symbolic interactionism are presented in order to explicate the assumptions underlying subsequent analyses throughout the book. In addition, some major differences between the symbolic interactionist perspective and other theoretical approaches will be mentioned later in the chapter. For the present, discussion of the premises below is designed to synthesize the position as previously stated and to highlight fundamental assumptions.

According to Herbert Blumer (1969, p. 3), the symbolic interactionist position rests upon three premises. They are:

1. "Human beings act toward things on the basis of the meanings that things have for them."

2. "The meaning of such things is derived from, or arises out of, the social interaction that one has with one's fellows."

3. "These meanings are handled in, and modified through, an interpretative process used by the person in dealing with the things he encounters."

The first premise shows the rational and pragmatic bias of the symbolic interactionist perspective. Meaning is related to *utility* and to the *practical* aspects of experience. Although the premise is simple, it is an important one, and as Blumer states, one that is frequently overlooked by social scientists. Also, the symbolic interactionist position highlights the *rational* side of human nature implied in Blumer's first premise. Rationality is shown in the premise that meaning and action are linked rather than separate. To illustrate, a pediatrician assumes that it is his obligation to do everything medically and surgically possible for a child, as long as there is some hope of saving life or forestalling death. Hence, he may prescribe radical and sometimes mutilating surgical procedures when he decides they are justified. Occasionally, however, what seems like a rational course of treatment to him appears to be a cruel prolongation of suffering to the parents. In this case, the pediatrician's meanings are tied to his beliefs about sound medical practice from his experience. From the vantage point of his meanings, the rationale for treatment makes sense to him, although it may seem disturbing or even irrational to the parents.

This illustration shows that meaning and action are rationally linked when seen from the actor's point of view. In other perspectives, such as a psychiatric perspective, rational meanings are believed to be verbalized by the actor, although irrational ones—hidden even from the actor, and thus unconscious—are typically thought to cause action. In contrast, when studying death and dying, the symbolic interactionist assumes that the individual's perspective has a certain rational basis even when meanings remain implicit and unstated. The interactionist will, for example, take the dying person's assessment of his or her situation and feelings as "real" in and of itself, whereas those espousing other, notably psychiatric, perspectives will attempt to determine meaning by looking beyond what is directly stated.

The second premise is an important distinguishing assumption since it shows how symbolic interactionism differs from other perspectives. In the interactionist perspective, the derivation, or source, of meaning is an *emergent*, creative process. Blumer (1969) shows this assumption concerning the source of meaning to be quite different from the two more traditional ways of attributing meaning. One traditional way of attributing meaning is to consider it as emanating from the object itself, as if meaning is intrinsic to the object. Consequently, this view grants an objective character to meaning because it becomes attributed to the object's inherent qualities or characteristics. To illustrate, practitioners often view laboratory procedures as objects with inherent meaning rather than as objects to which they *give* meanings from their shared set of understandings. From an interactionist viewpoint, meanings can be *conferred* only upon objects. To the extent that meanings are shared, people will relate to the object in much the same way. For example, when physicians agree to define certain readings on a lab test in the same way, they draw the same conclusions about the significance of them. Another more subtle example concerns viewing cremation as an "object." The meaning of cremation does not lie in the act but in what it symbolizes. Its meaning lies in the value and definition people give it vis-a-vis their own lives. For secular, ecologically minded persons, cremation is apt to be given a positive meaning since it does not use the valuable green space taken by cemeteries. In contrast, those who believe in an afterlife or in reincarnation may give it a negative meaning if they believe that it is necessary to have an intact bodily form. In any case, the meaning does not lie in the act of cremating; it lies in the *values* people have concerning the act and their *definitions* of what the act is.

As Blumer (1969) notes, the third premise is often misunderstood by sociologists. Blumer emphasizes the interpretative process through which meanings are derived; he says that it is a mistake to view them as merely an application of previously established meanings. According to Blumer, the interpretative process is an internalized social process in which people make "indications" to themselves through communication. Making indications to oneself means, in short, conversing with oneself.

Through the interpretative process, previously held meanings may shift and change. In one case, for example, a man of 85 had always assumed that he would die much sooner than his wife, who was 66. Since he held a view of death as a peaceful transition into another existence, he seemed to accept the inevitability of his own demise. Although his family had thought him to be remarkably accepting of death, they came to realize that his seeming acceptance had limits. Always having believed that his wife would survive him, he became shaken and distraught when he discovered that her death was imminent, a discovery made long after other family members knew of it. Since they wished to "protect" his fragile health, they did not inform him. After her hospitalization she was sent to a convalescent hospital to die, but he was told that she was sent there to recuperate. At first, he could not understand her listless fatigue. Heavily sedated, she seemed more apathetic than he had ever known her. Because he could not believe that she, who had been so full of vitality, could give up so easily, he pleaded with her to live and return home with him. But she slipped into a coma and soon died. He saw her death as a travesty, a failure. For him, the failure had two dimensions: her failure to struggle against death and the practitioners' failure to permit her to try. He blamed the staff for keeping her over-sedated and immobilized, which he believed contributed to her weakened condition. In essence, his interpretation of her death was rooted in the context and his experience of it.

Because the symbolic interactionist emphasizes the interpretative process, it is a particularly suitable frame of reference to use when the researcher wishes to learn the effects of experience on meanings or, alternatively, the effects of meanings on experience. In order to obtain a sense of the ways in which meanings shift and change, it is necessary to have access to the social worlds and social experiences in which they are situated. From a research standpoint, there are two major ways of studying the stability and change of meanings as they are interpreted by people in everyday worlds. First, one way to approach the study of meanings of death and dying is to conduct research in a social world where members confront it. In studying the views of student nurses, for example, one could begin when they are novices unfamiliar with what other nurses deem to be the appropriate ways to think, feel, and act toward death. Then through sustained participation in their world, one could make systematic observations leading to some assessment of the ways their socialization process alters their stance toward death. Second, many people have similar social experiences such as facing death or feeling intense grief but do not share the same social world. In this case, the other way of tapping the interpretative process of those studied is to complete in-depth interviews at different intervals to assess how and when individuals reinterpreted their experiences and subsequently developed new or altered meanings of death. In both approaches, the researcher seeks to discover the *conditions* contributing to the stability or transformation of subjective meanings through the individual's interpretations of his or her experience.

These approaches reveal possibilities for studying the empirical implications of Blumer's premises. To extend his position, two more premises could be added to form a more explicit statement. They are:

4. Meanings are interpreted through shared language and communication.

5. The mediation of meaning in social interaction is distinguished by a continually emerging processural nature.

The symbolic interactionist position has several notable strengths that are of particular import in the study of death. Obviously, studying death from a point of view that highlights the thoughts and ideas of the interacting individual is very useful. What death means to people cannot be taken for granted. Consequently, much of what follows in this book will open up major questions regarding the meaning of death to members of varied social worlds and interactional contexts. By looking at what real persons think, feel, and do as a starting point, the sociologist can better assess changing images of death and ways of dealing with it. In the examples above, meanings of death were situated in experiences that made them directly significant to the actor. But, meanings of death may also be derived from those who are not believed to currently face it as well as from those for whom it is imminent. For example, death may mean quite different things to the same person at different points in the life cycle, as well as at different points in the dying process. One woman who saw death as forbidden in middle age redefined it in old age. She then saw it as reunification bringing her back together with her deceased husband. (Her views may also reflect the social-historical times in which she developed them. Death as forbidden was a common theme when she was middle aged; death as unification is perhaps more widely held now.) Another woman who was dying of cancer first viewed death as the enemy to struggle against when she was told of her diagnosis. Shortly before her death, it became apparent that she now viewed death as a peaceful release from the anguish caused by her pain.

An important implication of the perspective is the kind of research which is congenial to it. For the symbolic interactionist, the natural world is the world of inquiry; exploration, inquiry, and observation all take place within it. Consequently, this perspective is particularly useful for small-scale studies in which firsthand data are obtained. The sociologist's intimate knowledge of the situation enables him or her to study hidden aspects of group existence. For example, taken-for-granted but patterned ways of handling interaction with survivors of patients who died on a medical ward may be discovered by the sociologist, although participants actually are not aware of the patterns. In an area such as death, where so much of social reality remains tacit and unstated, this task is particularly important.

The symbolic interactionist perspective also emphasizes how the social actor makes sense of problematic situations in everyday life. Interactionists are curious about the kinds of ideologies people hold that help them make sense of their situations. For purposes of clarification, an ideology is a *shared* set of values and beliefs held by a group, which provides a *justification* for prior actions and a call for future actions. In any case, symbolic interactionists are interested in the ways in which ideologies focus attention on some issues and discourage raising questions about others. For example, some physicians espouse the following ideological beliefs: (1) the physician should be totally responsible for the patient's treatment, (2) the medical aspects of the case are the most significant, and (3) patients who are seriously ill cannot be expected to be fully rational. As a consequence of their ideology, these physicians take the active role in decisionmaking and, hence, do not question the patient's passive role in the treatment process.

Ideological views are also important in the study of the self, a major topic of research for symbolic interactionists. I contend that, in American society, the self is inherently *evaluational*. That is, selves are fundamentally defined through values, often in deceptively simple terms such as a "good person" or a "poor patient." More subtly, the self-images of physicians who hold the above ideological view are evaluated on their ability to actively intervene with the disease process and thus control it.

For the dying, maintaining a positive sense of self can often become a significant problematic issue. Since selves are socially created and socially maintained, the social identity *conferred upon* the individual typically has profound implications for any personal identity the individual claims. Often, when a person is dying, the self that the person had claimed throughout his or her life is stripped away by the institutionalized procedural ways in which dying typically is handled in the medical setting (cf. Goffman 1961). For example, in one case a woman dying of burns was virtually abandoned by her husband and those who had known her before the accident. Her last few months were spent in intensive care wards, where she was given an identity by nurses as someone who was manipulative, emotionally unstable, and undesirable to work with. This identity was ascribed to her partially because she was unable to fit her pain into "appropriate" institutional routines. She complained of "too much" pain "too often," much to the irritation of the nurses. Whatever she had been before her injury, her social identity in dying was reduced to that of a "whining sniveler." One wonders if she was able to retain any threads of a more positive personal identity from the past, since no visible remnants of her prior existence were available to her in her terminal months—even her face was drastically changed.

Because the self is so central a concern of symbolic interactionists, attention will be given to it throughout the book. Consequently, the self-images of various participants in diverse arenas where death is an issue will be examined.

The dramaturgical approach One approach derived from the general perspective of symbolic interactionism, the dramaturgical approach, holds much promise of illuminating issues concerning death and dying. This approach uses the *metaphor* of the *drama* to analyze interactional encounters. By invoking this metaphor, these analysts highlight certain dimensions of reality that might otherwise not be brought into view. In particular, dramaturgical analysts highlight the *construction of action* and its *context*. That context includes the temporal and spatial dimensions of the scene in addition to the social staging of action.

Consistent with the general symbolic interactionist approach, those employing the dramaturgical method aim to study meaningful action. As Kenneth Burke (1945), the originator of this approach, stresses, it begins with theories of action rather than theories of knowledge. That is, the dramaturgical approach takes as a starting point of analysis the problematic features of the *action* of the individual. Other approaches, including the general symbolic interactionist perspective above, begin with the problematic features of the *knowledge* of the individual. While the dramaturgical analyst asks first, "What does the social actor do?," the symbolic interactionist asks first, "What does the social actor think and know?"

Since the dramaturgical approach focuses squarely on the ongoing construction of action by participating social actors, the analyst must make a close examination of the dialectical relationships between purposes and actions. It is assumed that actors continually makes sense of their interactions and the context in which they occur, thus causing purposes and actions to be continually modified and changed.

Rather than inquiring into the definition of the situation as held and verbalized by each individual actor, the dramaturgical analyst emphasizes the definition of the situation that seems apparent in the *event*, that is, the one that is given in the structure of action. Hence, when someone commits suicide, the dramaturgical analyst would look at how family members acted afterwards. The dramaturgical analyst would assess the meaning of the death to the family as it is visible in what they actually do, rather than in what they might say about it to an interviewer.

Quite clearly then, the dramaturgical approach explicitly takes *nonverbal behavior* into account. Taken-for-granted meanings may then become visible. In this way, dramaturgical analysts are often in a position to make distinctions between the actual performance of actors in an event or scene and their later rationalizations or justifications of their performance in that event or scene. For example, in the situation cited above, a case history by a participant observer of the events following a suicide may look very unlike the accounts given by relatives. Their views of their actions might be cast in explanations that not only absolve themselves from any responsibility for the death, but also justify how they handled it.

The suicide of one college student revealed to me by someone who was not directly involved illustrates the point. Before the student's death, she had aroused the concern of her housemates numerous times. After her boyfriend broke off their relationship, she became very depressed. At first, her housemates were sympathetic and tried to talk with her about her problems, which began to multiply. Being uninterested in her classes, she rarely attended them. Later, she quit her part-time job. By greatly diminishing her activities without adding new ones, she spent the days sitting around the house. For a time her housemates tried to distract her from her preoccupations by suggesting outings or attempting to engage her in conversations. But it wasn't long before they became quite angry with her. They felt that she wasn't doing anything to help herself. Even the two women who had been especially supportive and solicitous of her began to exclude her. One moved out, saying she couldn't "take it anymore." The other said, "I hate to go into the living room anymore because she's always sitting there waiting to glom on to anyone who will listen to her; she is such a downer." Although the others decided to ask her to leave, no one had the chutzpah to make the request. Besides, the pressures all felt at the end of the semester caused them to attend less to matters at home. One Saturday night when the others were gone, the woman took an overdose of sleeping pills. After her death, her housemates reconstructed their interpretation of what had happened before. They emphasized their earlier attentiveness and gave the impression that it lasted for a much longer period than it actually had. Further, when questioned about their later exclusion and rejection of her, they claimed that they were trying to encourage her to become "more independent and resourceful."

What is significant here is the ways in which the participants' views changed after the woman's suicide. If a sociologist were to interview the woman's housemates after her suicide, quite a different response would be obtained than the one gained through the eyes of the observer who witnessed how members of the household actually dealt with this woman. After the suicide, their interpretations of what happened were essentially shaped by their need to justify their actions toward their deceased housemate.

Because of their sensitivity to the subtle uses of rationalizations and justifications and other self-absolving statements to explain behavior, dramaturgical analysts have greatly enriched insight into human motivation. These analysts do not accept the social determinist view that social forces motivate the individual to act. They believe that motives are invoked by social actors as a way of explaining or *accounting* for past actions. Dramaturgical analysts assume that much of social life does not necessitate articulating reasons for behavior. In that way, acts may not be consciously defined. But when actions are frustrated or called into question, then the issue of motivation arises. Actions become *problematic* when actors become self-conscious about what they are doing. For example, terminal patients may not be questioned about requests for painkillers until staff realize that they are on the point of addiction. Then, they may call these patients' motives into question and seek accounts from them in order to "explain" the questioned behavior.

Consequently, providing explanations for behavior occurs only when taken-for-granted activity is challenged or interrupted. By interpreting prior action, a stated motive answers the question of "why" behind that action. In short, motives provide a way of rationalizing or justifying actions when an account is defined as necessary. As Brissett and Edgley (1975, p. 7) put it: "human beings are consciously rationalizing, not consciously rational."

Dramaturgical analysts assume that people first *act*, then, as a *consequence* of action, define meanings. To illustrate, the possibility of suicide arises in the course of action rather than through long premeditation. As a case in point, a woman recounted her suicidal experience as building up during a weekend bout of drinking and taking sedatives. She did not begin the episode with suicide in mind, but as events progressed she decided to seek what for her was later described as rebirth through the "transition of death" by cutting her wrists.

Dramaturgical analysts typically employ more of an objectivist approach to social reality than those who adhere more purely to the symbolic interactionist perspective described above. Behavior is analyzed from the standpoint of the *observer*, who has a close view of the scene, with stress on the observable played roles and the discernible actions taken, rather than on the subjective meanings of participants. In that way, nonverbal aspects of behavior are brought into view as well as verbal ones. Similarly, the analyst pays more attention to the analysis of the event than to the thoughts of various protagonists within it. For example, a researcher studying funeral directors may describe and analyze in detail the observable role played in front of the bereaved without any elucidation of what the participants actually think and feel while playing that role (see Turner and Edgely 1975).

Because dramaturgical analysts often study behavior from the outside, they carefully record those expressions, gestures, body movements, and cues that are unwittingly revealed by the actor in the course of action, in addition to those explicitly strategized to elicit a desired effect or response. Since persons often indicate their "real" intentions through such unwitting disclosures, dramaturgical analysts may then impute specific intentions to those observed (see Goffman 1959). For example, a man was discussing the death of a family friend who had developed heart disease in middle age. He no doubt believed that the statements about his friend were sympathetic. Yet, through the glint in his eye, the combined smugness and nonchalance in his voice, and the erect position of his head, he unwittingly gave me the distinct impression that he felt victorious that his friend had died and not he.

Goffman (1959) emphasized the actor's *presentation of self*. In this approach, the analyst attempts to identify what and whom is being presented, the ways in which roles are being played, and how both fit into the ongoing scene. Questions one might ask include: Is the presented self consistent with the role played? Is the role a routine performance or an extraordinary one? For whom is it routine? The role of announcing death, for example, is routine for a physician, but it results in an extraordinary event for the bereaved.

The significance of the *audience* is now apparent: Any drama must have its audience. But what is the nature of the audience? What kind of reciprocity exists between audience and performer? What relationship does the audience have to the ongoing scenes? In formal relationships such as in hospitals, the relationship between audience and performer tends to be more static than in informal, intimate relationships. Currently, however, we are witnessing something of a reversal in audience-performer roles with the dying. While the stage is typically set for dying patients to constitute the audience for various performances played out around them and on their bodies, some dying persons are refusing to remain in the audience! Instead, they wish to take the leading role as the *performer* who gives shape and content to the unfolding drama.

Examining the audience raises other questions: Under what circumstances are there different audiences? Is the same performance played to all of them? Quite clearly, audiences differ and performances must be changed accordingly if they are to be taken as credible and real. For example, the exaggerated deference of a funeral director is quite inappropriate with peers, as is any reference to the deceased as a "stiff" or "corpse" to the bereaved. Similarly, hospital staff often shift their performances according to their assessments of the social class background of the clientele. To illustrate, I noticed that in one convalescent hospital the staff were much less careful about their actions in front of the families of Medi-Cal (state-supported) patients than the private patients. In this particular institution, the aides sometimes had coffee and cigarettes in the rooms of patients whom they deemed to be senile or comatose. When the registered nurse was elsewhere, they would occasionally turn up the patient's radio and practice dance steps. When families visited the Medi-Cal patients, the aides would stop dancing, but unless work was immediately pressing, they finished their coffee and cigarettes while conversing with the visitors. The registered nurse who supervised them did not seem to object to this behavior, but if similar behavior was witnessed by the families of private patients, she chastized them heavily and even threatened to fire several of them (see Sudnow 1967, for similar incidents).

The way in which the performance is given is then intertwined with whom, where, and when it is given. Generally, dramaturgical analysts have paid more attention to *spatial* and *temporal* arrangements than have their symbolic interactionist counterparts. Hence, they study the effects of territorial arrangements on the scene. In particular, they differentiate between public, or frontstage, territories and private, or backstage, regions (see Goffman 1959). Of course, vast discrepancies are apt to exist between these two arenas of action. For example, nursing homes might be considered the backstage of the medical care system since what goes on within them is largely outside the purview of the public. Or, to use the term more concretely, hospital staff may attempt to put forth one type of impression in the presence of patients and families, but immediately drop it when observed by peers. Similarly, dramaturgical analysts focus on the timing of actions and events.

Whether or not the timing of a performance is "correct" affects its credibility with the audience. For example, Shneidman (1973) tells of a Greek immigrant who was admitted to the hospital with advanced leukemia. When Shneidman interviewed him, he seemed depressed. The patient disclosed that a young doctor had asked him, "Are you afraid to die?" (p. 31). Shneidman discovered that the doctor had asked the question *before* the patient knew what the term "leukemia" meant. Obviously, the timing of the doctor's performance was wrong although, no doubt, the question was meant to show concern.

In concluding this discussion of the dramaturgical approach, I need to comment on the conception of human nature implied within it. In the foregoing discussion, one might see human nature as opportunistic, self-interested, and strategic. However, the value of the method of analysis does not need to be limited to the study of manipulative performances calculated to have the "edge" on other participants. What happens in everyday life is simply more obvious when actors behave strategically. In any case, by using the dramaturgical method, the analyst gains a sense of the ways in which individuals attempt to *control* their situations, interactions, and most importantly, themselves.

Both the dramaturgical and symbolic interactionist approaches begin with analyses of the individual. While the dramaturgical analyst emphasizes action, the symbolic interactionist emphasizes intention. Both perspectives lead to an examination of meanings derived from interaction. Although these perspectives have in the past primarily been used to study the self and interaction, they may also provide a framework for analyzing larger social units.

Structural-Functional Approach

Basic to a structural approach is the question: How is death related to the *society* as a whole? In asking that question, structural-functional theorists would examine the functions of the ways of handling death that serve the wider society. Since they view society as a social system or organism maintained by the balanced *functioning* of its parts, this approach is based on an *equilibrium model*. The emphasis is placed upon how society maintains its equilibrium such that *social integration* is preserved. The parts of the social system contributing to the maintenance of the equilibrium are the *social institutions*. If social integration is to be maintained, institutionalized ways of handling death would have to be consistent with the maintenance of the present social structure. From this perspective, the ways in which death is handled would necessarily have the consequence of providing continuity in the ongoing social structure.

Adopting a structural-functional approach leads one to look closely at the institutionalized cultural foundations of contemporary attitudes toward death. In order to understand these attitudes and place them in perspective, one must look at ritual meanings held by members of society. Explication of meanings about death provides some insight about the reciprocal ways in which death and social structure are linked. For example, Ivan Illich (1974) argues that ritual meanings about "natural" death become institutionalized into the social structure of medicine as well as in the everyday expectations of lay persons. Even though meanings of a "natural" death become transformed by the institution of medicine, according to Illich, they remain significant for the structuring of actual care by paradoxically creating a pool of passive consumers who then are subjected to a technologized dying process.

A structural perspective necessitates an analysis of the *development, structure, functions, consequences of,* and *interrelationships* between dominant institutions. Then, an analysis must be constructed of the connections between institutional forms and death. Parsons and Lidz (1967) invoke this line of reasoning when they explore the effects of awarding secular institutions major value in modern society. They propose that the rise of science has had the consequence of diminishing the significance of death. Values supporting science have taken precedence over those supporting religious institutions, which Parsons and Lidz claim provide the framework for interpreting death. Further, they imply that such interpretations must be consistent with beliefs supporting science if social integration is to be maintained.

A more subtle interplay between science and death perhaps centers on the area of *death expectations.* People hold institutionalized expectations concerning the "appropriate" type of death, that is, a natural death, and the "correct" timing of it (old age). For example, it is neither proper nor natural to die from a fall at age 30. The significance of these expectations may readily be discerned when they are not met. Lifton's observations of the survivors of the atomic bomb on Hiroshima (1968) shed some light on the profound disruption occurring when not only individual death expectations are shattered but also when institutional arrangements are broken. He found that the survivors were so overwhelmed by their experience that they did not and could not respond to their situations with anything resembling a "normal" grief response. Instead, they were left numb as their worlds literally collapsed. Although Lifton's intent was to explore the psychiatric implications of such an experience, the careful study of such dramatic disruptions of institutionalized expectations may reveal much about the preexisting social structure.

Another means of making structural patterns more visible is to conduct comparative studies of diverse cultures. By conducting systematic comparisons of the beliefs and norms of another society with our own, the structural-functionalist may make hidden dimensions of culture more visible. For example, Parsons and Lidz (1967) compare the abbreviated and privatized contemporary mourning rituals with those in preindustrial societies wherein death caused much greater disruption of social structure. They hypothesize that the modern approach of brief rituals and private grief may be functional for society as structural continuity is maintained if the survivors quickly resume their former roles and tasks.

Since social structural analysis examines values and practices in relationship to the functioning of society, some positions arrived at stand in stark contrast to those taken by other intellectuals and the public alike. For example, Parsons and Lidz (1967) take issue with the commonly accepted view that the dominant cultural attitude toward death in American society is death-denying. In contrast, they claim that the ways in which death is treated are consistent with dominant values requiring *activism* of the individual. Hence, they imply that life in American society presupposes active, forward-looking members whose primary task is to fulfill their social roles. (Later, Parsons, Fox, and Lidz [1973] qualify the earlier argument by stating that much of what passes for "denial" actually is a type of apathy perpetuated by both the stoicism of the Protestant Ethos and everyday medical practice.)

Having set forth some of the major concerns of a structural-functional approach to the study of death, I will now examine the potential of death for disrupting the equilibrium of social life. Blauner (1966) points out that this potential exists in any society although its extent varies with the type of social structure and the significance of the participation within it of those who die. Thus, standardized practices including customs, norms, and laws are developed to handle death in ways which *minimize* the potential disruption and foster the *reintegration* of the group. A modern example of such standardized practices consists of the rituals surrounding the death of police officers who are killed on duty. The full participation of an officer's peers as well as other law enforcement officials in the funeral and burial rites serves to reaffirm the solidarity and purposes of the members. Moreover, the scenario of the procession with uniformed members of their respective agencies marching or riding their motorcycles and horses is a concrete symbol not only of their affiliation but also their strength. As one policeman commented to me, "I think the real function of the procession is to re-establish a sense of order, particularly for the members of the force of the guy who was killed."

Blauner emphasizes that a disruptive consequence of death for ongoing social life is the social vacuum that is created by death. He argues that a death creates a gap in the social structure, and possibly in the institutionalized functioning of a particular group. How serious the social vacuum is depends upon the social and symbolic importance of the person or persons who died. One individual in our society whose death created something of a social vacuum was John F. Kennedy. Quite clearly, in smaller groups or societies in which face-to-face interaction between its members is characteristic of the society, the potential disruption caused by death is much greater than in a mass society. Blauner posits that elaborate funeral, burial, and mourning rites were developed in these societies to lessen the disruption of the society as a whole. Through these rites, the duties and rights of the survivors were clearly spelled out. Blauner astutely recognizes that death in these societies could have devastating effects upon the kinship and community structure since death frequently occurred while the deceased was an integral part of the group. That is, women died in the midst of their child-raising years and men died while involved in their work. In short, mortality had a grave impact upon the society since those who were responsible for the functioning of the society were affected by it.

Blauner's basic thesis is that fundamental determinants of the impact of death are the *age* and *social contributions* of those who die. According to his argument, those who are younger and who are directly contributing to the functioning of the society are going to create larger social vacuums upon their deaths. It must be noted, however, that social contributions must be given full credit since in some societies the most important social contributions for maintaining the moral beliefs and norms of the group are made by the elders who rule the group. In our society, most elderly people are afforded little opportunity to contribute to others and are not given much respect for their prior contributions. Consequently, they have a different kind of status in the social structure than is often observed in traditional societies. Blauner's study represents a typical structural-functional approach because it emphasizes the effects of social roles and social functions on society.

Although death occurs at all ages, functional theorists have been particularly concerned with institutional relationships between death and the elderly, since the death rates in industrial societies are increasingly constituted by them. In our society, retirement, without compensatory tasks and status combined with child raising in early adulthood, results in a situation where elderly persons no longer are an integral part of the functioning of the society. Further, the elderly have become segregated from the rest of the community in retirement apartments, planned communities, mobile home courts, nursing homes, and downtown hotels. Consequently, even their presence is less visible to those who are contributing actively to the maintenance of the society. Blauner points out that a way of reducing the impact of mortality is to reduce the real or ideal significance of those who die. In this vein, he cites the classic example provided by Aries (1962). Historically, Aries found that French children were not highly valued when infant mortality was high. At that time, children were not seen as individuals until they had attained an age after which their chances of survival became more promising. Consequently, their social loss to the family and to the larger society was kept minimal. Thus this *attitude* was *functional* for a society in which natural biological forces made the experience of infant mortality likely. Blauner sees an analogous situation emerging with the elderly in our society. Not only do they not contribute to the vital functions of the society, but they are also systematically deprived of their individuality and certainly represent a devalued group. In short, according to this argument, deaths of elderly persons would not necessitate any serious disruption and accommodation by the society. In contrast, in a society where the elderly are fully integrated, institutions would have to arise to distribute their functions, to repair the group of their loss, and to treat death as a visible fact of life.

In the structural-functional approach, the individual and the society exist in a delicately *balanced relationship*. Since death could conceivably alter this delicate balance, social mechanisms are developed that are assumed to be *adaptive* for both the society and the individual. Because aging and death are facts of life, functionalist theorists, such as Blauner, raise questions about the adjustment of the society and individual to these facts. Blauner has provided a cogent analysis of how the society adapts to the deaths of members who are most likely to die. Structural-functional theorists also raise questions as to how the individual adapts so that the fragile equilibrium between self and society is maintained. Since death rates are inevitably high in old age, functional theorists assume that both the society and the individual must prepare for it.

In their theory of *disengagement*, Cumming and Henry (1961) provide a theoretical explanation of the development of this preparation. Disengagement means that once-active individuals gradually give up their former social roles that contributed to the work of the society. Disengagement is advantageous, according to the theory, to both the society and the individual. Society gives individuals the freedom to withdraw, something structural-functionalists assume individuals desire. Society then benefits because others can assume the vacated social roles. The advantages to the society are clear— the work of the society is carried out and the unpleasant fact of death is minimized. But how is disengagement satisfying for the individual? Cumming and Henry propose that individuals want to withdraw since death can be accepted with greater equanimity once they no longer have deep social ties anchored in adult responsibilities. Because they are motivated to disengage, their life satisfaction is assumed to be based on prior accomplishments and an increasing concern with inner needs. Structural-functionalists assume that older people voluntarily initiate their disengagement during middle age as they become aware of their decreasing life span. Hence, according to the theory, people gradually relinquish social roles and bonds in order to *prepare for death*. By giving up social roles and reducing the number and intensity of social ties, older people become socially and psychologically prepared for death. Relationships are ended or are resolved; detachment and passivity are permitted as it is assumed that these people do not feel pressured to remain involved. Then, what Cumming and Henry imply is that the social situation of the aged is a *satisfactory* arrangement. Since individuals may prepare for death through their gradual withdrawal, the society does not have to concern itself with either heavy social obligations to the aged, nor does the presence of the aged impede the smooth working of that society. Clearly, individuals do not withdraw with the *motive* or *intent* to "help society out"—reasons are varied. They include apathy, lack of money and, most importantly, I think, ill health. The ultimate *function* of disengagement, however, is that it does "help" maintain the current social structural arrangements.

Cumming and Henry view the process of disengagement as a natural process which is irreversible once set into motion. Psychological and social age are merged in this framework into a developmental conception of a linear process that culminates in death. The first major step of the process usually begins with retirement. But gradually, as individuals withdraw, a new equilibrium is established between them and the society. The type of balance between self and society when individuals are disengaged is qualitatively different than that experienced in middle age. By the time illness and dying are experienced, disengaged people are assumed to be able to accept their inevitable fate.

In a framework such as Cumming and Henry have provided, what is typically observable within the society is elevated to a "natural" and "universal" status. Because older people are usually forced to disengage and may currently accept the social pressure to play their passive and often segregated roles does not necessarily mean that the disengagement process we discern reflects anything more than the social structuring of economic existence. Further, on a social psychological level, the passivity and withdrawal of older persons may simply be something of a self-fulfilling prophecy that is socially produced. Hochschild (1975) insightfully notes that forced economic disengagement itself fosters passivity and loss of emotional intensity, two conditions which, according to Cumming and Henry, are supposed to be criteria of successful psychological disengagement. Thus, Cumming and Henry elevate an economic necessity within a certain type of society into a functional prerequisite of society itself. The disengagement theory raises some intriguing questions for students on death. Does, in fact, disengagement in old age prepare people for their deaths, or does it perhaps so demoralize them that they no longer have much interest in living? Is resignation confused with acceptance? Does death become viewed as an escape, a way out? Do disengaged persons give more conscious thought to coming to terms with their own deaths than people who are more involved? In order to examine these questions fully, one must look at the empirical world of living, thinking beings, rather than being satisfied to posit explanations that may make sense theoretically but are not clearly assessed empirically.

In order to study the implications of this theory empirically, two important questions must be asked from two other perspectives. From a symbolic interactionist perspective, one must ask what disengagement subjectively means to the social actor. The investigator must look at how the individual defines involvement and withdrawal and determine what explicit and implicit criteria the person has for both. Then, too, from a Marxian perspective, disengagement must be studied in conjunction with power arrangements. By and large, old people do not yet have much choice about engagement, and their very lack of choice must be made an object of study. Hence, the structural-functional perspective, by focusing on the functions of processes such as disengagement tend to ignore the subjective feelings and intentions of individuals, which are emphasized by symbolic interactionists. Structural functionalists also tend to view the current structural arrangements as necessary. This results in an acceptance of the social order as it is, which Marxists call into question. As will become apparent in the next section, a Marxist structural analysis raises a contrasting set of questions to ask of the social order.

A Marxist Perspective

Perhaps because death is something which happens to the individual, sociologists have, for the most part, neglected to study it from a radical structural critique. However, I propose that any serious sociological treatment of death in American society raises radical issues about its structure. From a Marxist perspective, the institutions supporting American society need restructuring to obtain an equitable distribution of wealth and power. A radical analysis of social structure would then go to the roots or foundations of that structure and seek to transform them. Simply because most sociological studies of death and dying are social psychological in focus does not mean that the issues are limited to the individual or the interaction process. Besides, the ways in which the individual's concerns and arena of interaction fit into the larger social context are of major significance. (Although to date there are no Marxist sociologists who study death, there are a number of studies which suggest dimensions of the issues raised by this perspective.) In the following analysis, I shall attempt to show how death in American society might be dealt with from the perspective of Marxist humanism (see Fromm 1962; Giddens 1971; Zeitlin 1968).

One of the obvious issues to be addressed in a Marxist approach to death is that of *inequality*. Inequality is apparent in the availability and quality of medical care, as well as in differential death rates. For example, Sudnow (1967) documents the moral decisions made in a county hospital. These decisions result in practices which systematically deprive lower income patients (particularly the elderly poor) of optimal care, in general, and of lifesaving procedures, in particular. From a statistical point of view, lower income people, including most minority people, are shown to have substantially higher death rates for each age bracket than middle-class males (see Goldscheider 1975). Similarly, in one of its recent publications, the Department of Health, Education, and Welfare (1977) reported that the age-adjusted death rate in 1973 for minority men was one-third more than the corresponding rate for white counterparts, and the rate for minority women was 50 percent more than the rate for white females.

The inequality observed in mortality rates suggests the kinds of relationships between death and a social structure predicated on a class system that sociologists might further study. Marxists assume that the class system divides people into groups having widely discrepant and often mutually exclusive economic interests, whether or not members of these classes actually recognize their interests. When they do not, it is assumed that they have accepted the dominant ideas and values of the society, which are the ideas of the power elite. Marxists then posit a crucial relationship between social structure and those ideas held within a society. With that crucial relationship in mind, a discussion of ideas about death and social structure may begin.

As a starting point, Marxists would assume that neither the process of dying nor the modes of handling death can be separated from the larger social structure in which they take place. Thus, from a Marxist perspective, a major tenet is that "psychological" reactions seemingly caused by intrapsychic processes are actually fostered by larger social processes. In this view, then, it is a mistake to examine only the subjective view of the individual or, for that matter, the psychological processes that professionals observe in dying patients or the bereaved. The thoughts and feelings that are both unstated and directly expressed by people who may in some way confront death are shaped by their experiences within the society and their exposure to the dominant ideologies and institutions within it. For example, the sister of a woman whose husband was dying in a local hospital made the following statement:

> She [her sister] wants to be with him when he dies, whenever it occurs. I think that she's being unrealistic. Most people die alone today. You live alone and you die alone—that's the way it is. Dying is something you have to do on your own.

This woman's statement reflects her ideological view, one shared by many who believe that the living and dying should be separated. It also shows that the excessive individualism characteristic of a competitive economic system, and the ensuing loneliness, carries over to death as well.

One might raise further questions about how death and ideologies are related. As observed earlier, ideologies not only justify past actions but also foster the creation of future actions. Since death is usually conceived of as a unique experience belonging solely to the individual, at first glance there may seem to be no connection with ideologies. But from a Marxist perspective, most of what we "know" about death represents ideological views rather than a "true" picture of reality. In addition, from this perspective dying cannot be separated from living and what living is all about is also shrouded in ideological beliefs. If so, our modes of conceptualizing death, dying, and grieving would be intimately related to our ideological conceptions of living and life. And from a Marxist perspective many parallels can be drawn.

Marxists claim that what is taken for granted to be "true" and "real" by a group of people typically reflects an *unexamined ideology*. Many of our assumptions about death and dying then reflect ideological stances. Ideologies are not necessarily false beliefs or myths that totally obfuscate reality, but they do tend to be partial in character and limited in the scope of reality that they accurately portray. For example, the current belief among some practitioners that the patient must pass through the psychological stages of dying, as first outlined by Kübler-Ross (1969), is an ideological perspective (see Chapter 5 for an extended discussion of this). Many terminally ill patients do go through the stages, although those who would acknowledge that the stages reflect their own experiences of the dying process might be a much smaller number than Kübler-Ross's followers might expect. Or, like the belief in romantic love in this culture, to the extent that an ideology about death becomes dominant throughout the society, then people become socialized into making attempts to validate the belief in their own everyday reality.

In any case, when a view of reality is taken as "real" and "true," it tends to become *reified*, or treated as a concrete and stable entity. Major interpretations of the dying process have become treated as if they were fixed and stable entities which then take on a universal character. They are treated as "natural," rather than habitual or culturally defined.

As beliefs take on ideological weight, they provide a form for seeing and understanding reality. The framework through which death is usually studied and understood tends to be a psychiatric framework. This framework, like other conceptual frameworks, highlights certain aspects of reality and blinds its user to others. From a Marxian view, our perspectives on death and dying have blinded us from seeing the ways in which they are ideological and when acted out in practical reality, perpetuate certain power interests. For example, ordinary people who believe in giving relatives the maximum amount of medical intervention possible are unlikely to be aware that the stance they take also supports the pharmaceutical, hospital supply, and convalescent hospital industry interests.

Furthermore, from a Marxist perspective, it becomes clear that ideologies serve to mask the divergent interests that different sectors of the society have. Since in this perspective it is assumed that different groups often have *mutually exclusive* interests, it follows that many so-called services for the dying and deceased, such as funeral planning or terminal care, may be designed for the economic interests of those providing services rather than the clientele being served.

Ideologies that reflect more widely held cultural values are also played out in the scenarios surrounding death. Beliefs in individualism, self-reliance, privatism, and stoicism are ideological and justify the ways in which dying is handled. The ideological view of dying as a private affair, something that *should* be the responsibility of the family, relieves other social institutions, notably health and welfare organizations, from the necessity of providing comprehensive services. This view is consistent with more generally held beliefs that individuals must handle their own affairs. Such beliefs are justified by ideological views that human beings deserve privacy in their problems, and in order to maintain self-respect, they wish to rely on themselves to handle them whenever possible. When it is not possible, failure may be conferred upon those unable to handle their situations. These beliefs give some indication of the ideological power of the Protestant Ethos that is still embedded in the American consciousness (cf. Gorer 1965).

Such ideologies serve to work against the "objective" interests of many individuals. For those who hold these beliefs, feelings of failure are likely to develop when responsibilities cannot be handled by a single-family unit or, likely, a spouse or adult child. The difficulties in taking care of a terminally ill person tend to multiply and spiral as the person's disease sets in. Hence, the stage is set for the ill person to feel guilty for the burdens on intimates, and then, too, intimates are apt to feel overwhelmed and angry. For example, one elderly woman was afraid of going to an institution. Her middle-aged daughter took care of her as she progressively deteriorated. Since there were no community resources for terminal care, the burden of home care fell on the family, primarily her daughter. For a period of time, the daughter attempted to manage both her job and her mother's care. However, with the downhill course of the disease it became impossible, so the daughter took a leave of absence. The care steadily increased to the point that keeping her mother clean and reasonably comfortable took more than the daughter (whose back was literally giving out) could handle. The mother felt guilty for the strain her daughter was under. The daughter began to feel and, occasionally, express anger at her mother for being so unwilling to go to a nursing home. And by that time there were no available slots at any of the nursing homes the family thought were suitable placements. Yet, this family and often others similarly involved still define the situation as "our" problem and attempt to respond to it only in the most individualistic manner, such as seeing the solution solely in terms of personal expression of negative feelings elicited by the situation.

But a personal and private crisis has public consequences and political implications. What is privately felt and experienced could be changed when brought into the public arena. So long as experiences remain "private matters" they will not be given much public attention. Thus, even when discussed in the realm of public policy by practitioners and concerned citizens, the problems are narrowly defined and the solutions stop-gap and partial.

More common, however, is the tendency for practitioners to reaffirm the definition of the problem as a private one, the solutions for which are to be developed individually, case by case. Hence, for the most part, the experiences of the dying person are not seen in the context of larger social meanings.

In the discussion above, I have emphasized how ideologies are related to our current practices concerning death. Now I wish to offer some ideas about how these practices might be related to everyday life. The Marxian conception of social reality holds the position that human beings are basically creative and reflective beings although social systems, most notably those predicated on advanced industrial capitalism, produce alienated beings who cannot control their fates. In this view, the very form that human nature takes in this historical epoch is twisted into a type of being to correspond to the needs of the system. It is believed that human beings are fundamentally shaped by an alienating, dehumanizing social structure that encourages people to lead atomized, fragmented lives. Competition and the quest for personal gain are believed to feed the isolation and alienation that characterizes life in this society. As a result, people do not recognize their common interests with others and are unlikely to feel secure in challenging their existing mode of life. Thus competition and alienation give birth to the kinds of *controlled individualism* that symbolize the American spirit and, subsequently, mitigate against the development of concerted collective action that would radically change both the structure of society, in general, and the experience of dying, in particular.

In many ways, dying in this society dramatically symbolizes an underlying theme of the alienation and powerlessness of its members that is obscured by the appearance of freedom in everyday life. Dying patients are often left alone, abandoned by relatives, forgotten by friends, and feared by practitioners. They may be treated as dead or nonpersons while they are sentient. Their feelings and wishes are subjugated to institutional routines, treatment trends, and their relatives' decisions. Not only are they usually powerless, but they are also stripped of their selves as they become objects to be manipulated by those who control them. An example from a case history may help. One old man was discharged to a convalescent hospital to die. (Nursing aides in the acute hospital had told him that he would be going "home," but his son had not visited in several weeks.) Because he had outlived his friends, his life had been mostly limited to his T.V. in his boarding house room. Other boarders paid little attention to him. After the transfer to the convalescent hospital, he had virtually no contacts with the outside world except for occasional hurried "visits" from his daughter-in-law. Eventually, those also ceased. He had no control over treatment, though at first he complained much. Because he became a source of staff irritation and resentment, they sedated him heavily. By the time he died, he had become a symbol of death itself to the staff.

The powerlessness of this man surely contributed to a loss of self while he was dying. But his experience is not unique. Perhaps then, the treatment of the dying symbolizes the hollowness of life in an alienated society. And the systematic alienation and isolation of the dying patient shows in bold relief the fundamental premises on which existence in American society is based. But if one attempts to control one's life and take responsibility for that control one might, in turn, decrease one's alienation and, simultaneously, foster conditions which may give rise to a more humane social order. Thus, as alienation decreases, the construction of personal meaning would increase in life as well as in death.

Now I will return to more concrete instances which demonstrate how death may be related to power interests. From a Marxist perspective, one can argue that although we hold ideologies espousing the value of individual life in this society, those in power have little respect for the collective life of the society and particularly for those in the lower classes. Hence, working-class youths find themselves being used as cannon fodder during military crises, factory workers are exposed to life-threatening chemicals in their everyday work, and the aged poor suffer a slow starvation from malnutrition. Economic prerogatives taken by the few in power then may supersede the interests of the larger community. Those in power act in their own interests at the expense of those who do not have it, often without their full awareness of the implications of doing so. Even when those who are affected are dimly aware that extreme hazards might affect them, they may not press for changes. Factory workers, for example, may be aware that studies indicate that those who work daily in contact with harmful substances have a higher incidence of certain lethal cancer. But if the studies are not conclusive, and if the predictions of disease are made for twenty or thirty years hence, then workers may shrug off the ominous implications of their work because they need to make a living now. Besides, corporation representatives can threaten closure of the plant if working conditions are changed. If other possibilities for work are few, the workers are apt to be controlled by such tactics.

Returning to the issue of risks to which the worker is exposed, Hesslink and Steinman (1976) trace the history of one type of harmful substance, asbestos. They show that a wide gap exists between medical discoveries of harmful chemicals and the implementation and acceptance of government rules. In their example of the asbestos industry, they found that dangers associated with its use were suspected as early as 1906! By 1930 the suspected risk had been confirmed, yet not until 1972 were regulations established. Furthermore, to date, the public has only very recently become at all informed about the dangers of the substance.

According to Hesslink and Steinman, several factors may be operative in the delay of information. First, the industrial physicians who are most likely to first encounter indications of danger seem to identify themselves more as management than as physicians. Second, these physicians may be in danger of demotion or harassment when they take stands that undermine the corporation's objectives. Third, corporations sometimes exert censorship over the publications from their medical employees precisely for protection from lawsuits, raised insurance premiums, and workers. This suggests that corporate officials knowingly will place their own economic interests over the general welfare of their workers and the public. Fourth, Hesslink and Steinman demonstrate that beyond the private sphere, government bureaucrats take steps to keep information inaccessible to the public. Government agents, like workers, may at times find it preferable to continue exposure to dangerous materials both for the workers and the public alike than to make drastic changes that could affect the general economic situation at the time. Fifth, even if regulations are passed and public information is made available, the government may not enforce regulations or, if enforced, they may be so weak that corporations break them regularly.

The contradictory interests of different groups of people are shown in the asbestos example. Underlying the issue is the fundamental dilemma of whether the public good is worth more than disrupting the present social arrangements.

When dilemmas like this are examined, it becomes apparent that the life and well-being of the people is not necessarily the first consideration of those who shape public policy. Another example of such a dilemma arises in the area of earthquake prediction. Some people take the position that it is "dangerous" to inform the populace of these predictions since the economy will be disrupted if predicted locations are evacuated despite the fact that without advance notice thousands may be killed.

Although the intentional acts of individuals to serve their own interests is a major concern of a Marxian theorist, this perspective also reveals how the limited point of view some people have because they occupy a particular position in society can shape their actions within it. Subsequently, an individual's actions may unintentionally cause or perpetuate an undesirable situation, such as more people becoming critically ill from exposure to asbestos. When dealing with complex medical issues involving interpretation of highly sophisticated data, many of those involved see the situation only from their positions. Hence, however unintentionally, important aspects of the problem at hand are often overlooked, though the costs of these blunders may be paid in human lives.

This discussion suggests some of the central questions that might be asked from a Marxist framework. The strength of a Marxist humanist approach is that it links the underlying social structural problems with the psychological responses of individuals. In conclusion, the symbolic interactionist, structural-functionalist, and Marxist perspectives when used concomitantly, provide powerful insight into meanings, individual group relations, underlying root causes, and sources of order and change. A sociological investigation into death will profit from all three perspectives.

PHILOSOPHICAL AND PSYCHOANALYTIC PERSPECTIVES

In this section, I will analyze two perspectives long related to death: *existentialist philosophy* and the *psychoanalytic perspective*. While existentialists claim that one must face one's death, psychoanalytic observers question whether it is possible to do so. Both perspectives hold that a more common response is to deny one's mortality. In any event, these perspectives constitute important conceptual contributions to the study of death. Because the *phenomenological method* of inquiry is ordinarily used in conjunction with existential philosophy, I introduce that approach in relation to the provocative questions it raises when applied to death. Although these perspectives do not represent the core of sociological thinking, they have all influenced sociological endeavors and have much promise for influencing our future research and thinking about death.

Existentialist Philosophy

It is imperative to examine existentialist perspectives on death since these philosophies have focused on the confrontation with death as the central issue in human existence. Furthermore, in certain ways existentialist premises have permeated some of the new movements in death education and death counseling that have emerged in the last decade. Implications of an existentialist approach for these movements will be mentioned later in the book. For the present, I will concentrate on an explication of the existentialist approach to death.

A common thread among the quite diverse existentialists is their acknowledgment that human existence is finite; we all must face death. And unlike other theorists, existentialists contend that as individuals we *can* face death. The entire thrust of the existentialist position is directed toward the individual. It is posited that individuals are inextricably linked with their deaths. As Kenneth Harris (1971) notes, the individual's death is the personal property of that person and consequently has great personal significance.

Since the existentialists take personal existence as the central feature of reality, it becomes the locus of studying that reality. As Harris explains, existentialists do not view society, scientific thought, or historical process as having a greater level of reality then the subjective experience of the individual. Basically, existentialists refute presuppositions that assume the prior or greater reality of such things.

Since personal existence is the level of reality, there is no other locus of responsibility than oneself. Hence, existentialists view personal existence as fundamentally *free*. The notion is put forth by Sartre, a noted existential philosopher and novelist, that the human being is condemned to freedom. In this view, our personal freedom is the fundamental characteristic of human existence. Those who espouse an existentialist view believe in assuming responsibility for their actions. In this view, one cannot seek regulation from external authorities such as those provided by science, society, or religion. The search for external authorities is viewed as a denial of our freedom to choose to act, and take the responsibilities for our actions. From the existentialist position, one cannot escape one's *isolation* in freedom and responsibility. Consider, for example, Mrs. A., the social worker who refuses the patient's request for assistance on the basis that the patient's condition does not fit the appropriate categories. This worker expresses regret by saying, "Well these are the rules and I have to follow them." From an existentialist view, that worker is denying her freedom by claiming that she is forced to implement the rules. Rather, she *chooses* to implement them. Other possibilities include attempting to stretch the rules, pushing for changes in them, or if need be, taking the consequences of refusing to follow them. From this perspective, individuals are always responsible for their moral choices and actions.

Since individuals alone have the moral responsibility for the kinds of acts they construct, and acts are given to the self only in their immediacy, existentialists believe that human beings ultimately are isolated in their freedom. As a consequence, this inescapable isolation gives rise to alienation. Existentialism, according to Sartre, views alienation as an inevitable *condition* of human existence rather than as a consequence of socio-historical conditions that could be ameliorated with a transformation of the basic economic structure of society (as Marxists would contend). Existentialists proclaim that we are alone, and death is something we ultimately must face.

Although the existentialists have postulated the significance of confronting death, they have noted that in the realms of both traditional philosophy and everyday existence, people have shied away from confronting the inevitability of death. Existentialists claim that many people attempt to deny or circumvent death rather than confront it directly and subjectively. From the existentialist position, this stance toward death represents an attempt to flee from reality and also constitutes a means of avoiding the construction of meaning out of subjective experience.

Existentialists argue that the construction of meaning in life is central to the possession of a fully human experience. In order to experience subjectively, and subsequently affirm life, individuals must continually remain aware of their mortality. When the possibility of death, particularly in the immediate future, is held in the individual's consciousness as he or she constructs daily life, that construction is believed to take on greater meaning. Experience becomes sharpened, more intense, and more fully lived when considerations of possible death underlie individual's choices concerning how to live. It is assumed that facing death and handling the subsequent overwhelming anxiety leads to clarifying one's priorities. This assumption appears to be borne out by many who face imminent death. For example, in a news interview reported in the *San Francisco Chronicle*, writer Susan Sontag made the following observation:

> It sounds very banal, but having cancer does put things into perspective. It's fantastic knowing you're going to die; it really makes having priorities and trying to follow them very real to you (Sontag 1978).*

Consciousness of death is assumed to break through the routinization of ordinary existence and call into question the subsequent demands that are placed upon individuals from external sources. Then, a tacit premise in the position is the belief that many people are the victims of social pressures and social forces precisely because they are unable to face subjectively the meaning of their deaths and, therefore, their *lives*. Nonetheless, it is clear that existentialists see ordinary people as taking refuge in the meanings supplied by others because they lack the courage to examine their lives and, possibly, to abandon the form and direction their lives take when prescribed by others. Surely, when one lives on the surface of existence, to confront death subjectively has great risks since an examination of it and one's life might lead to a conclusion

---

*From "Looking Through the Black Hole of Death," by Susan Sontag, February 1978. © 1978 by The New York Times Company. Reprinted by permission.

that it has been "worthless" and will continue to be so unless drastic changes are made.

The emphasis on subjective mortality cannot be overstated from this perspective. To put it into the subjectivist terms of existentialism, the realization that I must eventually die, and may indeed die soon, reflects a different level of consciousness than the knowledge of "death-in-general." Death-in-general may be kept external to the self. People may not need to be concerned about it. Indeed, they may show a good deal of fascination for death that remains external and does not permeate their personal realities.

Existentialists argue that many flee from death by separating it from actual experience; in effect, they depersonalize it. Olson (1971) notes that a technique of depersonalizing death consists of transforming and reducing it to an abstract universal category by treating it in ways devoid of personal meaning. Hence, the concrete experience of the individual that everyone must undergo is hidden. Our "modern" institutionalized modes of handling dying provide numerous illustrations of that. Heidegger (1962) uses Tolstoy's *The Death of Ivan Ilych* to illustrate how the impersonal categorization of death breaks down for Ivan and gradually takes on personal meaning. The term "death," previously a general term that had been one label or category weighted no more or less than others in casual discourse, then begins to take on new, unique, and deeply personal symbolic meaning. The transition from the previously shared indifferent view of death in general to Ivan's construction of subjective meaning about death is shown in the following statement.

> All this was just what Ivan Ilych had himself brilliantly accomplished a thousand times in dealing with men on trial. The doctor summed up just as brilliantly, looking over his spectacles triumphantly and even gaily at the accused. From the doctor's summing up Ivan Ilych concluded that things were bad, but that for the doctor and perhaps for everybody else, it was a matter of indifference, though for him it was bad. And this conclusion struck him painfully, arousing in him a great feeling of pity for himself and of bitterness toward the doctor's indifference to a matter of such importance (Tolstoy 1971, p. 76).

Moving from an indifferent depersonalized view of death to one that is subjective and immediate is not sufficient to lead the examined life. The person who confronts death must *accept* it. According to Koestenbaum (1971), the first acceptance is the acceptance of "my death" as a different kind of thing than the deaths of those around us. Death can vitalize and affirm life only when it is accepted and when people subsequently organize their lives with this acceptance in mind.

Acceptance of death has some intriguing dimensions. Since death is something that is certain to happen to everyone, it appears to be a commonplace event beyond our control (cf. Guthrie 1971). However, when contemplating my death, the commonplace character of death shifts. No longer is death ordinary; it becomes an extraordinary event when it is mine; moreover, it is an event which marks the boundaries of my finite existence (Guthrie 1971). When we seriously consider our death and the boundaries it necessarily places upon our experience, the meaning of death takes on new and powerful dimensions. Envisioning the end of my experience is virtually impossible to consider with the same type of indifference, nonchalance, or objectivity I experience when I think of the deaths of others. In Western culture, however, although we know we are going to die at some point, we often have difficulty conceiving it. In short, knowledge of my own death is more likely to be understood only abstractly and not concretely.

The thought of my death thus causes great anxiety. The possibility of my death means the *end* of my world, my knowing. The thought of not being in the world and having no way of knowing the world can be extremely disconcerting and personally threatening. When I die, my world disintegrates, it is no more. The feelings that such thoughts elicit are exemplified by the following comment by a student:

> *I laid awake during the night in a cold sweat. To think of not taking care of my children, not knowing—not being was terribly upsetting, overwhelming. I had never thought before of death as the end of my experience. I now think I took comfort in the illusion of being able to watch myself, or somehow experience, after death.*

Existentialists postulate that the type of anxiety induced by a subjective confrontation with death transforms the *value* of things in my world (see Koestenbaum 1971). Whereas before, trivial pleasures and forms of competition may have seemed significant as they consumed my thoughts, the potential threat of death shows the banality of such pursuits.

When viewing reality from the vantage point of the disappearance of my world with my death, I am apt to wish to construct a life that has personal significance rather than pursuing what is significant to others. Although contemplation of death in general does not jar or disturb us, I contend that the closer death intrudes upon our personal worlds, the more aware we will be of our mortality. The death of a close friend or relative can alert us to our own vulnerability. When deaths of others disrupt our personal, social worlds, the fundamental basis through which we know ourselves and understand the world is subsequently disrupted. Then the possibility of dying becomes more real.

The strength of the existentialist position is its emphasis on the *anticipation* of death and the effects of that anticipation on everyday life when the possibility of death is confronted directly and subjectively. In constructing *expectations* of death we may then come to our own understanding of how death and life are linked. But by being aware that death has a certain mystery, we recognize that we can only know about death and not what it is. According to this line of thought, the upshot of such understanding affords us much greater autonomy in our lives for making choices and taking responsibility for them.

In Sartre's analysis (1956), the escape of the ordinary person into the routines of everyday life stands as witness to his or her inauthenticity. Such an escape surely protects that individual from confronting who and what he or she is. The institution of medicine is replete with possibilities for escaping into the routines of everyday life. Consider, for example, these lessons in inauthenticity given to nurses who deal with dying children. To children's questions, suggested responses include: "Why do you ask that?" "What makes you think you are going to die?" or "Do you feel badly today?" (Bright and France 1972, p. 228) Or, when children respond to their mother's tears, nurses are told they can satisfy children with statements like: "It makes mothers very sad when their children can't go out and play." (Bright and France 1972, p. 228) Ironically, these pat statements are much more honest than the typical deceptions, including statements I have overheard, such as: "Oh, you'll feel better in no time," or "If you try very, very hard, you'll walk out of here and go home."

What is ordinarily unrealized about deceptions and blatant lies is that those who give them lead an inauthentic existence, as well as any who are taken in by the fictions. By providing the means to escape reality, inauthentic persons fail to confront either their situations or their feelings about them.

A consequence of inauthenticity is an existence defined by others. The selves of inauthentic persons rests on criteria that they actually may not share and certainly do not participate in forming. Tolstoy's Ivan Ilych (1971) provides the classic case of someone who built a self on the criteria put forth by polite society of his day. He did not examine those criteria; he just followed them. He chose his vocation, his wife, and his life-style all because they met the external criteria.

In a sense, inauthentic existence fosters the conditions under which personal integrity becomes a negotiable commodity. From this perspective, whatever ethical principles might have provided the foundation for personal integrity become compromised when someone leads an "inauthentic" existence. As ethical principles become compromised and negotiable, so does personal integrity.

The issue of personal integrity is raised by Sartre (1956) in his discussion of inauthentic existence. Here individuals are blind to their alienation as they hide behind social roles. In turn, this blindness reveals what Sartre calls "bad faith," which consists of failure to acknowledge what one is and what one is doing. Exemplars of bad faith are functionaries who choose to impose special rules and procedures upon others but refuse to acknowledge their own complicity in their actions. Like the social worker described earlier, these functionaries claim to believe that the rules act rather than themselves. In contrast, "authentic" persons refuse to hide behind social rules and roles. What Sartre tells us is that one may responsibly refuse to follow orders or implement policies that are inconsistent with one's moral convictions and ethical principles. Those who hold this perspective would say that one may dissent and take the consequences of being autonomous. The costs of autonomy may be high; for example, one may lose one's job, country, or life. But persons who are willing to take a principled stand, for which others who are less principled will punish them, understand and accept the costs. For someone who holds this position, enduring the wrath of those who support the commonplace interpretation of the rules and those who make them is a better choice than sacrificing personal integrity and the moral principles upon which it is based.

Authenticity in Sartre's perspective is then intertwined with his conception of freedom. However, in Heidegger's view, death offers the human being the possibility of human freedom, but paradoxically, since death is unavoidable, it limits human freedom (see Molina 1967). In Heidegger's work (1962), the subjective confrontation with death is a personal one that has all kinds of ramifications for the emotional being. The confrontation with death is for Heidegger as well as Sartre steeped in emotional responses such as anxiety, dread, or nausea. But particularly with Heidegger and those who follow his line of thought, the emphasis is on subjectivity and the personal reflection upon the inevitability and possibility of one's mortality and, then, the possibility of living and dying authentically.

For Heidegger, authentic existence as subjectively experienced means that the individual is linked to or is based in Being (what it means to "be"). Anxiety is positive in Heidegger's work in the sense that it makes people aware of their estrangement with Being (Briesach 1962). Although it can be a profoundly disquieting experience, that anxiety gives individuals an awareness of their aloneness as they are "thrown into existence," to use a Heideggerian phrase. Death, then, for Heidegger offers the possibility for people to incorporate the finiteness of life into their beings. By bringing the possibility of death into immediate existence, a transformation of conventional definitions of time occurs. People who bring death into their subjective experiences take responsibility for the past and do not separate themselves from the future. Past, present, and future become intertwined into a coherent process. The future is part of the present because of death. Existential being in this framework then means that the uncertain date of future death permeates the present. Hence, the objective character ordinarily granted to time is transcended by the experiencing subjective being.

In contrast to Heidegger, Sartre (1956) does not view death as a possibility but as a situation that ultimately must be confronted by each individual. For Sartre, death is *absurd*; it cannot be experienced or anticipated. Sartre's disagreement with Heidegger lies in the issue of death as individualizing the human being. For Sartre, death in itself does not give meaning to human existence. Rather than presenting possibilities, death destroys human possibilities. Sartre emphasizes that the fact of death cannot in and of itself ever give meaning to life. Instead, for Sartre, awareness of death reveals the human *condemnation to freedom.*

Themes that are discernible in Sartre's and especially Heidegger's work, loom large in Koestenbaum's analysis of death (1971). He, too, emphasizes the difference between the death of others and the death of oneself. Koestenbaum also stresses that trivial concerns, petty competitions, and everyday problems that underlie so much of ordinary existence become meaningless in the face of the overwhelming issue of death. Consequently, Koestenbaum contends that individuals may feel some urgency to find meaning in life. Taken to its logical extension, Koestenbaum's position would be better stated if he emphasized that individuals then felt the urgency to *create* meaning in their lives since meaning is subjective and can be known only, in this sense, subjectively.

In contrast with Heidegger and Sartre's emphasis on emotions, Koestenbaum's position has a rationalistic bent. He emphasizes that individuals who are continually aware that they are condemned to die will have a sense of urgency about their daily activities. But according to Koestenbaum, this sense of urgency is liberating since those individuals focus on projects that provide *direction* and *meaning* in their lives.

Koestenbaum's position is based on the assumption that repressing the knowledge of one's death leads to self-deception and the unexamined life. In his view, repression of death is essentially repression of fear based on the acceptance of what he calls a "fraudulent promise: *symbolic immortality*." For Koestenbaum, symbolic immortality implies living through others instead of for one's self. To illustrate, Mrs. G. is an exemplar of a woman who lived through her husband rather than for herself. Having no children or special interests of her own, she devoted her life to him and his interests. In a very real sense, he provided a world for her.

The acceptance of self offered by significant others holds the promise of immortality in the sense that that acceptance gives one a life and a world. If the world created through symbolic immortality is threatened, the loss of that world becomes the threat of *symbolic death*. When Mrs. G's husband died suddenly, she suffered a symbolic death. Her world literally collapsed. Rather than losing part of herself and her existence, she felt that without him she was no one and had no life.

Koestenbaum's rationalistic bent is more observable in his assumption that the freedom to make decisions will be directed toward making plans and projects in life. In this view, living takes on businesslike properties and those plans and projects appear to be ones that are, at least for the most part, socially validated as purposeful. Koestenbaum's perspective may be highly suitable for the educated upper middle classes who are able to exert control over their destinies and plan their projects according to traditional conceptions of purposeful activity. But his form of existentialism in particular, and the form of others more generally, may make little sense to the less privileged person whose options in life are narrower. Taken to its logical extension, Koestenbaum's position stresses individualism to the point where persons and their social context become separated. That is, this type of analysis fails to take into account the systematic ways in which everyday social and power relationships restrict and inhibit many members of society from controlling their destinies. Granted, members can conceivably attempt to follow their consciences and create purposeful projects and subsequently make explicit whatever barriers exist to fulfilling them. But to the extent that real social barriers exist along racial, class, and sex lines, Koestenbaum's brand of existentialism may overlook the "real" issues that are subjectively defined by many members of society.

Existentialism has some important insights for sociologists; in particular, the emphasis on the subjective construction of meaning is significant. This emphasis, of course, converges with that of the symbolic interactionist, although the interactionist would assume that individuals construct meanings despite their willingness or lack of it to face their deaths. Both the emphasis on meaning and the moral responsibility demanded by existentialism diverge considerably from structural-functionalism since the latter perspective emphasizes a rather mechanical performance of the expected social role without consideration of the meaning of the actor or the moral consequences of the act. Like Marxists and symbolic interactionists, existentialists believe that human beings are capable of reflection. Therefore, they also believe individuals may question the nature of their routinized actions and, subsequently, change them. Still, the approach does make central assumptions about a conception of human nature in relationship to social structure that may be questioned from a sociological perspective. Since existentialists tend to be asocial and ahistorical in their assumptions, they see alienation and anxiety as part of the human condition. From a sociological view emphasizing the social nature of existence, including dying, precisely what constitutes existence is contingent upon the interplay between selves and social structures during specific historical eras. If this assumption is correct, then alienation and anxiety are not necessarily part of the human condition. And perhaps meanings of death themselves are tied only to particular social structures and thus could possibly change under different social conditions.

Phenomenology

Particularly in the study of death and dying, existentialism is linked with the phenomenological method of inquiry, despite the fact that in other realms of inquiry they are often treated independently. At this point, existentialism may be cast as a "dated" philosophy except in the crucial questions that its adherents raise about death and the quality of existence. Currently, sociologists appear more interested in using phenomenological methods to study a variety of concerns (including death) (see Bogdan and Taylor 1975; Psathas 1973; Filmer *et al.* 1973). The phenomenological approach starts with an examination of the point of view of the experiencing person. Experience is studied from the *inside*—from what it appears to be to the involved person, who may also be the social researcher. For example, a phenomenological study of dying would necessitate discovering what dying is to those who are experiencing it.

The priority given to subjective experience contrasts with more objectivist perspectives that detail information *about* people or situations from the standpoint of a relatively uninvolved observer.

Put most simply, the thrust of the phenomenological method is twofold: (1) to study the phenomenon directly and (2) to discover how it is constituted (see Phillipson and Roche 1974). First, the investigator must go directly to the phenomenon to be studied, hence, the phenomenological dictum: "to the things themselves." If for example, the process of suicide is the phenomenon, or "thing" to be studied, the investigator must go directly to people who experience that process. Seeking the views of clinicians or suicide prevention volunteers who work with suicide attempters would not suffice because they have views of the process rather than direct experience *within* it. Second, the investigator must explicate how the phenomenon or thing is constituted. In order to do this, one must study the perceptions of conscious individuals. Then the investigator would have to discover the concerns and perceptions of individuals as they move toward suicide. Moreover, an analysis would need to be made detailing the shape individuals' concerns and perceptions give to events and later actions. The following hypothetical case illustrates the methodological approach. A researcher becomes interested in studying suicide after a close friend "suddenly" kills himself. The researcher reflects upon his friend's situation to record all the events and feelings that could have conceivably led to the action. The researcher then reappraises his own self-destructive thoughts and fantasies. He attempts to explore how they can be differentiated from other experiences and feelings. Next, he gains permission to observe at the local crisis clinic where suicidal individuals are taken. Following his observations, he conducts a series of depth interviews with persons who previously attempted suicide to discover what they were thinking during their crises. By comparing the patterns and themes, he is able to discern parallels between the suicidal experiences of diverse individuals.

Now, turning to a more sophisiticated explanation of the phenomenological method, I will discuss the relationship between the phenomenon and consciousness. According to Phillipson "a phenomenon is that which is given or indubitable in the perception of consciousness of the conscious individual" (1974, p. 121). Thus the phenomenologist most fundamentally attempts to describe the objects of perception or those held in *consciousness*. From a phenomenological point of view, consciousness is always of something. Hence, it is *intentional* in the sense that it is *directed* toward objects and events. Nonetheless, consciousness cannot be equated with purpose or planning. In contrast, the concept of intentionality is used to link consciousness with the *relationship* between the thinking subject and the perceived object. The conscious individual attributes meanings to the objects of perception. But the meanings of different participants sometimes reflect different intentions. In the hospital situation nurses often attempt to keep the emotional level of the ward even and manageable through superficial pleasantries. Reflect upon the different intentions indicated by this account:

> *A staff member came into the room and cheerily said, "Well, Mrs. J., how are we today?" (I noticed questions directed to elderly dying patients are often phrased with a "we" as if the patient lacked the dignity of a separate identity as "you" and also perhaps because using "we" implies concern about one's own feelings as well as the patient's.) Mrs. J. moved herself up in bed with her elbows and said in her most regal best British accent: "Well my child, I don't know how we are feeling but I am doing something I shall not do again. I am dying" (Mervyn 1971, p. 1990).*

As is implied by the account, intentions are revealed in taken-for-granted commonsense meanings. The commonsense meanings held by members of everyday worlds and their construction become the special interest of sociologists who take a phenomenological stance in their work. A corollary of this is that mind and action are intentional rather than externally determined. Hence, the phenomenological view of human nature assumes that individuals are capable of reflective thought; they are not simply products of social forces. The construction of commonsense meanings would then be an ongoing process developing out of the actor's conscious attempts to make sense of his or her experience. At this point, a convergence with symbolic interactionism and Marxism may be readily discerned.

In order to understand the commonsense meanings of the social actor, the phenomenological sociologist must understand the *logic* of the actor's experience from his or her particular perspective. The phenomenological method assumes that the researcher often does not share this experience or understand its rationality. Hence, a major task of the researcher is to explicate the taken-for-granted rules invoked by actors to make sense of their experience. By doing so, the researcher takes as problematic rules and meanings taken for granted by individuals sharing the experience. Looking at an actual situation may clarify these tasks. Medical instructors commonly develop a series of interactional rules for handling the process of arriving at an accurate diagnosis. To illustrate, one intern told me about a staff physician who instructed his flock of residents, interns, and students by developing rules of discourse at rounds. The intern said that when the staff physician felt someone had slipped up but did not choose to embarrass his subordinate he would ask what the results of a specific lab test were. All those present would know the test had not been ordered, but the proper answer was, "It's not back yet from the lab, sir." Then, immediately after rounds, the responsible subordinate would hasten to write the order. The sociologist would first need to know what the bona fide members knew, that the cover-up of an omission was the interactional issue. Then the sociologist would need to ferret out the interactional rules to handle it. Next, the sociologist would need to discover what the omission meant. Were such omissions handled so politely when they resulted in a life-threatening situation? Or were distinctions made between patients? If so, what kinds of distinctions were made, and when were they made? In these ways a sociological researcher taps the taken-for-granted rules and meanings of members of a specific group.

Moreover, in keeping with phenomenological premises, researchers must question their own methodological rules for discovering the commonsense rules of those involved. For example, researchers who study bereaved persons reporting some kind of contact with the deceased would necessarily question both scientific methodology and the commonsense rules of the bereaved for identifying and making sense of their experience.

Phenomenological sociologists assume that the way of knowing any experience gives researchers a particular slant on what is known. Hence, they stress that researchers attempt to examine their own taken-for-granted assumptions so that they are not imposed upon the people who are being studied.

Phenomenological sociologists aim to study the properties that constitute the characteristics of the phenomenon being examined. Thus, this type of analysis is intended to discern the *essences* or basic forms of the social phenomenon that distinguish it from other objects or events. As Bruyn (1966) notes, the term "essence" suggests those social or cultural characteristics that, for the actors involved, fundamentally define the basic properties of the phenomenon and make it what it "is." Hence, these properties constitute a quality intrinsic to the phenomenon. The essences the phenomenologist seeks are not some Platonic *ideal* essences but socially constituted and socially recognized phenomena. For example, if grieving were chosen as the phenomenon to be studied, one would attempt to discern those properties that make grieving what it is and thus distinguish it from other responses. The essence of a phenomenon may not necessarily be discerned in its external characteristics, which can be empirically observed. Instead, the essence of the phenomenon may have to be intuited for it to be understood. For example, the external characteristics of dying constitute recordings of observations that practitioners make, such as the patient's vital signs. But the external characteristics, per se, do not constitute the essence of what dying is. The essence of dying must be seen in its uniquely human and social properties since what dying means can only be understood in relation to the subjective meanings of those who are actually dying and those who share that experience.

Although this method starts with the viewpoint of the individual social actor, a major goal of the sociologist's phenomenological research is to discover how *intersubjective social worlds* and *shared views* are constructed in everyday life. Thus, those taking this point of view may begin research by investigating a topic related to death, such as grief, and start by asking themselves questions about the nature and experience of grief. Some phenomenologists espouse the view that students who wish to know about an event or phenomenon must first experience that kind of event or phenomenon themselves. Others believe that it is sufficient for those who are engaged in phenomenological research to either experience the event or phenomenon vicariously or learn of it through empathetic understanding of the experience of others as they reveal it. If one were to study grief from the first perspective above, one would have to experience grief before embarking upon research. Basic questions would then be reflected upon. What did grieving feel like? What did it mean to me? How did I know that the feeling felt was grief and not some other response? In which ways can it be distinguished from other kinds of emotion? How is it related to anger, depression, remorse, and self-pity? By asking such basic questions about the experience of grief, the phenomenologist begins to question taken-for-granted assumptions about the nature of that experience. The value of starting from the inside lies in being able to make qualitative distinctions between events or experiences that would be otherwise obscured or unknown if one were to emphasize only the external characteristics of the phenomenon.

When applied to the study of death, the phenomenological critique of behavioral science raises two interrelated and provocative issues. First, with this perspective comes an imperative to obtain data directly through *first-hand experience*. When it is not possible to obtain the data directly, researchers must devise methods to bring them as close to the phenomenon as possible. Since for many issues surrounding death, collecting data from first-hand experience is difficult, researchers may use depth interviews, descriptions from literature, popular media accounts, and so forth.

Second, the phenomenological approach raises *critical methodological questions*. From a phenomenological approach, a central methodological problem consists of analysts demonstrating how they construct their explanations. In this framework, those explanations should be directly related to the subject that was researched. In the previous example concerning suicide, the "scientific" explanations of suicidal behavior should be directly grounded in the themes discovered in the suicidal persons' accounts of their motivations and experiences. (But since they provide an *analysis* of the actors' accounts, analysts' explanations will not be the same as the actors'.)

Taking this line of thought further, the phenomenologist would ask: How are concepts arrived at in death research specifically, and thanatology generally? For the most part, it can be argued that our central ideas are not derived from rigorous analysis of the commonsense notions of people who are confronted with the practical issues that death poses. Instead, the store of ideas constituting the field of death largely consists of work founded on speculation or preconceived theoretical orientations. Since whatever questions are asked of reality give shape to the answers "found," much research in death and dying may more closely reveal the researcher's biases and proclivities than the empirical world presumably brought into view.

With the subject of death, as well as other topics, preconceived scientific concepts are often laid over the empirical reality rather than arising from it. Preconceived psychiatric categories perhaps generate the most common type of interpretations of issues surrounding death. When this occurs, what constitutes the commonsense understandings of the scientist are raised to an abstract conceptual level where they are purported to take into account and explain the empirical reality addressed. In any case, when abstract theoretical schemes are imposed upon empirical reality rather than being derived from that reality, the likelihood of distortion becomes greatly increased. This constitutes a major problem in the study of death. So much of what we professionals "know" is shaped from our preconceived, commonsense notions about what topics like dying, mourning, and suicide are.

Hence, if we take a phenomenological stance seriously, then the descriptive terms and concepts used to define and describe the study of death need to be systematically clarified. What does "acceptance of death" mean? To whom? Under what kinds of conditions? What constitutes a "social death"? What are the parameters of it? How can it be compared to "psychological death"? Such questions indicate the incisiveness which a phenomenological critique of current conceptions of death and dying could conceivably bring about, but it remains to be undertaken.

Psychoanalytic Perspective

Because the psychoanalytic perspective has dominated the study of death, it is important to explore briefly some of its major tenets and the assumptions supporting them. First, I will summarize some of the main assumptions underlying the psychoanalytic perspective according to Freud, and second, I will analyze his central ideas dealing directly with death.

One of the first assumptions of psychoanalytic theory is that only a small portion of the mind is conscious; the rest remains *unconscious*. In the unconscious exist all kinds of impulses, desires, images of repressed experiences, and feelings that may be highly contradictory. For example, a man may hold unconscious death wishes toward his powerful father of whom he is sometimes jealous while, simultaneously, he depends on the help his father gives him with his business. Irrationality characterizes the unconscious. According to the psychoanalytic perspective, the unconscious plays a dynamic role in human *motivation*, as it is assumed to give impetus to behavior. But this behavior is later rationalized with socially "acceptable" motives.

Still, Freud contends that our unconscious wishes or thoughts about death replicate those of primeval humans. While civilization has caused humankind to view killing with horror, underneath our conscious exteriors lie death wishes, not only toward strangers but also toward intimates. Unconscious *ambivalence*, then, is believed to characterize our stance toward death. Freud (1977) observes, for example, that "exaggerated" concern for another or "unfounded self-reproaches" after a death indicate the extent and significance of unconscious death wishes.

From this perspective, it logically follows that underlying our thoughts and feelings about death is a store of psychic material that we do not consciously confront or understand. Because it is believed that many of our ideas are only partial and symbolic representations of repressed anxieties, tensions, and unresolved intrapsychic conflicts, it follows that a person's stated feelings or intentions about illness and death are not taken at face value by those who subscribe to this perspective. Inherent in any psychoanalytic inquiry is the questioning of the stated motivation of the patient and the consequent search for hidden or latent meanings in the patient's statements, gestures, or actions. Consider these events from a psychoanalytic perspective. A little boy throws a terrible tantrum in the face of his mother's refusal to grant him permission for a particular activity. She later disclosed to the father that the boy had never been so unmanageable. The next day the mother dies suddenly without having fully resolved the earlier conflict with her son. Overwhelmed with grief, the boy becomes isolated from other adults and children. As an adult, he gives no indication of remembering the events preceding his mother's death, but displays to his therapist a heightened fear of death and disruption. From a psychoanalytic perspective one would wonder if the boy's apparent repression of the scenario that caused him intense guilt contributed to his response as an adult. Whatever conflicted feelings he held about his mother were possibly transformed into the anxieties still plaguing him.

Quite clearly, those who use the psychoanalytic perspective typically look back into the patient's past and reconstruct those events which now appear to have caused problems. Because they believe the first five years of life are most important for personality development, psychoanalysts assume that traumatic experiences during this period cause individuals problems throughout their lives. In order to ferret out such problems and their implications, the analyst looks for latent meanings, hidden from the patient's conscious awareness.

In the psychoanalytic framework, the psyche is taken as the primary locus of reality as contrasted with a sociological viewpoint that takes social existence, or ongoing interaction, as the primary locus of reality. Not only is the psychological response of the individual then given most emphasis but, moreover, the unconscious motivation believed to underlie that response is seen as most significant. Further, the psychoanalytic perspective assumes that psychic energy drawn from inborn instincts plays a more important role in the dynamics of personality than external stimulation from the environment. Nonetheless, according to the psychoanalytic view, environmental stimuli may have powerful effects on developing children, particularly when children are unable to cope with the situations confronting them. Considerable stress is placed in the psychoanalytic framework on early childhood development, during which intrapsychic conflicts are played out within the structure of personality. Conflict is generated by the child's need to reduce tension and satisfy impulses but without the ability to do so directly and immediately.

Thus such situations give rise to anxiety that produces repression of the original impulse or wish. Unresolved repressed conflicts or traumatic experiences, then, are assumed to account for present anxieties. For example, experiencing the death of the mother is viewed by psychoanalysts as having severe repercussions for the child's later development.

Quite clearly, the psychoanalytic view assumes that our thoughts and feelings about death are not straightforward. Instead, these ideas and feelings are believed to be *obscured* by symbolism, repression, and conflicting attitudes. To carry further the implications of repressed conflicts, consider a psychoanalytic view of the effects of an "abbreviated" period of mourning. If that period is not sufficient for the bereaved to extricate themselves from the previous relationship, then the unresolved relationship is assumed to affect future relationships and forms of adjustment. The fact of a short mourning period itself, from a psychoanalytic view, indicates a certain stance toward death. That stance would consist of a denial of death in which the survivors did not adequately assess the significance of death and then respond to it "appropriately" (see Rakoff 1973).

The *denial of death* as a dominant orientation toward death not only is a strong theme in the psychoanalytic literature but also has permeated conventional thinking about death. Since a full discussion will be devoted to it in Chapter 3, I will outline here only the general ways in which it is related to this perspective. Those of a psychoanalytic persuasion hold that we cannot easily face our deaths. They contend that denial of death is a typical response to one's demise even when it seems imminent. Thus in working with dying patients, for example, they might attempt to discover to what extent someone holds "false" hopes or tries to prolong life by seeking forbidden drugs of questionable medical value.

At any rate, denial of death in everyday life is linked to unconscious motivation in the psychoanalytic framework. It is believed that the realization of death is so difficult because people cannot imagine themselves dead. The assumption of *unconscious immortality* enters here. In Freud's view, a concept of natural death is an intellectual abstraction since death does not exist in the unconscious. Instead, an animistic belief in unconscious immortality is a fundamental part of the structure of personality. Hence, according to Freud, children and what he called "primitive" people were unable to understand the concept of a natural death since they do not possess this type of intellectual reasoning.

The belief in unconscious immortality is related to the fear of death. Freud assumes that the unconscious has no representation of death since the person has never experienced it. Fear of death in the psychoanalytic framework is imbedded in fears that are more directly related to experience and the intrapsychic conflicts that have resulted from those experiences. Fear of death is often taken to be the result of *repressed guilt*, which may be traced to unresolved earlier experiences. Because there is no unconscious representation of death, fear of it represents fears of infantile powerlessness that has been experienced in losing parental protection. As Gifford (1971) points out, fears of death then stem from fears of helplessness, injury, or abandonment initially aroused by separation.

Belief in unconscious immortality has been more widely accepted than another major theme in Freudian theory, the assumption that human beings have a *death instinct*. In the Freudian perspective, death is an intrinsic part of life; it is as much a part of human nature as is Freud's postulate of the existence of life (or libidinal) instincts. In Freud's view, the death instincts exist in conflict with the life instincts in a similar way as the asocial id is in conflict with the socially imbued superego. The death instincts then become mediated by the ego into aggressive acts outside the self. For example, in our culture, a competitive, aggressive stance toward certain types of business activities such as selling is an "acceptable" way to mediate such aggressive tendencies. By fusing the death instinct with the life instinct, the tendency toward self-destruction is averted. What is ordinarily called the death wish exists when such fusion does not take place. Since human beings are propelled toward death, the death wish is a normal part of the human condition although it is more typically transformed and expressed as aggression.

Norman O. Brown (1959) suggests that the consequence of repressed death is to spawn cultures. He states that while animals use the death instinct to die, human beings use it aggressively to build civilization and make history in their efforts to fight death. Paradoxically, civilization turns the human being against itself. In *Civilization and Its Discontents*, Freud argues that we would be happier if we gave up civilization and returned to more primal conditions. His argument is based upon the premise that the demands of civilization are irreconcilable with the demands of instinct. Not only is sexual gratification channeled and deferred due to the demands of society but also aggressiveness is channeled and ultimately turned inward on the self in the form of guilt and neurotic symptoms. In order to have civilization at all, we must be willing to give up our spontaneous gratifications and hostile aggressive impulses and channel our energies according to the *reality principle*. Basically, the reality principle means the ability to accommodate oneself to the demands of the external world through deferred gratification. In accommodating to the external world, individuals are then able to differentiate what is actually or objectively *external* to themselves and what is derived from subjective wishes and desires. Yet, by following the demands of the external world, one gives up one's preferences and essentially subjugates oneself to the needs of the society. It stands to reason that according to Freud, the aggressive instinct poses the greatest threat to the maintenance of civilization. In times of war, for example, our murderous impulses toward strangers become unleashed and perhaps uncontrollable. Given the nature of the human psyche posited in this perspective, we are ill-prepared to be peaceable beings since war provides an outlet for these impulses. In more ordinary times, however, society holds spontaneous expression of aggression toward others in check, though it may be a fragile one. Thus, the energy from that basic instinct will be turned inward against the self when civilization makes stringent behavioral demands upon the individual.

A brief summary of a case history may help to illuminate the complex ways that the aggressive instinct is viewed from the psychoanalytic perspective. In this case, Pincus (1974) describes the dynamics in what superficially might have looked like a complementary relationship. The wife was a successful career woman who assumed most of the responsibilities in the marriage despite her lifelong immobilizing bouts with asthma. The husband, irresponsible and disinterested in his work, played the role of the charming host. Pincus analyzes the choice of the husband as symbolizing the wife's attempt to resolve her relationship with her father, a charming, imaginative, and irresponsible man who died when she was eleven. The marriage became more conflicted with time. The wife had an affair and considered leaving her husband. Though she did not leave for that reason, she accepted a fellowship necessitating their separation for a year. Just before her departure, the husband fell critically ill with asthma attacks though he had never before exhibited these symptoms. It was discovered that he had had a recurrence of T.B.—this time of a life-threatening nature. The wife stayed with him day and night through several crises. Just after his release from the hospital, she began to have similar asthma attacks. She died unexpectedly the third night after her admission to the hospital. Pincus suggests that the wife's ambivalent wishes for her husband to die, consciously unacceptable, but nevertheless present, were turned inward, and thus she died.

Perhaps, then, the woman paid for her repressed guilt and ambivalence with her life. In more ordinary circumstances, the internalization of aggressiveness is believed to result in a punishing superego with a heightening of the sense of guilt. The superego may become so coercive that it is impossible for the individual to live up to the norms and values prescribed by it. Aggression turned upon the self may lead to self-destructiveness in various forms, of which suicide is a dramatic example.

A few sociological comments are in order. From a sociological perspective, the search for latent meanings within the psychoanalytic tradition has several consequences. Foremost among them is a tendency to discount patients' views of their interpretations of reality since interpretations made from the vantage point of the psychoanalytic framework are given greater significance. Presumably, analysts have "objective" stances in their interpretations as contrasted with patients' subjective ones. Accordingly, those objective stances are believed to result from the specialized training and expertise that analysts possess. Beliefs in objectivity of this sort do lead to a social distancing between patient and practitioner that may result in the patient becoming primarily an "object" of study instead of a person of equal value. Furthermore, this perspective rests on instincts, which are unable to be empirically documented. Because sociologists typically give more credence to socialization than instinct or internal conditions of the psyche, both the initial premises and the logic of the psychoanalytic perspective are frequently called into question.

In contrast, to summarize Freud's view, the growth of civilization proceeds with greater and greater instinctual renunciation but at the cost of more and more impoverishment of the self. Consequently, civilization has caused individuals to give up some of the possibilities for happiness in exchange for the security possible through participation in society. In turn, civilization is built upon repressing the death instinct. The psychoanalytic position that we cannot confront death directly has had much influence on intellectual and commonsense reasoning about our relationship to death. Hence, the debate still being waged about whether we deny death and, if so, to what extent, fundamentally stems from psychoanalytic notions of unconscious immortality.

SUMMARY AND IMPLICATIONS

The six conceptual approaches outlined in this chapter have two major emphases. They are: (1) emphasis on the *individual* as the subject of analysis and (2) emphasis on the meanings of death and dying for the larger *society*. The symbolic interactionist takes the actor's meanings as the starting point of inquiry and analysis. In contrast, those taking a dramaturgical approach take action as their starting point. Both approaches view human existence in terms of *processes* constructed out of everyday actions. In these approaches, it is believed that thinking actors make choices about their actions. Hence, these approaches view actors as reflective and creative. Because actors reflect upon their situations, rather than responding automatically, social interaction is somewhat indeterminant. And society itself may change as the actions and interpretations of its members change. Importantly, adopting this perspective leads to discovering the meanings of those who confront death and dying.

The structural-functional approach contrasts with the symbolic interactionist perspective and its derivative, the dramaturgical approach. Structural-functionalism emphasizes an *institutional* analysis of the structure of society, a structure assumed to be rather fixed and stable. Hence, individual choice is not emphasized; the institutionalized roles with their corresponding expectations and obligations are. Because of their structural focus, these analysts ask how dying affects the institutional structure, rather than specifying how it affects the individual dying person's psyche. While they attempt to explain observable behavior, they do not address the consciousness of the individuals studied.

Marxism, however, provides a potential tool for combining institutional analyses of the structure of society with studies of the consciousness of individuals. Marxists emphasize the role of power, particularly economic power, in controlling both the social structure and the ideas held in the minds of the masses. From this perspective, questions would be raised about the powerful institution of medicine in relation to alienated consumers and patients. By changing the social structure, with consequent changes of the distribution of power and goods within society, Marxists argue that alienation will be reduced.

That position is challenged by existentialists, who argue that alienation is an inevitable part of the human condition. For them, individuals are alienated because they are free to choose their acts. With this freedom to choose comes an awareness of one's isolation and moral responsibility. Abdication of that responsibility is seen by existentialists as a refusal to face one's death and therefore one's life. In order to construct personal meaning in life, one has to confront death subjectively. The importance of constructing meaning parallels the symbolic interactionist perspective (although prescriptions for any a priori confrontation with death are not made by symbolic interactionists). Also in both perspectives, a strong phenomenological theme demands examining the consciousness of individuals as the topic of study. A phenomenological approach emphasizes studying the topic directly and discovering its essential characteristics. To do so, the researcher must discover the taken-for-granted rules and meanings of those who experience the phenomenon. The objective of the phenomenologist is then to understand from their point of view or how it is given in consciousness to them. To study death from this perspective means that one must get as close to the experience studied as possible and experience it in the way that those studied experience it.

In contrast, the psychoanalytic perspective emphasizes the individual but does not examine the objects of consciousness from the individual's point of view. While psychoanalysts work with the material provided to them by patients, they do not view the conscious actor's interpretations as reflecting the real issues and sources of problems. Instead, they argue that individuals' conscious thoughts often represent a denial of the "real" and unconscious reasons for their actions and feelings. Because they believe that the unconscious cannot face death, they assume that much of our thought and action in regard to it represents a denial of death.

After reflection upon the perspectives outlined in this chapter, I believe that the analysis holds special significance specifically for research directives and, more generally, for social and political action. First, by showing the potential for sociological analyses of death, a case has been made for making fresh observations in the area of death and dying. The symbolic interactionist and phenomenological approaches, particularly, hold potential for developing new ideas about what death means and how dying is handled in everyday life without being tied to narrowly defined psychologistic explanations. By studying processes and elucidating the multiple social realities affecting the actor's actions and ideas, new ways of knowing and making sense of death may be developed.

Second, implications for social and political action may be derived from analyzing the existentialist and Marxist approaches together. In combining an existentialist and a Marxist approach to death, we can link a refusal to face mortality subjectively and political reality. That is, if members of society actually confront the fact that they will die and thus attempt to control the quality of their present experience, there might be less willingness to accept current social, political, and economic realities. Possibly, a general reluctance to confront mortality subjectively may have larger political consequences. It is conceivable that current social, political, and economic institutions are, however unwittingly, perpetuated by a lack of willingness to confront and accept death since the logical sequel of doing so is to take action in life.

When people avoid any confrontation with finitude, they act as if time were endless, as if they were essentially immortal. Consequently, they may not face the fact that time is continually slipping away. I contend that if more people took seriously existentialist concerns about death, we might become more active in demanding changes that improve the quality of lives. But as a society we may be immersed in the everyday routines to the extent that we keep putting off our objectives and settling for what seems to be available.

If this argument is tenable, then it follows that not confronting death is part of a more general passive stance toward the world that contributes to the maintenance of current power arrangements. By accepting authorities as they are, by accepting the social world as given, individuals are unlikely to take hold of the potential power that they possess. In sum, hiding one's death from oneself also carries the consequence of hiding one's life. Conversely, to confront and accept one's death from an existentialist position means taking control over one's life and one's actions with conscious acknowledgement of one's moral responsibility for whatever choices are made. If this position gained widespread collective appeal combined with growing political awareness, the construction of a more humane social order would be possible.

In this chapter, I have outlined intellectual approaches. But these ideas are not wholly confined to esoteric discussions. Rather, some of these ideas have permeated everyday social thought. As such, they have provided the source of commonsense meanings held by ordinary members of society who may remain entirely unaware of the intellectual antecedents of their views or of the parallels between them and more theoretical positions. In particular, existentialist and psychoanalytic thought have influenced everyday conceptions and concerns with death. In the following chapter, the significance of their influence becomes discernible.

REFERENCES

Aries, Philippe (1962). *Centuries of Childhood: A Social History of Family Life*. New York: Knopf.

_____ (1974). *Western Attitudes toward Death*. Baltimore: Johns Hopkins University Press.

Blauner, Robert (1966). Death and social structure. *Psychiatry* 29:378-94.

Blumer, Herbert (1969). *Symbolic Interactionism*. Englewood Cliffs, N.J.: Prentice-Hall.

Bogdan, Robert G., and Stephen Taylor (1975). *An Introduction to Qualitative Research Methods*. New York: Wiley.

Breisach, Ernest (1962). *Introduction to Modern Existentialism*. New York: Grove Press.

Bright, Florence, and Sister M. Luciana France (1972). The nurse and the terminally ill child. In Mary H. Browning and Edith P. Lewis (eds.), *The Dying Patient: A Nursing Perspective*. New York: American Journal of Nursing Co.

Brissett, Dennis, and Charles Edgley (1975). Introduction. In Dennis Brissett and Charles Edgley (eds.), *Life as Theatre*. Chicago: Aldine.

Brown, Norman O. (1959). *Life Against Death*. Middletown, Conn.: Wesleyan University Press.

Bruyn, Severyn (1966). *The Human Perspective in Sociology: The Methodology of Participant Observation*. Englewood Cliffs, N.J.: Prentice-Hall.

Burke, Kenneth (1945). *A Grammar of Motives*. Englewood Cliffs, N.J.: Prentice-Hall.

Cumming, Elaine, and William Henry (1961). *Growing Old*. New York: Basic Books.

Department of Health, Education, and Welfare (1977). Parameters of health in the United States. In Howard D. Schwartz and Cary S. Kart (eds.), *Dominant Issues in Medical Sociology*. Reading, Mass.: Addison-Wesley.

Filmer, Paul (1973). On Garfinkel's ethnomethodology. In Paul Filmer, Michael Phillipson, David Silverman, and David Walsh, *New Directions in Sociological Theory*. Cambridge, Mass.: MIT Press.

Freud, Sigmund (1935). *A General Introduction to Psychoanalysis*. New York: Simon and Schuster.

_____ (1962). *Civilization and Its Discontents*. New York: Norton.

_____ (1975). *Beyond the Pleasure Principle*. New York: Norton.

_____ (1977). Thoughts for the times on war and death: our attitude toward death. In Sandra Galdieri Wilcox and Marilyn Sutton (eds.), *Understanding Death and Dying*. Port Washington, N.Y.: Alfred Publishing Co.

Fromm, Erich (1962). *Marx's Concept of Man*. New York: Frederick Ungar.

Giddens, Anthony (1971). *Capitalism and Modern Social Theory*. Cambridge: At the University Press.

Gifford, Sanford (1971). Freud's theories of unconscious immortality and the death instinct. *Journal of Thanatology* 1:109-25.

Goffman, Erving (1959). *The Presentation of Self in Everyday Life*. Garden City, N.Y.: Doubleday, Anchor Books.

_____ (1961). *Asylums*. Garden City, N.Y.: Doubleday, Anchor Books.

Goldscheider, Calvin (1975). The social inequality of death. In Edwin S. Shneidman (ed.), *Death: Current Perspectives*. Palo Alto, Calif.: Mayfield.

Gorer, Geoffrey (1965). *Death, Grief and Mourning*. Garden City, N.Y.: Doubleday, Anchor Books.

Guthrie, George P. (1971). The meaning of death. *Omega* 2:299-306.

Harris, Kenneth (1971). The political meaning of death: an existential overview. *Omega* 2:227-39.

Heidegger, Martin (1962). *Being and Time*. New York: Harper and Row.

Hesslink, George K., and Howard K. Steinman (1976). Social awareness of environmental health hazards: the lag between medical discovery, governmental regulation and public acceptance. Paper presented at the meetings of the Pacific Sociological Association, March 1976.

Hochschild, Arlie (1975). Disengagement theory: a critique and proposal. *American Sociological Review* 40:553-69.

Illich, Ivan (1974). The political uses of natural death. In Peter Steinfels and Robert M. Veatch (eds.), *Death Inside Out*. New York: Harper and Row.

Kalish, Richard A., and David K. Reynolds (1976). *Death and Ethnicity*. Los Angeles: University of Southern California Press.

Kaufman, Walter (1959). Existentialism and death. In Herman Feifel (ed.), *The Meaning of Death*. New York: McGraw-Hill.

Koestenbaum, Peter (1971). The vitality of death. In Frances G. Scott and Ruth M. Brewer (eds.), *Confrontations of Death*. Corvallis, Oreg.: Continuing Education Publications.

Kübler-Ross, Elisabeth (1969). *On Death and Dying*. New York: Macmillan.

Lifton, Robert J. (1968). *Death in Life*. New York: Random House.

Lindesmith, Alfred, Anselm L. Strauss, and Norman K. Denzin (1975). *Social Psychology*. Hinsdale, Ill.: Dryden.

Marcuse, Herbert (1959). The ideology of death. In Herman Feifel (ed.), *The Meaning of Death*. New York: McGraw-Hill.

Mervyn, Frances (1971). The plight of dying patients in hospitals. *American Journal of Nursing* 71:1988-90.

Molina, Fernando (1967). *Existentialism as Philosophy*. Englewood Cliffs, N.J.: Prentice-Hall.

Olson, Robert (1971). Death. *Omega* 2:273-86.

Parsons, Talcott, and Victor Lidz (1967). Death in American society. In Edwin S. Shneidman (ed.), *Essays in Self-Destruction*. New York: Science House.

————, René C. Fox, and Victor M. Lidz (1973). The "gift of life" and its reciprocation. In Arien Mack (ed.), *Death in American Experience*. New York: Schocken Books.

Phillipson, Michael (1973). Phenomenological philosophy and sociology. In Paul Filmer, Michael Phillipson, David Silverman, and David Walsh, *New Directions in Sociological Theory*. Cambridge, Mass.: MIT Press.

————, and Maurice Roche (1974). Phenomenology, sociology, and the study of deviance. In Paul Rock and Mary McIntosh (eds.), *Deviance and Social Control*. New York: Harper and Row.

Pincus, Lily (1974). *Death and the Family*. New York: Random House, Vintage Books.

Psathas, George (1973). *Phenomenological Sociology*. New York: Wiley.

Rakoff, Vivian M. (1973). Psychiatric aspects of death in America. In Arien Mack (ed.), *Death in American Experience*. New York: Schocken Books.

Reinhardt, Kurt (1970). *The Existential Revolt*. New York: Frederick Ungar.

Sartre, Jean-Paul (1956). *Being and Nothingness*. New York: Philosophical Library.

Shibles, Warren (1974). *Death*. Whitewater, Wis.: The Language Press.

Shneidman, Edwin (1973). *Deaths of Man*. New York: Quadrangle Books.

Sontag, Susan (1978). As quoted in "Looking into the black hole" of death. *San Francisco Chronicle,* February 8, 1978.

Strauss, Anselm L., ed. (1964). *George Herbert Mead: On Social Psychology.* Chicago: University of Chicago Press.

Sudnow, David (1967). *Passing On.* Englewood Cliffs, N.J.: Prentice-Hall.

Tolstoy, Leo (1971). The death of Ivan Ilych. In Frances Scott and Ruth M. Brewer (eds.), *Confrontation of Death.* Corvallis, Oreg.: Continuing Education Publications. (First published in 1886.)

Turner, Ronny E., and Charles Edgley (1975). Death as theatre: a dramaturgical analysis of the American funeral. *Sociology and Social Research* 60:377-92.

Zeitlin, Irving (1968). *Ideology and the Development of Sociological Theory.* Englewood Cliffs, N.J.: Prentice-Hall.

CHAPTER THREE

DEATH CONCEPTIONS AND CONCERNS IN EVERYDAY LIFE

Any sociological treatment of death needs to take into account the understanding of death in the everyday world. Even though human consciousness of death takes incredibly diverse forms, we can discern major themes and patterns in American society. I will attempt here to tap those themes and patterns.

Some questions arise as I undertake this task. What sense do people make of death? What relationships can be found between consciousness of death and social experience? For that matter, the long-debated question may be raised anew: *Are* we really conscious of our own mortality? To answer these questions, I begin by analyzing *death conceptions* held by persons in everyday worlds. A discussion of death *language* and *meaning* follows. Last, I explore the concerns of *fear* and *denial* of *death*.

DEATH CONCEPTIONS

In the assessment of responses to death, patterns in the diverse conceptions held by individuals emerge. I address these patterns first. Following this, I outline death conceptions throughout the life cycle. Although age is surely not the only significant category related to death conceptions, it is the one most explored in research. Other categories, such as ethnicity, are just beginning to be tapped by researchers (see Kalish and Reynolds 1976). Although it would be equally fascinating to conduct a systematic inquiry relating death conceptions to other categories, such as the occupational, marital, and health status of various individuals, these tasks remain to be completed.

Types of Death Conceptions

The ways in which individuals conceptualized death are no doubt as diverse as conceptions of life. But conceptions of death are particularly intriguing, since, despite the claims of some who presume to know what death is, there are no ways of verifying them. While some who view death as a mystery, an unknown, may emphasize their unformed thoughts and feelings about it, others develop remarkably intricate conceptions. Though death conceptions are rich and varied, major discernible themes constituting general types link seemingly contradictory conceptions. Death may be categorized as an *event* or *state*, or it may be related to *purposes* and *hopes*. Because current dominant conceptions are treated throughout the book, I shall attempt to outline only major types.

Views of death as an *event* encompass divergent meanings about the nature and character of that event and what, if anything, follows it. Although in all views, the event means the cessation of biological life, the commonsense notion is that the event occurs in a *specific* point in time. In contrast, some scientists are beginning to view the event as a process possessing *duration* (with somewhat ambiguous boundaries). In everyday life, however, the cessation of biological life may be viewed as a complete *ending* of the person. As one person commented, "Death signifies an ending, going away, leaving, departure, not particularly *to* anything but *from* a life, friends, family, experiences." On the other hand, the event may be viewed as a *transition*. Even those who view death as the end have different themes and concerns. A quasi-scientific theme, for example, is shown by lay persons who use almost clinical descriptions of death without indicating subjective concerns. Others suggest a merging of "scientific" and personal and social concerns, such as a student's view of death as a "bio-social disconnection." Or, while some view death only in relation to the dying process, as a release, others view it in largely personal terms as failure (to be able to survive) or loss of self-control.

Similar diversity may be discovered in the conception of the event as a transition. The transition may represent a passage, departure, or a shift into nothingness. Major interpretations of the event as transition assume that death elicits a *verdict* on the deceased after their lives are reviewed, appraised, and judged. Here, death is essentially represented as a "day of judgment" followed by eternal rewards or punishments.

Whether or not death is viewed as an end or a transition, those who conceive of death as *severance* from life emphasize the *nature* of the event. In this view, the person is torn away from the living and life itself. In his historical analyses of Western attitudes toward death, Aries (1974) posits the roots of this conception in the sixteenth century, but it remains prevalent today. According to Aries, death was thought to be a paroxysmal "rupture" or "break" devoid of its earlier erotic characteristics, although defined as romantic. Death as severance constitutes for Aries a shift from earlier conceptions of death as familiar and tamed to contemporary views of death as *shameful* and *forbidden*. In any case, themes of severance may be discerned when death is conceived of as an event marked by separations and loneliness. To illustrate, a woman remarked that she saw death as a "wrenching away" from her family and friends into the "ultimate isolation." She envisioned death as an event that would separate her from all that she had previously known and leave her lonely and isolated.

In contrast to death as an event are conceptions of death as a *state*. While the former usually refer to a point in time, the latter tend to emphasize *infinite* time. The two are not, however, exclusive categories since the state may be viewed as a *sequel* to an earlier transition. That state may be defined as a "void" or "emptiness." For example, one person remarked, "Death evokes images of a void, an empty space, the absence of a presence—an empty chair, not hearing that voice or feeling that touch—similarly a wide expanse of ocean, a canyon, a seemingly empty space." In contrast, others who assume continued existence propose that death is a state of being. Typical statements include those contemporary images of death as a higher plane of existence or consciousness or a state of "perpetual development" (see Kastenbaum 1977). These statements reflect an underlying assumption that something occurs and that, moreover, one may still *experience* it since it is seen as a form of life. Conceptions of this order are put forth by some proponents of the death and dying movement who posit their views as unalterably true (see L. Lofland 1978).

The next type of death conception may be broadly cast in terms of *purposes*. Here, stress is given to both the *effects* of dying and what it presumably *accomplishes*. Depending upon the individual's proclivities and concerns, the effects of death may be seen as peace, reward, unification, loss of others, personal loss or, for that matter, a loss of persona. Other consequences of death are thought to be an *elevation* or *reduction* of *status*, a return to God, nature, or deceased kin.

The effects of any purposes attributed to death are often *personified*. Thus, throughout history death has been viewed as the great destroyer, grim reaper, gay deceiver, lover, or comforter. These personifications are external forces who *take* the dying person, often after an entangled relationship. While the image of the grim reaper suggests a hostile confrontation with death, the image of gay deceiver implies that the dying are lured through chicanery. The comforter image connotes a peaceful departure into death. Though these personifications may be linked to specific historical periods, we might possess our own contemporary personifications, such as death as the "enemy," a less personal, more anonymous, but no less ominous or external image than earlier ones. At that, the less personal, less definitive, and more anonymous character of death as the "enemy" perhaps reflects the character of contemporary social relationships in contrast to those of earlier periods.

The effects of death are strikingly portrayed in the medieval concept of death as an *equalizer*, or leveler. Since death was ever present then due to plague, epidemics, and wars, a uniquely social conception of death developed that obliterated worldly social distinctions at the time of death. Death, then, humbled the mighty and thus accomplished an equality unknown in everyday medieval life.

The last category of death conceptions is based on *ideals, hopes,* and *wishes,* that is, what individuals think death *should be*. Though many of the views above purport to describe what death is, these views often reveal what their possessors hope or wish it to be. When we look into the realm of ideas, hopes, and wishes in everyday conceptions, demarcations between dying and death become blurred. Since the conception of a *"natural"* death typifies this and is particularly salient in handling the dying, I will treat it further.

An idealized conception of death, a *natural* death, is an *easy* death without agony, pain, lingering, or undue inconvenience to self or others. Moreover, death is typically assumed to occur at the *"correct"* time, old age. In addition, in order for death to be natural, its cause is typically believed to be *old age,* an amorphous condition thought to be a *spontaneous* way for the body to fade into oblivion. But a paradox occurs. In order to have such a death one must preserve oneself until the proper time comes to die "naturally." That means that one must seek medical care, at least in the interim before death. And ultimately, people do not die naturally, rather, they die of something. As long as they have some medical problem, they are likely to remain under the purview of medical specialists who are apt to be in full control when decisions about handling death occur.

Illich (1974) contends that the "dominant image of death determines the prevalent concept of health" within a society. In seeking a "natural" death, individuals come into the purview of medical specialists. Illich argues that although the dominant image of death is a natural death, in actuality, many patients experience a prolonged clinical death constructed by the institution of medicine. His argument rests on three major premises. First, modern medicine possesses a ritual nature that obfuscates the fundamental contradiction between what people desire and what actually occurs in medical institutions. Second, medical institutions foster the dominant image of death by giving the masses the death image held by elites. Third, a greater number of consumers are created who become dependent on medical services. Because consumers accept the idealized image of natural death and subsequently become dependent on medical services, Illich argues that the medical institution gains coercive control over its clients. Simultaneously, it provides the dogma that supports the fundamental ritual on which society is organized. Illich's argument then rests on the premise that the powerful institution of medicine is a basic source of social order. Hence, a conception of natural death may serve these coercive functions that negate the original ideals, hopes, and wishes of its adherents.

Dominant conceptions of death are more than interesting ideas held by individuals, since they also shape and are shaped by institutional forces. Further, whatever particular death conception is articulated, "appropriate" attitudes and actions follow from it. In that sense, we are reminded that our views shift and change, as it has been observed historically. Finally, as L. Lofland (1977) proposes, a marked change may be presently occurring since some groups are developing new ways of thinking, acting, and feeling in the face of death.

Death Conceptions and Age

Do death conceptions shift and change over the life cycle? If so, how does that occur? Although current research is highly tentative, it appears that death conceptions are, to an extent, age graded. But why are they age graded? Those with a psychological bent usually assume that human life consists of a *developmental process*, fundamentally *biological* in origin with psychological implications. In contrast, others assume that whatever similarities are discovered are due to *socialization*. Also, in an age-graded society, life experiences of people of the same age bear certain similarities. Moreover, those life experiences tend to be heavily influenced by the social structuring of everyday life. This section will deal with the relationships between age and death conceptions by exploring biological and social influences on different age groups.

Whether or not children possess a view of death at all has been a source of debate among psychologists. Those who adhere to Piaget's structural analysis of conceptual development propose that children should not be expected to have a concept of death until they have attained a level of mental development that allows for *abstract reasoning*. Here, these theorists assume that: (1) mental development is primarily biological, (2) abstract reasoning is dependent upon levels of development, and (3) death is an abstract concept unable to be fully understood until the level of development necessary for abstract reasoning is reached.

Those who adopt Piaget's theory assume that there are substantial differences between the reasoning of children and adolescents. Similarly, they propose that there are qualitative differences in the thinking of a child and that of an adult. From this perspective, adults do not simply know more than children, but are instead distinguished by the quality of their reasoning. The level of understanding is the crucial factor in assessing reasoning ability. Menig-Peterson and McCabe (1978) support Piaget's theory. In their analysis of narratives provided by children, they discovered that children under 5 and a half years virtually do not discuss death. Yet, lack of discussion does not necessarily indicate that these children have no knowledge or conception of death.

In contrast to younger children, Menig-Peterson and McCabe found children over 5 and a half to be extremely curious about death. They talked about it frequently in the same offhand way that they might chat about a television program. Only after 9 years of age did these children show some emotional response. A 7-year-old child whose mother had died related narratives about it with "inappropriate" emotional responses (she laughed when talking about the man who had killed her mother). Her response was taken by the authors to indicate massive denial.

But to go back to Piaget's theory, even children as old as 10 years display concrete cognitive patterns that do not specify abstract relationships. The following statement made by a boy of 10 is categorized as representing concrete mental operations:

> Death is when your body just turns off. It just refuses to function any-more—you just die. When you are older, your blood cells and stuff like that go bad. Your skin gets wrinkled. Last Friday in Mr. T's room we were talking about blood cells and skin cells (Kraai 1975, p. 8).

In this perspective, it makes no sense to try to teach a child what death means, since understanding death necessitates making abstract connections between largely unobservable events and processes. Although a younger child like the one above can make some statements about the state of being dead, his connections between phases of the process of becoming dead suggest a lack of understanding.

The development of an increasingly more intricate view of death was also found by Nagy (1959) in her postwar study of children's concepts of death. She found that children from 3 to 5 saw death as a gradual or temporary *departure* or *sleep*. For these children, death is often *reversible*, since it is not clearly distinguished from life. In contrast, she found that children between 5 to 9 tended to *personify death* with dangerous and powerful attributes. A typical conception is death as an evil-intentioned male figure, frequently in skeleton form, who carries people away with him.

Nagy emphasizes that in this stage the child accepts the existence of death, but it is *external*. After age 9, however, Nagy concludes that the child reaches the point of understanding that death means the *cessation* of the body. At this point, the child comes to realize that death is a process that is *inside* someone instead of an external event.

Other psychologists who do not take a developmental approach and most sociologists question the premises of that approach. Although the area needs further research, there are some important indications that children are capable of abstract thought, in general, and abstract conceptions of death, in particular, at an early age (see Kastenbaum and Aisenberg 1972).

Any social psychological investigation of the child's view of death would have to take into account the *social context* in which that view is constructed. Rochlin's psychiatric investigation (1967) gives weight to the significance of the social context. He points out that adults commonly *prohibit* children from becoming aware of death. Surely, shielding children from the facts of death must have some impact on the child's developing view of it. Conversely, being exposed to death must have some effect on the child, especially since that exposure may have occurred in emotionally laden circumstances.

For his study of very young children's views of death, Rochlin (1967) selected 3- to 5-year-olds who were capable of organized thinking. He chose urban children who had well-educated parents without any religious affiliation since he wished to avoid prior exposure to death and indoctrination into a particular view through organized religion. Rochlin argues that, at this early age, children already defend themselves against the knowledge that life may end. According to him, children engage in magical thinking and alter their realities to correspond with their wishes. To illustrate, similar to Nagy's earlier work (1959), the child may believe that the dead person will live again or that sleep and death are equivalent. Interestingly, Rochlin discovers that morality is introduced by the child very early; the "bad" die before the "good," and the "good" may return from the dead. Death itself is viewed as the outcome of human relations such as strife and hostility.

More importantly, Rochlin's data indicate that these young children appear to understand the finite nature of life, in general, and of their own lives, in particular. He maintains that these children's conceptions are heavily influenced by their conscious and unconscious emotions. Rochlin comments on this issue in the following way: "What is remarkable is not that children arrive at adult views of the cessation of life, but rather how tenaciously throughout life adults hold on to the child's beliefs and how readily they revert to them" (p. 63).

Other studies (Anthony 1971; Furman 1974) support Rochlin's conclusion that young children develop a concept of death. Furman's psychiatric research demonstrates that it is easier for very young children to understand the death of a parent when they already hold a concept of death. Concrete evidence of death was found to help bereaved children in understanding it. In contrast, Furman found that understanding the death became much more difficult when adults intentionally or unintentionally hid or misrepresented the facts.

Kastenbaum and Aisenberg (1972) point out that ambiguities in adult language and thought may confuse the young child who only uses words and ideas in one context. Thus, when the same word is used in another context the child becomes confused. The transposition of meaning the child makes may be quite complex. For example, Sandor Brent (1978) discovered that his 2-year-old son equated a car motor with the human body. The boy concluded that when the car was out of gas or the battery had no charge, it was "dead" though it could "live" again. The boy then insisted upon having a bottle of sugar water to keep his own "motor" running during the night. This example suggests that the use of language gives shape to the child's emerging concept of death. But what other evidence can be found to support the view of the child's response to death as social in origin rather than developmental?

Bluebond-Langner's findings (1977) show that the developmental perspective does not hold up when terminally ill children are studied in the context of their experience. Rather, she argues that the children become aware of their impending deaths and possess death conceptions remarkably similar to

those of adults. She discovered that the ability to synthesize information cor-
responded to *experience* and not to age or intellectual ability. For example, she
found 3-year-olds with average intelligence to know more about their impending deaths than 9-year-olds known to be of exceptional intelligence.

According to Bluebond-Langner, this difference may be attributed to the
child's relative placement in *stages* of *information acquisition*. That terminally
ill children do acquire information even when their parents expressly shield
them from it was discovered by Waechter (1971). She found that these children
perceive nonverbal cues of their conditions despite parental evasiveness. She
proposes that the false cheerfulness and evasiveness of adults may lead the
child to conclude sadly that disclosure of fear of impending death may result in
further loss of already diminished human contact. Waechter discovered the
children's loneliness not only in their dying but also in stories the children told.
These stories reflected the extent to which they had accurately pieced together
information. Consider this little girl's story:

> *She's in the hospital, and the doctor is talking to her mother and father.*
> *She's sick—she's got cancer. She's very, very sick. She's thinking she*
> *wishes she could go home. She's had an operation at the hospital, but she*
> *didn't want it because she wanted to get out of the hospital. This little*
> *girl dies—she doesn't get better. Poor little girl. This girl at the hospital—*
> *she has cancer. Her hip is swollen and her bone's broken. This little girl in*
> *the picture died, and then they buried her. And then she went up to*
> *heaven. She didn't like it there—because God wasn't there (Waechter*
> *1971, p. 1172).*

Two provocative issues are raised by these studies of terminally ill children. First, Bluebond-Langner takes issue with earlier conclusions that
children do not have conceptions of death. She argues that earlier writers mistakenly took what children *say* for everything they *think*. By situating children's comments in their experience, greater insight is gained into their views.
Second, these two studies imply that children may be strikingly responsive to
the feelings of adults. That may also be true of the children in the other studies
conducted under diverse circumstances at different times. If so, studies of
children may actually *mirror* the *thoughts* and *feelings* of *adults* rather than
those of the children purported to be studied! Further, it follows that conceal-
ing death information from children affects the views of death they hold. In
any case, the social context of the child's experience seems to be significant,
regardless of the particular findings obtained.

There seems to be more interest in the death conceptions of children and
the elderly than in those of other age groups. One of the few papers on adolescents (Kastenbaum 1959) strongly suggests that they are deeply affected by
the socio-cultural matrix in which they live. Kastenbaum emphasized that
adolescents are not passively determined by external forces, but exist in a
dynamic relationship with them. These adolescents lived in an *intense present;*

the past and the future remained vague by contrast. Kastenbaum reports that they viewed death as *empty*, not active; it represented the *end* to them.

Although little has been written about death conceptions held in middle age, Jaques's developmental analysis (1969) has become something of a classic. He posits a correlation between death and what he called the "midlife crisis." According to Jaques, midlife represents the turning point between growing up and growing old; death lies in the future. He claims that midlife crisis begins roughly with the onset of menopause in women and the reduction of sexual intensity in men. Jaques contends that the crucial dimension of middle age is the subjective awareness of one's eventual death. A 36-year-old patient of Jaques's compared his earlier view of life as "endless slope" with his new realization of death. He said, "Now suddenly I seem to have reached the crest of the hill, and there stretching ahead is the downward slope with the end of the road in sight—far enough away it's true—but there is death observably present at the end."

Subjective awareness of death may also lead to the realization that the future is circumscribed and much of one's hopes, dreams, and plans will not materialize. Of course, that realization alone might be enough to warrant the kind of psychological depression that Jaques maintains characterizes the midlife crisis. If so, the crisis described as ultimately biological by Jaques would actually be *social psychological*. Further, it is difficult to accept Jaques's developmental argument since it is based on such a vague notion as a midlife crisis. Whether or not there is a discernible decrease of sexual intensity in the male at around 35 is questionable. In addition, the crisis conventionally associated with menopause in women has been shown to correspond with the role loss of "empty-nest" mothers (Bart 1971). What Jaques may have mistaken for a developmental crisis may more accurately reflect age-graded and age-related events elicited by social processes.

In addition, certain events are more likely to happen to someone at particular age levels. The loss of one's parents is one critical event apt to happen in midlife. Another is the loss of friends due to terminal illnesses. Such losses no doubt cause any adult to think about death more subjectively, at least for a period. However, the loss of parents in midlife has another significant dimension—the effect on adult awareness of knowing that there is no generation beyond them. As one woman talked about it to me,

It is such a hollow feeling knowing that there is no generation before you; you are it now, the oldest generation in your family. That is a scary, empty feeling.

It is conceivable that the death conceptions of the middle-aged are directly related to their social functions within the society. Since they constitute the group largely responsible for maintaining the social order, their death conceptions would naturally reflect their involvements. Hence, their views could be expected to differ from those views of the young and the old.

Although these observations are highly speculative, more concrete information is available on the conceptions of the old. Kastenbaum and Aisenberg (1972) propose that elders (and women and minorities) are more apt to have what they call a "participating" response to death. In this conception, death is viewed as being *within* the individual. Persons who hold this conception view death as a form of *honor, fulfillment,* or *reunion.* Themes of reunion may be with nature or, in the case of elderly widows particularly, with their dead husbands.

Kastenbaum and Aisenberg remark that they have known geriatric patients who speak of death as a familiar *presence* or *companion.* This response is consistent with Swenson's finding (1975) that institutionalized elderly look forward to death more than those who are not institutionalized. Kastenbaum and Aisenberg observe that the aging process itself causes the elderly to have fewer illusions about the locus of death as within them. Kastenbaum and Aisenberg show two kinds of active participatory responses to death by the elderly. In the first, a merging occurs between the person and death. This merging is due to partnership or *union,* rather than dread or sorrow. According to Kastenbaum and Aisenberg, if this stance is taken, older persons may reject nourishment, medication, or surgical intervention that might extend their lives. In the second participatory response, the individual treasures death. It becomes a personal possession, perhaps the only remaining one on which the person's self-image can be based. Kastenbaum and Aisenberg (1972, p. 105) tell of a 93-year-old man who made this statement about his death: "It's mine," the elder rejoined. "Don't belong to nobody else." Death may then symbolically represent to the aged a last claim to *uniqueness.*

The aged seem to be willing to talk about death more frequently and openly than people in other age categories. Some studies indicate that the aged feel less fear about death than others. Kastenbaum and Aisenberg believe that the aged approach death with more acceptance than apprehension, although Feifel and Branscomb (1973) suggest that they repress their fear. Interestingly, Swenson (1975) found that those who lived alone had a more negative or fearful view of death than other elderly persons. In contrast, Jeffers and Verwoerdt (1977) found that anger was conspicuously absent from the responses of elderly subjects in their North Carolina study. Instead, death was seen as appropriate, although some did not wish it to occur in the near future.

These somewhat contradictory findings raise the perplexing question: Do the views of the elderly reflect their age status? Swenson (1975) concludes that age level, per se, has no predictive value in the individual's concept of death. Different social circumstances proved to be more definitive variables for him. In those studies where age does seem to be predictive, one needs to ask whether differences result from age alone or from historical circumstances shared by the same cohort. For example, Kalish and Reynolds (1976) wonder if the emphasis of the elderly on family and tradition stems from early socialization or from actual increased emphasis on these values with age. As Kalish and Reynolds suggest, without detailed studies of the entire lives of a group of individuals, it is impossible to determine the meanings of their responses. In short, the investigator has no context in which to make sense of the responses.

Experiential concerns also are important to note in connection with the death conceptions of the elderly. Kalish (1976) emphasizes that the limited life span of the aged requires continual readjustment of allocation of time and effort. He posits two important conceptions, death as an *organizer* of *time* and death as *loss*, as possibly of special significance to the elderly. Those elderly who make plans and rely heavily on a future orientation are apt to be highly aware of the possibility of impending death. Kalish remarks that the coming of death accelerates the feeling of the elderly of being "devoured" by time when remaining time is thought of in weeks or months. But according to Kalish, in the immediate present death makes moments creep by because one hesitates to involve oneself in meaningful activities that may never be completed.

Death as a loss may not differ so much in kind from conceptions held by persons in other age groups. But the older person may have already sustained many losses such as spouse, social identity, home, and income. These losses may shade the extent to which death is perceived as a loss. If losses deprived individuals of major sources of valued experience, such as loss of spouse or health, they may become apathetic about death. According to Kalish, elders are less reluctant to give up life because less potential exists for satisfying future experiences. Kalish insightfully notes that a special type of loss significant to the elderly is the *loss* of *control*. In my previous research projects (Calkins 1972; Charmaz 1973), aged persons often confided their fears of a loss of control. For them loss of control meant becoming a *burden*, a fate worse than death because of the consequent diminishing of their personal dignity. One elderly woman disclosed,

> *I don't know what I will do when I can no longer take care of myself. I just hope I go quickly—I don't want to be a burden to my children. I don't want them to have to take care of me. There's no room in their lives to take care of an elderly person and besides, I've been around long enough and seen enough to know what that's like. . . . I certainly don't want to become one of these mindless old souls who don't know sic 'em from come here. There's nothing sadder than those poor things out at X [a local convalescent hospital]. Some of those old people don't even know their relatives. As far as I am concerned, I'd rather be dead than be like that.*

In any investigation of age-linked conceptions of death, the degree of awareness of finitude is essentially a *social comparison* process (Marshall 1975). Marshall found that elderly persons living in a retirement community compared themselves with friends and associates who were dying and dead. Death then became an explicit concern of the living. Similarly, Hochschild (1973) found that the elderly women she studied constructed social comparisons as they attempted to guess how long other residents would live.

These observations suggest strongly that concepts of death and concerns about it are most fundamentally linked to the *interaction process*. How death is treated in interaction and, subsequently, how it is *interpreted* would then assume much more importance than age. Similarly, comparisons of interaction would seem to provide crucial information in the development of a concept of death. Such concepts are not wholly idiosyncratic. Rather, they arise out of the interpretations actors make of their realities as interaction takes place within them. If so, concepts of death must be more explicitly linked to the social worlds in which they are found.

To conclude, it stands to reason that the views of different age groups represent the symbolic ordering of their worlds. Children who are shielded from death may not reveal their views or may not develop them explicitly. Adolescents remain in the intensity of the lived present. The middle-aged confront who they are and will become. And for those aged who face visible reminders, death becomes increasingly an explicit concern.

LANGUAGE AND MEANING

Experience is given shape through word and gesture. The shape of death in a society is framed by the words and gestures used to account for it. In this section, I will first identify and discuss key components of American *death language*. Then I will provide an example of the imputation of meaning largely through gesture. That example consists of a discussion of implied meanings elicited by the concept of *symbolic death*.

Death Language

The language with which we describe and denote death reflects our culture, the structure of personal relationships, and experiences associated with death. In the analysis that follows, I emphasize two aspects of death language: conventional *words* and *meanings* and the emerging *death talk* characteristic of the death and dying movement (see L. Lofland 1977).

Conventional words and meanings appear to me to suggest three major themes: *neutralizing, euphemizing,* and *ridiculing* death. As existentionalists imply, because we have no term to distinguish death in general from death of the self (Koestenbaum 1971), meanings of death are made more ambiguous. I suggest that the absence of such a term neutralizes death's meaning in part by keeping it separate from oneself. Death is neutralized by eliminating emotional experience from our death terms—an actual event becomes a general, *abstract* category. Professionals in particular neutralize death by using abstract terms that reduce living beings to objects.

Statements such as "the patient exsanguinated" or "the patient expired" show the kind of abstract objectifications that are made. Real people, actual events, the character of that person's final moments (if known and shared at all) become transformed into a neutral and quasi-technical term like "expired" (a term which does, in some sense, seem the opposite of "inspired").

Everyday euphemisms, such as "passed on," "faded away," "gone," and "promoted to Glory" (a Salvation Army term), also serve to neutralize meanings of death. All denote death as an amorphous and vague transition. Such terms imply that the harshness of finality is neutralized. Importantly, however, a major intent of euphemisms is to demonstrate the "proper" *respect* for the deceased and the family. In that way, a kind of *etiquette of death* has developed. The imagery evoked by these everyday terms is less harsh, definitive, and final than that of others like "died." Hence, it is easier and more "polite" to acknowledge a death by using these terms when talking about an intimate or acquaintance. Euphemisms themselves give rise to ridicule when members of the audience deem them to be inappropriate or incongruous with the actual situation. For example, when a young man gave a public eulogy for an esteemed elder and repeatedly referred to his death as "untimely," he was met with stifled giggles from the audience because the deceased was 85.

The last conventional meaning of death centers directly on the kind of ridicule intended to mock ordinary proprieties surrounding death. By offending and even shocking others, those who ridicule display their indifference or disdain for these proprieties. As that ridicule is often impersonal, it gives rise to practical jokes that may be played on an unsuspecting victim. For example, when crossing a tollbridge, some medical students took great delight in slapping a hand from the Anatomy Department's "spare parts" box with a quarter in it into the awaiting palm of the tollkeeper. In another instance, friends who were enticed by an anatomy student to see her new "kitty," presumably hiding under the bed, were shocked to find a preserved and skinned cat there. While some believe such escapades reduce human anxiety about death, others view them as a means of poking fun at the silence and seriousness with which death is usually treated. Although ridicule is perhaps more likely to be general and impersonal, it also may be specific and personal. For example, a woman who essentially abandoned her dying brother discovered that her later conspicuous show of grief at the funeral was the subject of ridicule by other friends and family. She was thereby informed of her lesser status within the group elicited by her own behavior.

In contrast to these more conventional words and meanings, those involved in the death and dying movement make concerted efforts to talk about death in as *direct, subjective,* and *emotional* a way possible (cf. L. Lofland 1977). Rather than using terms to neutralize death and separate it from self, movement proponents advocate spontaneous, verbal expression of intense feelings about death. And they often promote immersion in these feelings, possibly as a reaction to the lack of intense feeling in conventional words and meanings.

While death talk obviously differs from conventional words and meanings, several similarities may be discovered. First, death talk is taken as a *positive* or preferable way to deal with the issues posed by death, a posture similar to that taken by those who use euphemisms or attempt to neutralize death. Second, death talk is treated with a *seriousness* ordinarily attributed to the conventional words and meanings. In fact, members of a group often compete to have their situation recognized as the most serious. For example, in a grief group organized by Kavanaugh (1972), members competed for the acknowledgment that their loss was the worst of all. Ridicule and criticism may also emerge but have different objectives. Rather than ridiculing death per se, individuals ridicule and criticize motivations and ways of handling it by others. Thus, those who do not respond in "appropriate" ways may find themselves the objects of ridicule and criticism. For example, in another instance in Kavanaugh's group, a member who liked to peep at others grieving was labelled a "grief voyeur."

Death talk is not merely the province of professionals concerned with the issues. It also has become more common among the dying. Terminal illness clubs and organizations have sprung up, sometimes under the aegis of professionals, but increasingly initiated by patients. A main objective of these organizations is to give mutual support. The intensity and frankness the Jaffes (1977) call "terminal candor" characterizes relationships among members. Sometimes members become local celebrities (a few are nationally known) by making themselves available to groups to discuss their feelings and concerns about dying (L. Lofland 1977). So some of the dying almost literally spend their final days and hours talking themselves to death.

Having outlined the ways in which death language is used, one might ask: What analytic sense can be made of it? Clearly, individuals' stances toward death are indicated by the words they use to describe them. *When, how* and *in what context* terms are employed reveal assumptions about death. In short, the *timing* and *pacing* of words may reveal as much about a stance toward death as the meaning of the words.

In the above discussion I focused primarily on what constitutes a death language. Now I will turn from the meaning of language to a language of meaning.

A Language of Meaning: Symbolic Death

Meanings arise through interaction, but what is communicated often goes beyond the content of words alone. Intentions are also imparted through gesture and symbol. By examining the concept of symbolic death, we can see the stated and unstated meanings that constitute a special language of *intention*.

Symbolic death refers to certain interactional circumstances in which valued aspects of the self are invalidated, violated, or otherwise *negated*. Symbolic death essentially is a *death* of *meaning* through loss of face or self, usually stemming from a lack of acceptance. Obviously, symbolic death differs considerably from biological death, since one feels symbolically dead at any time when one's symbolic world is extinguished. The loss becomes more devastating as more aspects of self are called into question. For example, it was one thing for a chronically ill patient to have her role as patient called into question and quite another to have the very essence of her being undermined (see Charmaz 1973). One chronically ill woman had an extremely difficult time recovering from pneumonia. She had lost the gains in strength and endurance that she had previously made. After several more episodes of flu, bronchitis, and drug reactions, her physicians began to wonder if she was really motivated to improve her health and financial status. At first they saw her as a some-what recalcitrant patient whose physical status created difficulties in respond-ing quickly to medical intervention. But as she continued to have setbacks, they began to suspect that she was not motivated to improve. They thought that she was trying to work them in order to qualify for social security dis-ability. When the woman accurately sensed their suspicions through their intonations and gestures, she was devastated. Having been a fiercely indepen-dent person in the past, she felt that she was being wholly discredited. Because these physicians played such a significant role in her life at that time, her self-image was directly affected by their actions.

Since the structure of the self is often built on a taken-for-granted founda-tion, people may remain unaware of how much their self-images are tied to specific symbolic worlds until these worlds collapse. For example, a man failed to realize how much structure his marriage gave to his life until it suddenly broke up.

Symbolic death is situational. Persons who are not significant in our intimate social worlds still may cause our symbolic death in specific situations. For example, by making a fellow worker's mistake publicly known an asso-ciate causes him to feel great embarrassment and mortification. Thus he is given a symbolic invitation to die. When personal slights such as being dis-counted, ignored, or snubbed are experienced, the individual is not granted an equal status. Further, by diminishing persons by treating them as non-persons, we extend a symbolic invitation to die (Jourard 1971).

Symbolic death is dramatized by a defined *incongruity* between the selves reflected in the encounter and the selves persons had previously assumed themselves to be. As Koestenbaum (1971) points out, subtle forms of symbolic life and death revolve around the issue of *personal acceptance.* Accepting per-sons by being receptive, open, understanding, friendly, and so forth, is, according to Koestenbaum, to act as if they were alive. Conversely, rejecting persons by being cold, unfriendly, critical, or indifferent is to threaten them with symbolic death. Whether or not the threat is taken seriously depends upon the situation and the relative significance of those who give it.

Powerlessness in the situation enhances and fosters the experience of loss of one's symbolic world. The person who feels powerless is unable to im-mediately reconstruct a devastated symbolic world. When one is relatively powerless to change the initial loss or situation, this realization of one's inability to alter the circumstances may be as immobilizing as the initial experience itself. For example, the chronically ill woman mentioned earlier felt herself powerless after being denied benefits by social security personnel. She made the following statement:

All I can do is dissolve in tears—there's nothing I can do. I just get im-mobilized—you sort of reach a point, you can't improve, can't remedy the situation, and you're told you aren't in the right category for getting the services you need and can't get for yourself. It makes me madder and madder at myself for being in the situation in the first place (Charmaz 1973).

To take this line of thought a bit further, it is clear that some individuals contribute to their own symbolic deaths by being, for example, unwilling to take the risks involved in reconstructing their social worlds. Or, if tacitly aware of the possible loss of their present, albeit limited, symbolic world, they may accept their present situation. And others create a type of symbolic death by not transcending the limits of their present circumstances. Instead, they opt for a limited but familiar life and personal identity rather than trying to realize what might be possible for them.

Symbolic death is socially constructed in other circumstances as well. In the educational system, for example, institutionalized practices of racism and sexism invite large numbers of children to die symbolically before they have lived (see Kozel 1970). Other examples abound in our society. For one group in particular, the elderly, symbolic death is especially striking.

Since not all old people have valued social roles or construct social identities valued by others as well as themselves, they may receive continued messages that they are no longer useful or wanted. An extreme example is the Englishwoman who tried to persuade her 86-year-old mother, a woman of some means, to commit suicide (*New York Times*, August 27, 1977). A hidden camera recorded the daughter handing her bedridden mother a massive dose of pills in a bag of candy. In this case, the invitation to die was explicit. The daughter told her "mum" that taking the pills with a big drink of whiskey was always fatal. When her mum demurred to take them, her daughter reassured her that people did it all the time and there was nothing to it. When her mum at last accepted the pills, the daughter left with the parting instruction to her mother that she not make a "mess of it this time."

In other situations, expectations of death are held only because of age. In Sudnow's *Passing On* (1967), he noted that old persons who were emergency cases were often cast in the dying role simply because they were old. The staff felt that the person was old enough to die anyway, so why not have this be their last admission to the hospital? In this instance, a symbolic death may become a real one. When others hold such expectations and especially when the stigma of the wider society toward old age is accepted and endorsed by the aged themselves, it is not surprising that they simply give up and die. Accepting the invitation to die becomes easier than attempting to live if symbolic life is such a struggle.

Symbolic death shares some properties with *social death*. Social death refers to treating people as if they are incapable of social response, or already dead before biological death occurs. A significant parallel between symbolic and social death is that they are both founded in the responses of others more powerful (at least in the specific situation) than the individual. Quite clearly, both reflect a *lack* of *human acceptance* of one person by another. When persons are socially dead, for all intents and purposes they are already symbolically dead to the person casting them in that role. But in contrast to symbolic death, people considered socially dead may not accept the definition. Nevertheless, they may not be in a condition to confront the issue; usually the term social death refers to patients who are in the final stages of dying although they may still be sentient.

Finally, those who do not wish interaction with the dying may use these tactics to avoid it. By treating a dying patient as already dead, people can avoid taking the patient into account *as a person*. In short, when treated as socially dead, the moribund are symbolically invited to hurry their dying.

In the analysis of symbolic and social death, the "little" deaths that people suffer in everyday life, but often attempt to gloss over become apparent. Recognition of these deaths can become a source of exerting control over them. However, recognizing them and *accepting* the definitions of others may lead to actual deaths.

FEAR AND DENIAL OF DEATH

La Rochefoucauld's famous seventeenth century saying, "One cannot easily look directly at either the sun or death," (see Wahl 1959, p. 19) is still meaningful to many today, perhaps because of the intellectual rationale founded in psychoanalytic theory. According to this view, facing death elicits a natural fear, and denial of death is believed to be a result of this fear. Thus, fear and denial are viewed as two sides of the same coin. Whether they represent an *inherent* human condition or are responses produced by social and cultural conditions will be explored below. In any case, fear and denial are often viewed as the typical American responses to death. As such, they become major concerns for practitioners, patients, and students of death. But whether these concerns accurately portray the empirical world remains another issue to be introduced below.

Fear of Death

Definitions and sources Writers from different schools of thought disagree about the extent, source, significance, and consequence of a fear of death.

Perhaps more importantly, the precise nature of the fear of death and how it is identified, known, and experienced are taken for granted by most writers who have been concerned with it. Their ideas may, in turn, reflect taken-for-granted definitions of death held in the wider society.

Though the phrase, fear of death, has been used in diverse ways in both the literature and lay speech, the exact source or cause of fear often goes unspecified. Ordinarily, psychologists use the term "fear" in conjunction with a specific source or cause. "Anxiety," in contrast, is used to denote the discomfort elicited by pervasive or unknown sources. What is called a fear of death is sometimes indicated by a highly specific source of that fear that is readily identifiable, such as a fear of flying or fear of dying from cancer. At other times, the source may remain unspecified and amorphous. Since the phrases "fear of death" and "death anxiety" are not always distinguishable in the literature, they will be used interchangeably in this section.

A closer look at the meanings implied in "fear of death" is needed. First, fear consists of painful feelings characterized by *alarm, consternation, dread,* and *expectation* of *danger*. As Choron (1964, p. 71) elucidates, the phrase is used in a broad sense to indicate "aversion, strong dislike, uneasiness" when thinking generally about anticipation of death. Hence, it is necessary to distinguish between those kinds of situations in which the fear of death refers to general thoughts about finitude and those in which it refers to immediate threat. Further, it may mean a *fear* of *loss* of *experience, fear* of *decay, fear* of *irreversibility,* and *fear* of *loss* of *self* (see Gordon 1970). What is often overlooked is that persons may have particular meanings in mind when they say "fear of death," but those meanings become obfuscated by the generality of the phrase. In any case, fear is, essentially, an evaluational term rooted in the symbolic understandings of the individual. My view of fear, including the fear of death, is that it is something defined by the individual rather than an automatic response or an inherent characteristic of human nature.

A general fear of death may actually stem from a more specific fear. As Choron (1964, pp. 72-83) clarifies, several different sources of fears fall under the general rubric "fear of death." His breakdown of the types includes: *"fear of what comes after," "fear of the process of dying"* and *"fear of ceasing to be."* It is important to note that someone may show marked fear about one source and be comparatively unconcerned or accepting of others. For example, one man claims to be unconcerned about an afterlife as long as he dies quickly. The thought of a lingering, painful death is extremely frightening to him. Another claims not to be frightened of the dying process but finds the thought of ceasing to experience unsettling and frightening.

As I note in Chapter 5, there are ample reasons to fear the process of dying because it is often marked by pain, powerlessness, isolation, and abandonment. And the fear of ceasing to be is sometimes melded with the fear of what comes after. That is, one fears ceasing to be because one feels that nothing comes after death. Walton (1976) contends that a certain amount of anxiety in the face of death is rational for those who view death as a cessation of all experience, as long as that anxiety does not disrupt their lives.

In contrast, one might expect those who hold a religious orientation to be confident in the face of death since death would be viewed as a transition from one form of existence to another. Lester (1967) examined a number of studies on the relationship between religion and the fear of death but found the results to be inconclusive. Since then, greater attention has been given to the *depth* of *religious belief*. Kübler-Ross (1969) mentions that those few who possess an "intrinsic faith" show less fear than others. Similarly, Templar (1972) finds that those who are extremely involved in their religions show less death anxiety. Kalish and Reynolds (1976) propose that those without a coherent belief system to provide meaning to life and death are apt to fear death the most. In their view, then, atheists as well as devout persons may evince little fear of death when their views are sincerely believed.

Traditional views In taking a closer look at views that assume death fear is an intrinsic part of human nature, I must draw upon ideas from the psychoanalytic tradition. According to Freud, the fear of death, though pervasive, is a secondary fear due to guilt or separation. However, many psychoanalysts now see it as a basic or *universal* fear. Nevertheless, most are in keeping with Freud in their belief that civilized humans have not progressed much from their primitive ancestors in the face of subjective death (see Wahl 1959). Similarly, they believe that on an unconscious level we live in terror of our deaths. Thus, psychoanalysts propose that individuals have several major ways of coping with the difficulty of facing death. First, they believe that it is necessary to *repress* anxiety about death in order to live with a modicum of comfort and security. Second, individuals are thought to engage in *magical thinking* in order to cope with death. Thus, individuals are believed to maintain an unconscious belief in *infantile omnipotence* since death is treated as if *reversible*. Third, a heightened fear of death is thought to underlie neurotic behavior, although it may surface in *oblique* or *distorted* ways. Thus, fear of death is thought to be *transformed* into such feelings as anger, fear of isolation, or separation.

With his emphasis on repression and unconscious motivation, Slote (1975) combines psychoanalytic insights with existentialist ideas to explore and explain the fear of death. His argument goes as follows: Because people do not wish to live in fear, they live in the external, objective world. They are essentially driven toward activities. Their activities divert them from themselves; that is, their subjectivity which, if realized, would bring them in touch with their "actual" death anxiety. Slote contends that people deceive themselves about their motives for these activities. According to him, they repress their fear of death through activity but unconsciously do not wish to live.

Ammon's discussion of the "unlived" life (1975) reveals similar themes. He argues that a "pathological" fear of death founded in repression and flight results from an "incomplete" development of identity. For Ammon, un-achieved identities develop when individuals try on identity after identity without attaining self-realization through any of them. An example of some-one with an unachieved identity is a man who undertook many activities without realizing either excellence or fulfillment in any of them. At one point he wrote poetry; then for several years he attempted to write a play. Next he tried sculpture, followed by an abortive teaching career. Each activity was characterized by his lack of intense involvement. He went through the rituals of appearing to be a poet, playwright, sculptor, and teacher. Although he claimed to believe in his creativity, he appeared to escape from it more than develop it. As he became middle-aged the problem intensified. Also, since many of his friends became accomplished in their various pursuits he felt his lack of achievement more keenly. Sadly, as his anxiety increased, he seemed even less able to realize an identity meaningful to him.

The unlived life and unachieved identity are part of a self-perpetuating process. Because of death fear, neurotic individuals attempt to hide them-selves and escape reality through activity. Since this activity does not provide fulfillment, and life is therefore unlived, death becomes even more feared. Further, as Ammon remarks, "neurosis is the way to avoid non-being, by avoiding being itself" (1975, p. 95).

Some empirical support exists for the psychoanalytic notions of a re-pressed fear of death. For example, Feifel and Branscomb's findings (1973) suggest that on a conscious level individuals deny fear of death, while on a fantasy level they are ambivalent and unconsciously negative toward it. While these researchers' evidence may be suggestive, it is not definitive. And that speaks to a larger issue. In my view, the lack of definitiveness of psycho-analytic reasoning about the fear of death is a central problem. Although psychoanalytic notions offer provocative insights, it remains unclear to what extent they are empirically valid and under what conditions they may or may not reflect central death themes and concerns of specific groups.

Relationships to social structure and culture In the preceding discussion, I examined views predicated upon the assumption that the fear of death is a fundamental or inherent part of the human condition. Now I will look at the other possibility, that the fear of death is socially created.

In his analysis of American values and social structure, Slater (1974) addresses the fear of death. According to him, the rise of individuality with the illusion of self-sufficiency heightens consciousness of self while fostering an *emergence* of the fear of death. What Slater implies is that in societies where individuality is a high cultural priority, the fear of death logically follows. He theorizes that community and privatism are *mutually exclusive* goals and, while a given social organization may support one goal, it cannot support both equally. From Slater's perspective, people in industrial society lose the con-nectedness based on community provided in other societies. Dying becomes an ultimate form of loneliness, and the perception of the depth of that loneliness may become merged with the fear of death. From this line of thought it becomes clear that the fear of death may be a price paid for living in a society whose ideology rests on the type of individualism experienced in America.

Given Slater's argument, the fear of death would logically be related to social, cultural, and historical conditions. Some evidence for this position is available. Rzhevsky states, "The Chinese look upon death not with fear, but with pleasure" (1976, p. 38). Rzhevsky also comments that the Indian whose outlook toward life is pessimistic sees death as "deliverance." Rzhevsky further observes that Russian fatalism toward death is marked by a seemingly contradictory attitude of indifference toward and contempt for life. He analyzes the Russian stance toward death as emanating from its pagan cultural history, which gave rise to an attitude fostering fraternity, conformity, dependency, and despair.

Possibly, the fear of death is most noticeable in western cultures characterized by industrialism and individualism. Further suggestion of a contrast between industrial and rural society is provided by Douglass's description of life in a Spanish Basque village (1969). He observes that individuals are "calm in the face of death." Here, the cultural response to death is characterized by openness and candor in general and resignation by individuals in particular. Similarly, Roberts (1977) finds that the rural people of Appalachia hold a fatalistic view of death notable for its apparent absence of death fear. Kalish and Reynolds's quantitative findings (1976) suggest that American blacks, particularly elder males, may have less overt death fear than members of other cultural groups.

All these studies imply that the extent to which a people may hold a fear of death varies with social and cultural conditions. Perhaps a consequence of the current concern with death will be more detailed investigations into the nature and quality of the response of different groups to death.

Effects on interaction: an illustration Psychoanalysts have long contended that the fear of death is played out in interaction. Bermann (1973) offers a remarkable observational study of the interactional effects of the fear of death. In his case study, Bermann found that family members felt a real terror of death but did not acknowledge it. The source of their fear was the knowledge that the father might die at any time. Although Bermann states that everyone in the family knew of the possibility of the father's impending death, the only way the anxiety was clearly shown was through the behavioral aberrations of the young son, who showed signs of "mental illness." He portrays the boy as a scapegoat for the pressures within the family.

Bermann suggests that the construction of a scapegoat within a family takes years to develop through a multitude of repeated reinforcements. He implies that the symbolic construction of the scapegoat can be divided into two phases: (1) the creation of an *expendable member* of the family and (2) the *ascription* of *blame* to that member by other members and treatment of it as "fact" by the scapegoated member as well.

Through the degrading process of becoming the family scapegoat, this child was essentially redefined in ways that resulted in his bearing the burden of each member's fear of death and guilt about the father's illness. Part of their effective construction of him as a scapegoat depended upon the boy's increasing behavior problems. Bermann maintains that the boy's self was virtually "annihilated" by other family members, particularly the mother. The boy was raised as if he were a twin of his older brother, who typically outshined him in every way. By being faced with continual failure to measure up, the boy suffered uninterrupted humiliation. Consequently, his capacities were seriously undeveloped and undermined. Bermann proposes that the scapegoating of the one child became a palliative for the family's inability to deal openly and directly with their fear of death.

An underlying problem with Bermann's analysis is his tendency to look at the behavior of family members as if they were actually part of middle-class culture. Both parents had what are essentially working-class jobs and no education beyond high school. Perhaps in part because they were not bona fide members of the middle class, the fear of death played a more significant, though unacknowledged, role in the family. Because the family were members of the working class, giving vent to their fears might have been perceived as even more inappropriate than in the middle class, where greater latitude is given to verbal expression of this kind of feeling.

Nevertheless, Bermann dramatically shows how embracing typical American values based on individualism, privatism and, self-reliance leads to internal stresses within the family, despite the normal public image that family members portray to others. Bermann maintains that our social system and the values supporting it place such tremendous strains on the nuclear family that it cannot confront and manage an impending crisis of this magnitude. Thus casualties are created although the responsibility for them is laid squarely on the casualties themselves. (As Bermann points out, social values and mental illness converge in ways that insure that those who need help the most are the least likely to get it.) In this case, Bermann analyzes the boy's entire existence as a symbolic testimony to the other family members' fear of death. At that, their fear appears to have been intensified due to their unwillingness to deal with it directly. And as we shall see in the subsequent section, this stance tends to be defined as "denial."

The Social Construction of the Denial of Death

General reflections What is the denial of death? How is it known and to what extent can it be found to exist? To start with, we need to examine the kinds of contexts in which the term is used. First, denial of death is used to indicate *disbelief* in the possibility of death of self. Second, it is used to describe a *negation* of death as a part of human existence. Third, it is used to depict a *cultural stance* toward death. In all contexts, it is typically compared unfavorably with "acceptance of death," a term with equally elusive meanings.

With each usage, one needs to distinguish denial of death from deception, avoidance, and concealment. The term has in the past been used in general ways with different indicators. For example, avoidance of the topic of death may be taken by one investigator to indicate denial, but other investigators disagree. Then, too, when issues of deception of information or reality arise, one needs to ask in whose interests those deceptions serve. Similarly, if the fact of impending death is concealed, one needs to ask by whom, for what purpose, and whose attitudes are affected.

Probing questions are not always asked in actual situations. Rather, imputations of denial are readily given as "reasonable" accounts of behavior and as "logical" explanations of cultural traits. Consider now the kinds of cultural traits and individual behaviors that are commonly taken as evidence of "denial."

Dumont and Foss (1973) have attempted to construct a thorough inventory of the evidence in support of the denial or acceptance question regarding the American stance toward death. They cite violent death and its magical reversibility in children's stories and games as one indication of denial. Similarly, children's cartoons on Saturday morning TV programs are action-packed episodes during which the main characters are systematically obliterated only to magically reappear intact. Quite clearly, judging by the popularity of violence in the entertainment field, there is an audience for death. We could go further than this and claim that Americans are fascinated with death, or at least the image of it provided in the media. On an impersonal, uninvolved level, death has become normalized and even accepted by many persons.

Death language characterized by euphemisms that circle the touchy issue of death is often taken as evidence of denial. Other indications of denial might include seeking high-risk occupations, purchasing unsafe automobiles or consumer goods of questionable safety, driving carelessly, or tacitly accepting escalation of the nuclear arms race.

The treatment of death, dying, and bereavement by representatives of the funeral industry and medical practice is often defined in terms of denial. Because I deal with them in detail later, I only mention them at this point. But Dumont and Foss take special note of the ways the funeral industry and the floral industry have tried to curtail practices unfavorable to their vested interests. These researchers suggest that the mere existence of a custom does not necessarily imply general agreement with that custom. This issue arises in any circumstance where a group has been able to maintain power. Therefore, whether certain practices of the industries dealing with death, dying, and bereavement indicate a public demand for denial is equivocable.

But consider other issues. American attitudes toward the aging process and the aged are often believed to be part of a stance of denial. The logic goes: since our society is action- and youth-oriented, we do not like to have visible reminders of inaction and death. Blauner (1966) and Fulton (1967) emphasize the importance of age-segregated communities for reducing the impact of death on the wider society. Fulton explicitly sees such efforts as ultimately designed to avoid direct confrontation with death.

If the aged are segregated and ignored, then the dying are even greater outcasts. Further, Dumont and Foss (1973) emphasize the *relative infrequency* of deaths of intimates. The fact that death is typically an extraordinary event surely must contribute to the American view of death. If, for example, a middle-aged woman first experiences a death in her family when her father dies, she may not have thought much about her response to death. Under these conditions, the term "denial" may not fully describe the experience and affective response of the individual.

These reflections take into account general themes ordinarily believed to be significant in the debate on the denial or acceptance of death. Essentially, however, they are conjectures from different points of view. To understand these views, it is necessary to examine further the social experience and conceptions of human nature that give rise to them.

Illness and medical care   If experience with death is limited, then experience with serious illness is also likely to be limited. Some people have come to believe that science will conquer illness, the effects of aging, and even death itself (see Dumont and Foss 1973). Thus, any examination of the denial of death needs to take into account how illness is viewed and handled within the society since it is usually the direct precursor of death. Certain myths about health and disease have been fostered in Western society. A belief in natural death generally ignores the fact that death has a cause—ordinarily an illness. Perhaps because the chronically and terminally ill remained largely invisible in the past (or died considerably sooner), only recently have people begun to view death as following a long-term, downhill spiral. (Of course the recent increased availability of terminal role models to teach ways to handle dying may also have increased public awareness of dying [see L. Lofland 1977].)

The antecedents of denial may be found in the social structuring of illness. The obfuscation of the dying process has been at least partially fostered by the medical profession in its dual emphasis on *rapid intervention* and *acute illness*. By forcing the dilemmas raised by the experience of chronic illness into the model of acute care, medical practitioners have, however inadvertently, been guilty of mystifying the nature of death. With this comes the commonsense tendency to view disease as something that is ameliorated rather than as something that progressively develops over time. Hence, I am suggesting that the kind of response labeled denial is *socially constructed* and the supports for that construction are founded in medical care itself.

The patterned ways in which institutionalized medicine fosters a response of "denial" from the patient are examined in Chapter 5. I contend that such responses may be built into the interaction process long before the patient becomes terminally ill. Maintaining hope and optimism while withholding bad news are postures which do not apply to death alone. They are part of a more general response to illness. In my earlier research on chronic illness, I discovered that patients initially develop ideologies to account for and handle their illnesses (see Charmaz 1973, 1976). The dominant ideology emphasizes an initial optimistic response to illness characterized by conceptions of *recovery, individual responsibility,* and *achievement.*

When patients base their ideology on conceptions of acute illness, they believe that they must combat the disease and conquer it, not accept it. This belief tends to be encouraged by practitioners since it simultaneously leaves the patient responsible for the outcome and encourages hope despite the fact that not all diseases can be "conquered" or "overcome." Most importantly, an attitude is fostered by both practitioner and patient that comes very close to what is usually referred to as "denial."

An example of such a situation is revealed by a woman who is severely disabled with multiple sclerosis. False hopes of conquering her illness were encouraged. One of her first doctors, a devout Christian, professed to discuss her case with God in his prayers. Afterwards, he suggested to her that if her belief in God was strong enough, she would get well. The woman realized that he was making the inference that her recovery was ultimately her responsibility. Although she rejected his suggestion of how recovery might be possible, she embraced the notion of recovery. Having been informed that she would very gradually deteriorate and perhaps in twenty years or so require a wheelchair, she did not anticipate the rapid downhill course that she actually experienced. Adamant that she would not be "defeated" by this disease, she made valiant efforts to maintain a normal existence. Between her lack of anticipation of immediate disability and her belief that she should win out over her illness, she pushed herself to handle activities long after she had exhausted her physical capability of handling them. Hence, she got leg braces only after many falls and was prescribed a wheelchair only when she could no longer walk across the street. Not only was she losing mobility but also she was becoming blind and incontinent within three years of her initial diagnosis. Since she did not expect permanent problems that soon, she experienced repeated episodes of each sign of deterioration before she identified them as something genuinely alarming and not a transitory inconvenience.

In another case, the daughter of a woman who was dying of cancer stated that she thought the practitioners encouraged her mother to deny her illness and impending death. She described her mother's response to a biopsy in the following way:

> She'd just say, "I'm going in for surgery, uh, you know they are going to do a biopsy and that's it." She wouldn't discuss it even when we pressed

it with, "How do you feel about that?" and "What do they think is there?"
She'd say, "Well, I don't know" or "they don't know."

The daughter described the physicians as giving both her mother and the family "platitudes" as they were optimistic about the possibility of recovery up until the last six weeks of her mother's illness. As her mother's condition worsened, her daughter felt that she knew she was going to die but would not accept it. She remarked:

She just wouldn't accept it for herself. She said, "If I take the radiation
treatments and the chemotherapy and just wait, if I can hang on long
enough, maybe they'll find a cure." I think this came from the doctors, I
really do. They told her that "maybe they'll find a cure, Lida and in the
meantime, if you take the chemotherapy, perhaps things will be better
and it might work, we've known it to have a remission before and it might
work in your case."

If denial is fostered in illness and dying, what kind of response can be expected from patients? That answer is partially supplied by Kastenbaum and Aisenberg (1972) in their discussion of the "overcoming" response to death. Though this is not the only response to impending death, it is an important one to discuss in relationship to denial. There are significant parallels with my own findings of the optimistic ideology of the chronically ill. In this response, death is viewed as external to the person; it is something to be overcome. In order to overcome it, power must be exerted. Importantly, the person who wishes to overcome it has a need for independence and achievement. The inability to overcome death is viewed as a failure. And, as will be seen in the next chapter, the overcoming response of the patient is an exact *complement* to the conception held by many practitioners of death as an enemy. Kastenbaum and Aisenberg (1972) suggest that men are likely to espouse the overcoming response. And since male values have dominated the culture, it stands to reason that many women will also espouse it. For example, when a woman was told she had lung cancer, she responded that she was going to fight it and not "give in" to the disease process. Critical illness may seem to offer a chance for heroism, since it is assumed that only the heroic are sufficiently brave to fight it. When the patient's emphasis is on overcoming disease and death, then what is called "denial" is heightened. It is ironic that practitioners generally encourage the overcoming response as long as they retain a clinical interest in the patient. But when they decide that the patient will die, the same response is apt to be labelled denial. In short, both the form and content of interaction are logically connected with attitudes of "denial."

Becker's denial of death Both the ideas presented about social structural sources of denial in medical care and the next discussion of political implications stand in contrast to established views of the denial of death. In which ways are these established views conceptualized? Ernest Becker elucidates and extends these views in his much-acclaimed book, *The Denial of Death*. Because Becker synthesizes major perspectives that posit and explain the denial of death, his work merits special consideration.

His analysis begins with a discussion of the fear of death, because it is taken as the underlying determinant of the denial of death. For Becker, the fear of death is a *universal* phenomenon that makes intelligible human motivations that otherwise remain hidden. In addition, he seems to accept the assumption that the fear of death has a biological basis because he links it to self-preservation. Becker takes the following traditional psychoanalytic notions for granted: (1) human beings cannot face their deaths, (2) this fear of death and the inability to face it cause the individual to avoid it or attempt to overcome it by denying that it will occur, and (3) the fear of death itself becomes repressed.

For Becker, a full confrontation with death would cause someone to become psychotic. Consequently, he argues that the symbolic world constructed in human existence serves to deny the fact that death is ultimately our fate. Part of the symbolic construction in this ongoing denial of death is that of *human character*. Character is socially constructed for Becker and, most significantly, it is a "vital lie." By this Becker means that individuals avoid despair (and the truth of death) by building defenses that allow some sense of meaning and personal power. The gist of the matter is that Becker sees this construction as *necessary*. In actuality, however, he views the sense of meaning and personal power gained as falsifications. To Becker, the belief that we control our lives is false since we exist in a social system that supports us. He remarks that the paradox in needing the lie in order to live results in having a life we do not control.

One of Becker's main contributions is that he links denial of death to the quest for *heroism*. To begin his analysis of heroism, Becker assumes that narcissism, or self-absorption, is inherent in the human condition. This narcissism is twofold. On the one hand, it causes us to assume that everyone but us is expendable, which again leads to an inability to confront finitude. On the other hand, narcissism gives rise to a struggle for self-esteem manifested by the quest for heroism. While children may show their quest for self-esteem, heroism, or recognition by others openly, it becomes more disguised with adults. Becker states that, although the need for heroism is not easy to admit and remains unconscious, it is nevertheless acted upon. While some individuals may attempt to radically alter the boundaries of ordinary existence in their quest for heroism, Becker observes that others attempt the "safer" tactic of following the roles that society has laid out for them. Regardless of how one attempts to realize heroism, for Becker it is the central problem of human existence.

Becker explains fascination with someone who holds or symbolizes power as a type of *transference* in which magical powers are projected on the leader.

Thus, the individual both identifies with and is dependent upon that leader, who is then given a heroic parental role. In following this leader, the individual shares in magical transformation of the world, but in doing so gives up personal autonomy. In addition, unequal social relationships contribute to the lack of personal autonomy when loyalty and obedience are given to the leader.

Becker finds that the essence of transference is the *taming* of *terror* of one's *individuality* and of one's *death*. According to him, transference is a necessary means of infusing human life with value. Through "transference heroics," one takes on the immortal qualities of the other.

The crux of his argument is contained in his assertion that glorification of the hero becomes a way of denying one's creatureliness. Becker highlights his thesis when he says, "Sex is of the body and the body is of death" (p. 162). What he means by this is that sex reduces us to our creatureliness, represents a negation of distinctive personal traits and therefore holds a degree of terror. But, Becker argues, the human being cannot tolerate being a creature like any other; the human being must create meaning.

Becker contends that the crucial problem of the modern individual is the difficulty of creating meaning that is, heroism in everyday life. Thus he sees mental illness as the consequence of failed attempts to attain heroism. He argues that we cannot overcome our creature anxiety unless we are gods, so we seek the god in the other. And according to Becker we must overcome our creature anxiety since otherwise it brings us face-to-face with the intolerable—death.

Becker's analysis is given as an explanation of a *universal* characteristic of the human condition. No doubt what Becker presents is a cogent, provocative statement of the condition of many human beings in Western society. He speaks to the fragmented relationship people sometimes have with their bodies in Western societies since the creatureliness of the body may not only be denied but may also become separated from the "self." Although it was not his objective, Becker's portrayal might be seen as testimony to the amount of alienation experienced by human beings in industrialized societies. Individuals may be separated from their bodies and unaware of their repressed feelings, conflicts, and death-denying feelings. But these indications of alienation may stem from sources other than innate human proclivities. They may arise out of the fabric of societies in which they are observed. What Becker describes may then be a direct reflection of social-historical conditions that are concrete and specific, not diffuse and universal.

Becker's analysis of the denial of death and, correspondingly, the nature of human beings, ends by being profoundly pessimistic. In his intent to put forth an existentially informed psychoanalytic perspective, he concludes that it is essentially impossible to alter what he takes to be basic biological conditions. If Becker's argument is taken to its logical conclusion, then it would be unrealistic to attempt to change the denial of death, which many observers believe is the dominant stance toward death. Essentially, Becker separated the individual from the social structures in which that individual existed. In doing so, Becker took the traits that he posited in individuals to be fixed and stable. While his criticism of contemporary society is aimed at the lack of viable structures wherein heroism can be attained, he fails to realize that the quest for heroism itself is a reflection of a society based on individualism and competition. Similarly, he fails to acknowledge that the social structuring of death and dying has profound implications for our conceptions of it.

Political implications of the denial of death Though Becker's argument is compelling, my earlier discussion suggested an alternative explanation of the denial of death as social in origin. If so, it is conceivable that it has political implications.

Social conditions related to our stance toward death are given more significance by other writers. Strong arguments are made that Americans in particular avoid death, even when it intrudes upon their immediate worlds (see Blauner 1966; Fulton 1967; Kastenbaum and Aisenberg 1972; Kübler-Ross 1969; Sudnow 1967; and Weisman 1972). Dumont and Foss (1973) remark that the concentration of death among the elderly encourages the majority of Americans to view death as something that will occur in the distant future. If they are correct, the term "denial" may not fully describe the stance taken toward death. Death may seem irrelevent in the present but still be anticipated in the future.

Dumont and Foss (1973) conclude that it is untenable to assume that there is a single attitude toward death. Thus they argue that individuals in this society both accept and deny their deaths. Specifically, they propose that persons will accept their deaths on a rational, conscious level, but deny it on an emotional, unconscious level. This is possibly so, but here again it seems necessary to examine the type and quality of experience the person has had and is presently having. When death is certain and all openly acknowledge it, it would seem that emotional content might conceivably take a different form than when it is kept "uncertain" and hidden.

More important than the argument about whether death is accepted or denied is a clarification of what is meant and the context in which the terms are used. As existentialists aver, it is one thing to be able to talk about death openly in abstract, general terms and quite another to be able to confront one's death. Similarly, acceptance of one's death in the far distant future is of quite a different order than facing the possibility of it now. And the conditions under which one faces it appear to shape responses to it. For example, before becoming ill a man expressed a wish to live to be 100 years of age. But when tormented by excruciating pain in his terminal phase of illness, he said he was ready to die. In any case, whatever attitudes toward death are espoused, the researcher should examine those attitudes within the context of the experience that may have shaped them.

What are the implications of the denial of death? One overriding implication raised by existentional thought is that a denial of death serves to obfuscate crucial issues of human existence such as the quality of life. If individuals deny their deaths, they are apt to see themselves as immortal; by assuming they will die in the distant future, these individuals do not question their everyday lives. Toynbee clarifies this when he states, "Death is 'un-American'; for if the fact of death were once admitted to be a reality even in the United States, then it would also have to be admitted that the United States is not the earthly paradise that it is deemed to be (and this is one of the crucial articles of faith in 'the American way of life')" (1968, p. 131).

In a larger sense then, the denial of death may have political implications. Killilea takes this reasoning further. He argues that the denial of death "is positively required by the assumptions and incentives of our political ideology" (1977, p. 206). In explicating John Locke's political philosophy as the most significant for American institutions and public policies, Killilea contends that Locke's hidden assumptions about the human condition give rise to his acclamation of the unrelenting pursuit of private property and profit. Specifically, Killilea emphasizes Locke's assumption that the purpose of life is to exhibit greater competition, accumulation, and productivity than others.

Killilea proposes that acknowledgment of death leads to a sense of limits and both, in turn, lead to a new perspective on human existence with fundamentally different priorities than those that shaped the American consciousness. Rather than the Lockean pursuit of individual gain, Killilea proposes that the new perspective will result in the recognition by the individual of social responsibilities and mutual dependence.

Surely the potential exists for the development of a new perspective along the lines that Killilea suggests. But whether it will emerge is ultimately an empirical question. As long as those involved with the issues that death poses limit themselves to considering primarily the immediate thoughts and feelings of the individual, it is unlikely that a radical restructuring of individual and social priorities will occur. In that case, the concern with death and dying generally and denial of death specifically may instead remain a profitable enterprise.

SUMMARY AND IMPLICATIONS

What people think and feel about death is revealed in their everyday conceptions and concerns about it. Death conceptions include those categorized as an event or state, as well as those categorized in relation to hopes and purposes. Views of death as an event emphasize either the end of experience or the transition to another type of experience. Views of a particular state may be conceived of as the sequel to the event or as infinity. When conceived in relation to purposes, death is viewed in terms of what results from it such as loss, peace, or reunion. Purposes are also cast in personifications of death such as the gay deceiver, grim reaper, or today's personification, the enemy. Death is also conceived in relation to hopes; an example of this is the widely held idealized conception of a "natural" death.

When examining death conceptions in relation to age, we question whether they reflect developmental or social causes. Although many studies of children's conceptions of death conclude that they are related to mental development, recent studies of terminally ill children challenge this position. Researchers have discovered that these children correctly recognize and interpret signs given by others to indicate their impending deaths. They argue that children's views of death reflect the information available to them and the situation in which it is acquired. Because children are remarkably aware of and responsive to the feelings of adults, studies of children's views of death may reflect the thoughts and feelings of adults with whom they are associated.

The other extensively researched group, the aged, seem to be relatively accepting of death. They often hold death conceptions that assume death is within them, a familiar presence rather than something external to struggle against. Thus the aged appear to exhibit less fear about death than others, although they fear losing control and burdening others while dying.

Meanings attributed to death are revealed through the language used to depict death and describe death-related events. While conventional death language neutralizes death or hides it in euphemisms, the new death talk is aimed toward directly and emotionally confronting it. Meanings of death are also imparted through gesture. In that sense, a symbolic death results when valued aspects of self are invalidated or negated in interaction. Symbolic life and death are contingent upon personal acceptance. Lack of acceptance subsequently leads to the extinguishing of one's symbolic world. Sometimes, as with the aged, a symbolic death is the precursor to actual death, when, for instance, the loss of the aged person's symbolic world results in a literal invitation to die.

Meanings of death often are believed to be predicated on the dual concerns of fear and denial of death. Fear of death may include fear of loss of experience, self, or one's body. In addition, it is possible to fear one aspect of dying, such as what comes after death or ceasing to be, without fearing all. Consistent with the psychoanalytic tradition, many individuals believe that fear of death is repressed and subsequently denied. Denial of death is believed to be both an individual adaptation to one's mortality and a cultural response to the issue of death. Although the issue of denial is repeatedly raised when someone is dying, what is typically forgotten is that the social-structural supports of the patient's response of "denial" are founded in medical care. Further, a social structure based upon individualism and competition may in general foster in its members a heightened fear of death and subsequent avoidance of it.

What are the implications of the issues and concerns outlined above?

Death conceptions and concerns clearly influence their possessors. What is not clear is how researchers arrive at their analyses of them. Although such topics as the fear and denial of death have spurred considerable research, much of it has been conducted through survey research. By the nature of survey research, the questions posed to the subjects are preconceived. As with any other type of research questioning, the answers received are, in part, shaped by the questions asked. Frequently, the more "rigorous" the survey, the more the answers are forced into preconceived categories. And, I maintain the more the answers are forced, the less they reflect the experiences, thoughts, and feelings of the subjects.

On the other hand, when researchers attempt to *situate* their observations in the lives of their subjects, different types of interpretations are made. In order to so situate research observations, it is necessary to gather firsthand data about the lives of the subjects as they construct their everyday worlds. The concepts and concerns they hold about death are more apt to be made visible through their actions rather than through responses elicited from them by the researcher. What individuals check on a questionnaire or explain to an interviewer does not represent all they think and feel. Consequently, the closer the researcher comes to the world of the subject, particularly when events in that subject's world pertain to death, the more complete the image the researcher will obtain of the subject's concept of death.

However, individuals' concepts and concerns with death may be expected to change as their experiences change. Moreover, the concepts of death held by a group may be expected to change as their social-historical experience changes.

In this chapter, the discussion of death conceptions and concerns focused on everyday life. But their significance goes beyond everyday meanings and actions. Practitioners, too, develop death conceptions and concerns. Typically, evidence of their conceptions may be discovered in their practices. In the next chapter, I turn to an analysis of a medical conception of death widely believed to be the dominant one and the ethical issues related to it.

REFERENCES

Ammon, Günter (1975). Death and identity. *The Human Context* 7:94-102.

Anthony, Sylvia (1971). *The Discovery of Death in Childhood and After.* New York: Basic Books. (First published in 1940.)

Aries, Philippe (1974). *Western Attitudes toward Death.* Baltimore: Johns Hopkins University Press.

Bart, Pauline (1971). Depression in middle-aged women. In Vivian Gornick and Barbara K. Morgan (eds.), *Women in Sexist Society: Studies in Power and Powerlessness.* New York: Basic Books.

Becker, Ernest (1973). *The Denial of Death.* New York: Free Press.

Bermann, Eric (1973). *Scapegoat, The Impact of Death Fear on an American Family.* Ann Arbor: University of Michigan Press.

Blauner, Robert (1966). Death and social structure. *Psychiatry* 29:378-94.

Bluebond-Langer, Myra (1977). Meanings of death to children. In Herman Feifel (ed.). *New Meanings of Death.* New York: McGraw-Hill.

Brent, Sandor B. (1978). Puns, metaphors and misunderstandings in a two-year-old's conception of death. *Omega* 8:285-95.

Britain is shaken by the TV film of woman urging suicide on her mother. *New York Times*, August 27, 1977.

Calkins, Kathy (1972). Shouldering a burden. *Omega* 3:23-36.

Charmaz, Kathy Calkins (1973). Time and identity: the shaping of selves of the chronically ill. Ph.D. dissertation, University of California, San Francisco.

_____ (1976). Ideologies and the politics of constructing identity. Paper presented at the meetings of the Society for the Study of Social Problems, New York.

Choron, Jacques (1964). *Modern Man and Mortality*. New York: Macmillan.

Douglass, William (1969). *Death in Murélaga*. Seattle: University of Washington Press.

Dumont, Richard G., and Dennis C. Foss (1973). *The American View of Death: Acceptance or Denial?* Cambridge, Mass.: Schenkman.

Feifel, Herman, and Alan Branscomb (1973). Who's afraid of death? *Journal of Abnormal Psychology* 81:282-88.

Fulton, Robert (1967). The denying of death. In Earl A. Grollman (ed.), *Explaining Death to Children*. Boston: Beacon Press.

Furman, Erna (1974). *A Child's Parent Dies*. New Haven, Conn.: Yale University Press.

Gordon, David C. (1970). *Overcoming the Fear of Death*. New York: Macmillan.

Hochschild, Arlie Russell (1973). *The Unexpected Community*. Englewood Cliffs, N.J.: Prentice-Hall.

Illich, Ivan (1974). The political uses of natural death. In Peter Steinfels and Robert M. Veatch (eds.), *Death Inside Out*. New York: Harper and Row.

Jaffe, Lois, and Arthur Jaffe (1977). Terminal candor and the coda syndrome: a tandem view of fatal illness. In Herman Feifel (ed.), *New Meanings of Death*. New York: McGraw-Hill.

Jaques, Elliott (1969). Death and the mid-life crisis. In Hendrik M. Ruitenbeek (ed.), *Death: Interpretations*. New York: Dell.

Jeffers, Frances C., and Adriaan Verwoerdt (1977). How the old face death. In Ewald W. Busse and Eric Pfeiffer (eds.), *Behavior and Adaptation in Late Life*. Boston: Little, Brown.

Jourard, Sidney M. (1971). The invitation to die. Chapter 11 of *The Transparent Self*. New York: D. Van Nostrand.

Kalish, Richard A. (1976). Death and dying in a social context. In Robert Binstock and Ethel Shanas (eds.), *Handbook of Aging and the Social Sciences*. New York: D. Van Nostrand.

_____, and David K. Reynolds (1976). *Death and Ethnicity*. Los Angeles: University of Southern California Press.

Kastenbaum, Robert (1959). Time and death in adolescence. In Herman Feifel (ed.), *The Meaning of Death*. New York: McGraw-Hill.

_____ (1977). *Death, Society, and Human Experience*. St. Louis: C. V. Mosby.

_____, and Ruth Aisenberg (1972). *The Psychology of Death*. New York: Springer.

Kavanaugh, Robert E. (1972). *Facing Death*. Baltimore: Penguin Books.

Killilea, Alfred G. (1977). Some political origins of the denial of death. *Omega* 8:205-14.

Koestenbaum, Peter (1971). The vitality of death. In Frances G. Scott and Ruth M. Brewer (eds.), *Confrontations of Death*. Corvallis, Oreg.: Continuing Education Publications.

Kozel, Jonathan (1970). *Death at an Early Age*. New York: Bantam Books.

Kraai, Marian C. (1975). Children and death, developmental process. Unpublished paper, University of Nebraska, Lincoln.

Kübler-Ross, Elisabeth (1969). *On Death and Dying*. New York: Macmillan.

Lester, David (1967). Experimental and correlational studies of the fear of death. *Psychological Bulletin* 67:27-36.

Lofland, Lyn H. (1977). The face of death and the craft of dying: individual and collective constructions. Unpublished manuscript, University of California, Davis.

_____ (1978). The happy death movement: reform goals and ideological elements. Paper presented at the annual meetings of the Pacific Sociological Association, Spokane, Washington.

Marshall, Victor (1975). Awareness of finitude. *Omega* 6:113-29.

Menig-Peterson, Carol, and Allysa McCabe (1978). Children talk about death. *Omega* 8:305-318.

Nagy, Maria H. (1959). The child's view of death. In Herman Feifel (ed.), *The Meaning of Death*. New York: McGraw-Hill.

Roberts, Cecilia M. (1977). *Doctor and Patient in the Teaching Hospital*, Lexington, Mass.: D.C. Heath, Lexington Books.

Rochlin, Gregory (1967). How young children view death and themselves. In Earl A. Grollman (ed.), *Explaining Death to Children*. Boston: Beacon Press.

Rzhevsky, Leonid (1976). Attitudes toward death. *Survey* 22:38-56.

Slater, Philip (1974). *Earthwalk*. Garden City, N.Y.: Doubleday.

Slote, Michael A. (1975). Existentialism and the fear of dying. *American Philosophical Quarterly* 12:17-28.

Sudnow, David (1967). *Passing On*. Englewood Cliffs, N.J.: Prentice-Hall.

Swenson, Wendell M. (1975). Attitudes toward death among the aged. In Robert Fulton (ed.), *Death and Identity*. Philadelphia: Charles Press.

Templar, Donald Irvin (1972). Death anxiety in religiously very involved persons. *Psychological Report* 31:261-62.

Toynbee, Arnold (1968). Changing attitudes toward death in the modern western world. In Arnold Toynbee, A. Keith Man, Ninian Smart, John Hinton, Simon Yudkin, Eric Rhode, Rosalind Heywood, and H. H. Price, *Man's Concern with Death*. New York: McGraw-Hill.

Waechter, Eugenia H. (1971). Children's awareness of fatal illness. *American Journal of Nursing* 71:1168-72.

Wahl, Charles W. (1959). The fear of death. In Herman Feifel (ed.), *The Meaning of Death*. New York: McGraw-Hill.

Walton, Douglas (1976). On the rationality of fear of death. *Omega* 7:1-9.

Weisman, Avery D. (1972). *On Dying and Denying*. New York: Behavioral Publications.

_____ (1978). Misgivings and misconceptions in the psychiatric care of terminal patients. In Charles A. Garfield (ed.), *Psychosocial Care of the Dying Patient*. New York: McGraw-Hill.

CHAPTER FOUR

ETHICAL ISSUES AND EUTHANASIA

Technological progress in medicine has brought about new ethical dilemmas for practitioners, patients, and relatives. Although the dilemmas are many and complex, two types illustrate the kind of ethical issues that arise today. First, some patients are without brain function; their bodies are maintained by technological devices. Second, other patients are waiting for organ transplants; the success of their transplant is greater if the donated organ is taken from a body with a functioning heart and respiratory system. Clearly these dilemmas show the importance of the kinds of decisions that are made.

Consider the following dilemma: A young man is brought into the emergency room with massive injuries sustained in an automobile accident. After hours of surgery using the best technical skill available and repeated tests, he lies unconscious with little indication of brain function although he still has a heartbeat. What course of action should practitioners take? Should he be maintained through artificial means? Or is he already "dead"? The Karen Ann Quinlan case publicized the problematic features of taking action in these types of circumstances and brought a number of ethical issues inherent in dying today into sharp focus (see, for examples, Berger and Berger 1975; Kastenbaum 1977).

In this chapter, I will illuminate these issues. First, I will analyze the relationship between the medical conception of death and the ethical issues involved in using highly technologized forms of treatment on the dying. Second, I will discuss the controversy of euthanasia. And third, I will examine the movement to legalize the rights of the dying patient.

TECHNOLOGICAL DYING

As the previous example indicates, dying sometimes takes on dramatic new dimensions in our time. The character of technological dying is, I think, related to a conception of death widely believed to be held by medical practitioners. The extent to which this conception was held in the past or is held today remains an empirical question. Although it probably was more generally held among practitioners in the past, an important point is that it is *believed* to be their dominant conception of death today. In addition, it is believed to be a taken-for-granted conception. If so, then the dilemmas and ethical issues stemming from it have developed inadvertently, by default for the most part, rather than by explicit or strategic intent. But to the extent that taken-for-granted assumptions and everyday practices are called into question, they may be reassessed and perhaps changed. I now turn, with that intent in mind, to the medical concept of death and its implications.

The Medical Conception of Death

Over the past few decades members of the medical profession have been thought to hold a particular conception of death. That conception begins with an image of death as the *enemy* to be met, struggled with, and overcome. If death is the enemy, it logically follows that all means at one's disposal should be employed to overcome it.

A conception of death as the enemy is perhaps the logical conclusion of what Friedson (1970) calls "the clinical mentality" of practitioners. The clinical mentality is characterized by active intervention, pragmatic solutions, and clear-cut judgments based on clinical experience. The practitioner seeks to act aggressively and definitively against the possibility of death. Quite conceivably, "winning" against death when the odds are slim serves to reaffirm a conception of death as the enemy.

Is death an enemy feared by practitioners? Feifel *et al.* (1967) suggest that physicians possess a heightened fear of death when compared with groups of healthy and ill lay persons. Kasper's psychoanalytic study (1959) lends tentative support to this finding, and Schulz (1978) reports that his initial investigations on the topic corroborate the earlier research.

Whatever underlying attitudes and feelings give rise to the physician's conception of death as the enemy, clearly, since death is not always overcome, it may indeed "win out." What happens then to the physician's conception of death? I suggest that it shifts to one of *failure*. At this point, death may symbolize to the physician the failure of the current status of medical *knowledge*. But the conception of failure is likely, moreover, to have a more personal tone. First, death may be seen as the patient's failure to struggle hard enough. Second, the physician may sense his or her failure to motivate the patient to fight death effectively. Third, and perhaps most importantly, death may be seen as a failure of the physician's skill and judgment.

Attempting to keep the patient alive then becomes the physician's personal responsibility and moral battle. Abdication of that responsibility to struggle to maintain life is linked to failure. In the Rabins's reflections on the socialization of the physician (1970), they contend that medical students are subtly imbued with a view of death as failure.

The failure of *self* leads to the next shift in the medical conception of death. Death becomes *forbidden*. Aries (1974) sees forbidden death as the logical conclusion of American medical and social practices. In this sense, death becomes something inadmissable. Evidence of it must be negated or at least concealed. And, of course, concrete indications of Aries's argument are visible in everyday medical practices. Often, once patients fail to improve or fail to be interesting terminal cases (thus becoming plain, routine deaths), the physician fails to care for them. Consequently, if accurate, the three-phased medical conception of death fundamentally *shapes* and *reaffirms* everyday practices in the care of the dying. Quite possibly the concept had widespread validity in the past, particularly among medical researchers and powerful leaders, and emerged in a historical context favorable to its development. Some indication of this is given by Berlant (1978), who argues that the conservative code of medical ethics adopted in 1876 assumed paternalism, fostered exploitation of the dying for learning, and legitimized a lack of accountability. It stands to reason that this concept developed hand-in-hand with beliefs in medicine as a technical science. Likely, this conception gave license for other vested interests in terminal care to flourish. The extent to which the medical conception of death is currently supported is not as important for the present analysis as the institutionalized practices it has fostered and maintained, such as technological dying. More importantly, these views and practices led to a stance in which physicians often failed to take into account the ethical implications of their actions.

Ethical Implications of the Medical Conception of Death

Conceptions of death are closely related to views concerning what constitutes an "appropriate" or proper dying. Such views are, of course, steeped in assumptions based on value positions whether or not they are stated or recognized. Rather, current views of dying tend to be accepted at face value. When a particular view of dying has currency, it may be taken as objective or true without recognizing its underlying value premises. Over time, the underlying values are forgotten and the moral issues posed by the human experience of dying become obscured. It is likely that, in this way, a view of dying that held *prolonging life* as the "proper" way to handle it developed. This view has only recently been called into question.

With the advent of great technical advances in medicine, a belief system has emerged that defines problems, of which dying is an important one, in relationship to *technical solutions*. Basically, they are seen as providing the answers to human dilemmas faced by practitioners.

Current institutionalized views of dying developed in the technological context. *Scientism*, the worship of science in general and technology in particular, has fundamentally shaped the mentalities of practitioners, and often, I might add, those of patients. Hence, both practitioner and patient may place their faith in technical procedures as a way of preserving life. This faith may be extended to practices that result in prolonging the dying process. Built into this mentality is the belief that, through technological progress, the problems of today will be conquered tomorrow. Taken to its logical extension, then, this mentality may lead to attempts to prevent death at all costs.

The upshot of scientism in medicine is that dying has been taken out of the *moral order* and placed in the *technological order* (Cassell 1974). That is, it has been moved from the realm of values, dominated by concepts of right and wrong, to the realm of usefulness, effectiveness, and expediency. It is this shift to which advocates of "death with dignity" object. Yet it should be noted that the assumptions of the technological order, however unexamined, have become what is "right" for some.

But to return to the argument, the human experience of dying becomes subsumed by the technological order in which it occurs. What once might have been defined as a moral question becomes a technological problem. To illustrate, consider the question of whether the patient should die in a familiar setting with intimates. When participants believe that patients have the right to have all the technological assistance that can be brought to bear on their cases and that the physician has the responsibility and obligation to order it, the question becomes irrelevant.

Although in recent years court decisions have not been consistent, rulings have supported the use of maximum technological intervention. For example, recently the young parents of a small boy with leukemia wished to refuse technological intervention and massive chemotherapy. Instead, they wanted to treat him at home with natural foods and affection. The judge not only ruled against them but also threatened to place the child under foster care if the parents did not comply with the treatment regimen set forth by physicians. This decision was made despite the uncertainty of survival or prolongation of the boy's life through technological intervention ("Leukemia Dispute—Parents Lose Case" 1978).

Death occurs when technology *fails*—it almost occurs by default. Underlying the transfer of death to the technological order is the unstated and unacknowledged assumption that moral matters can be made technical. By treating moral issues *as if* they were technical, a reality is constructed that minimizes the importance of moral judgments and questions in a given situation.

Formalized, technical care in a bureaucratic organization is a consequence of a shift in the setting in which dying occurs. In earlier times, care was given at home, where the patient died in familiar surroundings. Quite conceivably, the dying may then have had both more control of their situations and more social support than is ordinarily the case now. The formalized setting in which people now die tends to limit the control that the patient might have and to minimize social support from intimates and staff. Joseph Fletcher (1977) succinctly states the differences between past and present modes of handling death:

> *Novels in the classic tradition have drawn a picture of the deathbed scene where the elderly "pass on," surrounded by their families and friends, making their farewell speeches and meeting death instead of being overtaken or snatched by it. This model of death has become almost archaic. Nowadays, most of the time, death comes to people (even the young and middle-aged) in a sedated and comatose state; betubed nasally, abdominally, and intraveneously; and far more like manipulated objects than like moral subjects. A whole fascinating array of devices—surgical, pharmacological, and mechanical—is brought into play to stave death off clinically and biologically. Yet ironically, by their dehumanizing effects these things actually hasten personal death, i.e. loss of self-possession and conscious integrity. They raise in a new form the whole question of "life" itself, of how we are to understand it and whether the mere minimum presence of vital functions is what we mean by it (pp. 354-55).*

As Fletcher suggests, a whole gamut of new issues is raised as dying becomes situated in the modern hospital.

Hospitals are formalized settings organized to provide specialized, technical services otherwise difficult to obtain. Since the hospital is a formal organization, rules are developed concerning the actual services rendered and the nature of interaction. Assumptions that place high priority on technical considerations are written into the rules. Similarly, the nature of interaction is subjected to rules that emphasize the formal aspects of the relationship between practitioner and patient.

Consequently, technical procedures and styles of interaction are not separate entities; they are melded together in ways that are mutually validating and perpetuating. An impersonal attitude toward the patient symbolically affirms the practitioner's greater interest in the technical aspects of the patient's case. Similarly, both interest and attitude constitute an "objective" stance toward the patient. This stance is exemplified by some physicians in teaching hospitals. Roberts (1977) maintains that in the teaching hospital patients are hardly perceived as persons at all, although they are well known as *cases*. To illustrate, she argues that the patients' only personal attributes are age, sex, obesity, and intelligence level (usually judged to be low, a label more readily given to women than men). Further, she notes, as does Millman (1977), that once a patient's vague symptoms are diagnosed as psychological, they are dismissed. The impersonal, objective attitude legitimizes dismissing psychological symptoms in favor of focusing on what are defined as the real medical problems of the patient. That this technical stance, although intended to be objective, sometimes has lethal consequences cannot be denied. A young man whose case Millman discusses was mistakenly diagnosed. After being dismissed by the doctors as an unlikable crock, they assumed some of his complaints were psychogenic in origin. Even though there were several prominent clues to real and serious distress beyond their initial diagnosis, they did not pursue further tests or exploratory surgery until the patient was almost dead from widespread cancer.

This type of stance does limit the physician's involvement with the patient in ways that support organizational objectives of efficiency. This is, of course, one of the consequences of the change in the character of care as formal organizations take over care of the dying. Further, as a parenthetical note, one might observe that the impersonal stance serves to distance death from the professional.

As a result of these changes in the organization of care, with their accompanying changes in attitudes, dying is placed squarely in the realm of technological decisions. Ethical issues become obscured as decisions are made on the basis of interest in technical procedures. The matter of interest is significant since physicians may evince an interest in a particular procedure and subsequently perform it on the patient without seriously deliberating the implications of the procedure for the patient's life. For example, a somewhat risky procedure, ostensibly designed to be "life extending," is performed on an aged, chronically ill man, who had been self-sufficient prior to his surgery. But the procedure takes such a toll on him that he becomes wholly debilitated, dependent, and despondent and dies soon after. Because the risks involved were never explained to him, he did not anticipate the possible consequences of the procedure. Despite this, the resident's interest in practicing the technique was served.

The physician's interest as it is reflected in institutionalized practices affects the patient as well. Clearly, institutional practices in medical education facilitate the establishment of priorities based on technological interest at the potential expense of the patient. It is tacitly understood that the poor offer their bodies as "clinical material" for educational use in exchange for treatment. The espoused, and usually realized educational objectives, emphasize mastering the full gamut of technological innovations. These patients' bodies become a field to be invaded by an onslaught of up-to-date technical armamentarium. When technical priorities are laid most bare, stark clinical situations exist such as one in which a patient is kept alive until the end of the semester in order to allow medical students to become adept at using the machines that keep the patient alive (Glaser and Strauss 1965). Or the critically ill man who is being seen by virtue of a grant to study his rare disease may discover that practitioners have little interest in examining his other developing symptoms when they are evaluated as unrelated to his "interesting" condition. Even the willingness to tinker with technology and the patient's organ system may then be circumscribed by the physician's interest.

Dilemmas between the physician's interest and the consequences for the patient are not always softened by the physician's exposure to medical ethics. Lally (1978) reports, for example, that physician investigators who are socialized to be compassionate and ethical exist in a setting where the valued results are research publications. Paradoxically, giving the kind of detailed information to the patient necessitated by an ethical stance leads to much less willingness on the part of the patient to participate in research. When physician investigators establish research as the first priority, they are likely to resort to "salesmanship" techniques to ensure the "proper" participation (Lally 1978). Not surprisingly, Lally's physician respondents reported that "ethical concern for research subjects" was their lowest priority. Quite clearly, these priorities pave the way for development of a highly limited type of interaction between physician and patient.

A closer look at the operative social mechanisms needs to be taken. Specifically, what kind of interaction process leads to death being subsumed under technology? As implied above, the *social relationship* created between practitioner and patient reflects the technical, formalized settings in which dying frequently occurs. The character of that relationship is of course partially dependent upon the objectives of the hospital milieu. Roberts (1977) observes, for example, that the teaching hospital she studied is characterized by *"structured transiency,"* actually of both physicians and patients. That transiency contributes to the physicians' lack of awareness of their patients as *persons* and heightens their efforts to be highly knowledgeable about them as cases. While this difference by no means implies that patients are necessarily treated unkindly, it does indicate, as Roberts discovered, that problems emerge when the participants' contrasting world views and definitions of priorities come into conflict (see Chapter 5).

When decisions are made within a highly complex institution such as a university hospital, the formal aspects of the case tend to be highlighted. Patients are identified and known primarily by their diseases. Decisions are made regarding the way the disease may be handled by the current state of technology. When patient and practitioner are known to each other only through fleeting, fragmented encounters, the practitioner is unlikely to know the patient's real concerns and choices. From the practitioner's perspective, it may not seem necessary to know those concerns and choices since the handling of the case is contingent upon external factors founded in technical skills.

It stands to reason that the more the institutional milieu is characterized by structured transiency, the more practitioners will define their social relationships with patients in technical terms. Such definitions typically assume that the physician's responsibilities justify dominance in the relationship. Most importantly, an objectified, routinized, and formal practitioner-patient relationship serves to validate a conception of death that tends to reduce it to the level of mechanistic, technical considerations.

Values that support technologizing death include beliefs in the *sanctity* of *life, expertise* as the basis of decision making, and the locus of *responsibility* in the physician. Beliefs in the sanctity of life set the stage for using technical procedures to prolong life and, moreover, to prolong the dying process. Crane (1975b) points out that physicians uphold the belief in the sanctity of life, but arguments develop among them about when "life" ends. Essentially, these arguments question the *definition* of life. One group of protagonists defines life in *social* terms, the other in *physiological* terms, but both agree on the sanctity of life. This belief has been used as a powerful justification for maintaining life-support systems on terminal patients. When arguments for the sanctity of life are invoked in defense of maintaining the dying process through technical procedures, the practitioner may ask, "Who am I to take away whatever life this patient now has?"

Despite the immediate dilemma that such questions pose, in a larger sense they may provide rationales for abdicating moral responsibility. A paradox develops: as physicians take responsibility for the patient and technical procedures, they may abdicate responsibility for consulting with the patient and intimates and following their wishes. Again, moral decisions have been transformed into technical issues. Similarly, the availability of equipment and resources seriously affects how decisions are made, yet the underlying moral character of those decisions may remain unacknowledged. In a local hospital emergency room, for example, a nurse expressed her resentment over an unacknowledged moral issue. With the addition of trained paramedics giving emergency cardiopulmonary resuscitation, she claimed that an unprecedented number of patients who suffered brain death were "revived." Thus, they were subjected to what often became a lengthy "dying." Also, their families suffered from the emotional and financial strain of their situations.

Correspondingly, a related issue arises when doctor and patient have different conceptions of the proper use of technical equipment. If, for example, a hospital has an extensive cardiac care unit with the latest cardiac monitoring systems, the chances are that some heart patients will be sent there by their physicians, even if they have expressed wishes not to have that kind of care. These patients' wishes might be buttressed by the fact that there are no firm indications that this highly technical care increases the length and quality of life. However, physicians who take it as their responsibility to provide the maximum medical intervention may choose to disregard those wishes.

Lest the impression be given that the power taken by the physician is entirely a one-sided affair, the responses of patients and families need to be outlined in greater detail. First, patients and intimates typically wish to believe in their physician's judgment, especially in times of crisis. Second, for some, the physician may symbolize the kind of external authority they have always followed. Third, other patients and intimates may possess a greater belief in scientism and technological solutions than their attending physicians!

In any event, many individuals are enamored with medical scientism. Public awareness of the success of some procedures often leads to a more ready acceptance of others. But when enamored with medical scientism, many will seek the most technically precise and advanced forms of treatment—even if this treatment is known to be of questionable value for the specific case. When this position is taken to its logical extension, families may opt for prolonging an agonizing dying process instead of removing the hardware that keeps the patient (barely) alive. Ironically, at this point, the practitioner may suggest removing the equipment but the family may refuse.

A parallel theme is reported by Dorothy Paulay (1977), a social worker who was called to the hospital after her husband's car accident. Because of the extent of his injuries, the emergency care physician told her he was terminal. She was advised not to see him in his current swollen, injured, comatose state. Even though the doctors told her it was hopeless, she and her son were determined that he would survive and recover. Much later she reinterpreted her stance then as denial, but at that point, she wanted everything done to sustain him, despite the prognosis of his physicians.

Why does the use of technological support strike such a responsive chord in some individuals? The standard answer is that they deny death or refuse to face it. But one might also consider the extent of socialization in scientistic values, as well as the high value placed upon prolonging "life." Still, if impending death is not dealt with openly by all, whatever ambiguities or dilemmas exist in the situation are apt to become resolved in favor of prolongation of the dying process.

In subtle ways, general cultural assumptions, as well as those specifically about death, enter into the kinds of decisions made. Conceptions of death held by individual participants have been observed to play an important role in making moral decisions that shape the dying process. Those conceptions rooted in fear of death, for example, may lead to practices in which personal responsibility is minimized and technical intervention is maximized. In an event, implicit in any conception of death is a set of practices that logically emerge from it. For that reason, it is especially necessary to address the implications of practitioners' conceptions of death since they ordinarily have the power to realize their conceptions in everyday actions.

Determining Death

The creation of a sophisticated, life-sustaining (otherwise known as death-prolonging) technology calls into question previous criteria for determining death. Earlier determinations of death made on the basis of cessation of respiration and heartbeat were clear-cut indicators of death. They ordinarily still are; however, in a small but significant number of cases, these criteria are insufficient (see Institute of Society, Ethics and the Life Sciences 1977).

Because comatose patients can be maintained artificially, what constitutes death and when it occurs are now problematic issues. Conversely, when reflecting upon what constitutes life, Devins and Diamond (1977) raise the question: Can vital functions necessary for life be taken as a determination of what is *sufficient* for life?

According to Devins and Diamond, the transplant issue has provided the major impetus to form a new determination of death. About 60 percent of the kidneys for transplants are "donated" by cadavers. Prior to this type of organ transplant, the time of death was not as significant because tissues were usable for a longer time after death. The advent of kidney transplants brought the dilemma of the determination of death into sharp focus. For the transplant to be successful, Devins and Diamond specify that kidneys must be removed while still functioning, and frequently this is done *before* the donor's heart and respiration functions have ceased. These new problems in determining death raise not only the spectre of malpractice but also profound moral and ethical dilemmas.

Though what it is to die has not been agreed upon, it is generally agreed that older determinations no longer suffice. As heartbeat and respiration are no longer definitive, physicians and ethicists alike look to other organs, particularly the brain, as the locus of death. Yet terms such as heart death or brain death do not accurately portray the intent to define the *person* rather than a bodily function as dead (see Veatch 1976).

As suggested by Crane's comments (1975b), determinations of death increasingly take into account the extent to which the patient retains *human* characteristics, such as the ability to comprehend. When human characteristics form the criteria for life and their absence the criteria for death, a different set of concerns develops than when the basic differentiation between life and death is the biological functioning of the organism. If human characteristics are taken into account, a much higher level of functioning is assumed. In contrast, the organism may be maintained in a vegetative state (see Institute of Society, Ethics and the Life Sciences, 1977, for a more extensive discussion). For example, in one county hospital where I conducted research, a ward was organized to treat comatose patients who had been in that condition for years, some for over a decade. At any rate, the crux of the issue of determining death is stated by Veatch (1976). From his observations, what constitutes a determination of death according to one physician's practical policies does not necessarily constitute it for another.

Obviously, a set of readily testable criteria for determining death is needed. Those criteria would have to be sufficiently complex to account for what are not commonly taken to be key dimensions of death. Hopefully, such criteria would not only provide physicians with definitive guidelines but would also make for greater congruence between medical and legal definitions of death. Devins and Diamond (1977) assert that cases can now be clinically

evaluated to ascertain that the patient will never again possess human characteristics due to the type and extent of brain death.

Such criteria would help clarify directions to take in everyday practices.
Significantly, the point when a person's organs may be legitimately removed
for transplants would be clarified. In one case a few years ago, the family of
the deceased transplant "donor" sued the surgeons who removed the organs
since they employed a different and earlier determination of death than had
the family and their physicians. In this situation, it is correctly proposed that
the potential transplant donor not be pronounced dead by the same surgeon
who needs the organs since there may be a conflict of interest (see Devins and
Diamond 1977; Veatch 1976)!

Another area that might be clarified by more complex criteria for determining death encompasses those comatose cases in which the patient demonstrates minimal brain activity. Although the medical status of these patients is
not explicated, Kastenbaum (1977) reports two instances when physicians
wished to abandon the use of machines, but the families refused and the
patients markedly improved. Such occurrences, though rare, demonstrate the
difficulty in making decisions regarding the moment of death. Besides, these
cases come to symbolize hope for others whose comatose relatives do not
respond, even when they have dissimilar medical conditions. Few individuals
wish to die "prematurely," or want to submit a relative to a premature demise.
(This discussion raises, of course, issues similar to the medieval concern about
being buried alive.)

More common, however, are the situations in which comatose patients
are supported for months through technical intervention. Usually, no earlier
written directives signed by the patient are available. The situation is, as
noted, further complicated when the patient still possesses minimal brain
function. Such situations obviously cause great anguish for families and,
sometimes, practitioners. But what it could "mean" to the patient remains
another issue. Advocates of death with dignity say that it is this type of situation that robs patients of their dignity. But if the patient no longer possesses
human characteristics, then dignity would seem to be a misplaced issue. As
Kastenbaum (1977) points out, the issue of death with dignity in these cases
may lie more squarely with the real distress the family experiences. He
suggests that the pressure to remove life-sustaining devices may be derived
from this distress and the family's subsequent need for action. And that raises
the question: In whose interests is the patient sustained in a state between
living and dying? Whose interests should be taken into account? In short, the
issue of the determination of death raises crucial issues for everyday practices.

THE CONTROVERSY OF EUTHANASIA

The ethical dilemmas inherent in determining death lead to some of the questions raised by the controversial issue of euthanasia. To the extent that dif-

ferent criteria are employed to determine death, one person's determination of death may constitute another's definition of an act of euthanasia. Such discrepancies also raise the issue of the "right to die." I will explore these and related issues in the following discussion.

First, a bit of clarification needs to be made. Though the term euthanasia means "the good death," its original meaning has become both expanded and obscured. It has also come to mean assisting the dying in hastening their deaths. Further, it has come to mean actively killing the patient. As Veatch (1976) remarks, the contradictory nature of the various meanings given to the term warrants elimination of its use. However, since the term commands a vast literature as well as public concern, I will use it while attempting to make its various meanings clear.

Because much of the current public controversy about euthanasia may be traced to confusion about its meanings, we need to look at precisely what is being addressed under that topic. Two distinguishing themes used to analyze euthanasia include (1) the type of *action* performed and (2) the *role* of dying persons in making decisions about that action. The type of action performed is labeled either positive or negative. *Positive euthanasia* implies that definite steps are taken to produce death. *Negative euthanasia* means that death is not actively prevented.

The role that dying persons take in making decisions about their deaths forms the basis for ascertaining whether the choice is *voluntary* or *involuntary*. Most of the current discussion of living wills and right-to-die laws is explicitly directed toward individuals who voluntarily choose how their dying should proceed when death is imminent. Controversies concerning euthanasia include at least three interrelated ethical questions. First, should individuals have the right to *elect* and *control* death? Second, at what *point* might an individual legitimately exert these rights? Third, whose *interests* are going to be given priority, those of the individual or those of the society? These questions will be addressed throughout the discussion.

These moral and ethical questions are inherent in any examination of euthanasia since it is closely related to both killing and committing suicide. Positive euthanasia by the dying person might be defined as suicide; when someone else acts, as a type of murder. Certainly, involuntary euthanasia in which death is essentially arbitrated by someone else may be construed as a type of homicide. Presumably, euthanasia is performed with the best interests of the patient in mind and not the advantage of those who commit the act (although the extermination centers in Nazi Germany belie this [see Steiner 1976]). For this reason, physicians may go to the opposite extreme to avoid giving any evidence of having caused a patient's death.

Voluntary euthanasia, positive or negative, is closely related to suicide. From the standpoint of protagonists against euthanasia, voluntary euthanasia is simply a way of "giving up." In their view, condoning this means that the individual is given the right to commit suicide, although the death is not always self-inflicted.

Negative euthanasia essentially means that medical intervention in the natural processes of dying will not take place. As Glaser (1975) points out, patients affected by this type of decision are ordinarily those with severe, irreversible brain damage or in the terminal stages of disease. The latter have exhausted all currently available treatment.

The distinguishing characteristic of negative euthanasia is that it consists of acts of *omission* rather than *commission*. That is, death is not forced by the commission of specific acts that definitely lead to it. Rather, practitioners simply do not provide further therapeutic intervention. In most instances, this means that no radical, life-sustaining techniques will be used once the physician has determined that the patient is clearly moribund.

In practice, as Bok (1975) and Crane (1975b) both suggest, decisions about which measures to omit may be highly problematic. While choosing not to resuscitate may constitute an omission aimed to avoid prolonging dying in one case, eliminating intravenous nourishment may be such an omission in another case. Where and how to draw the lines may then pose knotty problems for the physician who fundamentally does not believe in prolonging the dying process. Then, too, other staff may have great difficulty in following the physician's orders. Consider this case: A severely deformed baby with Down's syndrome (commonly known as mongolism) was born. The physician was certain not only that the child's brain was extremely damaged but also that he was terminal. After a soul-searching decision was reached by the parents, they elected to let the baby die rather than try to preserve his life for a few weeks or months through surgical intervention. To do that meant eliminating nourishment. But the baby's cries caused the nurse great anguish. While she was aware of his condition, and some of his deformities were grotesquely evident, her feelings led her to want to sustain his life and keep him comfortable.

A similar case that raised knotty problems is reported by Maguire (1975). When the parents of a Down's syndrome baby refused permission for the surgical procedures necessary for his survival, the child was ordered to have nothing by mouth. After fifteen days the baby died, but in the interim the staff had to watch the child's struggle for life. Maguire points out the many ethical questions that arose in this case. Since the parents made the decision, should they have been held accountable for the death watch? Should the state have taken the baby and placed it under legal guardianship for the surgery to be performed? Should the physician have ordered drugs to ease the child's suffering and, most importantly, hasten its death?

Maguire then gets to the crux of the issue. Cases like this call into question whether acts of *commission* are not, under certain conditions, more humane than acts of omission. In the case above, hospital staff were certain that the baby suffered greatly. For many, in these kinds of circumstances, it is the patient's suffering that makes the death such a problematic issue, rather than the fact of death itself.

The situation above is somewhat paradoxical since so often decisions to let someone die are made to reduce suffering (although one might question whether it is the child's or parent's suffering that is intended to be reduced in these two cases). The issue of pain is addressed by those who support prolonging life. They sometimes argue that euthanasia is unnecessary since the very last stages of dying are ordinarily painless. But, as Bok (1975) specifies, their definitions are limited to the physical pain caused directly by the disease. She emphasizes that there may be other sources of physical discomfort; moreover, much suffering may be caused by fear, uncertainty, and loneliness. In addition, it should be noted that a short period of "painlessness" might follow a lengthy period of extremely painful dying.

The arguments in favor of voluntary euthanasia from the viewpoint of the individual are suggested throughout the book. Since they are imbedded in the preceding sections, I will simply outline them here. First and foremost, individuals have the right to choose their deaths. Second, this right is underscored by the fact that technological medicine obscures the moral dimensions of the dilemma and usurps choice. Third, individuals may decide that suffering is of a magnitude to warrant release through death. Fourth, individuals may specify that they do not wish dying to be prolonged when irreversible brain damage results in the loss of human attributes.

Briefly, the arguments against voluntary euthanasia are ordinarily based on one of the following points. First, one of the most compelling arguments against euthanasia rests on religious grounds. Although this argument has several variations, the major theme centers on the immorality of killing self or others. Subsidiary arguments (cf. Kluge 1975; Maguire 1975) rest on notions of God's will or ultimate purposes and the value of earthly suffering. Second, though not specifically religious, arguments against euthanasia are often based on beliefs in the sanctity of human life. The gist of these arguments is again that euthanasia means taking lives and thus is viewed as tantamount to murder. Obviously, even if death is voluntary—either self-imposed or assisted—there may be abuses. But Maguire (1975) argues that, despite the possibility of abuses, it does not logically follow that every specific act is immoral. Third, arguments are constructed about the *state of knowledge*. The possibility of error in information or judgment is a compelling argument for many when the moral stakes are so high. Perhaps more important is the argument sometimes made by physicians that a new medical breakthrough suddenly may radically alter the circumstances. The case most often cited of this is the situation of Dr. George Richard Minot (see Glaser 1975), who was suffering from diabetes when insulin was discovered. Not only was he saved, since he was among the first to receive insulin, but also he and his associates later made the discoveries that reversed the course of pernicious anemia. The drama of Minot's case and his subsequent contribution provides a powerful justificatory symbol to physicians of the value of life. Fourth, arguments are made that there is no way of knowing what patients would want once they are unable to communicate. This argument raises the possibility that prior wishes such as those expressed earlier in a "living will" might no longer be desired by the individual at the time when they are due to be realized (see Kluge 1975). This argument will be dealt with in more detail later.

Recognizing the complex argument raised by voluntary euthanasia alone, let us consider for a moment the greater ethical problems raised by involuntary euthanasia. As Bok (1975) and Veatch (1976) both observe, the definition of euthanasia as a good, quiet, and easy death is not necessarily limited to suffering or incurable illness. They note that it does not exclude the kind of "euthanasia" practiced in Nazi Germany. Because the concept of the good, easy death may be socially supported in ways that lead to systematic exterminations, safeguards must be applied to any legitimation of euthanasia through social policies or laws.

The utilitarian doctrine of the greatest good for the greatest number figures in discussions of euthanasia, especially when the needs of society are considered. Presumably, this sort of justification supported the Nazi extermination program. Maguire (1975) relates that all those who were socially unproductive, as well as those who were Jewish, were categorized as "useless eaters" by Hitler. Although the Nazi experience stands as the extreme example of involuntary euthanasia in modern times, the same criterion of social productiveness applies to other categories of people. Of course, the first question to arise is: Who invokes the criterion of social productiveness and with what specific standards? In a society based on diversity, there may be little agreement about what exactly social productivity is and which groups are not productive. Nonetheless, it is conceivable that those in power might also have the power to make their definitions stick.

In our society, at least three categories of people stand out as ones that are easily labeled "unproductive." They are the congenitally disabled, severely retarded, and the "senile" aged. They are socially unproductive, and their maintenance is costly to society. In a broader sense, however, such individuals may impart to others, if not to themselves, some understanding of what it is to be human. Hence, while function may clearly be divorced from production, it still may remain a contribution to the wider society. Further, one might ask if function is necessary at all. In view of these concerns, any policy on euthanasia that stems primarily from utilitarian premises is likely to be fraught with ethical problems.

Yet, the interests of society are important, too. Consider what problems would ensue if the medical care system became inundated with betubed comatose patients who lay interminably between life and death. The dilemmas are both complex and perplexing, and they point to the kinds of fundamental issues that emerge when any policy on euthanasia is considered. Thus, we are back to the question: Whose rights take precedence, those of the society or those of the individual? From my perspective, the potential abuses of euthanasia loom much larger when the needs of society are given greater priority than the *choices* of individuals. Yet, as we shall see in the next chapter, practitioners often make tacit calculations to determine who shall live and who shall die (Simpson 1976; Sudnow 1967).

Clearly, social control may be increased when positive euthanasia is policy. As mentioned before, positive euthanasia rests on those acts that hasten dying. Extremely technical medical management of a patient's condition may rest on a delicate equilibrium. In such problematic cases, whether euthanasia is socially defined at all or is defined as positive or negative often rests entirely on the *intentions* of the practitioners. Even in less complex cases, practitioners' intentions are often taken as the most significant basis for interpreting their actions. For example, performing surgery on a terminal cancer patient is usually seen as legitimate if performed with the hope or intent of retarding the disease process, although death is believed to be hastened if the procedure is not successful.

Positive euthanasia might be more widely employed than is ordinarily supposed, particularly if acts that lead to a hastened death may be interpreted in several ways. Persons other than the physician may be the ones to take the action. For example, a depressed boy, newly quadriplegic, begs to die, so his brother shoots him in his hospital bed. In other cases, however, hospital staff decide to hasten death. For example, a nurse who works in a terminal cancer ward in a small hospital lets some patients know that she will act to shorten their dying if they so wish. Another young nurse who also worked with terminal cancer patients was shocked to discover how frequently physicians ordered lethal doses of narcotics for these patients. She said,

> It is an awful position to be in. It makes you feel like you are pulling the trigger—like you are an angel of death. Anybody could figure out what the dosage means. But what was so strange was that none of the other nurses would talk to me about it.

Because of social, moral, and legal sanctions, it stands to reason that persons who perform these acts usually would be unlikely to talk about them. Information on the extent and nature of such practices needs to be carefully researched, it it can be at all.

From my perspective, the crucial problem with positive euthanasia lies not in the acts per se, but in the *decision-making process*. When such acts are performed without the expressed desire of the patient, or at least with the concurrence of an intimate who interprets the terminal person's preference, then the practitioner is on extremely shaky ethical and legal grounds.

Earlier in the discussion, two ambiguous but related issues were raised regarding euthanasia. The first concerns whether competent individuals will wish to have earlier stated preferences specifying euthanasia acted upon when they know that death is actually imminent. The second area concerns what the terminal person who is comatose or otherwise unable to respond would wish. The first concern could be made into an empirical question that may be investigated. Dempsey (1975) reports that those who advocate euthanasia are the middle-aged and late middle-aged since these age groups constitute the majority of the membership of the Euthanasia Council. He suggests that the elderly are much less predisposed to consider euthanasia than are younger people. On the other hand, aged nursing-home patients sometimes beg for death. It seems, then, that a number of conditions might influence how persons feel about euthanasia in general, and specifically, what their wishes are for themselves.

The second ambiguous area cannot be researched. We simply don't know what, if anything, comatose terminal patients might "think" about euthanasia when actually dying. In my view, the fact that communication with the dying is impossible does not necessarily mean that no action should take place. It seems reasonable to follow whatever previous wishes were specified by the patient.

Quite clearly, the context of the patient's situation figures in the kind of approach the physician will take, and that approach may hasten death. Crane's analysis of physicians' attitudes toward death (1975a) shows strong indications that under certain circumstances physicians will act in ways that bring about earlier death. Specifically, the majority of her respondents stated that they were willing to incur a high risk of respiratory arrest in terminal cancer cases by increasing narcotics. In contrast, a question put to pediatricians about giving a lethal dose to a baby born without a brain was answered overwhelmingly in the negative. But Crane observes that in the first case, physicians have the *alternative explanation* of intending to relieve pain despite the possible consequence of death. In the second instance, the intention to produce death is much clearer. Perhaps, the social construction of meaning plays the most significant role in determining how an act will be defined. It stands to reason that different meanings will be attached to different categories such as the disease entity, patient age, degree of intimacy with the patient, and so forth. Although they may be taken for granted, these categories might congeal in predictable ways. Perhaps most importantly, shared ways of viewing and acting upon such categories lead to legitimizing certain practices regarding them.

Certain practices are already becoming common. For example, it may be very difficult to remove life from someone who retains the characteristics of a feeling, interacting person, just as it may be difficult to sustain the life of someone who is terminal and no longer exhibits these characteristics.

Kluge (1975) argues that euthanasia is permissible in three circumstances: (1) when the individual is not yet a person (that is, a social being), such as an aborted fetus; (2) when the individual is no longer a person; and (3) when an aware individual requests to be allowed to die because physical or psychological existence is unbearable, and intervention to alleviate the situation is impossible. Using these criteria, euthanasia for adults would be limited and the rights of the individual would be protected.

In conclusion, one paradoxical issue remains in the controversy over euthanasia. On the one hand, the impetus of the movement to legitimize euthanasia has emerged from the social structure of dying in a technological society. The grotesqueness of dying in an impersonal, formal setting hooked up to technical symbols of medical authority is not appealing. If dying were to be humanized and taken out of the technologicalized medical institution, then perhaps much of the concern about hastening death would be eliminated. But the paradox is that to do this would necessarily shorten existence, and that might be defined as euthanasia.

LEGALIZING PATIENT RIGHTS

Attempts in some states to codify into the law patients' rights to control their dying have arisen as a response to the dilemmas posed by practices consistent with technological dying. Such legal efforts are a direct response to the *loss of autonomy* the patient experiences in the dying process in particular and the experience of illness in general.

Without legal patients' rights, practitioners may not follow patients' wishes even when they are specified in writing. Signing a "living will" essentially requests that death-prolonging technical devices and procedures not be used when death is certain, but since the will may be ignored, it does not resolve the problem of choice. Family members who cannot accept death, feel guilt, or do not share the views of their dying relatives may urge the physician to sustain life. Or the physician may be unwilling to permit hastening a patient's certain death. Similarly, nurses may be caught in the dilemma. They may have standing orders to resuscitate the patient whenever "necessary." To fail to follow their official orders and risk discovery could cost them their jobs. Quite clearly, considerations other than the patient's wishes have figured heavily in how dying actually occurs.

The move toward codifying certain rights of the patient into the law is a move toward redress of some of the more flagrant abuses of human rights in medical settings. The loss of the usual rights of citizenship and those informal rights accorded adults is characteristic of everyday practices in medical settings. Typically, the right of the patient to autonomy has totally dwindled away by the time dying is certain. Consequently, to afford patients some rights to control their dying is a small step to reverse a process and mode of interaction that characterizes much of medical practice.

The movement to legalize patients' rights represents an important re-cognition that those rights exist. If they were codified into law, patients could choose to exercise them with greater certainty that they would be followed. Hence, if patients wished to shorten an agonizing death or save their families some of the strain of a lingering death, not to mention pro-hibitive expenses, then they might more easily do so than before.

However, the fact that laws have been passed in some states does not mean that no further problems are encountered by those who elect to use them. Several problems are readily apparent (see Veatch 1976). First, the wording of the laws is often vague. General terms like "death with dignity," "natural death," and "meaningful existence" are extremely difficult to inter-pret concretely and uniformly. Second, some of the proposed legislation actually contradicts and limits previously established legal rights of patients. Third, several acts give decision-making authority directly to the physician rather than to kin after the patient is judged to be incompetent. Fourth, other legislation, such as the California Natural Death Act, have cumber-some clauses such as the one requiring that a second directive be signed by the competent patient two weeks after a terminal diagnosis is made in order for it to be binding. The patient is frequently incompetent by then! Despite the problems with this type of legislation, the California act alone demon-strates that its enactment did not bring into being the widespread practices of euthanasia feared by its opponents ("Right-to-Die Form Demand Slackens" 1978).

The pressure to formalize statements of patients' rights into law has come from several sources. Some physicians feel that earlier court decisions inhibited them from making ethical decisions since doing so would make them vulnerable to malpractice suits. Notably, those who espouse the idea that euthanasia should be a choice have long supported such measures. Their efforts have been joined by increasingly vocal thanatologists, practitioners, and patients who support the view of "dying with dignity." They argue that technological "living" is not worth the human costs to the patient. Because of their views, they have been active in attempting to gain public interest in the plight of the dying patient.

Quite clearly, right-to-die laws and related acts are themselves *technical responses* to the technological bent modern medicine has taken. These laws may give patients a safeguard otherwise not available to them in highly complex medical settings. The extent to which the laws will actually be put to use is of course questionable. Greater public awareness of the plight of the dying and the possibility of recourse might generate use of right-to-die legis-lation. To the extent that the patient is influenced by the preferences of the physician, invoking legal rights is apt to be a moot point. In actual situa-tions, however, patients and family members tend to be persuaded by the mode of treatment or plans that the physician proposes. Crane reports that one of the research physicians whom she interviewed made the following remarks:

> You can't let the family influence you. But it is necessary to handle them diplomatically, so they will go along with your decisions. I steer them to my way of thinking. They don't want to make the decisions themselves (1975b, p. 193).

The influence of the physician will be heightened when the patient or family sees the practitioner as possessing extremely scarce resources and expertise. If the physician is studying the disease the patient has, and no other specialized treatment is available, the patient is apt to be highly responsive to the implicit or explicit wishes of the physician.

Formalized legal directives are probably unnecessary when the patient, family, and physician share a long-lasting and rather intimate relationship. If the physician and patient are accustomed to negotiating treatment plans, it seems likely that this ability to make agreements would carry over into the dying process. Besides, over the years the physician would develop a sense of what is meaningful to the patient and the kinds of priorities of the family. *Certainty* about what is genuinely desired and *mutual trust* would characterize the relationship. Under these conditions, the physician is apt to be more responsive to the wishes and needs of patients and their intimates. To illustrate, in ideal circumstances if a patient did not wish hospitalization, the physician would be aware of it and could be expected to help the family handle the situation at home. But the ideal often is not the real, and besides, many chronically ill patients change or outlive their physicians. In lieu of carefully worked out understandings based on agreements over the years, it seems logical that legal statements written by patients concerning their preferences are the most promising solution.

Right-to-die laws have arisen in part from the ambiguity of court decisions concerning terminal patients. The physician, in particular, is legally responsible for treatment even if the patient is going to die and begs to die to relieve suffering. Hence, mercy killing is punishable although in actual circumstances there have been few convictions of either physician or family member. However, a quirk in the law may be discerned in those situations when the physician acts to "preserve" life or give supportive care. Again, the physician's intentions or primary objective is given legal significance.

Though legal precedents concerning dying are ambiguous and in some ways contradictory, court decisions have typically served to uphold "life" through the use of technical procedures and equipment. Hence, the courts have taken medical intervention to be the physician's responsibility. Although the actual number of physicians who are challenged on their handling of terminal care in the courts is small, the symbolic impact on the minds and attitudes of physicians is apparently great. Legal constraints may impel the physician to continue treatment in hopeless cases. And hospital policies may take into account these legal constraints more than the physician might wish. An internist gave Crane this explanation for a response to a questionnaire item:

What I check what I would do, this is not always what I would do of my own volition. My check mark is often a concession to hospital demands and legal concerns (1975b, p. 21).

Because beliefs in the sanctity of life have been written into the law, there is some legal reluctance to leave the interpretation of "good medical practice" entirely up to the attending physician. The view that good medical practice means to cease or forego extraordinary procedures for the patient whose death is imminent is gaining wider acceptance. But from a legal perspective, codifying precisely what extraordinary procedures are can raise sticky problems. Simple maintenance care may at times be extraordinary depending on the patient's physical status. The legal problem, then, is that it is almost impossible to develop wholly concrete criteria by which actual cases may be judged. That problem will continue until a more uniform determination of death is arrived at, since bodily maintenance becomes extraordinary when the patient is without brain function. In any event, problems are intensified when the patient is no longer competent.

How are these situations actually judged? Clearly, attending physicians are the single most important party, although presumably their decisions are made in consultation with the family. Of course, that consultation occurs in a context in which physicians have control of the information. The research physician who calculated what he told families in order to maintain control over decisions (Crane 1975b) was acting highly strategically to further his own interest, the research investigation. The investigation might have had much higher priority to him than the desires of individual patients. In other situations, the practitioner may neither be aware of the patient's preferences nor have a specific stake in the outcome. Nonetheless, physicians may influence the family considerably simply because they are viewed as the experts.

Cantor (1975) notes that some hospitals use committees to assume the authority of decision making when the patient is no longer competent. Some of these committees include other professionals, such as members of the clergy or psychiatrists, who are apt to be more interested in the social and humanistic aspects of the case than the technical aspects of it. Cantor states that these committees are sometimes referred to as "God squads." To date, it is not altogether clear the extent to which death by committee actually changes the outcomes of decisions. But death by committee affords practitioners protection by *diffusing* and *objectifying* the responsibility for decisions.

Legal guardians are sometimes appointed who are expected to act in the best interests of the patient. Ordinarily, guardians are appointed when the patient is no longer competent and has no family to assess the situation. Or physicians may petition for a court-appointed guardian when they feel that family members are not acting in the patient's best interest. In cases of clear parental neglect of children, obtaining a court-appointed guardian is standard procedure. Parental neglect is defined in circumstances in which parents refuse medical intervention for their dying child, and practitioners believe the condition to be reversible with proper treatment. Numerous examples are provided by cases of Jehovah's Witnesses. Because their religious beliefs cause them to refuse blood transfusions, the children of Jehovah's Witnesses are frequently given court-appointed guardians when transfusion is at issue. Even with older children, it is generally believed that they should not have to decide against transfusion (and hence for death) until they are of age.

Although the courts have generally ruled in favor of "life," Veatch (1976) states that no court has ruled in favor of life-sustaining techniques for a child who will be left with severe mental or physical disabilities. Competent adults usually are legally permitted to make choices about their fates. The notable exception to this has been those cases when the adult has dependent children. Here, the assumption is that it is in the state's interest to rule in favor of treatment (see Veatch 1976). In a complex case, Veatch (1976, p. 157) tells of Mrs. Jones, who was brought in for emergency care by her husband. Because of a ruptured ulcer, she had lost two-thirds of her blood. Since she would not give permission for transfusion, a hurried bed-side hearing was arranged. The judge ruled in favor of giving the transfusion since she was 25 years old and had a 7-month-old baby. It was the judge's opinion that it was in society's interest to preserve the life of this mother so she could raise her child.

Although judges may place limits on them, patients possess some legal rights whether or not they have a right-to-die law in their state (though ordinary practices may not allow for exercising them). Right-to-die and natural death laws reaffirm and strengthen these rights. In that sense, they constitute an important step in providing greater public recognition that the patient has rights. They also provide legal justification for those physicians who are predisposed to follow the patient's wishes but feel constrained by earlier court rulings.

SUMMARY AND IMPLICATIONS

Problems of technological dying have emerged in a context in which beliefs in the preservation of life and the efficacy of technologized medicine are widely held. In turn, these beliefs are often viewed as related to the medical conception of death as an enemy to struggle against. Although this conception may currently be undergoing challenge, it is widely accepted as characterizing the dominant view of medical practitioners. Certainly it is related to the kinds of medical practices developed that favor length of life over quality of life. Greater interest in patients' cases than in their perspectives, as well as research and education, has contributed to technologized dying. Besides, the physician's relationship with the patient is often only a fleeting one in which technical aspects of the case dominate his or her concerns. Importantly, under these conditions ethical implications of treatment decisions are obscured and the patient is often left without knowledge or choice. Consequently, death occurs when technology fails.

Technological medicine has brought into being new dilemmas concerning the determination of death. In particular, kidney transplants have caused problems since it is necessary for the donor's heart and respiratory system to be functioning for the kidney to be salvageable. In addition, a small but growing number of patients linger between life and death while they are supported by life-sustaining (or death-prolonging) machines. Because of the new dilemmas in determining death that are posed by technological medicine, more physicians are assessing whether the patient retains human characteristics as a critical variable in determining life or death.

These issues lead directly to questions about euthanasia. Although euthanasia is defined as the good and easy death, its definition does not address whose good it serves and who chooses it. Voluntary euthanasia means the patient chooses it, and involuntary euthanasia means that it is imposed by someone else. The actions taken are also of significance. Acts of omission mean that measures are not pursued, and the patient is allowed to die. Acts of commission mean that measures are enacted to hasten death. In actual cases, the difference between acts of omission and commission is sometimes fuzzy, but acts of omission ordinarily indicate that life-sustaining equipment is removed when death is imminent.

Because patients have had relatively little control over their medical treatment and are often unable to express their preferences when decisions need to be made, their rights to express choices in terminal care are becoming increasingly codified into law. Right-to-die laws are themselves technical responses to technologized dying. They are unnecessary when the physician is certain about the patient's wishes and the patient trusts the physician. Right-to-die laws intend to give the patient the option to make decisions.

The most fundamental issue raised by technological dying and euthanasia concerns the power to make decisions. While some dramatic cases reveal the institutionalized prerogatives of practitioners, what is not so readily apparent is the lack of control experienced by most consumers of health care when the final phase of dying is neither so dramatic nor prolonged.

However, it seems conceivable that at least the dying person's relatives, if not also the patient, will be increasingly included in decisions to turn off life-sustaining machines. And with a growing public awareness of the dilemmas caused by technological dying, an increasing number of individuals will begin to exert their rights. Unfortunately, I suspect that a *minority* of physicians will encourage patients and relatives to participate in these decisions. When a greater openness toward death is achieved on the part of all participants, the topic will be broached more easily, particularly before it becomes an immediate issue. After all, for those strategic-minded practitioners, involving the family in decisions will offer a modicum of protection from malpractice.

The final decision to remove life-sustaining equipment is of course momentous. However, it is easily forgotten that turning off the machines is frequently the final decision in a *series* of decisions. And for patient and family to control the dying process, they must be involved from the beginning in the step-by-step actions that lead to the development of technological dying.

In this chapter, I discussed the ethical dilemmas posed by technological medicine. Clearly, the technological emphasis in medicine more or less shapes the dying process of those receiving terminal care. In the next chapter, I analyze the ways in which the problematic features of dying are played out in interaction. And because of the trend toward institutionalization, much of that process is shaped by the interaction between practitioners, patients, and relatives. The next chapter will thus treat the concrete, specific, and often much less dramatic issues that emerge in interaction as dying proceeds.

REFERENCES

Aries, Philippe (1974). *Western Attitudes toward Death*. Baltimore: Johns Hopkins University Press.

Berger, Patrick F., and Carol Alterkruse Berger (1975). Death on demand. *Commonweal* 102:585.

Berlant, Jeffrey (1978). Medical ethics and professional monopoly. *The Annals* 437:49-61.

Bok, Sissela (1975). Euthanasia and the care of the dying. In John A. Behnke and Sissela Bok (eds.), *The Dilemmas of Euthanasia*. Garden City, N.Y.: Doubleday, Anchor Books.

Cantor, Norman L. (1975). Law and the termination of an incompetent patient's life-preserving care. In John A. Behnke and Sissela Bok (eds.), *The Dilemmas of Euthanasia*. Garden City, N.Y.: Doubleday, Anchor Books.

Cassell, Eric J. (1974). Dying in a technological society. In Peter Steinfels and Robert M. Veatch (eds.), *Death Inside Out*. New York: Harper and Row.

Crane, Diana (1975a). Patients attitudes toward the treatment of critically ill patients. In John A. Behnke and Sissela Bok (eds.), *The Dilemmas of Euthanasia*. Garden City, N.Y.: Doubleday, Anchor Books.

_____ (1975b). *The Sanctity of Social Life*. New York: Russell Sage Foundation.

Dempsey, David (1975). *The Way We Die*. New York: McGraw-Hill.

Devins, Gerald M., and Robert T. Diamond (1977). The determination of death. *Omega* 7:277-96.

Feifel, Herman, Susan Hanson, Robert Jones, and Lauri Edwards (1967). Physicians consider death. *Proceedings of the American Psychological Association* 75:201-202.

Fletcher, Joseph (1977). Elective death. In Sandra Galdieri Wilcox and Marilyn Sutton (eds.), *Understanding Death and Dying*. Port Washington, N.Y.: Alfred Publishing Co.

Freidson, Eliot (1970). *Profession of Medicine*. New York: Dodd, Mead.

Glaser, Barney G., and Anselm L. Strauss (1965). *Awareness of Dying*. Chicago: Aldine.

Glaser, Robert J. (1975). A time to live and a time to die: the implications of negative euthanasia. In John A. Behnke and Sissela Bok (eds.), *The Dilemmas of Euthanasia*. Garden City, N.Y.: Doubleday, Anchor Books.

Institute of Society, Ethics and the Life Sciences: Task Force on Death and Dying (1977). Refinements in criteria for the determination of death: an appraisal. In Sandra Galdieri Wilcox and Marilyn Sutton (eds.), *Understanding Death and Dying*. Port Washington, N.Y.: Alfred Publishing Co.

Kasper, August M. (1959). The doctor and death. In Herman Feifel (ed.), *The Meaning of Death*. New York: McGraw-Hill.

Kastenbaum, Robert J. (1977). *Death, Society, and Human Experience*. St. Louis: C. V. Mosby.

Kluge, Eike Henner W. (1975). *The Practice of Death*. New Haven, Conn.: Yale University Press.

Lally, John J. (1978). The making of the compassionate physician-investigator. *The Annals* 437:86-98.

Leukemia dispute—parents lose case (1978). *San Francisco Chronicle*, July 11, 1978.

Maguire, Daniel C. (1975). *Death by Choice*. New York: Schocken.

Millman, Marcia (1977). Medical mortality review: a cordial affair. In Howard D. Schwartz and Cary S. Kart (eds.), *Dominant Issues in Medical Sociology*. Reading, Mass.: Addison-Wesley.

Paulay, Dorothy (1977). Slow death: one survivor's experience. *Omega* 8:173-79.

Rabin, David L., with Laurel H. Rabin (1970). Consequences of death for physicians, nurses and hospitals. In Orville G. Brim, Jr., Howard E. Freeman, Sol Levine, and Norman A. Scotch (eds.), *The Dying Patient*. New York: Russell Sage Foundation.

Right-to-die form demand slackens (1978). *Santa Rosa Press Democrat*, May 7, 1978.

Schulz, Richard (1978). *The Psychology of Death, Dying and Bereavement*. Reading, Mass.: Addison-Wesley.

Simpson, Micheal A. (1976). Brought in dead. *Omega* 7:243-48.

Steiner, John (1976). *Power Politics and Social Change in National Socialist Germany*. Atlantic Highlands, N.J.: Humanities Press.

Sudnow, David (1967). *Passing On*. Englewood Cliffs, N.J.: Prentice-Hall.

Veatch, Robert M. (1976). *Death, Dying and the Biological Revolution*. New Haven, Conn.: Yale University Press.

CHAPTER FIVE

THE SOCIAL PROCESS OF DYING

Though some may conceive of dying only in biological terms, it is an inherently social process. Physical dying is essentially without meaning until it is *recognized* and *defined*. Socially constructed definitions of issues and events give shape to the experience of the dying individual.

In preceding chapters, I have touched upon a number of important socially defined issues. The denial of death by the dying, social death, the loss of self among the dying are but a few of them. In this chapter, I bring these issues to the foreground by illuminating the ways in which they are played out in interaction. Toward that end, I explore the following topics: (1) the social milieu of death, (2) treatment of the dying, (3) death expectations, (4) dying in stages, and (5) the experience of dying.

THE SOCIAL MILIEU OF DYING

Dying is fundamentally shaped by the social milieu in which it occurs. Ordinarily, the milieu is the home, hospital, or nursing home. In the following brief discussion, I will discuss the major properties of the social structure of each milieu. Commonly, a distinguishing property is the *decreasing amount* of *accountability* for terminal care in each respective setting. As will be seen in the remainder of the chapter, that issue alone brings into focus many of the dilemmas caused by dying in today's society.

An emerging trend of keeping the dying at home challenges the common assumption that the medical milieu is the appropriate setting for the final stages of dying. Financial and humanistic concerns have questioned that assumption. Since dying is so costly, patients themselves sometimes seek to remain at home for as long as possible to avoid burdening their families with the high costs of institutionalized care. Occasionally, an elderly individual will avoid institutionalization so that financial resources are left intact for survivors.

Persons concerned with humanistic alternatives typically view the social milieu of institutions as dehumanizing and degrading to the patients. From this perspective, the loneliness and anonymity of dying among strangers in mechanistically run institutions symbolizes the alienation of the patient.

As a result, an acceptable way to handle the problem is to care for the dying patient at home. Patients at home usually have access to help and emotional support from relatives and sometimes trained workers. Relationships between family members are typically close when these kinds of arrangements are intentionally made, though they sometimes are made by default. Accountability for the patient's *psychological* as well as physical comfort is maximized when family elect to undertake care. Although some physicians and social workers will heavily discourage the family from undertaking the care of a terminal, bedridden person, others now attempt to assist the family in making arrangements they can handle.

But the amount of physical work alone, not to mention the social and psychological strain of dealing with the dying of a loved family member, is extremely arduous. Special diets, incontinence, skin care, and continuous observation indicate the kind of work involved (Calkins 1972).

Being accountable for the maintenance of a medical routine is a heavy burden for one person to handle. One of the hazards involved in home care with insufficient help is the deterioration of relationships between the dying and their caretakers under the pressure of arduous work. Thus, dying at home can be fraught with knotty problems, and it may not prove to be a workable choice when it occurs slowly or when relatives are unaware of the kinds of dilemmas they may face. This issue will be dealt with more thoroughly later. For the moment, keep in mind that the energies and resources of the caretakers may be depleted. Imagine, for example, the strain on a single middle-aged woman whose leave of absence from her job is almost up and her elderly mother for whom she is caring has not yet died! The strain is heightened by the fact that she is forced either to resign from her job when it would be difficult to find a comparable new one, or suffer the guilt of failing to fulfill a promise to her mother.

Certainly, dying at home is the best arrangement for many families since it allows more latitude for them to handle it in their particular way. Furthermore, patients at home may be integrated into the round of daily life and therefore be involved in *living* as they die. Perhaps the most important implication of dying at home is that the dying person and relative may come to feel that they have realized a *symbolic completion* of their shared relationship (see Calkins 1972).

Accountability becomes more diffuse in the formal organization of the hospital. But clearly there are differences between hospitals. Notably, the social class level of the bulk of the clientele in addition to the resources of staff shape the extent to which accountability for terminal care is a priority.

Even if dying is not openly acknowledged in the private hospital, physical care may be excellent and staff may encourage the family to remain present. Moreover, with greater professional interest in the psychosocial dimension of dying, some informal or formal resources for helping the patient and family are often available now. Under these conditions, middle- and upper-middle-class patients are treated sensitively and humanely.

On the other hand, as Sudnow (1967) demonstrates, care in a public institution might be neither sensitive nor humane. The dying are often low in the scale of staff priorities. Comfort care and conversation may be largely overlooked. Moreover, the patient becomes a "non-person" who is *socially dead* before biological death because of the volume of patients and because staff do not feel accountable for giving supportive care. The nurse Sudnow observed closing the eyes of a woman before she died is an exemplar of staff who treat patients as socially dead. Because it is easier to do this preparatory task for the morgue before death, this nurse routinely closed their eyes while dying patients were still alive.

Social death is then intimately connected with issues of professional and moral accountability. Social death permits doctors to turn away from their "failures." It legitimizes staff treating patients as nonpersons without human qualities. Most strikingly, social death serves to rationalize abandonment of the aged dying through banishing them to organizational repositories for terminal patients. These repositories can be found in the back wards of public institutions, or more commonly in nursing homes.

One might ask how the nursing home can be described. Nursing homes and convalescent hospitals attempt to replicate the mechanical efficiency of the hospital, typically with much less success. In the nursing home setting, the mere mechanics of physical care such as bathing, changing beds, giving medications, and so forth, are problematic. A mounting literature attests to the generally poor quality of care given in these institutions (cf. Mendelson 1974; Stannard 1976; Townsend 1971). Facilities often are understaffed and overcrowded and lack adequate supplies and services. I have witnessed several such institutions where the lack of fresh linen resulted in patients neither being bathed nor having their soiled beds changed. In one con- valescent hospital, the special diets were systematically ignored since the kitchen was run by people who did not speak or read English. The adminis- trator counted on the patients' "senility" and the lack of interest by family to hide the facts.

Because it is easier and cheaper to keep patients in bed than to work with them, many of these patients are helped along in their dying. They lose their strength more rapidly, and they lose the incentive to live (Townsend

1971). Their social milieu is characterized by occasional orders from staff interrupting the monotony of television shows selected by the staff. Sources of diversion, stimulation, and human interaction are apt to be limited. The aged dying sometimes have no living family left, others are geographically separated from their relatives, and others are virtually abandoned. The following excerpt from a letter to Congressman Pryor illustrates conditions within the social milieu of the nursing home:

> I'm sick of the smell of urine and feces and the silent eyes of old people who have no one left; forced to die in a place that has no regard for their dignity or worth as human beings. The owners of these places are merchants of human flesh whose only concern is profit.
>
> The patients have four walls to look at all day; and three meals and three doses of medication to quiet them down; and three shifts to note coming on and going off.
>
> But one day is no different from the rest and even the sane patients don't know what day it is when you ask them, although some have calendars to mark off the days like the days off sentences to which they have been forced to serve. I have had patients ask me why God doesn't let them die and I have no answer.
>
> There is a certain absurdity to the whole thing—these mainly rich old people left to decay and die in loneliness and rags. A woman with no one and nothing but a fortune in shares asked me of what use was all her money now. And the sad thing was it wasn't of any use except to pay her hospital bills (Townsend 1971, pp. 195-96).

By their very presence in the nursing home, some patients suffer social and symbolic death. Because of the *isolation* and *relative lack* of *scrutiny* of nursing homes by professionals and the public alike, it even becomes possible for staff members to treat an alert patient as socially dead. The less accountable the staff members in these institutions are to internal supervision and externally imposed standards of care, the more possibilities exist for them to treat sentient patients as socially dead. Patients often have no visitors to intercede for them or relatives to help provide them with the minimal comforts of life that might also demonstrate their individuality, such as wearing their own clothes. Further, some patients live in fear of staff members' reprisals if they complain (Townsend 1971). Clearly, many of these abandoned patients are serving a terminal sentence in poorly managed facilities that do not even meet minimal standards.

Last, however unintended by its participants, the organization of the medical care system has consequences. Notable among them is the tendency to hide failures. By sending the failures of technological medicine, the dying, to the back wards of public institutions, or increasingly to nursing homes, where they are no longer in view, the lack of accountability for terminal care is perpetuated.

TREATMENT OF THE DYING

Since most persons die in institutionalized settings, particularly hospitals, a closer look at the interactional dynamics within them is needed. Personnel in treatment institutions are fundamentally concerned with the *nature* and *flow* of *work*. This overriding concern sometimes results in the interests of staff and patient being at odds, especially when reluctant staff fear that giving the patient any information will generate more work. Hence, in this section, I will discuss the social structuring of work and evasive and direct interaction followed by some comments on why patients and staff sometimes come into conflict.

Social Structuring of Treatment

The treatment of the dying is fundamentally linked to the structure in which it occurs. Since hospitals are organized around work, work and how it is to be allotted are important. Traditionally, the staff's first priority has been to *physical care*. Only recently have committed professionals been able to gain widespread support for their stance that psychological support to the patient and social support to the family should become part of the routine work of terminal care. But the extent to which these services are actually given remains another issue.

In any event, the social structuring of terminal care and *work priorities* are intertwined. Both shape the patient's dying process. In addition, the structure of work often determines how much contact and help the patient can have from family members. Many intensive care wards are set up for the ease of nursing personnel to move swiftly from patient to patient. Particularly when the hospital administrator has calculated how to obtain the most efficient use of the nurse's technical skills on these wards, the patient's family is permitted to visit for only five to ten minutes an hour. When having relatives underfoot is not viewed as disadvantageous for ward work, relatives are permitted to stay as long as they like. Actually, nurses may come to prefer having relatives in the room since as close a vigil by nurses is then less necessary. Besides, having relatives in the room often relieves an unwilling nurse from sticky conversations with a sentient patient about dying.

By maintaining a continuous flow of work, emergency wards in large city hospitals are structured for the efficient care of those patients who need urgent attention. But at critical moments the volume of patients is too large for the staff and they stack up, even when some of them have grave conditions or are already dying. When the emergency ward is not equipped to handle the situation because of the volume of patients, understaffing, break-downs of crucial equipment, inability to locate the appropriate specialist, and so forth, what may have otherwise been a routine emergency becomes a crisis (Glaser and Strauss 1968). For example, a gunshot wound that ordi-narily would have been routinely handled becomes a crisis only because the patient was forced to wait several hours for the surgeon.

Crises also may occur when the *protective impersonality* of the emer-gency room breaks down. If the staff know the dying patient personally, then they may have difficulty mobilizing themselves to handle the crisis while there is still time to save the patient. This point is nicely illustrated in the following anecdote related by Glaser and Strauss:

> One case that paralyzed an emergency staff into crisis was the shooting of the ward clerk by a former lover, a deputy sheriff who was bringing the patient to the ward. Staff members were so shocked that they could not at first begin the routine for standard unexpected emergencies. They gaped and mumbled: "She was one of us." "It's different when it happens to an employee of a hospital." "We knew her and it's harder to lose someone you know." "Sheriffs don't do that." As the nonmedical features of this surprise subsided, and the staff could see pertinent medical aspects of what had happened, they could start to shift the crisis back to routine emergency treatment of a bullet wound. However, they were too late to save the patient (1968, p. 126).

More commonly, however, the *nature* of the *emergency* and the *patient's social status* affects the mobilization of the staff during the crisis. While the patient's social characteristics may not always affect emergency treatment, they tend to be taken into account when the volume of work demands making decisions about when the patient is treated. In addition, Sudnow's study (1967) and Simpson's replication of it (1976) show that physicians who work in hospitals serving members of different social classes treat their respective clientele in different ways. Further, in a hospital serving lower-class people, including drug addicts, prostitutes, alcoholics, suicides, and drifters, Sudnow found that physicians were more apt to classify these patients as "dying" and subsequently limit the amount of intervention they received, which in turn essentially facilitated their dying. In contrast, Sudnow found that physicians in a middle-class private hospital were reluctant to be thought of as "giving up." He points out that by "giving up" physicians fear endangering the doctor-patient relationship as it extends to the family. Then an important aspect of physicians' relative candidness about their predictions of death is the *audience* who receives the information. Whereas in the county hospital, it becomes common knowledge among the staff, in the private hos-pital it is the family who is likely to receive this information.

Two important implications can be drawn out of this discussion. First, patients who might be able to be "pulled through" may be left to meet an early demise. Sudnow recounts the case where the physician decides not to order transfusions for an alcoholic who was bleeding internally. The reason given was that, if pulled through this crisis, the patient would be back in a week needing another transfusion. Decisions of this order are, I believe, in part predicated on the scarcity and costliness of medical care.

The second implication concerns those who are "pulled through." Often when patients are "respectable" citizens, the physician will pull them through, but they will just take much longer to die. Similarly, Simpson (1976) comments that great leaders may ironically be forbidden the "unharassed death" that the indigent are assured.

This brings us to a crucial consideration in the care of the dying—the part played by the assumed *social value* of the patient. As Glaser and Strauss (1968) emphasize, social characteristics such as age, education, social class, race, and marital status, as well as the patient's objective physical condition, influence who will be treated and saved and who will be postponed and perhaps left to die. The following anecdote from Sudnow demonstrates the point:

> *Two persons in "similar" physical condition may be differentially designated dead or not. For example, a young child was brought into the ER with no registering heart beat, respirations, or pulse—the standard "signs of death"—and was, through a rather dramatic stimulation procedure involving the coordinated work of a large team of doctors and nurses, revived for a period of eleven hours. On the same evening, shortly after the child's arrival, an elderly person who presented the same physical signs, with what a doctor later stated, in a conversation, to be no discernible differences from the child in skin color, warmth, etc., "arrived" in the ER and was almost immediately pronounced dead, with no attempts at stimulation instituted. A nurse remarked, later in the evening: "They (the doctors) would never have done that to the old lady (i.e., attempt heart stimulation) even though I've seen it work on them too"* (1967, p. 101).

The social characteristics on which a person's social value is assessed subsequently become the source of the staff's appraisals. Combined with the appraisal of social value is the outcome of that appraisal—the staff member's implicit assessment of the amount of *social loss* incurred by the death of the patient (Glaser and Strauss 1968). In a crowded urban emergency room, work is literally organized around such appraisals (Glaser and Strauss 1968; Simpson 1976; Sudnow 1967). Patients who are evaluated as having low social value tend to be deferred until those rated as higher are helped, despite the fact that the former may be in much greater need. For example, an emergency room nurse recently stated to me that rarely has she observed anyone over 40 getting attention before a needful child, even when the adult appeared to be in worse condition.

Appraisals of social loss and social value are not limited to the emergency situation. Glaser and Strauss demonstrate that the patients to whom nurses become most attached tend to be ones given high appraisals of social value. A certain amount of *involvement* with patients seems to foster more effort to save them.

But a paradox may develop. Swanson and Swanson (1977) provide an anecdote about a terminally ill medical student who previously had worked with staff. Since he was known to staff and symbolized their world, they were very fond of him. Characteristic of a classical "good" patient, he complained little and expressed appreciation for their efforts. But as death became closer, staff seemed angry with him and avoided him. Why?

Two conditions appear to be operative here. First, since he was of the staff's symbolic world, his death appeared to be personally threatening to them. Second, because he had been known to them before his illness took its toll, they were directly confronted with marked changes in his appearance and vitality. Concrete reminders of dramatic shifts in an esteemed associate whose death is felt to be untimely cause some individuals too much distress to handle it in ways other than avoidance.

Ordinarily staff do not observe or *know* patients before they are defined as *patients*. When involvement is specifically patient-staff, a modicum of identification seems to be optimal for sustaining care.

However, staff do not always wish to become involved. In order to remain uninvolved, nurses often attempt to listen to the patient selectively. Thus, as Glaser and Strauss (1965) remark, they turn "a deaf ear" to details of everyday life that point to the potential social loss such as children, personal aspirations, or career. By controlling the information they have to contend with, the nurses are then more able to keep their work routine and maintain their composure. Clearly, when the nurse is able to neutralize or minimize appraisals of high social value, the kind of treatment the patient will get is likely to be limited to routine physical tasks.

Even patients with low social value become interesting and therefore valuable to staff if they are "interesting cases." Great lengths will be taken to keep an interesting case alive in the midst of crisis so that more can be learned about the specific disease or procedure. But those who attend the patient and perhaps the family do not always concur with prolonging death. When faced continuously with the patient's intractable pain or insurmountable anguish, some nurses will push for letting the patient die. Also, because they become ward fixtures, some interesting cases become an integral part of ward life. Nurses particularly may then become aware of the patient's thoughts and feelings about living and dying. Subsequently, they sometimes decide to act as mediators between patient and physician who interpret and promote the patient's preferences.

In the last analysis, taken-for-granted assumptions about the patient's social value shape the structuring of terminal care. Whether the patient becomes an individual to many a staff member or remains one of a numbered, often faceless, crowd depends upon appraisals of social value. In that regard, Michael Simpson (1976) remarks that preventive medicine is more extensive than traditionally conceived. He cautions, "If you want to maximize your chances of being rescued from catastrophic illness, perhaps a heart attack— strive to look as young as you can, dress well and traditionally (this is no time to be eccentric) disguise your deviancies, and keep your breath fresh" (p. 248).

Evasive Interaction

A prominent characteristic of interaction between staff and dying patients is the *lack* of *direct acknowledgment* of impending death. Physicians tend to be reluctant to disclose bad news to dying patients; their justification is that the patient would not be able to cope with it (see Glaser and Strauss 1965). Physicians are more likely to disclose their unpromising predictions to the family, who are apt to keep them a secret from the patient, not infrequently at the physician's direct request. When death is not disclosed directly, subsequent interaction is characterized by *evasion*.

Under these conditions, staff members attempt to manage dying patients' evaluations of their conditions and their circumstances so that they will not discover their terminality. Glaser and Strauss (1965) demonstrate the lengths that staff go to prevent the patient from knowing. They find that nursing staff create a *"fictional future biography"* so that patients will believe they actually have a future (Glaser and Strauss 1965, p. 33). Further, staff offer interpretations of signs to patients who question why they are not progressing more quickly.

Clearly, if patients have a good deal of trust in the staff, they are likely to be reassured by erroneous or partially true interpretations of their conditions. Glaser and Strauss (1965) report that skilled staff members may be able to manage their facial expressions and even their gestures to hide the truth from the patient. However, this is a problematic issue, as Erickson and Hyerstay (1974) point out. They argue that dying patients are in a double bind since *contradictory messages* are being given. Gestures, voice inflection and pitch, facial expressions, and non-responses all provide cues even if the verbal deception is handled well. At any rate, if dying proceeds slowly, patients will become increasingly aware of the inconsistencies and contradictions between what staff are saying and what they are experiencing—but it can take quite a while for this to occur.

Whether the patient "knows" is something of a controversy. Many doctors, including Kübler-Ross, assume that the patient "knows" but wishes to deny it, whereas Glaser and Strauss argue that the patient may indeed not "know." If the latter position is accepted, one of the problems that emerges is the amount of time and energy it takes for the patient to discover what is happening. As Erickson and Hyerstay put it: "Thus, it seems, an abundance of time and effort goes into producing an elaborate deception for an audience that 1) doesn't want to be deceived and 2) already suspects the grim denouement of the drama" (1974, p. 288).

Increasing isolation of dying patients is no doubt related to the attempt to maintain pretense about their situations. Nurses who feel less adept in discounting cues and in managing interaction are apt to drastically reduce the amount of time they spend with the dying one. They attempt to minimize conversation and stick to the more perfunctory aspects of their work in order to reduce the chances of giving off cues to the patient. Perhaps, too, the nurse does not want to be held accountable for imparting the bad news to the patient. Consequently, the patient may have less and less contact with staff.

As patients begin to experience contradictions, inconsistencies, and, often, increasing social isolation, their suspicions of dying begin to grow. At this point, patients may actively attempt to elicit information from the staff that provides evidence for their suspicions (Glaser and Strauss 1965). Patients may then continually question staff who try to avoid discussing their conditions. This is shown in a comment by a student nurse in Quint's study:

> She kept referring to all those purple bruises, and every time you'd walk in she'd say, "Why do I have these bruises?" She had two conditions (I can't remember what the other one was) but it certainly wasn't something that would cause these bruises. It just didn't correlate to the point where, if it were you or I, we would suspect something was seriously wrong. She was always asking questions. You always had to be on your guard (1967, p. 97).

Patients' attempts to get confirmation may then be met with further countermoves by staff to prevent disclosure of death. According to Glaser and Strauss (1965), nurses typically act as if the patient were ill but not dying. They retain cheerful bland countenances as they attempt to maintain the pretense. The upshot of these tactics is that some patients get angry and feel that they are being given the "runaround" (Glaser and Strauss 1965).

Staff are usually much more comfortable when patients form their own unobtrusive *silent* confirmations of imminent death. Perhaps maintaining the patient's silence, except when in the presence of a staff member who is able to talk about death, is the perferred mode of handling someone with a poor prognosis. A paradox may develop here. Patients become well-socialized to keep quiet about death, sorrow, and pain. Subsequently, they seem unwilling to express feelings to the one staff member who indicates an acceptance of them.

Yet the need for the dying to have human contact, even from strangers, cannot be denied. Ordinarily, if isolated patients without friends or family do not receive it from staff members, it is not forthcoming. The fact that in Los Angeles "death companionship" can be purchased from a commercial enterprise, Threshold, is testimony both to the needs of the dying and the cultural assumption that human needs may be fulfilled through entrepreneurial ingenuity (see "Death Companionship: Work of Threshold" 1975).

However, companionship through outside resources is not always available. If staff remain unwilling to talk with the patient and the patient does not press the issue, then both parties may pretend to ignore the impending death. Consequently, the *mutual pretense* of both staff and patient that Glaser and Strauss (1965) describe becomes a logical outcome of the kind of interaction the patient has with staff members. Social conventions may prevent patients from broaching the topic when they sense that nursing staff find it too uncomfortable to deal with. Similarly, relatives, chaplain, and physician may give cues indicating that they, too, do not wish to directly face the patient's feelings. Quite possibly these participants either unwittingly, or sometimes consciously, convince themselves that patients really do not want to talk about it. But when the issue of impending death is evaded, strain increases. Hence, staff may *increase* their efforts to evade since they feel that addressing the psychological issues is like opening Pandora's box. For staff, to open the box means being inundated with impossible needs and demands by dying patients (see Hertzberg 1977). Reluctance to deal with the issues openly is revealed in a physician's statement reported by Garfield:

> *I've recently realized that for the past 25 years when a patient of mine has been terminally ill, I'd walk into the room talking constantly, approach the bed, and back out of the room talking. I do this because I have nothing to offer medically and I'm not willing to deal with the patient's emotional stress. That's not my training so it's probably better if I handle the situation that way. The psychologist or social worker or psychiatric nurse spends time with the patient and opens up a whole emotional can of worms and then who gets the brunt of it, I do, the physician. I don't have time to deal with these issues. It's better if physicians give brief general reassurance and don't dig too deeply (1978, p. 105).*

So staff tend to justify evasion by saying that it is for the patient's own good, regardless of the patient's perspective on the matter. Under these conditions, staff members claim that the patient might not only "fall apart" if direct acknowledgment of death is made, but also if there is time, seek out faith healers, quasi-practitioners, or others unacceptable to the established medical profession. Staff members sometimes point to such actions as the illegal quest for laetrile by some cancer victims to illustrate what they mean about patients' knowledge of their diseases causing "problems." Laetrile patients will go to Mexico for treatments, engage in smuggling, and pay exorbitant black market prices to obtain the illegal drug. In the last analysis, evasive interaction tends to perpetuate the social control over the patient by the physician.

Direct Interaction

Although deception and evasion still commonly characterize interaction between dying patients and practitioners, more practitioners are beginning to advocate direct interaction with patients about their conditions (see Carey and Posavac 1978-79; Rea, Greenspoon, and Spilka 1975). Typically, properties of direct interaction include an *open* and *frank attitude* on the part of the practitioner. Basic to this stance is the assumption that patients have the *right* to know relevant facts about their conditions and to participate in whatever decisions are made. The logical extension of this position is that patients have the right to determine what kind of treatment, if any, will be conducted.

However, practitioners exhibit varying degrees of openness. As one local physician said,

> *I believe the patient has a right to know anything about his condition. Some patients don't want to know, so my policy is, tell the patient everything about which he asks. All they have to do is ask me. I am glad to sit down and have long talks with my patients about their conditions and what they mean. I never give them a time limit, that's like handing someone a death sentence. And it is often an erroneous estimate anyway.*

Other practitioners now support disclosure of a terminal diagnosis but feel that their primary obligation is to give patients an *opportunity* to ask questions concerning their prognoses. It appears that openness is becoming common with those who have kidney failure and cancer. But it may not be nearly as common with those practitioners who treat patients with injuries or circulatory and respiratory illnesses.

Although direct disclosure may be *forced* by the practitioner who takes the initiative to inform, it need not be insensitive. Clearly, those who inform a patient or relative in an abrupt and callous manner foster distress in that person (Glaser and Strauss 1965; Fischoff and O'Brien 1978). Glaser and Strauss (1965) provide this example: "One doctor walks into the patient's room, faces him, says, 'It's malignant,' and walks out." Such a forced disclosure is direct and frank; however, it results in an interaction process as *closed* as those characterized by evasion and deception. Consequently, direct interaction in the sense used here demands a willingness to be responsive to the patient's concerns.

Clearly, a major strategy for handling the disclosure of information is to place the burden of seeking out information on the patient. In actual situations, of course, this stance may prove to be a means of *evading* the issue of death, at least with certain patients. But the argument goes that patients will ask only as much as they can "take." And the assumption is that they *will* ask—an assumption without a solid empirical foundation. When some but not all information is disclosed, it is crucial that nonverbal gestures and cues are congruent with what is verbally stated. If the practitioner gives signs of discomfort, abruptness, or impatience, the patient will receive the latent message, "Ask, but don't ask." Further, according to Saunders (1978), the patient who asks no questions has sensed the "dangerousness" of the topic imparted by the practitioner. In short, many practitioners now disclose the nature of the diagnosis directly but evade or conceal its implications for the patient (see De Francisco and Watson 1977; Kaplan *et al.* 1978).

Yet others are discovering that a clear communication of what is known creates less distress for the patient and family since the patient's fear diminishes when things are explained well (Garfield 1978; Saunders 1978).

Saunders (1978) observes that physicians are often not the appropriate person to impart information to the patient since they often lack an understanding of the patient's subjective world and may not perceive unstated concerns. As Saunders suggests, a social worker, psychologist, or some other professional might be more suitable to discuss the illness and treatment with the patient. But for some patients a paradox might develop were this to occur. While a patient might have a stronger relationship with the other professional, those who hold doctors in awe are only convinced of the validity of medical information directly given by the physician. A solution to this problem might be to have the physician give the news first in the company of relatives and another professional who later handles further explanation and psychological concerns.

Not infrequently, practitioners feel uneasy about giving "bad news." One way practitioners neutralize apprehension is to begin a lecture on technical details. When this occurs, the patient is barraged with what seem to be ambiguous terms and meanings although they may constitute direct information. For example, when an initial disclosure of malignancy is unsuspected by patients, their concentration is especially apt to focus on that information alone instead of all the subsequent details. As Hogshead (1978) points out, for patients to "know," the diagnosis must be couched in terms that are meaningful to those patients. It is far preferable for a practitioner to have a relationship with someone prior to giving bad news than to give it to unknown patients whose responses would be judged only outside of the context of their lives. Another significant point is that bad news may need to be given gradually during several different encounters (Hogshead 1978). Since suddenly being forced to imagine themselves extinct constitutes a nasty surprise for many, it stands to reason that they will need time to adapt to such disquieting news. Unfortunately, patients' initial refusal to believe the news is sometimes taken as massive "denial" when they have actually not had the time to fully realize its meaning.

Rather than simply leaving the encounter open for questions addressed to the physician, Hogshead (1978) recommends asking questions of the patient. Specifically, he inquires about what was disclosed earlier by other physicians and what was just mentioned by him. By using such tactics, he is able to open up the interaction for clarification from the beginning and also encourage a working relationship between doctor and patient.

However, to get complete information it is typically necessary for the patient or relative to take an assertive stance by questioning the practitioner in detail. The tone of the relationship with the practitioner may again be established for fostering direct disclosures. Along similar lines, Carolyn Driver (1978) observed that she and her terminally ill husband had to create rapport with staff. Otherwise it was nonexistent. She further observed that few people possessed her husband's skills in achieving this rapport. Upper-middle-class persons are quite adept at drawing their practitioners into working relationships in this way. As a result, the responsibility of decision making becomes shared. One wonders, however, the extent to which the less educated are capable of initiating relationships to maximize open interaction and shared decision making.

Information, Priorities, and Conflict

What patients know about their conditions is a more complex issue than usually realized. Assuredly, whether patients are treated with candor markedly affects their understanding of the disease process, prognosis, and treatment. However, the biography of the patient also is significant. Values, world view, education, extent of prior experience with bureaucracies in general and medical institutions in particular all contribute to the patient's process of gaining information about his or her illness.

Part of the problem of gaining information is often understanding the "information" obtained. Even when information is obtained, patients interpret it from the vantage point of their own priorities and world views. As I will show, both may bring patients into direct conflict with the objectives of practitioners.

Glaser and Strauss (1965) observe that Americans are inexperienced at recognizing signs of impending death, and potential sources of information like the medical chart are carefully kept out of patients' reach. Even with the legal right to review their charts, staff typically fail to award patients the *symbolic right* to it. Thus they use informal means to preclude patients from becoming privy to medical interpretations of their medical status and response to it. Under these conditions, only the pushiest of patients take advantage of their rights, and they may be punished for exerting them.

The patient's failure to recognize signs of impending death is particularly significant. The subtle warnings of serious disease are often normalized by patients who then are taken by surprise when their conditions noticeably worsen. Social class differences are sometimes at issue here. People from lower class backgrounds tend to define symptoms at a later point than those who are more knowledgeable about diseases and can better afford medical care. Besides, according to Rosenblatt and Suchman (1964), lower class people do not view their bodies as machines to be kept finely tuned and repaired as do those from the middle class. Instead, they perceive their bodies as things to be enjoyed in youth and endured in old age. With these kinds of subtle beliefs, besides the costs of care, it is not surprising that lower class people tend to seek medical help later than their middle class counterparts.

Not infrequently, patients simply do not understand the medical implications of their conditions and the planned treatment programs. Further, physicians may fail to realize the extent of their lack of understanding, particularly when some attempt was made to inform them.

Roberts provides the following example of a man who may not have understood his condition and subsequently refused treatment.

> *Field Notes: Medicine. Jason Daniels is feeling very badly about a patient who is going home having refused dialysis. This is an elderly man and one they all seem to like. He doesn't seem to understand why they think he needs dialysis, let alone what they are talking about when they mention transplant. Like many people, he has his kidneys mixed up with his bladder, and thinks that as long as he can urinate everything must be all right. He says he wants to go home and go fishing, and "drink a little beer to keep the water works going." Fisher and Kerry Young (both third-year students) talked about this for quite awhile, finally coming to the conclusion that perhaps the old man wanted to go fishing for as long as he has yet to live, and really understands dialysis far better than they thought he did. They're being very sweet to him, helping him carry his things and reminding him he can come back if he wants to. Fisher says, "I hate it when I hear them tell people, 'If you go away now, don't come back.' If he wants to go fishing now, why shouldn't he? He'll come back when he wants to, if we let him." Kerry responds, "He won't though. Did you hear what the other doctor said to him?" Fisher says, "Yes. That was rotten." They both looked at me and changed the subject. They either don't think I heard, or don't think I remember hearing Doctor Trevor storming down the hall an hour ago shouting about, "These bastards who come in here and waste our time and then decide to go home" (1977, p. 95).*

In this case the patient is given the option to return for treatment when desired. Disobedient patients in teaching hospitals are often not given a second chance. A lengthy process of *negotiation* may follow, but negotiation frequently requires verbal and tactical skills the patient does not possess. Thus, in hospitals where the clientele are uneducated, poor, and unfamiliar with the values of scientistic medicine, negotiations take a different form than in those settings where doctor and patient have a greater basis for dialogue. In the former circumstance, the patient simply does not return or may refuse the next procedure. The physician might then resort to scare tactics. But scare tactics might backfire. When pressed to "fight" the disease in the medically prescribed way or suffer dire consequences, the patient's fright may result in flight (see Roberts 1977).

Those who have had little prior contact with institutionalized medicine are apt to be both frightened and bewildered when confronted with the technically oriented staff. In some instances, what is a routine procedure to insure survival and the only reasonable choice to the physician constitutes a devastating attack on the self to the patient, such as the woman who believes a hysterectomy will rob her of her gender.

Even when special efforts are made to reduce anxiety and to convince the patient of the value of the procedure, the assault on self-image may still be too great, and the patient may still refuse. For example, a woman stated that she opted for death rather than have an ileostomy. Only 25 at the time, she could not conceive of herself with a "bag." The possibility of odors or telltale bulges mortified her. Most importantly, she felt that her husband could not love her unless her body remained intact. So she went home against medical advice without the surgery. Until she was visited by an attractive young woman from a local ileostomy club, she remained adamant about refusing the procedure. With the support of this woman with whom she identified, she was able to accept the procedure.

Dilemmas are not always resolved so peaceably. What other differences contribute to conflicting views of staff and patients? Certainly the world views of patient and practitioner often radically differ. Negotiations are affected by hidden assumptions about time imbedded in contrasting world views. Hidden assumptions about time, for example, lead to different priorities and actions. Many people do not share the mechanistic linear progressive conception of time inherent in scientific medicine. Without this conception of time, treatment plans predicated on deferred gratification, hard work, and small increments of "progress" are unlikely to be followed. Moreover, the serious consequences of deferring the treatment seem incomprehensible to someone who does not possess a linear view of time.

Part of the linear view of time consists of a carefully mapped out and *predictable future*. Reality lies in the future as well as in the present. But not everyone views the future as real. For those who live in the present, the future remains vague, unknown, sometimes almost disconnected from the present. Thus what is an obvious connection between present actions and future consequences to staff may not be to patients. For example, after being told that his drinking would kill him, a diabetic continues to drink but later does not understand why he no longer feels well. Earlier pronouncements had no meaning to him until the seemingly imperceptible effects of drinking became disturbing.

A linear view of time often makes no sense to lower-class patients. Why plan? Plans are only thwarted and expectations crushed. Moreover, many lower class and chronically ill persons hold a *cyclical* view of time in which time moves from crisis to crisis in a cyclical fashion rather than progressing in gradual linear increments (see Calkins 1970). Crises consume one's actions, and they also draw the individuals involved inextricably into the present (Charmaz 1977). Then, when existence itself is characterized by constant crises, the person's consciousness of the future remains vague and uncertain.

Disparate conceptions of time held by practitioner and patient are apt to coincide with other dimensions of contrasting world views. For example, the active, pragmatic stance of the physician calls for intervention. But patients whose stance is fatalistic might not particularly believe in intervention. They reason that life is ordered by fate or predetermined by God (see Roberts 1977). In that sense, efforts by either patient or physician cannot be expected to alter the course of events. Such an attitude may be characterized by fatalistic statements as "If you are going to die, you'll die" or "Your time is up when God calls you." Until that time, the patient is apt to live according to priorities other than those set forth by practitioners.

Given these types of contrasting assumptions, it is not surprising that patients and practitioners have different interpretations of the patient's condition and what, if anything, should be done about it. But what is important to note is the fact that deep-seated values of various participants are played out through interaction.

DEATH EXPECTATIONS

When people are identified as dying, a new identity is conferred upon them. Subsequently, relationships may radically change. Of particular importance are two main issues: *certainty* of *death* and the *projected time* of dying. Further, *who* knows *what* at *which time* during the course of events shapes the unfolding social reality. In the following discussion, I explore three key dimensions of death expectations in situations characterized by their *absence, uncertainty*, and *certainty*. Last, I will comment on expectations made on estimates of *time*.

An Absence of Death Expectations

When are there no expectations of death? Sudden deaths are ordinarily thought to be without expectation. (The following remarks pertain only to those sudden deaths characterized by no particular anticipation, suggestion, or wish. Accidents, disasters, or acute illnesses all give rise to sudden deaths of this order. Even when death is not immediate, but happens within a few hours or even a day after the initial trauma, it can be viewed as a sudden death.)

Sudden death of any type is disquieting; it temporarily disrupts the character of ordinary events. The transition from life to death may occur so rapidly that dying seems to be without process. Instead, it may appear to be a state that has simply overwhelmed those involved, particularly the dying person. Without forewarning or cues, aware dying persons may be faced with making sense of their rapidly approaching demise. Yet without forewarning of immediate death, these individuals may be as unprepared and shocked as those around them. Thus one occasionally learns of persons having sudden myocardial infarctions and dying with an expression of surprise on their faces.

Sudden death becomes shocking for the relative who expected the illness or injury to be minor. Imagine the shock to a woman who discovers that her husband's earlier complaints of nausea were actually signs of a lethal myocardial infarction! Similarly, Bergman (1978) provides the statement by a mother whose expectation of the extent of her son's injury was only that of a broken leg. Without any preparation, she was abruptly told, "He's gone." As a parenthetical note, sensitive staff usually try to rapidly build up cues in order that the relative is not caught entirely unaware of the coming death.

An absence of death expectations is not limited to patients who suffer sudden illness or injury. Occasionally, someone dies whose condition did not seem serious enough to cause death. In that case, the sudden death causes survivors and staff as much disbelief as when there had been no visible physical problems at all. And even in those cases when death is certain but occurs much earlier than anticipated, the sudden closure of the relationship may cause much anguish. In short, an absence of immediate death expectations poses different problems for participants than circumstances wherein expectations are defined as certain or uncertain.

Uncertain Death

Dramatic cases of life or death crises dominate the conventional view of uncertainty about a particular patient's possible death. In this view, it quickly becomes apparent whether the patient will "pull through" or die. Thus the *projected time* of dying is *imminent*, if it will occur at all. For example, a profusely bleeding man with a knife wound in the chest is rushed into emergency surgery. He has lost substantial amounts of blood, and it is uncertain if the surgeons can save him, but whether he lives is expected to be determined during the next few hours.

The belief in a will to live commonly held by both practitioners and lay persons alike enters here. Pattison (1977) proposes that the will to live is linked with *something* or *someone* to live for. The will to live is often taken as the pivotal variable in the successful resolution of the uncertainty. Occasionally, practitioners marvel at a patient's tenacious desire for survival against high odds. Conversely, they sometimes observe that a patient who could survive does not. Their explanation of the death is contingent upon the lack of a strong will to live.

Surely the combination of a strong will to live and rapid, sophisticated medical intervention enhances a patient's possibility of survival. Sometimes the uncertain crisis is immediately resolved as the patient lives or dies. But things are not always so simple. Sometimes the resolution of the current crisis develops into *chronic uncertainty*. For example, the patient with the serious myocardial infarction survives the initial attack but is faced with chronic uncertainty about the future.

The issue of chronic uncertainty has perhaps become a more prevalent issue in the past decade or so. Often that uncertainty rests on whether treatment procedures will be effective and thus stave off death for an unknown period, sometimes months or years. Or the treatment may be predicted to simply retard the dying process and for those patients who elect to take it, might result in several years of dying. Clearly, then, the point at which "dying" is defined is open to divergent views.

People often distinguish between having a terminal illness and entering the final stages of dying only when death is imminent. Yet sometimes they do not. In the past, differences between those who defined the final stage of dying earlier and those who defined it later may not have been remarkable because of the smaller amount of time elapsing between these intervals. Now such differences sometimes become quite striking. These differences may of course lead to crucial differences in opinion on handling specific situations. Some participants may prefer to define dying as occurring only when death is imminent while others may define it as beginning with the *disclosure* of a very serious illness. Toch (1977) provides the extreme example of this situation. To the chagrin of the staff, the entire extended family of a 7-year-old girl convened at her bedside attired in mourning clothes. For the several months before the bewildered child died, they maintained a vigil in her darkened room. The staff felt that their crying and chanting resembled a wake. Such actions not only challenge the staff's taken-for-granted assumptions about the proper care and management of a terminally ill child but also challenge assumptions about when dying may be said to occur. These kinds of divergent views are apt to occur whenever death is ultimately certain but the time it takes to die is not.

One might then ask: What does the patient's outlook reveal about the dilemma of uncertainty? Practitioners often observe that uncertainty is met with vast swings of emotion corresponding to the patient's condition and prospects at the moment. Since the patient's prospects are linked to available resources and response to treatment, they sometimes radically shift. For example, kidney dialysis patients face both an uncertain length and quality of life (see Beard 1977). Their hopes are raised by the prospects of transplants, then dashed when the transplant fails. After a period they may become so debilitated that they cannot withstand the trauma of another transplant procedure. Certain death expectations may be formed only after several such shifts. Typically, certain death expectations eventually develop out of situations characterized by chronic uncertainty. Thus the patient moves from facing the threat of death to facing the reality of death.

Certain Death

Certainty of death has a finality ordinarily believed to eliminate ambiguity despite the fact that such certainty is essentially a *prediction*. Basically, certainty of death means the conviction held by a key interactant that the person will die (Glaser and Strauss 1965, 1968). Ordinarily, the physician's conviction is taken as the defining one, but it may also be held by nurses, relatives, or even patients, without necessarily being shared by other participants. In fact, the conviction of certain death is usually not shared equally by all participants. Sometimes not even all the physicians agree. More commonly, a lack of clear information about the attending physician's opinion is the problem for other participants early in the terminal illness. Often, the relative is told the "truth," but reality is mystified or softened for the patient. Not wishing to squelch all hope in the patient, the physician may inadvertently cause problems between family members who already experience considerable emotional distress. DeFrancisco and Watson comment on the effects of deceptive communication:

> One of the things that happened early in the case was that the doctors would talk to Mike and Kathy separately. They would give one story to Mike, which was sugarcoated, and they would give another story to Kathy, which was more factual. Then when Mike and Kathy would try to discuss things together, it frequently led to discord. Kathy would feel that Mike was denying and not wanting to face up to things. Mike, on the other hand, felt that Kathy was being unnecessarily pessimistic and was just trying to bring him down. They would at times end such discussion by accusing the other of lying (1977, p. 240).

The extent to which the definition that certainty of death holds or becomes evident to others is of course based upon the recognition of increasing signs. Once the definition of certain death has been made by medical authorities and accepted as real by patients and relatives, then the subjective worlds of the patients change as the realization of death pervades their consciousnesses.

Just as more patients live with chronic uncertainty about death and its timing, more are living in the face of certain death but with an *unknown* though abbreviated length of time. Thus, death might occur in three weeks, three months, or three years. Sometimes patients are informed of an outer limit of time but do not know when their deaths might occur within that period. For example, several years ago a Vietnam veteran mentioned to me,

> I've been told that people with my type of kidney failure generally don't live longer than seven years on dialysis. I've already lived four of them.

Knowing one's life is foreshortened causes some patients to struggle to be the exception to the predicted life span and thus "win" against death if only for a short time. As a dialysis patient, Lee Foster commented, "The record for longevity on a kidney machine, the last time I checked, was fourteen years, and if I stay on dialysis I aim to break the record" (1977, p. 526).

Foster as well as other patients whose futures are questionable express a profound hope that some new breakthrough will occur in the interim before their certain death, so that more time will be gained. Such hope might sustain these patients through pain, loneliness, and discouragement. But it may also cause them to pursue treatments of questionable value. By doing so they may expend great amounts of their limited energy and money. That may cause them great sorrow when they discover that they have run out of time, and other priorities, such as finalizing an intimate relationship, will never be realized.

Whatever else, those who are able to live with their diseases and share their concerns with a loving intimate talk of an intensity, clarity, and appreciation of life that transcends their prior everyday existence. No longer is the lived world taken for granted (see Foster 1977; Jaffe and Jaffe 1977; Kelly 1977, 1978). Instead, it takes on new dimensions of vitality and clarity.

When death is defined as certain and *immediate* but yet does not occur, felt, but often unarticulated, dilemmas arise. These dilemmas include reorganizing the family unit, resolving feelings about the impending loss but continued presence of the family member, and living with the nagging feeling that death might occur at any time. Under these circumstances, participants correctly feel that they are living in an unsettled state of affairs.

The sustained intensity of crisis may take its toll in the relationship with the dying. Sadly, some lash out in anger at the dying one for taking so long, for becoming such a burden. Once said, the deepest regrets do not ease the nagging pain and guilt over having rejected one's intimate at the last. As one man said,

> I'll never forgive myself for telling her she was a burden. I literally asked her to die . . . after twenty-five years of marriage and being so close all through it. Maybe I tried too hard to handle her dying alone. Maybe they kept her alive too long. But I'll never forget the way she looked at me when I came out with that.

Other relatives are able to state openly and with equanimity that death is overdue. When somehow convinced that the body lying there is no longer the person once loved, they are able to wish for death without remorse. Hence, social death is most likely to be ascribed to a patient who is unable to communicate when death is *certain* and *overdue*. An extreme example of social death is revealed by a nurse who telephoned the son of a comatose woman for permission to cut her hair. His response was, "Goodness, is she still alive?" (Calkins 1972, p. 34).

In contrast, even when death is certain and overdue, a definition of social death may not be sustained when the patient is able to communicate and remains linked to past and or present social world. In one case (Calkins 1972), a man whose wife was placed in a nearby nursing home could not consider her socially dead since she was nearby. Friends continued to inquire about her, visiting was continued, and she had limited speech despite her considerable brain damage. Her repeated question was, "Where's Daddy?" during the time he was attempting to establish a new life without her. Subsequently, it became impossible for him to treat her as if she were socially dead. This example illuminates one of the major issues, to be considered next, arising when people do not die at the "correct" time.

Expectations of Time

Death expectations are founded on *estimations* of *time* (Glaser and Strauss 1965, 1968). When death is sudden, it seems "untimely." When someone lingers, death seems "prolonged." Estimations of time tend to become joined with expectations of what should or should not occur.

Practitioners, particularly, tend to form fairly specific estimations about the predictable length of the patient's life. These estimations may be based entirely on unshared personal observations, although at times they may be fully articulated. Experienced staff build their estimations on what for them are easily recognizable physical signs. Consequently, definitive expectations are sometimes developed that calculate the patient's estimated demise. Yet these expectations may not be borne out, so physicians are often hesitant to disclose them. Making the wrong prediction can cause the physician embarrassment and result in strained interaction. Patients may even come to feel that everyone around them is waiting for their deaths to occur and is getting bored in the process!

Though they may not be articulated, estimations of remaining time shape interaction. The patient may sense them anyhow and respond accordingly. In addition, these estimations have implications for managing dying. A result of such estimations, for example, is to send the patient to a nursing home to die, rather than keeping the person in an acute hospital.

The upshot of estimations is that participants develop notions of a "correct" time for specific patients to die (see Glaser and Strauss 1965, 1968). According to Glaser and Strauss, the "correct" time to the physician may be the period between the expectable limits of time previously estimated. For example, as in the case of a cancer patient, the "correct" time is actual death within the two to four months the doctor had expected. The "correct" time to the social worker or psychologist might be after the point when the patient has finished what psychologists call his or her "death work" or achieved insight into neuroses and adjustment problems (Shneidman 1978). To the patient, the "correct" time might be the point at which special tasks are completed, relationships are resolved, and pain is unbearable. In any event, all the participants' definitions of "correct" time may be at odds and that may result in conflict.

Problems emerge when participants decide that the patient has either died too quickly or too slowly. When the patient has died too quickly, staff have nagging doubts about whether the correct procedures were competently followed, and whether the problem was fully identified in the first place. Glaser and Strauss (1965) describe a situation where the patient died unexpectedly on the operating table and rumors of negligence were rife until the pathology report revealed that the death had been of natural causes. In this instance, staff experience the kind of shock, dismay, and distrust more frequently felt by relatives who did not or could not read the same cues available to medical practitioners.

Sometimes, of course, negligence or incompetence causes or contributes to the death. Accountability and blame may then be attributed to various staff participants. Some members intimate or openly express their convictions about the lack of responsibility or ineptness of others to family. (I suspect these indiscretions are made only when staff feel sure that the family will not bring charges of malpractice.) Statements like "She shouldn't have died in surgery" or "The nurses should have called me sooner" or, more blatantly, "The technician prepared the wrong substance and it was injected" indicate the irritation and ascription of blame. More commonly, however, staff will close ranks to minimize the disclosure of actual events precipitating the death to avoid litigation.

Staff might then be expected to investigate informally, possibly with much speculation and gossip, a death that is otherwise inexplicable. But, formally, a death that was possibly avoidable might not be opened to public review. Millman (1977) demonstrates that physicians share an understanding to overlook each other's mistakes even when they hold private review conferences ostensibly to oversee and monitor each other's work. In the rush of crisis, then, staff may look to themselves for informal accountability when death occurs at a dramatically "incorrect time." But in the final analysis, they may take as little formal responsibility for it as is typically taken for ordinary dying.

DYING IN STAGES

Reflect upon the following situation. A 50-year-old woman is brought into the hospital for a battery of tests. She is informed thereafter that a cyst on her ovary was discovered. After further testing, a diagnosis of ovarian cancer is confirmed. Though not explicitly informed that her condition is terminal, she is informed of her diagnosis. The patient's response to the news is that she will fight it all the way. But her condition worsens over the next year and she becomes withdrawn and depressed as her physical status deteriorates.

Medical personnel often observe similar shifts and changes in the patient's perspective and attitude as dying ensues. Why might these changes occur? By accounting for such changes, Kübler-Ross's first book, *On Death and Dying*, provides the major articulation of an analysis of the dying process.

Because Kübler-Ross's early analysis brought dying into the public eye, it is extremely significant, although it may be critically examined from a sociological perspective.* The ideas critiqued below are not by any means limited to

---

* Portions of the following analysis were taken from my paper entitled, "A Symbolic Interactionist Critique of Kubler-Ross' Stages of Dying," presented at the Annual Meetings of the American Sociological Association in New York, September 2, 1976.

Kübler-Ross's stage analysis but may be placed in a more general context of a critique of those stage analyses based upon psychological responses with little or no examination of the social context in which they are situated.

Kübler-Ross's Stages of Dying

Based on her clinical observations and interviews of over two hundred terminally ill patients, Kübler-Ross's argument rests on a framework of five sequential psychological stages of dying. These stages are *denial, anger, bargaining, depression,* and *acceptance.*

Denial and isolation are terms used by Kübler-Ross (1969) to characterize patients' disbelief in the seriousness and specific nature of their illnesses. She states that denial is at least partially used by all patients at some time, usually at the initial stages of the disease or when it has been clearly diagnosed. She characterizes the patient's response of denial as "No, it cannot be me" (1969, p. 42).

Denial is an elastic category in that it consists as much in what the viewer *perceives* as the patient's actual behavior. From a sociological perspective, one wonders if "denial" is apt to be defined by practitioners when they sense or ascertain that the patient has a different viewpoint that conflicts with professional objectives. If so, there would be little agreement between patient and practitioner about priorities and plans for handling the situation.

When Kübler-Ross states that all patients use denial at some point, she is implying that the defense mechanism of denial is in some way universal. Since denial is a judgment conferred upon the patient by someone in authority, and at that it may be a judgment based upon fleeting interaction and the reported observations of people who are strangers to the patient, it is a judgment that is frequently made without intimate knowledge of the patient's inner world. The behavior labeled "denial" may constitute a rather natural response to what patients see as a highly unnatural state of affairs. Indeed, those events immediately following patients' discoveries of the unpromising information that they may be dying may appear to be highly unnatural and bewildering to them, particularly when their initial complaints were thought to be minor. A patient's response to his or her illness is likely to be observed in professional or institutional settings, thereby placing it in an unnatural context for him or her. Moreover, the patient's means of communicating personal thoughts and feelings about the developing events is shaped by his or her prior social experience. Many patients attempt to handle their feelings nonverbally rather than through chatting with staff members or discussing their feelings with a visiting psychiatrist. But those nonverbal cues that are a taken-for-granted part of cultural experience may not be read by practitioners who do not share that experience. Lower-class persons and ethnic minorities may be much more attuned to the nuances of facial expression, intonation, and body language than middle-class practitioners whose understanding of such cues may be highly limited and understood only within the context of their own cultural paradigms. Furthermore, if the patient comes from a social world in which verbal disclosures are given only to those with whom one has had an intimate relationship, then talking with strangers about one's reactions to dying would be unseemly, alienating, and perhaps frightening.

While the staff views the patient's behavior as denial, the situation may have quite different meanings for the patient. It may represent an attempt to deal with the situation by normalizing it for others, if not for oneself. Conventions of polite conversation enter here. Patients may view their proper roles in terms of what they see as "appropriate" responses to those with whom they are interacting. Their conception of the practitioner as an authority figure is apt to figure heavily at this point. Patients sometimes feel that important hospital authorities should not be burdened with their cases. They define the situation a "private problem" even if they trust the practitioner, but occasionally they do not. (Of course, the practitioner's scrutinizing for hidden meanings and probing for reasons may set the stage for mutual distrust to develop. But the specific grounds taken by each participant for such distrust differs.)

Moreover, patients may quickly pick up on the fact that the *practitioner* is skirting the issue of dying. Since patients often grant the practitioner the right to define the terms of interaction, they may knowingly follow suit and actively continue to skirt it or otherwise try to make the practitioner feel at ease. Quite conceivably, the psuedo-cheerful manner of practitioners contributes to the patient's lack of disclosure of impending death. That cheerfulness is apt to be interpreted by the patient as a request to avoid burdening practitioners with his or her concerns.

Judgments of denial by staff members tend to stick when the patient has become a management problem for them. Put simply, the patient is not following the program or is not complying with staff rules. Thus patients who do not easily fit into institutional routines are the ones likely to be seriously questioned as to whether they are denying their diseases. Under these conditions, these patients become isolated from other participants in the ongoing scene. Consequently, the isolation that Kübler-Ross says follows denial may be largely a function of the patient's lack of meaningful relationships through which the ambiguity of the current situation can be handled.

It seems curious that the issue of the denial of death by the patient is a resounding theme in the literature when such a response categorized as denial may also be viewed as a social and symbolic reflection of the way *practitioners* deal with death. When it is not dealt with directly and personally, when cues are only sporadically discovered, when the words death or dying are so skillfully avoided, then it is not surprising that patients so systematically give indications that professionals take as evidence of the defense mechanism of denial. What is labeled "denial" must be scrutinized in the larger context of social interaction instead of being viewed solely as a psychological response of the patient. Whether or not "denial" adequately describes the reality at hand is dependent upon the data, and I contend that the data must encompass the ongoing structuring of the patient's social world.

Kübler-Ross's second stage is anger. She characterizes anger as the reaction, "Oh yes, it is me, it was not a mistake" (1969, p. 50). She states that the patient's anger may be displaced on the staff and family. Kübler-Ross insightfully notes that those who have been in control find intolerable the situation with which they are now faced. Losing control may simply enrage such persons. They are forced into a dependent and often demeaning role vis-a-vis others whom they now need for small comforts. Also, because they are dying, engaging in angry outbursts may not be personally problematic since self-respect may no longer be as valued by patients. When patients feel that they are not being treated with respect by others, they may feel that there is no stake in self-restraint.

More than the patient's anger, the anger of the staff may become apparent in this stage. The anger of staff members can be enormous when they feel the patient, particularly a disliked patient, is controlling them. This is shown in the staff's reaction to Mrs. Abel's weeping in Strauss and Glaser's book *Anguish*. They had attempted without much success to "set limits" on her crying spells. The fieldworker said the staff were angry toward Mrs. Abel for her attempts to "manipulate" them into increasing her medications. Curiously, staff felt that this abandoned woman, who was dying a painful, lonely death, was "using" them by placing her requests for help with pain control through them (see Strauss and Glaser 1970, pp. 58-59).

Quite clearly, life on many terminal wards is set up for the organization of work of the staff and not for the patient's needs. Consequently, what might be interpreted as an angry outburst toward dying by the staff may in fact be a response to an inflexible hospital structure and treatment approaches to the patient. Perhaps, a consequence of the structure of this type of care is that patients become keenly aware of their losses and the inconvenience they cause them. The subsequent inconvenience of their immobility for others is symbolized by delays, reluctance to help, lack of empathy, and so forth.

Staff members may easily interpret a patient's request or gesture as hostile when they do not share similar worlds or everyday routines. Differences in the subjective worlds of patient and staff member comes across clearly in Kübler-Ross's account of Sister I.'s request that Kübler-Ross read to her from the Bible (1969, pp. 80-81). Kübler-Ross acknowledged her discomfort in reading the Bible and raised the question as to whether or not the request meant that Sister I. was "acting out," or put more commonly, "angry." In this case, the patient was asked to explicate the meaning of the act, but not infrequently meanings are presumed since staff members often erroneously assume that patients share their meanings of actions and events. Paradoxically, such misinterpretation may then elicit genuine anger from the patient that, in turn, could be taken as validation of the original psychiatric interpretation.

Kübler-Ross's third stage, bargaining, is characterized as an attempt to postpone death, often for a specified length of time. Kübler-Ross states that most bargains are made with God and are kept secret (1969, p. 84). But it is not inconceivable that a patient might bargain with the physician and family members either tacitly or explicitly as attempts are made to control life while dying. In her account of this stage, Kübler-Ross seems to have missed an important dimension of bargaining. That dimension addresses the impersonal nature of our institutions. Because the dying patient becomes an object to be worked upon, staff members may symbolically kill the patient's self in order for the routines of handling dying to be followed. Along this line of reasoning, Gustafson (1972) insightfully remarks that in the nursing home dying patients bargain for the *moral* and *social supports* for their self-images. That is, these patients wish to feel symbolically significant and socially alive. In short, they wish to remain persons with "selves." But given the structure of terminal care wards, dying patients cannot assume that they will be permitted to have selves while dying occurs. Since social death often permeates terminal care wards, the patients' bargaining may symbolically represent their desire to be treated as human while living under dehumanizing conditions. Thus the bargaining is not made for the length of life, but is aimed toward the quality of existence one has while dying.

Kübler-Ross argues that the fourth stage, depression, coincides with visible effects of the illness. The visible effects include physical signs such as additional surgery, disfigurement, weight loss, and the mounting financial burdens most terminally ill patients accrue as costs become unmanageable. Since the entire family is forced to make all kinds of sacrifices, Kübler-Ross observes that the patient is likely to feel remorse, sadness, and guilt. Wives of sick husbands must work, leaving even less time for the children and visiting; houses are remortgaged, and the structure of the everyday life of the family is altered in direct relationship to managing the dying process of one family member. Surely mounting crises and burdens only likely to be resolved by one's death are cause for depression. Despite such reasons for depression, Kübler-Ross emphasizes the preparatory aspect of the depression. She argues cogently that the patient has to experience preparatory grief in anticipation of leaving the world of the living. Kübler-Ross puts it succinctly when she emphasizes that the patient is losing everything and everybody. Consequently, she stresses permitting the patient to express sorrow. Kübler-Ross points out that the expression of sorrow while experiencing preparatory grief makes for a better acceptance of death later. She argues that only patients who have worked out their anguish in this stage will be able to die with acceptance and peace. In this stage, then, patients ideally resolve their relationships with those who are significant so that leaving them can be accepted.

According to Kübler-Ross, in the final stage, acceptance, the patient has few feelings and is now devoid of anger, depression, and envy for the living. Acceptance in this conceptual framework is characterized by a lack of struggle and a growing silence wherein most communication consists of nonverbal touching by someone whose presence alone is comforting. Kübler-Ross maintains that the more a person tries to deny imminent death and to struggle against it, "the more difficult it will be for them to reach this stage of acceptance with peace and dignity" (1969, p. 114). An example of Kübler-Ross's concept of acceptance is portrayed in a discussion with a terminal patient, Miss T., about acceptance by God.

> After a few moments of the most peaceful silence, she continued, "My time comes very close now, but everything is all right. I shared with you my concept of death, passing from this garden into the next. What is your concept?"
>
> I thought for a while, and still looking at her face, I said, "Peace." Her last words were: "I will pass into my garden very peacefully now."
>
> Miss T. died a few hours later in her sleep, (1970, p. 165).

In this case, the patient was a black woman who was denied treatment on the kidney machine, then a relatively scarce instrument. And according to Glaser and Strauss's analysis of social loss (1964), patients who are untreated are likely to be viewed as having a lower social value than others. Therefore, their loss to society is not so great. Although providing assistance to these patients to accept their fates gracefully no doubt is of great personal value to them, and more so to staff whose problems are then diminished, such practices do, in the last analysis, perpetuate discrimination within the wider society. Perhaps, then, the anger that some patients exhibit is a more fitting response to their circumstances than the kind of quiet acceptance that Kübler-Ross sees as the final stage of the dying process.

Implications of the stages What sociological sense may be made of the stages? As comprehensible and facile as they are, the stages point to some critical issues concerning the process of dying and their overall applicability in everyday situations. The applicability of the stages to specific critically ill individuals remains an issue. Although the stages provide a useful way of studying the process of dying, they in effect impose limits on our understanding of specific patients' experiences and, further, what the process of dying means in this society. The patients' views may become either reinterpreted or concretized to fit neatly into the stages. As poet Ted Rosenthal (1973) stated, "It's fiendish. No matter what you say, they all say uh huh, just what we thought you'd say." In short, the stages emanate from preconceived psychiatric categories that are *imposed* upon the experience rather than emerging from the data. The implications of such preconceptions have not gone unnoticed by practitioners. What originated as *description* of a reality often becomes *prescription* for reality. Kübler-Ross herself has publically expressed her dismay over the rigid adherence to the stages by some practitioners. More practitioners and professionals have recently taken issue with the sequential stage framework since the above critique was first formulated (see Garfield 1978; Pattison 1977).

Although Kübler-Ross aims to focus her interest upon the thoughts and feelings of the dying patient, much of her analysis is directed toward patient management. Paradoxically, her management strategies have the consequence of keeping death contained, preserving the equilibrium of the ward, and ultimately, taken to their logical conclusion, they lend themselves to a social construction of dying in which staff will not be disrupted by the unique responses of individuals.

Although Kübler-Ross ably provides us with a perspective on the reality of dying, it is but one view of that reality, and other views might be quite different and have different implications. Questions need to be raised concerning the meaning of the experiences from the point of view of the patient who experiences terminal illness. To what extent does Kübler-Ross's rendition of the five stages "make sense" and "ring true" to the patient? For that matter, to what extent do terminal patients undergo a subtle process of *socialization* through which this psychiatric paradigm becomes sensible to them?

Kübler-Ross's framework probably is highly applicable to the educated, psychiatrically oriented upper middle class although it might not be as useful for persons from other socio-cultural backgrounds. Some exploration of these issues through further research might shed some light on the extent of applicability of her framework (cf. Weisman 1978). Along that line, Schulz and Aderman's conclusion (1976) that most patients die in depression raises questions about the extent to which the stage theory is sequential.

One also wonders if there are perhaps some alternative stages that more closely reflect the experiences of people from different cultural groups or strata in society. For example, is the bargaining stage a general phenomena or does it perhaps more closely reflect middle-class ideologies wherein negotiation and exchange are part of the cultural assumptions of everyday life? Or is bargaining skipped or replaced by another stage by those elderly who claim to be ready to die? Is the staff member's definition of acceptance equivalent to the patient's definition of resignation? Kübler-Ross's stage of acceptance seems to be related to a lack of management problems for the staff. Given the narrow range of experiences and sources of intense relationships available in contemporary institutions, it seems possible that patients and families might have quite divergent definitions than staff of what constitutes and symbolizes acceptance.

One crucial issue raised by Kübler-Ross's analysis is the relationship between psychological responses and the patient's economic situation. Since dying is expensive and may economically devastate an otherwise comfortable family, it is clear that the sentient patient would have major concerns about the costs of care. Indeed, the patient and family's economic plight may shade their interactions with each other, staff, and their social worlds as they attempt to manage their situations.

An unresolved issue underlying these stages of dying concerns the patient's awareness of impending death. To what extent does clear knowledge of ensuing death affect the patient's course through the stages? If patients are not clearly informed that they are dying or if the issue is skirted, ignored, minimized, or camouflaged by those surrounding them, then it seems reasonable that their responses would mirror the ambiguity they perceive. What seems clear and even obvious to staff may remain problematic and undefined to patients. Thus, while staff may feel that dying patients have had ample cues about the nature of their diseases and their moribund course, these patients may not have correctly perceived or interpreted all the cues. Consequently, the patients may not have a clearly articulated prediction of death. Simultaneously, the staff may feel they are denying what is obvious. Although patients may ultimately "know" that they are dying, it may take them much longer to piece together the cues than staff members anticipate. If they are not told directly, their behavior witnessed in the stages may reflect their process of discovering the truth. Denial may occur when the patients have not yet put together the cues, isolation follows when they realize that things are not quite right, anger when they learn that everyone else knew long before, depression when there is not much time and so much is unfinished, and acceptance when they realize that nothing more can be done.

My argument then is briefly this: Kübler-Ross's stages of dying may be an accurate reflection of the patient's responses under *specific social conditions*. The social conditions discussed previously are characterized by the *lack of direct disclosure* of death to the patient. A close reading of Kübler-Ross will show that she, like other practitioners, prefers the subject of death to be introduced by patients. This sets the stage for their ambiguity to persist since, as noted above, patients frequently feel that all important news will be handed down to them. In turn, this ambiguity tends to work to the advantage of a practitioner who wishes the patient to remain manageable. But the most important point is that the stages of dying as portrayed by Kübler-Ross may indeed be a *consequence* of how illness and dying are socially handled in this society, rather than a psychological process of adjustment to death. Although others might draw the conclusion that Kübler-Ross has discovered a process reflecting universal qualities about the human condition in general and of dying in particular, I contend that her analysis reflects the socio-historical conditions in contemporary society in which a psychiatric paradigm has become a dominant perspective both in medical care and the wider society.

THE EXPERIENCE OF DYING

Dilemmas posed by dying, particularly when it is a lengthy process, shape the experience of both the individual and the intimate. In the following discussion, I will first explore further the problems facing the family and then analyze the sources of the patients' isolation in the dying process. Next, I will outline how the patients' experiences affect their self-images. Last, I offer some remarks on clinical death.

The Family and the Dying Process

Casual observers often forget that much of the dying process in chronic illness is imperceptible and occurs while the patient is home. The care of an ill, debilitated, potentially dying person is, for many families, a difficult matter since conventional American existence structured around the nuclear family is largely incompatible with such activities. In many households, no one is home during the day to help with even such minimal activities as getting out of bed or preparing lunch, much less giving round-the-clock nursing care. As couples become old and have a series of chronic diseases, the arrangements through which they carve out their daily existences become fragile since their problems often simultaneously spiral. Problems compound when people have chronic diseases—physical problems often lead to economic problems—and becoming more physically immobilized leads to a diminishing number of social relationships (see Charmaz 1973).

When the death of one partner becomes imminent, the fragile relationships and reciprocities holding together the everyday life of both are disrupted, if not destroyed entirely. Realizing the additional loss and strain on the spouse is likely to cause the dying partner much anxiety. This is suggested in one of Kübler-Ross's interviews with a woman whose husband was also chronically ill. The woman said:

> I just feel that the only one I have left at home now is my husband and he is a bigger baby than all the babies put together. He is diabetic and it has affected his eyes so he cannot see too well (1969, p. 236).

Slightly later in the interview, the doctor says to the patient: "At home who takes care of whom?" The patient replied:

> Well, he made a promise with me when I came out of the hospital last October that if I would be his eyes, he would be my feet and that's our plan (Kübler-Ross 1969, p. 236).

After a short discussion of how they managed this, the doctor commented:

> It sounds like at home you are chipping in for each other and each one does what the other one can't do. So you must have a lot of concern about how he's coming along when you are in the hospital (Kübler-Ross 1969, p. 236).

Similarly, Victor Marshall (1975) found that elderly respondents reported a desire to live in order to take care of another relative, usually a spouse, although the relationship occasionally was one between siblings or an adult child. Knowing that their relative could not live without them gave these people a reason to live.

Fulfilling a commitment to give care was frequently found to be accepted as a matter of course among working-class families since these obligations remained *unquestioned* by the respondents (Calkins 1972). Such plans were sometimes years in the making with the full participation of the person who was then dying. A relative's unquestioned obligation to take on the care of the dying one hinges on three central social conditions: *close kinship ties, proximity of residence,* and *frequent face-to-face interaction.* Frequent visiting and reciprocal assistance have sustained family relations over the years. For example, one grandmother had not only taken in her granddaughter as a child but had also provided housing for her when she married. The reciprocity was demonstrated when the granddaughter took on the care of both grandparents (Calkins 1972).

Sometimes, however, taking on the care of the dying frequently strains the family unit. Affection, duty, and privacy are commonly called into question and renegotiated. The exigencies of everyday life sometimes pulls participants into new relationships. For example, a son-in-law is requested to help his terminally ill mother-in-law into the bathtub as his wife struggles to maintain care at home for as long as possible.

Tensions arise not only between the dying and family members but also between members of the family themselves. One member views another as reneging on promises to help. Or another is accused of encouraging false hopes. So often with the aged dying or lingering terminally ill, family fights develop about the proper disposition of the patient. By this time in the dying process, patients are apt to be left out of the decision-making process even when they are still capable of participating. Instead, family take over, saying, "What shall we do about Mother?"

Yet more often than realized it is the dying aged who will not agree to the home care offered by adult children since they do not wish to impose on them. One terminally ill woman who lived with her two single, middle-aged daughters hinted this to me,

> What worries me so is becoming a burden to my daughters. I feel so useless around here. It's a terrible thing to become a burden to your children. In some ways, I'd rather go to a nursing home, not that I'm not grateful for all the girls have done for me.

Whether the dying know about their forthcoming demise plays a crucial role in family relationships. When dying is slow and family members feel compelled to hide the imminent death from the dying one, maintaining pretense may consume the thoughts of the other family members, particularly the spouse, who takes care of the patient. Wives, especially, try to minimize their husbands' symptoms by camouflaging the signs that symbolize their coming deaths. Minimizing the meaning of symptoms is shown in the following statement from an interview in one of my earlier studies:

> The hardest thing was to know and keep it from him (dying). Watch him slippin' away day by day. Then he'd say things like, "Wonder why my

food don't stay down?" and I'd have to say something like, "Well, my
food don't always stay down either," and you'd have to be able to give a
reason every time he said something like that, always have to have some-
thing to say when he said something (Calkins 1972, p. 31).

Family members may become so engrossed in giving care and maintaining their pretense that they do not handle either theirs or the dying member's feelings about impending death. Nonetheless, what may seem like the easiest path to take can generate problems later. In some cases, it is clear that the relative's acceptance of the death and resolution of the relationship becomes extremely difficult. In the example above, the wife was a working-class black woman who could not believe that her husband had died long after his death. Her charade had seemed unreal to her; she openly stated that she could not accept his death. A similar response is discernible in Robert Anderson's comments. He, too, had given long-devoted care while guarding the secret that his wife was dying. He said:

I have a new life; but though I have a new life, I have an old relationship
still struggling in my mind toward some resolution I know it will never
find. It has been fifteen years—the struggle still goes on, and I imagine
it will go on as long as I live (1974, p. 82).

Paradoxically, all participants may realize that death is imminent but, for a period, remain unaware of the others' knowledge. Thus a common cause of withdrawal and increased depression of dying persons is their perceived obligation to "protect" the others from the bad news. Members are left alone to handle their sorrow, remorse, or fear. Family often wait for the dying to disclose the news, and the dying may wait for family to become aware of the developing signs of impending death. Participants are then likely to begin feeling helpless in the face of their unfolding crisis.

One might ask if death is handled differently depending upon which member of the family is dying? There are some initial indications that age, sex, and family position affect the family's response to the dying of one member in predictable ways. For example, in their recent study, Cohen, Dizenhuz, and Winger (1977) found that men are likely to be directly informed of their terminal prognoses. In contrast, women usually are directly informed neither by practitioners nor by family members. Yet women tend to provide the sources of emotional expression and integration within the family unit (see Cohen, Dizenhuz, and Winger 1977). Consequently, the communication patterns within a typical family may become abruptly distorted or changed. Cohen, Dizenhuz, and Winger's finding of a strong trend toward increased illnesses of other members when the mother rather than the father is terminal indicates the stress within these families.

The discussion has centered on a dying patient in the family. But sometimes deaths are multiple, as in an accident or fire. What happens to the family then? An unbearable amount of stress is placed upon the adult who attempts to keep the remaining members together while also attending to the dying. Under these conditions, the relative may elect to keep the terminal family member unaware of the death of another member (see Seligman 1977). The pain of facing death multiple times may even result in an otherwise concerned family member abandoning the scene.

Abandonment may also be subjectively defined by a terminally ill person whose spouse dies suddenly. Reflect upon the following situation. A husband faces a certain death within months from cancer. All household activities are centered around managing his illness and his completion of several unfinished projects of great personal significance to him. Though saddened by his suffering and burdened by the strain of care, his wife proves to be a constant source of comfort to him. Imagine his anguish when she dies suddenly three months before his own demise! An already poignant departure becomes tormented by his feelings of abandonment, guilt, and remorse.

Though families may be broken by the disruption and strain caused by one or more deaths, some families become more tightly integrated in the face of death. Under which conditions does this occur? It seems that it is necessary for members to face death, acknowledge its inevitability, and attempt to control how dying is to be handled. I suspect that this sometimes occurs on a nonverbal level between devoted kin who have built up shared understandings over the years. Most importantly, it seems necessary that members share ideas about the "proper" way of handling things. Increasingly, families are defining the "proper" way as encouraging the dying person to set the tone of what is to occur. But however decisions are made, by physician, patient, spouse, or offspring, concurrence promotes family unity and personal commitment on the part of the members.

Interestingly, the dying person's fortitude during the crisis often becomes a point of stabilization for other members who suffer distress. As Nancy Harjan said of her son's terminal phase, "If Michael could face his death, I guess I can face my life" (1978, p. 85).

Isolation

Even with the current openness toward death, the dying commonly experience isolation as they become terminal. As a result, many dying patients spend their final days and hours in great loneliness. With that may come a feeling that they are already as good as dead; that is, they have died socially in the minds of others.

Isolation stems from at least three major sources: (1) the *consuming nature* of the *illness*, (2) *withdrawal by the dying* themselves, and (3) *social avoidance* of the dying. When terminal illness becomes consuming, patients are often forced to break the formal ties with their prior worlds (see Charmaz 1973, 1977). Jobs and community activities may be relinquished as the illness steadily intrudes upon the existence of the dying and their intimates. Frequent hospitalizations followed by arduous out-patient treatments often deplete the energy of terminal patients. When no longer participating in the conventional world of everyday life, dying persons may seem to others to be left behind; no longer do they share the same reality. When the event of dying becomes prolonged, these differences are apt to be heightened and intensified. Because of the consuming nature of the illness, the dying may appear to others to live in the past (see Charmaz 1978). (These problems contribute to the reasons why some of the dying make such concerted efforts to live as normally as possible while dying.)

The separation from one's former symbolic world may not be explicitly realized when individuals are experiencing a crisis. At those times, only the most intimate are usually involved or are desired to be involved by the dying. The social actors are drawn inextricably into the present during the crisis (see Charmaz 1977). Yet, clearly, much of dying is characterized by gradual deterioration and is handled by maintenance care. During these intervals patients' isolation from ordinary worlds becomes a pressing problem to them. They are too ill to participate fully in ordinary worlds and too well to be totally immersed in illness. Moreover, the boundaries of prior worlds are often such that full participation within them is demanded or nothing is permitted.

Because of the nature of the patient's illness, isolation may in effect be imposed by others. When the patient is referred to a treatment center some distance away from home, breaks with former associates tend to begin. And when trips to the hospital become repeated over time, others who initially took much interest tend to fade away (see Charmaz 1973). In addition, isolation may be concretely imposed upon some patients such as those receiving special or intensive care. Some conditions like severe burns demand that exposure to others be limited. Moreover, a common practice resulting in the patient's isolation, especially near death, is to keep the patient sedated on high doses of medication.

Becoming consumed by the illness often marks the beginning of the second source of isolation: withdrawal by the dying person. Withdrawal is obviously fostered by excruciating pain, discomfort, or lapses of consciousness. But frequently, the dying are also unable to concentrate on prior relationships when they are immersed in illness and what it portends for the future (Charmaz 1973, 1977). Interaction then becomes strained. The other feels even more uncomfortable in the presence of the dying patient, who now seems so estranged. Estrangement and strain are of course greatly heightened when both parties are aware, but do not acknowledge, that the illness is terminal.

Withdrawal from interaction by the patient is often due to fear and sadness. Fear over the possible relinquishment or abandonment by others, fear of losing self-possession before death, fear of the pain, and fear of what happens after death all figure at this point. But again, the source of the most important isolation is probably the fear of disclosure to one's intimates. Thus, when the dying feel they have to remain stoical for the family, they may not share the bad news, much less their other fears.

Fears are felt to be unable to be articulated to the intimate when they center on the shared relationship. Fear may be deeply felt about losing sexual attractiveness or, more basically, losing the partner before death occurs. So fear and isolation are self-perpetuating. Moreover, they tend to contribute to a disintegration of former ties before death actually takes place (Kelly 1978).

The third source of isolation, the social avoidance of the dying, is perhaps the most significant. That avoidance tends to permeate the dying's everyday existence. Treatment staff, friends, and relatives all may shun the terminal patient. When dying is lengthy, avoidance becomes most visible. Thus isolation is imposed when others fear that the possibility of a person's lengthy terminal illness may cause a sustained *burden* on them. Consider the following statement made by a woman who had several extremely serious illnesses with poor prognoses:

> *And, the friends drift away, the relatives forget you, even your closest ones, when you are sick. Oh, everyone is all concerned when something sudden happens and you are sick for a while, but if it lasts, if it is chronic, then they forget you and don't help you. Even my own children have never said, "Mother, is there anything I can get you?"* (Charmaz 1973, p. 35).

When death is predictable, the dying are surrounded by an *"emotional quarantine"* (Weisman 1978). In that sense, relatives attempt to shape a situation in which the dying cannot disclose their feelings and concerns. By uttering platitudes, insisting upon hope, or busying themselves with trivial concerns, they impart to the dying that the real issues must not be confronted. In addition, a feeling may be imparted to the dying that if struggle is no longer possible, facing death with a calm and, above all, quiet resignation is their proper role.

Some relatives cannot face the coming loss when death is certain and imminent. As a result, they occasionally leave their relatives in isolation. For example, the mother of a single woman now without other intimates also abandons her since she cannot handle her daughter's need to express her feelings about her coming death. Another poignant situation is that of the abandonment of a terminally ill child whose parents never visit the hospital though staff prod them to. More often, perhaps, the dying have the presence of an intimate, but are left in *emotional isolation*. The notable exceptions are those like the elderly who outlive intimates or are already isolated due to geographical, social, or emotional distances.

How do the dying cope with their isolation? While some reach out for almost anyone whom they are able to engage, others passively give up. Those who give up typically live out their final days without the opportunity to share their feelings or review their lives. In other situations, sensitive staff members may become a surrogate family. Occasionally, however, the hurt of abandonment is too great; the patient cannot accept a substitute, even when offered one, for the one intimate whose presence is desired.

One way of handling isolation is by making it *public*. By giving public expression to their feelings of isolation and loss, some terminally ill persons have not only elicited concern from the wider community but also built a social network among other terminally ill patients. For example, Jory Graham has a Chicago column explicitly directed toward sharing the emotional responses and problems of the terminally ill (see Cimmons 1978). Orville Kelly (1977) founded the organization, Make Today Count, as a result of the response to an article he wrote about the need of a forum to discuss problems of the terminally ill, family, and practitioners. Some make appearances at seminars and community meetings (see Lofland 1977).

For others, community projects in many areas are being developed based on volunteer services to the dying. The volunteers are called to assist either the dying person or the intimate. In the Shanti Project (Garfield 1978), for example, a volunteer may be requested by the patient or, as is often the case, by the physician. The volunteer may be requested to be primarily an ear for the dying. Or the volunteer may be asked to mediate between intimates. In some organizations, the volunteer may also help with household and caretaking tasks.

In any case, going public or requesting a volunteer is a way of creating a meaningful existence while dying. And that, in short, is the central problem posed by isolation.

The Dying Self

Like anyone else, patients who know that they are dying still need to present some kind of self to their social worlds since, after all, they are living as they are dying (Glaser and Strauss 1965). The self presented to others by the dying person is a self that in some crucial ways is shaped from the social circumstances in which he or she now exists. Thus the self that the dying person presents to others emerges from his or her present conditions as well as reflecting the self the person was in the past (Charmaz 1973, 1978). That is, the self that the person may show to his or her small social world (sometimes now only a few nurses) reflects the *social experience* of dying.

That social experience frequently results in a *diminished self*. The self tends to suffer diminishment or negation from at least three sources while dying: (1) the characteristics of *physical dying*, (2) *institutionalized uniformity*, and (3) *isolation*. Physical dying alone sometimes constitutes an unmitigated assault on the self when deterioration occurs in parts of the body necessary for the preservation of the patient's self-image. For example, becoming blind and bedridden causes the young mother much anguish when she can no longer see or care for her child. She feels that she is no longer a mother. For others, the loss of vital functions causes them much distress and embarrassment. To illustrate, a woman mentioned that being incontinent of bowel and bladder with subsequent cleanups by strangers was for her a degrading and mortifying experience.

Institutionalized uniformity results from those practices that reduce the self to an object. In this sense, the self that is permitted to be revealed to others may reflect only a narrow range of experiences and categories. Indeed, in some institutional settings dying patients are not allowed to have selves; they have essentially forfeited their right to possessing a unique self by virtue of dying. The patient's body becomes institutional property. Moreover, in many respects the patient's *self* also becomes institutional property. The lack of regard for the patient's self becomes apparent as staff take over the patient's body. The remarks below written by a new nursing assistant in a convalescent hospital reveal this type of disregard for the patient. He describes the death of a very proper, private woman as follows:

> In the third week I was asked to be next to Mrs. L. while she died, so that she would not have to be alone in her last hours. Unfortunately, it was at the end of the shift and all the aides were able to gather about for curiosity. They were able to show each other what they knew about checking for life signs—they stopped once she died . . . Mrs. L. had had her last rites with her sister present the night before and was alert until the last fifteen minutes (this was when the aides converged with wisecracks and probing fingers, to which she just closed her eyes). This convergence put her entire lifestyle up to mockery. It was humiliating for me to watch and, unless she died upon closing her eyes, a total humiliation to her (Austin 1976, p. 6).

When patients become essentially objects to staff to be worked on but not with, their ability to project selves over which they have control is vastly limited. The fact that having control over one's self is contingent upon the *cooperation* of others becomes starkly apparent when one is dying. If one is not treated as being anything more than the terminal cancer case in room 334, then one may come to accept that definition with resignation as one silently gives up what little sense of self one may have earlier possessed. Resignation is felt not only because of dying but also because of the symbolic loss of self and, consequently, one's humanness before death occurs.

Although the self may be symbolically obliterated by institutional practices, no new self is developed. Instead, the self by the dying patient is transformed into an entity regarded as no longer human.

That transformation process often begins long before the last hours of dying and is reflected in the growing isolation of the person. Due to the isolation, the burden of remaining socially and psychologically alive falls squarely on the dying individual. In her interview with Marlene Cimmons (1978), terminally ill Jory Graham observed that any pulling away by another confirms the dying person's suspicions of no longer possessing human value. Because of her awareness of the readiness of the dying to make this interpretation, Graham attempts to reassure the dying that they still have selves despite the destruction of a part of their bodies.

The poignancy of an isolated, dying student nurse who sought to maintain her sense of self through sharing her fears and reaching for human concern is shown below.

> But for me, fear is today and dying is now. You slip in and out of my room, give me medications and check my blood pressure. Is it because I am a student nurse, myself, or just a human being, that I sense your fright? And your fear enhances mine. Why are you afraid? I am the one who is dying!
>
> . . . Don't run away . . . wait . . . all I want to know is that there will be someone to hold my hand when I need it. I am afraid. Death may get to be a routine to you, but it is new to me. You may not see me as unique, but I've never died before. To me once is pretty unique! ("Death in the First Person" 1972).

In contrast to the development of a diminished self, other claim *uniqueness* in the face of their dying. In fact, their only claim to uniqueness may be that they are known to be approaching death (Lofland 1977). Their identities then are derived from and immersed in their illnesses (Charmaz 1973). Along this line, terminally ill Lois Jaffe (1977) remarks that being leukemic is as much a part of her sense of identity as being a woman or Jewish. Due to their special status of dying, these patients are recognized and sometimes sought out for their special "insights." Their stories of coping with dying—often sad but, increasingly, happy tales—become newsworthy human interest accounts (see Lofland 1977). But being catapulted in sudden stardom may have its less desirable effects, too. When attention wanes, staff sometimes complain that the dying are even more isolated than before becoming public figures. Important, too, is the tacit message that one's real value lies in dying rather than living. Seligman (1977) reports a case of a burned child whose sad story hit the national news. Seligman points out that the mother's emphasis on the subsequent gifts and attention imparted to her daughter that "illness and death have more value than life."

While it is clear that some achieve identities through dying, what is not clear is how long their special selves and statuses are maintained? Do these terminally ill also sink into silent obscurity in their final phase of dying? And are they not only able to sustain their newly achieved identities but also continue to *control* their dying processes?

In order to sustain the patient's prior identity, and therefore *preserve* the self through controlling the dying process, at least two often coinciding conditions appear to be necessary. First, the requests and wishes of patients with high *status* are apt to be taken into account more readily by staff, particularly when their physicians support them. By controlling their dying, they exert control over themselves. Second, and perhaps more important, is the *sustained support* of another (Lofland 1977). Although more practitioners are increasingly sensitive to the needs of the dying, a devoted family member, especially a spouse, typically plays the role of creating a situation wherein patients may retain possession of their selves while in the final stages of dying. Fortunately, current trends support the creation of organizational structures wherein the preservation of the dying self becomes more possible. Whether those who give support are family members or organizational agents, they not only support the emotional responses of the dying but also serve as interpretators of their wishes. When necessary on behalf of the dying, these individuals may need to pressure physicians for medications, refuse treatments causing unnecessary pain, or disregard hospital rules (see Driver 1978). When dying occurs at home, these individuals may give comfort and care in ways that demonstrate the continued symbolic significance of the dying person to others.

Consequently, the problematic features of maintaining a self while dying reveal in bold relief the *social nature* of the self whether the self is diminished or preserved. To the extent that a diminished self is neither nurtured nor validated as dying occurs, the patient is apt to be stripped bare of selfhood before death. While some dying individuals indicate that their innermost self still remains intact, it might be at the cost of a world so diminished that only unshared remnants of memory, fleeting perception, and feeling remain. Perhaps, then, one of the most significant aspects of the growing concern with death is that more of the dying may be encouraged to remain themselves as they die. If so, there might be far less emphasis on keeping the drug dosage so high that an otherwise sentient patient cannot experience dying. And with the new interest in relationships between consciousness and "clinical" death, more people might express the wish to be aware at the moment of death.

Moments of "Death"

What is known about the final moments of dying? Is there any way to tell what it is like to be dead? Recent interest in near-death experiences of those who were pronounced clinically dead has raised anew the question of life after death. Moody (1975, 1977) is perhaps most known for his controversial qualitative study of survivors of clinical death. He developed a model of the common elements of near-death experiences recalled by these survivors. Although any one survivor's experience may differ slightly from the model, Moody presents the following sequence as typical of a near-death experience.

According to Moody, these survivors are aware of being pronounced dead while they are in great physical distress. At that point, they hear a loud noise and experience extremely rapid movement through a long tunnel. Afterwards, these survivors become aware of viewing their bodies from a great distance. Many recall witnessing the attempts to resuscitate them. Moody reports that these persons state that they still have a form although they are separated from their physical bodies. They next become aware of being greeted by dead relatives or friends who come to help them. They feel a loving spirit represented by a bright light. Although communication with the being transcends language, the being asks for an evaluation of the person's life. To assist in this, a panoramic, sequential review of the images that constitute major life events is experienced. Then, according to Moody, these individuals move to a border or barrier between this world and the next. While wishing to go on, they realize that they must return. Often, unfulfilled duties such as raising children tug the unwilling back to life.

The notion of panoramic memory in Moody's model is particularly interesting since it coincides with commonsense beliefs about the moments directly preceding death. In their study of 205 accounts of life-threatening danger, Noyes and Kletti (1977) found that 60 persons reported panoramic memory. Most of these persons felt that death was imminent as their lives were threatened either by accident or drowning.

Panoramic memory is characterized by the *intensity* and *rapidity* of *vivid imagery*. The images of the past are so vivid that some persons felt they were actually reliving the scenes. Ordinary ways of relating to time and space have no meaning. The progressive reliving of events may seem endless but occurs in a relatively short time, a few seconds or minutes. Noyes and Kletti state that the images include views of the future as well as the past. Noyes and Kletti suggest that immersion in the images of the past is a way of easing the reality of death. One of their respondents viewed her panoramic memory as a last attempt to hang on to life. Noyes and Kletti view panoramic memory as the attachment individuals have for the *symbols* of their existence.

What does this type of experience mean? While some may claim that near-death experiences of this sort offer incontrovertible "proof" of a hereafter, others are not so convinced. Though there is no scientific proof that consciousness is sustained over time after "death," intriguing parallels between near-death experiences as related by contemporary researchers and notions of death in diverse religions may be discerned (see Holck 1978; Lee 1974). The loud reverberating noise is mentioned in *The Tibetan Book of the Dead*, as is the emphasis on pure consciousness. At least several Indian cultures view death as journeying across a river or boundary beyond which someone's deceased relatives are waiting to help. And the dazzling light at the end of the tunnel has strong parallels in *The Tibetan Book of the Dead* as well as in Christian thought. The classic illustration of the mystical light comes at the end of Tolstoy's *The Death of Ivan Ilych* with the statement, "In place of death there was light" (1971, p. 92).

Given these parallels, some may conclude that Moody has tapped a universal experience. But other perplexing questions arise. In looking at the religious and quasi-religious descriptions of death one might ask whether they say something universal about human existence or share some properties that converge in their respective treatments of death? For that matter, is the consciousness reported in these near-death experiences a *reflection* of a shared myth or *evidence* for it? And one might wonder if these experiences alone indicate that earlier definitions of death are inadequate.

Interestingly, researchers in this area are divided on the explanation of near-death phenomena. Noyes and Kletti (1977) propose that panoramic memory is related to the temporal lobe function of the brain. Moody (1977) reports a colleague who makes a point of talking to the patient after "death," not because he believes in a hereafter but because consciousness after death represents residual brain activity to him. Nevertheless, Moody's conclusions are based upon a religious conviction that there is a life after death.

Whatever else, these studies raise provocative issues about the nature of living and dying. Whatever conclusions one makes of them ultimately rest upon faith whether it is in science, religion, or mysticism.

SUMMARY AND IMPLICATIONS

The experience of dying is closely tied with the social setting in which it occurs. Ordinarily, dying takes place in a medical institution, although recent trends show that more families are interested in caring for their dying relatives at home. Keeping the dying at home not only affords them greater psychological comfort but also is sometimes less costly than institutionalized care. Characteristic of institutions that specialize in terminal care is their lack of accountability for it. Clearly, institutions serving the middle and upper classes provide more services for handling the social and psychological aspects of dying than are generally available to the clientele of public institutions. Even private patients in some nursing homes have difficulty obtaining basic maintenance care, much less emotional support while they die. Instead, terminal patients are often treated as if they are socially dead before their actual deaths. This is particularly prevalent because of the isolation and lack of scrutiny of terminal care in general and nursing homes in particular.

Whenever care is given in an institutionalized setting, the organization of work becomes a significant issue for staff. Hence, work priorities rather than patients' personal concerns shape their dying process. Work priorities not only monitor the flow of tasks but also preserve the protective impersonality often characteristic of patient-practitioner relationships. Work priorities are also shaped by the nature of medical problems at hand and the patients' social attributes. Staff tacitly evaluate the relative patients' social value as they gauge their efforts to save him or her particularly when they are faced with more patients than they can adequately serve. Typically, age and social class affect estimations of social value, and greater value is attributed to younger patients with high social status. Those patients whose medical conditions are interesting, however, are typically high on the staff's work priorities despite their low social value.

Although practitioners are handling terminal cancer patients with greater candor than in the past, evasiveness still characterizes much of their inter-action with other patients. Such evasiveness frequently results in the increas-ing isolation of patients as staff avoid them. Simultaneously, patients often seek further information. Over time both may be aware of the patient's im-pending demise, but pretend to ignore it. However, more practitioners are beginning to advocate direct and open communication with the dying. But they usually wait for the patient to initiate questions or comments about dying. Paradoxically, some patients who desire more information are reluctant to press questions and may also lack the verbal skills to effectively engage the practitioner.

Practitioners typically assume that the dying know more about their conditions than is often the case. Subtle indications of serious illness may be normalized by the patient. In addition, patients from the lower classes hold different views than middle-class professionals about their bodies, appropriate treatment, and the value of medical intervention. As a result, practitioners sometimes erroneously believe that patients are aware of their conditions and understand the medical rationale for treatment.

What a patient knows and understands is linked to death expectations based on the relative certainty of death and the projected time of dying. Without death expectations the dying may be as shocked as survivors. Un-certain death but a certain time of resolution of whether the patient will live or die often characterizes crises. In contrast, chronic uncertain time means that death may be continually imminent. Yet certain death is a prediction that may not be accompanied by estimations of exactly when it will occur. Some patients develop a reverence for life when they face certain death with or with-out a certain time limitation. The present is intensely lived as they cannot defer living until later. Thus living under the threat of death results in a new perspec-tive on life. The vitality of these patients contrasts greatly with many whose lingering deaths are certain but believed to be overdue. When this occurs, patients are kept alive by artificial means or remain otherwise dependent upon others. Implicit within death expectations are assumptions held by partici-pants about the correct or appropriate time to die. Hence, dying at the wrong time raises questions about the patient's will to live and the practitioner's competence.

During the dying process, patient's attitudes are believed to shift and change. Kübler-Ross's psychological stages are denial, anger, bargaining, depression, and acceptance. Although these stages were originally intended to be a description of reality, they have become a prescription for it. The stages seem to reflect a process of adapting to dying under conditions when practi-tioners choose to evade it. Denial is a judgment conferred upon patients when they are not aware (or informed) of the meaning of their illnesses. Isolation develops since impending death makes others uncomfortable. Anger is felt by patients when information is gained but time is lost. Depression comes when losses are realized and little time remains. "Acceptance" results when patients are resigned to dying according to the prescriptions of others.

Families also contribute to the social construction of the dying process. They too often feel compelled to hide imminent death from the patient and sometimes from each other. When this occurs, all members, including the dying person, are left on their own to handle it. Families who suffer multiple deaths have special problems. The stress is sometimes so great that one of the dying may be literally abandoned. In other situations the family derive strength from dying members who may give others more support than they receive.

Typically, the dying become more isolated as dying proceeds. Isolation is fostered by the consuming nature of the patient's condition, withdrawal by the patient, and avoidance by others. In the face of their growing isolation, some of the dying seek attention from anyone who will give it, while others give up. Increasingly, more of the terminally ill make their dying public or accept visitors who volunteer to help them. But these alternatives are not available to many.

Reducing isolation and increasing the physical and emotional comfort of patients constitute two conditions for preserving their selves. In the face of institutional uniformity and growing powerlessness, preserving a self is problematic even for those who remain sentient. Staff commonly assist the dying in relinquishing their selves by keeping them over-sedated. Staff may then more easily avoid anguished scenes and in effect claim the patient's self as institutional property to mold into their routine work of terminal care.

Despite the seemingly harsh dimension of dying in institutions, some research indicates that those who have experienced "clinical death" do not view the dying process negatively. Rather, they describe their experiences of rapid movement through a tunnel, separation from their physical bodies and panoramic memory as inviting. Their accounts of "dying" are remarkably similar to commonsense beliefs held about it in a number of cultures. Although some claim that these accounts validate beliefs in an afterlife, others see it as a reflection of a shared myth. In addition, scientific issues are raised since clinical death may not be a definitive equivalent to what death is, and, last, the images perceived by these individuals may not approximate "real" death.

Although many implications might be drawn from the preceding analysis, I wish to focus on those concerning the *patient's self* and the *social control* ordinarily exerted by practitioners. It may help to put the issue of denial of death into perspective by linking it with the patient's self-image. Cues of impending death or even direct statements forewarning the patient of its probability may be denied when they are discrepant with the patient's present self-image. What I am suggesting then is that the realization of one's impending demise must be integrated with one's self-image. And self-images tend to be somewhat entrenched; they often reflect the past more than present experience until individuals realize that they are identified by the present experience. Thus, when cues about bad news are given that do not reflect subjective views of self, they are unlikely to be understood, particularly when symptoms are not yet remarkable. Many patients then will only gradually integrate the knowledge of impending death into their self-images.

Patients' selves are also affected by the way practitioners control information. As patients begin to suspect the possibility of a poor prognosis, a *suspended self* may emerge. They are waiting to live or to die as they wait for news and decisions. But in the interim, as the patients feel the uncertainty of waiting, their self-images may become more open to definitions from others about who they are becoming. When information is delayed by practitioners or never given directly, but is gleaned by the patient, the self may no longer be suspended, but there may be too little time for living according to the patient's wishes, a realization that leads to depression.

There are other more tangible effects of withholding information. Not only is the patient's fear likely to be intensified, but also a certain lack of trust is displayed toward the patient. At a time when the patient's self-image may already rest on shaky grounds, the actions of practitioners may confirm self-doubts and undermine self-esteem. In addition, a paradox often occurs. Many practitioners assume that seriously ill patients revert to child-like behavior while simultaneously demanding passive and dependent roles from them. And because the practitioners view them as child-like and unable to cope, they are unlikely to inform them of bad news. Clearly, this ideological view justifies and perpetuates the kind of social control traditionally exerted by practitioners over their patients.

With the combined effects of prolonged dying and patient advocacy, practitioners may cease to play the role of social control agents to the extent they have in the past. But I think the amount of control they take will vary under different circumstances and in different milieus. While some patients may develop equalitarian relationships with staff, others might be relinquished to the care of other practitioners whom I believe may increase the amount of social control exerted over them.

REFERENCES

Anderson, Robert (1974). Notes of a survivor. In Stanley B. Troup and William A. Greene (eds.), *The Patient, Death and the Family*. New York: Charles Scribner's Sons.

Austin, Vaughn (1976). Life and death in a nursing home. Unpublished paper, Sonoma State College, California.

Beard, Bruce H. (1977). Hope and fear with hemodialysis. In E. Mansell Pattison (ed.), *The Experience of Dying*. Englewood Cliffs, N.J.: Prentice-Hall.

Bergman, Abraham B. (1978). Psychological aspects of sudden unexpected death in infants and children. In Charles A. Garfield (ed.), *Psychosocial Care of the Dying Patient*. New York: McGraw-Hill.

Calkins, Kathy (1970). Time: perspectives, marking and styles of usage. *Social Problems* 17:487-501.

_____ (1972). Shouldering a burden. *Omega* 3:23-36.

Carey, Raymond G., and Emil J. Posavac (1978-79). Attitudes of physicians on disclosing information to and maintaining life for terminal patients. *Omega* 9:67-77.

Charmaz, Kathy Calkins (1973). Time and identity: the shaping of selves of the chronically ill. Ph.D. dissertation, University of California, San Francisco.

_____ (1977). Time perspectives of the chronically ill. Paper presented at the annual meeting of the American Sociological Association, Chicago.

_____ (1978). Time and the situated self. Paper presented at the annual meeting of the Pacific Sociological Association, Spokane, Washington.

Cimmons, Marlene (1978). How a dying woman rages against her fate. *San Francisco Chronicle*, July 18, 1978.

Cohen, Pauline, Israel M. Dizenhuz, and Carolyn Winger (1977). Family adaptation to terminal illness and death of a parent. *Social Casework* 58:223-28.

Death companionship: work of threshold (1975). *Time* 105:68.

Death in the first person (1970). *American Journal of Nursing* 70:336.

DeFrancisco, Don, and Donald E. Watson (1977). A father with leukemia. In E. Mansell Pattison (ed.), *The Experience of Dying*. Englewood Cliffs, N.J.: Prentice-Hall.

Driver, Caroline (1978). What a dying man taught doctors about caring. In Charles A. Garfield (ed.), *Psychosocial Care of the Dying Patient*. New York: McGraw-Hill.

Erickson, Richard C., and Bobbie J. Hyerstay (1974). The dying patient and the double bind hypothesis, *Omega* 5:287-98.

Evans-Wentz, W. Y., (ed.) (1960). *The Tibetan Book of the Dead*. New York: Oxford University Press.

Fischoff, J., and N. O'Brien (1978). After the child dies. In Charles A. Garfield (ed.), *Psychosocial Care of the Dying Patient*. New York: McGraw-Hill.

Foster, Lee (1977). Man and machine: life without kidneys. In Howard D. Schwartz and Cary S. Kart (eds.), *Dominant Issues in Medical Sociology*. Reading, Mass.: Addison-Wesley.

Garfield, Charles A. (1978). Elements of psychosocial oncology: doctor-patient relationships in terminal illness. In Charles A. Garfield (ed.), *Psychosocial Care of the Dying Patient*. New York: McGraw-Hill.

Glaser, Barney G., and Anselm L. Strauss (1964). The social loss of dying patients. *American Journal of Nursing* 64:119-21.

_____ (1965). *Awareness of Dying*. Chicago: Aldine.

_____ (1968). *Time for Dying*. Chicago: Aldine.

Gustafson, Elizabeth (1972). Dying: the career of the nursing home patient. *Journal of Health and Social Behavior* 13:226-35.

Harjan, Nancy (1968). One family's experience with death. In Charles A. Garfield (ed.), *Psychosocial Care of the Dying Patient*. New York: McGraw-Hill.

Hertzberg, Leonard J. (1977). Living in a cancer unit. In E. Mansell Pattison (ed.), *The Experience of Dying*. Englewood Cliffs, N.J.: Prentice-Hall.

Hogshead, Howard P. (1978). The art of delivering bad news. In Charles A. Garfield (ed.), *Psychosocial Care of the Dying Patient*. New York: McGraw-Hill.

Holck, Fredrick H. (1978). Life revisited (Parallels in death experiences). *Omega* 9:1-11.

Jaffe, Lois, and Arthur Jaffe (1977). Terminal candor and the coda syndrome: a tandem view of fatal illness. In Herman Feifel (ed.), *New Meanings of Death*. New York: McGraw-Hill.

Kaplan, David M., Aaron Smith, Rose Grobstein, and Stanley E. Fishman (1978). Family mediations of stress. In Charles A. Garfield (ed.), *Psychosocial Care of the Dying Patient*. New York: McGraw-Hill.

Kelly, Orville Eugene (1977). Make today count. In Herman Feifel (ed.), *New Meanings of Death*. New York: McGraw-Hill.

_____ (1978). Living with a life-threatening illness. In Charles A. Garfield (ed.), *Psychosocial Care of the Dying Patient*. New York: McGraw-Hill.

Kübler-Ross, Elisabeth (1969). *On Death and Dying*. New York: Macmillan.

_____ (1970). The dying patient's point of view. In Orville G. Brim, Jr., Howard E. Freeman, Sol Levine, and Norman A. Scotch (eds.), *The Dying Patient*. New York: Russell Sage Foundation.

Lee, Jung Young (1974). *Death and Beyond in the Eastern Perspective*. New York: Interface Books.

Lofland, Lyn H. (1977). The face of death and the craft of dying: individual and collective constructions. Unpublished manuscript, University of California, Davis.

Marshall, Victor W. (1975). Socialization for impending death. *American Journal of Sociology* 80:1124-44.

Mendelson, Mary A. (1974). *Tender Loving Greed*. New York: Knopf.

Millman, Marcia (1977). Medical mortality review: a cordial affair. In Howard D. Schwartz and Cary S. Kart (eds.), *Dominant Issues in Medical Sociology*. Reading, Mass.: Addison-Wesley.

Moody, Raymond A. (1975). *Life After Life*. New York: Bantam Books.

_____ (1977). *Reflections on Life After Life*. New York: Bantam, Mockingbird Books.

Noyes, Russell and Ray Kletti (1977). Panoramic memory: response to threat of death. *Omega* 8:181-94.

Pattison, E. Mansell (1977a). The dying experience—retrospective analyses. In E. Mansell Pattison (ed.), *The Experience of Dying*. Englewood Cliffs, N.J.: Prentice-Hall.

_____ (1977b). The experience of dying. In E. Mansell Pattison (ed.), *The Experience of Dying*. Englewood Cliffs, N.J.: Prentice-Hall.

Quint, Jeanne C. (1967). *The Nurse and the Dying Patient*. New York: Macmillan.

Rea, M. Priscilla, Shirley Greenspoon, and Bernard Spilka (1975). Physicians and the terminal patient: some selected attitudes and behavior. *Omega* 6:291-305.

Roberts, Cecilia M. (1977). *Doctor and Patient in the Teaching Hospital*. Lexington, Mass.: D.C. Heath, Lexington Books.

Rosenblatt, Daniel, and Edward A. Suchman (1964). Blue-collar attitudes and information toward health and illness. In Arthur B. Shostak and William Gomberg (eds.), *Blue-Collar World*. Englewood Cliffs, N.J.: Prentice-Hall.

Rosenthal, Ted (1973). *How Could I Not Be Among You*. Evanston, Ill.: Eccentric Circle Cinema Workshop of Evanston, Illinois.

Saunders, Cicely (1978). Terminal care. In Charles A. Garfield (ed.), *Psychosocial Care of the Dying Patient*. New York: McGraw-Hill.

Schulz, Richard, and David Aderman (1976). How the medical staff copes with dying patients: a critical review. *Omega* 7:11-21.

Seligman, Roslyn (1977). The burned child. In E. Mansell Pattison (ed.), *The Experience of Dying*. Englewood Cliffs, N.J.: Prentice-Hall.

Shneidman, Edwin S. (1978). Some aspects of psychotherapy with dying persons. In Charles A. Garfield (ed.), *Psychosocial Care of the Dying Patient*. New York: McGraw-Hill.

Simpson, Michael A. (1976). Brought in dead. *Omega* 7:243-48.

Stannard, Charles I. (1976). Old folks and dirty work: the social conditions for patient abuse in a nursing home. In Cary S. Kart and Barbara B. Manard (eds.), *Aging in America: Readings in Social Gerontology*. Port Washington, N.Y.: Alfred Publishing Co.

Strauss, Anselm L., and Barney G. Glaser (1970). *Anguish*. Mill Valley, Calif.: Sociology Press.

Sudnow, David (1967). *Passing On*. Englewood Cliffs, N.J.: Prentice-Hall.

Swanson, Thomas R., and Marcia J. Swanson (1977). Acute uncertainty: the intensive care unit. In E. Mansell Pattison (ed.), *The Experience of Dying*. Englewood Cliffs, N.J.: Prentice-Hall.

Toch, Rudolph (1977). Cancer in the school-age child. In E. Mansell Pattison (ed.), *The Experience of Dying*. Englewood Cliffs, N.J.: Prentice-Hall.

Tolstoy, Leo (1971). The death of Ivan Illych. In Frances Scott and Ruth M. Brewer (eds.), *Confrontation of Death*. Corvallis, Oreg.: Continuing Education Publications. (First published in 1886.)

Townsend, Claire (1971). *Old Age: the Last Segregation*. New York: Grossman.

Weisman, Avery D. (1978). Misgivings and misconceptions in the psychiatric care of terminal patients. In Charles A. Garfield (ed.), *Psychosocial Care of the Dying Patient*. New York: McGraw-Hill.

CHAPTER SIX

DEATH WORK— PROCESSING THE DYING AND THE DEAD

Working with the dying and dead on an everyday basis poses dilemmas for the worker. In general, death workers tend to handle their situation by *routinizing* their work. In what way is death made routine? In this chapter, I shall attempt to answer this question. The effects of death work on the self-images of workers raise interesting issues. Some enlightened death workers not only advocate openness in the face of death but also predicate their self-images on helping others face their deaths. Nevertheless, I propose that the dominant stance of death workers is still to create barriers between their work and their self-images. From their perspective, then, who they are should not be defined by what they do, which is seen negatively. Having ruled out a definition in terms of function, death workers are left with tentative, often problematic alternatives. Like workers in other problematic work situations, they adopt similar strategies for defining themselves and handling their jobs: Primarily, workers deal with death work by making it *routine*. In doing so, they not only separate it from themselves but also *manage* the kinds of issues that death could conceivably raise at work.

Three major themes are addressed in this chapter: (1) the management of death in medical settings, (2) the routinization of ordinary death in the world of work, and (3) the work of the funeral director. In total, these themes constitute major areas in which the reality of death work is socially constructed by participants in their everyday work worlds.

THE MANAGEMENT OF DEATH IN MEDICAL SETTINGS

One area in which the consequences of institutionalized values are clearly discernible is in the medical management of death work. By sharing and negotiating meanings, a social reality is constructed that makes the management of death work possible in these settings. The physical plant, ward organization, and specialized treatment facilities all contribute to the ways in which meanings about death are revealed in death work. In different medical arenas, widely different values about death may be discerned in the management of death work. These values are played out in four major stances toward death work: (1) *minimizing*, (2) *hiding*, (3) *flaunting*, and (4) *acknowledging death*. Since minimizing and hiding death are central stances around which work is conventionally organized, greatest attention is given to them. Because minimizing the effects of death serves to hide it, these two stances will be treated together. While flaunting and acknowledging death may not be mutually exclusive, these stances have somewhat different implications for the management of death work and will thus be treated separately. These two stances deserve mention since they reflect changing meanings of death in the minds of the workers.

Minimizing and hiding death in medical institutions revolves around keeping it *invisible* and *separate* so that what is ordinarily construed as the real world of work takes on social and symbolic precedence. Under these conditions, death is kept separate and invisible from the wider community as well as from the patients. The values that keep middle-class people apart from aspects of life they deem unpleasant, such as living close to people who are disabled, old, poor, or ethnic, also are operative when we think of the dying and the dead. Consequently, establishments for housing the dying and the dead tend to be relegated to areas separated from residential communities. For example, a community was outraged when a funeral director wished to set up a funeral home for lower-income people in a neighborhood that had young children in it.

Often, medical institutions do not serve the locale in which they are situated. That is, they may be located in a particular area and business may be conducted on a routine basis, but their business remains almost incidental to the life going on around the institution. The institution remains enclosed and contained; hence, the dying and the dead remain invisible and separate. Furthermore, even when an institution is situated in the neighborhood it serves, social barriers are constructed to preserve the separation of the living from the dying and the dead.

In any case, when dying and ordinary existence take place within the same institution, such as within a retirement community or a long-term care facility, staff typically organize the areas of the institution according to the physical status (that is, relative distance to death) of those served. In retirement communities, then, one might find a marked social distance between the living and dying. Under these conditions, the period of being a patient before death may serve to decrease the impact of individuals' absences from their previously established groups since they may no longer be perceived a part of everyday life. Consequently, death work is made easier for staff, and the world of death is kept separate from other members of the community. That separateness is enhanced in those settings comprised primarily of single persons rather than couples. That is, when the institution typically serves only the person who is in need of care, separating the world of the dying from the world of those who will live is easier. In contrast, when both partners are integrated into the everyday life of the institution, one spouse's presence may come to symbolize the fate of the other. The character of the concern expressed for the dying spouse is apt to permeate both settings. That, in addition to the spouse's later bereavement, may result in a much lengthier symbolic tie than might have otherwise occurred between the resident group and dying persons, since the group is forced to take into account their presence for a much longer time. (Even when couples are recruited by the management of the establishment, their actual numbers may be quite small by the time they seek this kind of living arrangement. For example, in Victor Marshall's study (1975) of a retirement community, 78 percent of the residents were female, but only 15 percent of them were married.)

The greater the proximity of able patients or residents to those who are dying, the more work staff tend to devote to keeping death separate from them. In effect, death becomes more work. A fair share of that work results from the assumption that other patients and residents must not be exposed to what has happened or is happening. But staff members often do this because they perceive that hiding death and keeping silent about it are convenient ways of handling the situation. No doubt part of their reluctance to treat the situation openly is that doing so might force them to treat death in ways other than *routine*. If they could not routinize death, they might be confronted with more work. They might even question their beliefs and actions concerning death. Further, nursing staff typically attempt to remain silent about death in general and their own death work in particular. As one of the aides in Gubrium's study states, "It's not good to talk about death in front of the more alert ones. If they got frightened, it would just make your work that much harder" (1975, p. 207).

Thus, elaborate strategies and techniques may be developed by the staff to better hide the fact of death. For example, special codes are used over the intercom system to alert appropriate staff of a death without disclosing it to patients. The dead person is taken out by a rear entrance while the other patients are safely cloistered in the dining hall. Similarly, when rooms are shared, the nursing staff will often move the dying patient to a single room, if space permits, or make certain that the roommate is occupied elsewhere when the final stages of dying occur.

The extent to which these strategies are successful is contingent upon the *symbolic significance* of the person who is dying to others who are aware of the impending death. This brings up a crucial point. In those chronic care institutions serving as repositories for the dying, much of the anonymity of patients characteristic in acute care institutions is evident. To the extent that given patients have had significant identities within the institution, covering up their dying can become a touchy issue. The difficulty is further increased if, by virtue of their claims to maintaining prior identities, dying patients insist upon seeing old friends and acquaintances. This may cause strain for the staff since death work, as traditionally conceived in these institutions, must be conducted in private. (Over-sedation may, of course, be a direct consequence of such issues.)

Despite the work typically conducted by staff to keep death contained, noticeable lapses are apt to be evident when they define patients as "senile" or uncomprehending. Under these circumstances, nursing staff are likely to be quite graphic about the details of their death work. Gubrium gives an example of an aide explaining a crude technique of forcing stuck dentures out of the deceased's mouth in the presence of a presumably unalert patient. As the two aides left the room, the patient muttered, "What a thing to talk about" (1975, p. 207).

To the extent that divergent definitions are held between patients and staff about the process and proper etiquette of dying, dying can become a continual source of conflict between patients and staff. For less reverent patients, finding out what is being kept hidden from them can become something of a game. For example, in one of my earlier studies of a chronic care institution, some of the younger patients (who were not intimate with those who died) would take macabre delight in detecting deaths and confronting nurses with their discoveries.

Managing this type of death work in institutions for the aged appears to become easier when patients are socialized into passive roles. Marshall (1975) found that staff in a home for the aged viewed the residents as being "just like children," and they were treated as such. Under these conditions, residents or patients are apt simply to pass time until death. They become passive objects who are put through the institutional paces of everyday life by the management. Although such passivity may in the short run make death work seemingly easier for the staff, the kind of resignation Marshall saw in the residents does not necessarily lead to "acceptance" of death by patients. Death becomes viewed as preferable to living, simply because the constraints of living have become so great.

Because of the degree of specialization within the medical care system, different institutions vary in their service to the dying. An unintended consequence of the medical care system is that patients are systematically shunted through various kinds of institutions as their conditions worsen. Hence, not all medical organizations are equally adept at managing death, as it may not be a part of their everyday work. Interestingly, handling death would seem to be a natural part of life in medical facilities; but participants may view death as something beyond their domain of work and skill.

One often-heard statement in such establishments as chronic care hospitals, retirement homes, and even hospital wards is, "death does not occur here." Thus one might encounter (as I have) an administrator of an institution that primarily serves the elderly who states, "Nobody dies here—anyone who is terminal is transferred." The implication is that patients are not allowed to die there—dying in such a setting is an inappropriate mode of behavior. When they wish to present an image of their facility as one geared toward recuperation, not dying, administrators are particularly likely to utter this kind of statement. Besides, they may think it much better for public relations if aspects of the care of dying patients are minimized lest they earn a stigma for their association with death. An extreme example is shown by the hospital director of an institution for terminal cancer patients whose entire emphasis is upon the rehabilitative and treatment aspects of the program when talking with community members.

As indicated above, the ready solution to the problem of death in these situations is the transfer of the patient. Separating patients or transferring them ordinarily serves to make death more hidden or removed from others. In that way, death work becomes more circumscribed, *contained*, as it were, by territorial boundaries. Sentient patients, however, usually become aware of the meanings of different territories. Yet even the containment of death is not always successful. Slipups occur when staff make errors in their assessments of a patient's symptoms or when a patient dies suddenly from a cardiac arrest or stroke.

An unintended consequence of drugging patients heavily so they will not become management problems is that they remain unaware of dying and the death work going on around them. For example, in an earlier study I discovered old men living in a 10-bed ward who were so drugged and lulled by the institutional routines that they no longer bothered to account for others in the ward or the circumstances under which they had departed from it (see Calkins 1970). In this situation, the nurses felt they had to do very little to ensure that patients were socially separated from death, since they were already isolated subjectively from each other.

Alert patients in chronic care institutions organized on the principle of the seriousness of illness, rapidly begin to define transfers as symbolic of a change in their physical status. Transfer to a ward or area taken to be a certain indicator of dying may be met with great fear and recalcitrance on the part of a patient who refuses to be identified as moribund. Consequently, staff may be deceptive about the patient's destination. For example, in one case a patient was being sent to a nursing home to die, but the nursing assistant told her that she was going "home." Sometimes, however, staff give cues of the actual transfer. For example, in Remarque's *All Quiet on the Western Front* (1929), Peter is told by the Sister that he is going to the "bandaging room," but she makes the mistake of putting his clothes on the cart, a sure symbol of being sent to the "Dying Room" from which no one ever returned. The narrative reads:

Peter understands immediately and tries to roll off the trolley. "I'm stopping here!" They push him back. He cries out feebly with his shattered lung, "I won't go to the Dying Room" (p. 260-261). *

Clearly, managing death work is made easier for the staff if the patient does not make a fuss about being in the final stages of dying. The more the patient accepts the definitions of staff, the more likely dying will be as routine as the preparation of the body that follows it. Then, as noted before, dying is the intermediate stage in which one's body essentially becomes institutional property. If one's dying is viewed as inconsequential by staff, one may become institutional property rather early in the dying process. In this regard, Sudnow (1967) notes that liberties may be taken with the dying patient's body to expedite the later preparation of it for the mortician. Under these conditions, the patient has become integrated in the death work while still alive.

While the patient's body becomes institutional property in the context above, *death* becomes the property of the worker in another stance toward death work that I call flaunting. Flaunting consists of a new mode of handling death characterized by *ostentatious identification* with death and *forced confrontation* of others. No doubt flaunting has emerged in response to the more conventional stances of minimizing and hiding, and in that sense might be an overreaction to earlier ways of handling death work. Workers who flaunt death in this way display a superiority similar to those who saw themselves as sexually liberated not so many years ago. A feeling is imparted of having successfully dealt with a taboo that still plagues others. Consequently, these workers tend to be zealous in their attempts to force patients and workers to confront their feelings about death.

Flaunting is a stance ordinarily found in individual workers, although it could be an organizing principle for ordering the work of an entire group. Despite its comic properties, when flaunting death is a dominant stance toward work, patients may suffer unwarranted intrusions into the dying process by relatively powerful workers. Flaunting needs to be mentioned because it tends to deprive patients of *choice* about their dying and how it is to be handled.

Although not always entirely distinguishable from flaunting, acknowledging death is another emerging stance that workers (and patients alike) are increasingly taking. Acknowledging death makes for a different kind of death work. First, it enables patient and family to *participate* in decisions about how care is to be handled. Second, emphasis shifts to the quality of life experienced while dying, rather than the quantity. Third, pain control is likely to become

* Excerpt from *All Quiet on the Western Front*, by Erich Maria Remarque. "Im Westen Nichts Neves" copyright 1928 by Ullstein, A. G.; Copyright Renewed 1956 by Erich Maria Remarque. "All Quiet on the Western Front" copyright 1929, 1930, by Little, Brown and Company; Copyright renewed 1957, 1958 by Erich Maria Remarque. All Rights Reserved.

more individualized, reflecting the diverse needs of patients. Fourth, greater attention is given to the social-psychological aspects of dying. Fifth, when acknowledging death is a general practice, patients are more apt to become involved in each other's lives as there is no need to keep the dying separate and invisible.

Since the hospice is characterized by a direct commitment to providing care for the terminally ill without hiding it, we need to look at death work in this context. Hospices are designed to combine the skilled care of a medical facility with the warmth of the patient's home (Saunders 1977). Perhaps most fundamentally, death work in these settings is aimed toward creating conditions of physical and psychological comfort for the dying patient (see Kron 1977; Saunders 1977; Stoddard 1978). Because hospice care developed out of the medieval concept of hospitality extended to travelers, patients whom no one else can or wishes to care for are welcomed for as long as they need to stay. Embracing a community spirit, the hospice concept aims to give personal care while maintaining patients' relationships. In that way, the anonymity and isolation characteristic of acute care is diminished. The hospitality extended to patients is also extended to families, who work closely with staff in order that care may take place at home when at all possible (see Saunders 1977).

Because it is believed that a number of problems, such as fear, anxiety, and lengthy hospitalization, emanate from uncontrolled pain, hospice workers maintain a vigorous approach to pain management largely adapted from the techniques developed at St. Christopher's Hospice in London (see Saunders 1977; Stoddard 1978). Not all dying patients are selected for hospice care; for example, patients admitted to St. Christopher's are those who experience "unrelieved distress" (Saunders 1977). Because few hospice organizations in this country have physical plants at present, hospice care is provided for those who wish to die at home and whose physicians will refer them. Hospice care seems to produce highly successful results in making patients more comfortable and thus more able to live while they die.

From what little is reported on the hospice, it appears that the kind of experience patients have when death is acknowledged is markedly improved over other ways of managing death (Saunders 1977; Stoddard 1978). Stoddard tells of a young woman who felt self-hatred, arising from her belief that she was a burden to everyone before coming to the hospice. Not only did her sense of personal worth develop as she was given support from hospice staff, but she also became able to acknowledge her impending death openly with others because she was no longer viewed as a failure.

Personal worth is maximized by local hospice workers by giving the patient control over the dying process. For example, a volunteer from a hospice in Sonoma County is available to the patient on a 24-hour basis to help the patient psychologically (and often medically) and to do those mundane but necessary tasks of maintaining existence. In one situation a woman dying of cancer wished to remain in her home but only had one un-married daughter to help with her care. Hospice volunteer Barbara Anderson (1977) reported this woman's concerns: "Her fear was of being a burden rather than fear of dying. She knew that [death was imminent]; she was well-adjusted to it. She was afraid of being a burden to her daughter."

In this particular case, hospice workers served both the patient and her daughter. By providing assistance with nursing and household tasks, they enabled the daughter to care for the patient at home. Moreover, they enabled the daughter to maintain some privacy and continuity with her former life without feeling guilty about leaving her mother's bedside. Finally, they gave the daughter concern and support following her mother's death.

Whether or not the hospice concept can be fully realized in America remains questionable. Conceivably, the development of hospices could lead to increased fragmentation and specialization in a medical care system already plagued by poorly integrated care. Also, as Holden's (1976) interview with a leading cancer specialist suggests, the kind of community spirit that permeates the English hospice is notably lacking in America. Still, there are strong indi-cations that American hospice advocates share a similar quasi-religious fervor toward their work and are committed to improving the care of the dying. Whether the founders' commitment can survive the institutionalization of the hospice concept remains to be seen. It is even possible that, if fully realized, it may replicate some of the worst features of nursing homes. And all kinds of knotty problems may be anticipated if attempts are made to provide hospice care to all when the existing medical care system is largely based on profit. Still, it appears that hospice workers, both here and in England, construct a context wherein the *quality* of life takes precedence over the quantity.

THE ROUTINIZATION OF DEATH IN EVERYDAY WORK WORLDS

In contrast to hospice workers, who emphasize individualized care and personal concern, most death workers appear to treat death and dying as *routine* events. Now, I will address the characteristics common to the routini-zation of death in diverse settings. What similarities and differences might be drawn between the routinization of death in extraordinary circumstances and in more conventional work situations? In order to illustrate the dilemmas in both situations, I include a description of the death work done by the coroner's office since the work of the coroner's deputies in announcing an unexpected death to relatives highlights a common problem encountered in death work settings. There is a significant disparity between the meaning of a given death for the workers and for the relatives of the deceased. While a death may be routine for workers, they must deal with persons who are emotionally in-volved with the newly deceased and for whom the death constitutes an extra-ordinary event.

Routinizing Death Work

Clearly, death work has become increasingly routinized through bureaucratic procedures that make immediate tasks routine and foster a diminishment of the social and symbolic consequence of death and death-related events for the workers. Still, those who must work with the dying, dead, and bereaved confront many situations characterized by strained interaction. That problem becomes intensified when workers' specific tasks entail some level of attention, agreement, and participation from those who are immediately involved with the death. In the hospital situation, as noted in Chapter 5, many staff members, who do not like to discuss death, avoid dying patients and their families. Such avoidance may be justified in the worker's mind by giving higher priority to patients who are expected to live. This justification may be awarded support by staff and families alike when scarcity of time forces staff members to make explicit choices about who is to receive close professional attention.

One of the more dramatic portrayals of how death is handled through avoidance by death workers is Sudnow's description (1967) of the morgue attendant who was viewed by other workers as a *symbolic marker* of death itself. That there was only one morgue attendant and that he necessarily visited the wards reinforced the symbolic, death-linked definition of his identity. Typically, he was avoided by other workers or, if by chance they did interact with him in informal conversation, they plied him with intrusive questions so that he was not permitted to forget his association with death.

Sudnow's example of the morgue attendant is particularly striking since he was left on his own to manage the negative connotations of death that surrounded him. Without belonging to a group employed in similar tasks, such workers are unlikely to effectively counteract the stigma conferred upon them. In contrast, individuals who work in concert with persons performing similar death-related tasks are more likely to develop ideologies to explain and justify their work, regardless of whether they accept the potentially discrediting social identification that is often made with it. Thus when group solidarity is maintained, a degree of personal dignity can be fostered for the individual worker in the face of negative definitions by outsiders.

Two occupational groups that typically afford their workers this kind of support are coroners and funeral directors. In both occupational groups ties tend to be maintained with others who provide similar tasks. Coroners often work in an organizational unit with peers performing similar tasks, whereas funeral directors maintain ties with colleagues through their affiliations with occupational associations, if not always through daily work situations.

Since workers in most areas of death work emphasize routinizing activities directly connected with death, they develop styles of interaction that increase their control over the definition of the situation. By minimizing the potentially disruptive interactional features of confronting death, they accomplish two objectives. One objective is *self-protection* from anxiety, embarrassment, or other disquieting personal feelings that might emerge if deepest assumptions about life and death were to be challenged. The other objective is efficiency in completing the work. In the case of the funeral director, the profit motive may enter heavily into decisions to act efficiently, while for other workers, such as the coroner's deputies, motives may be slanted toward getting the tasks done without undue harassment or disruption from newly bereaved family members. In any event, these workers have powerful incentives for attempting to maintain control of the interactional situations in which they are involved.

Interactional Strategies for Routinizing Death Work

The routinization of death work is constructed in the everyday encounters of the workers. In the following pages, the interactional strategies that coroner's deputies use will be discussed to illustrate how death workers attempt to maintain the routine character of their work, despite circumstances that easily lead to strained interaction with involved members of the public. (The following analysis is taken from my study of coroner's deputies in three counties. All deputies were men who either had had prior experience in police work or had been embalmers.*)

In these coroners' departments, the ways in which deaths are announced to heretofore unsuspecting relatives are strategically constructed with an eye toward accomplishing the objectives of getting the relatives to quietly accept both the burial costs and the death without the deputy's personal involvement. Burial costs are likely to be the "real" issue in counties without access to inexpensive burials. Then, the deputies feel constrained to handle the notification of death strategically in order that the family readily assume the costs of disposal of the body. Consequently, the strategies employed in announcing the death to relatives differ according to the necessity of getting them to pay for burial costs. When this is necessary and therefore an important part of the deputys' work, special techniques are likely to be employed. Notably, strategic control of the encounter is enhanced by making the announcement in person. The deputies then lay the grounds for ensuring that an uneventful and speedy disposition of the body is made at the expense of the family. The other objective, to induce the relative to accept the death as real, coincides with the deputys' interest in making the announcement of death efficiently without eliciting a subsequent fuss from the bereaved or becoming involved themselves. Part of doing that means constructing situations in which the deputys' sense of self is protected in addition to their control over the encounter in

* Much of the subject analysis has been adapted from "The Coroner's Strategies for Announcing Death," by Kathy Calkins Charmaz, reprinted from *Urban Life*, Volume 4, No. 3 (October, 1975), pp. 296-316, by permission of the publisher, Sage Publications, Inc.

which they are engaged. Self-protection strategies are employed to maintain the routine character of the work and to keep the deputies from feeling personally involved in the ongoing scene. Clearly, the *distance* deputies place between themselves and death is potentially diminished while they are involved in making the announcement of death since possibilities arise for questions and concerns from survivors. Although deputies are more directly confronted with issues concerning death than most persons in everyday worlds, they disavow holding views about death different from those held by anyone else. Indeed, what is striking is the degree to which their views reflect typical cultural taboos. For the most part, the deputies show an avoidance of death, discomfiture over the expression of grief by survivors, and an absence of a personal philosophy about death in general and their own deaths in particular.

Yet the deputies have built up a set of fairly consistent beliefs that serve to perpetuate strategies that protect them from entertaining new meanings about the relationship between their work and death. An integral part of these beliefs is the view that death is an *external* event that is almost completely *separate* from the everyday worlds of the deputies. Death then becomes subjectively interpreted by the deputies as being the incidental *source* of their work, a by-product of the work rather than the focus of it. A main source of self-protection is based on the deputies' emphasis on the routine aspects of the work as the "real" activity. Constructing this definition of reality takes continued effort and is particularly problematic when the deputy is either with the deceased or the bereaved relatives.

The extent to which death is externalized and separated from the subjective consciousness of the deputy is exemplified by the statement one deputy made: "That's not a body lying there. *It's an investigation.* You have to look at it as an investigation, not a person lying there." By defining the deceased as an "investigation," this deputy is able to maintain his definition of the situation and, moreover, perpetuate his view of death as external and separate from himself.

Occupational ideologies held by the deputies support this view of death since it is generally believed that becoming involved in the situation prevents them from functioning properly in their duties. Since this view of death is shared and reaffirmed, it protects the deputies from experiencing the deaths they encounter in ways other than those officially prescribed.

Part of the self-protection strategy consists of the effort to remain the polite, sincere, authoritative, but basically disinterested, official. This stance becomes particularly apparent when the deputy's taken-for-granted notions of how the relative should respond are disrupted or negated. When the relative is lacking the usual proprieties of such occasions or fails to show the "proper" expression of grief, the deputies may feel constrained to normalize the situation for *themselves* instead of the relative. An example was given by a deputy whose taken-for-granted notions about grief were upset when he informed a young wife of her husband's death several hours before in a traffic accident. She said, "It couldn't have happened to a nicer guy and I'm not sorry." When the relative appears to take the "bad news" with so little seeming affect, deputies then have to make sense of the situation in order to integrate the discrepant information into their view of reality.

The strategies for making the announcement help the deputies remain in control of the situation and handle the special problems that emerge in the course of interaction. Not the least of these problems is the necessity of deputies to construct the *contextual properties* of the announcing scene besides constructing the *announcement* itself. In other words, they must create the kind of ambience and interactional circumstances wherein the announcement logically fits so that it is effective and believable; they have no ready-made scene to serve as an official backdrop for their proclamation.

Since they essentially have no organizational props or dramaturgical aids to create the proper atmosphere of the scene, the deputies strategically manage the encounter so that the scene is built up through their use of impression management and strategic disclosure of cues (Goffman 1959, 1972). Compared to physicians who announce "bad news" to the relative, deputies have a weighty problem. Besides their much lesser amount of authority and prestige, deputies lack the advantages typically possessed by physicians of a prior relationship with the relative, a fitting organizational setting for giving the news, and a series of prior interactional cues that serve to prepare the relative (Sudnow 1967).

Since deputies have neither the structural supports provided by the hospital situation nor the physician's status, they must devise tactics to get their work done without incident. Typically, their objectives are to announce quickly, to turn the responsibility of the body and its subsequent burial expense over to the family, and to determine that the person who received the news is holding up well or is with someone. But all these tasks may be embellishments to their main task of the disposition of the body and getting the family to assume the expenses, when this is their real objective.

Deputys' first strategic maneuver is to make certain that they have the correct person. Since high transiency rates exist in parts of urban centers, the deputies may, at times, feel compelled to ascertain that they have the right person. Similarly, when the announcement is made by telephone, deputies must first *ask* if they actually have the right party.

Once they are assured that the correct person has been located, they must then ensure that the relative accepts *their* identity as real. Thus a potential problem for deputies that occasionally arises is the refusal of the relative to recognize them as bona fide members of the coroner's office and the bearer of bad news. Consequently, through use of gestures, tone of voice, and body positioning, the deputies attempt to create a first impression of themselves that will set the tone of the following encounter (cf. Schwartz 1974).

A useful strategy that some deputies employ, particularly when they have confronted the issue of nonrecognition as a coroner's deputy, is to take a neighbor with them. Taking the neighbor with them is primarily a justification for more practical motives. First, the neighbor's accompaniment helps to establish the deputy's identity by legitimating their presence through demonstrating that the neighbor has accepted their identity as real. Second, the deputies protect themselves from refusal to enter the premises by the relative. Third, the neighbor serves as a buttress for the staging of the scene to follow. The concern and gravity written on the neighbor's face quickly cues the survivor that this is, in fact, a very serious occasion. Then, as the deputies introduce themselves and their job affiliation, "they know what is coming." However, from the perspective of the deputies, the most advantageous aspect of this strategy is that by virtue of the neighbor's presence, the deputies are not detained; they can get out almost immediately.

Cues are similarly built up when deputies are unaccompanied or notify by phone. One deputy said that he tried to talk to the relative for a few minutes before making the announcement. He said, "I ask if they have received any phone calls about the member of the family before telling them." The timing of cues is also controlled by officials who phone; they identify themselves, but not their office, since they think that they should give the relative a few cues of lesser weight before getting to the point of the call. They prefer to stall slightly by giving some general statements concerning the fact that they are informing the relative of very serious news. In this way, they strategically set the circumstances wherein the relative will attend to the deputy's interpretation of the news. The deputy supervisor said he usually tells them that "I have some terrible news for you," and he repeats it before going on to the actual announcement.

In both situations, the deputies create the context by rapidly supplying one meaningful cue after another that brings the relative into interaction as they prepare to move into the announcement. Compared to the medical scene, the cues come much more rapidly and sharply. Thus, the cues cannot be easily dismissed, although the survivor has little time to think about them.

Skillful deputies can be expected to handle the situation in such a way that cues will neither be missed nor misinterpreted. The relatives are not permitted enough time to disattend to them and, should they attempt to, the deputies will alter their presentation accordingly. For example, a deputy stated, "Sometimes I'm stern, sometimes I'm sympathetic, sometimes I even shout a little bit louder than they can."

The deputies who telephone find they get a better response when they successively lead the relative into questioning them. By doing so, the officials set the conditions wherein they can impart progressively unpromising news. For example:

> I tell them that he collapsed today while at work. They asked if he is all right now. I say slowly, "Well, no, but they took him to the hospital."

They ask if he is there now. I say, "They did all they could do—the doctors tried very hard." They say, "He is dead at the hospital?" Then I tell them he's at the coroner's office.

Most deputies expressly avoid the word "dead" when first imparting the news, since they feel it is too harsh. Substitutes are used, such as "fatally injured" and "passed away," if they must refer directly to it at all. A preferred technique is to control the interaction so that the relative refers to the person as "dead." Those making telephone announcements attempt to manipulate the conversation so that the relative says the word, "dead." Several deputies remarked that having the survivors themselves say it made the announcement more meaningful to them and the death more "real." Describing a close family member as "dead" becomes symbolic and sets the stage for treating the deceased as such. The deputies then reaffirm the survivor's statements and elaborate on them. Consequently, when the deputy's strategies work, the transition from perceiving one's relative from alive to dead can be made rapidly. The symbolic shift is likely to occur so quickly during the encounter that the relative may remain unaware of how the interaction was managed. Indeed, in an encounter deputies deem successful, the relative is likely to express appreciation for their "sensitivity."

Deputies state that the relatives always ask about the circumstances of dying. The coroners give them what information they have and can release, then turn the situation around by asking about funeral and burial arrangements. To illustrate: "They always ask what happened. Then we reverse it and ask what type of arrangements *they* are going to make."

Or in the case of the telephone notification, the relative typically inquires, "What can I do [to help]?" The deputies simply state, "All you need to do now is call your family funeral director, and he'll direct you." In both situations, this approach gets the relatives down to business and usually results in their agreement to "help" while in the midst of the initial encounter with the deputies. Likely, the relatives have unwittingly volunteered to underwrite the expenditures before they have any conception of the implications or expense. Simultaneously, the deputies have played the role of officials who cut through the survivor's grief and shock by pointing to the work that has to be done. Moreover, the deputies have strategically managed the interactional situation in ways that foster the relative's acceptance of their directives.

THE FUNERAL DIRECTOR'S DEATH WORK

The work of the funeral director ranges from the sales of ceremonial accouterments like wrinkle-free funeral fashions and satin-lined caskets to the preparation of the body with chemical preservatives. In any event, the tasks of the funeral director are set into motion by the selections and preferences of the survivors. As such, death work for the funeral director may be characterized by three basic dimensions including sales, technical skills, and interpersonal relations. After I outline the development of these tasks in the traditional American funeral, I will analyze the work of funeral directors. First, I will clarify their occupational status. Next, I will discuss the significance of selecting arrangements for the work, followed by an examination of the work, which culminates in the funeral ritual. Finally, I will comment on the social meanings of rituals.

The Development of Contemporary Funerals

While funerals have shown some diversity in form and character in recent years, traditional funerals organized by a funeral director remain the common ritual of separation between the living and dead. Social and historical trends that emerged with industrialization appear to have combined in ways that shape contemporary funerals, including (1) urbanization, (2) development of the nuclear family, (3) economic practices, (4) decreased direct exposure to death, and (5) the development of skills in handling the dead. These will be explored throughout this discussion.

A brief historical exploration should clarify the social and cultural trends that gave rise to the emergence of contemporary funeral practices. Philippe Aries (1975) describes these practices in America as "built upon the ruins of Puritanism, in an urbanized culture which is dominated by rapid economic growth and by the search for happiness linked to the search for profit." Still, the American way of handling funerals did not differ markedly from European counterparts until the rapid growth of urbanization following the Civil War. Before then, the funeral was largely a family affair in which members participated in a ritual that was a familiar part of life (Pine 1975). The emergence of the undertaker was spurred by the growth of cities, since the undertaker performed several of the tasks previously conducted by different members of the family. The custom of embalming was given great impetus by the Civil War, since it afforded the transport of the dead back to their home areas without as much odor of decaying flesh. Some thinkers, such as Aries (1975), question whether the development of embalming marked a certain refusal to accept death. Aries notes that in order to sell death, it had to appear to be "friendly." The emphasis on cleanliness, lack of odor, and long-term preservation potentially afforded by embalming presumably became appealing to the American public. Additionally, the shift from the family home to the funeral parlor developed as houses became smaller and more equipment was needed for embalming. And, of course, business conducted in one central location makes for a more efficient enterprise. Quite possibly then, the rise of commercialism in the funeral business began as death became more removed from the home. Nevertheless, the emergence of the funeral director is but one *instance* of a larger trend of *allocating functions* previously performed by intimates to officials in formal organizations.

We must also look at the role of the clientele in the emergence of contemporary funerals. I suggest that funeral rituals are in part our creations, despite the readiness to attribute full responsibility for them to the funeral industry. Though certain aspects of disposing of the dead have become institutionalized by being written into state laws, most states allow much greater flexibility and choice in making funeral and burial arrangements than the populace knows. Lack of public awareness, interest, and collective action perpetuates funeral customs that do not always reflect the preferences of individual clients. Similarly, the funeral industry would not have developed in the ways we can observe in this society if it did not serve some basic social needs, such as providing ritual methods of handling and disposing of the body that leave the bereaved uncontaminated by the "dirty work" involved (see Warner 1977). Gorer (1965) suggests that a social need has arisen to insulate ourselves from death. From a perspective like Gorer's, the role of the funeral director has been constructed so that we do not become preoccupied with death even when we are closest to it.

Nonetheless, aspects of a refusal to let the dead die have proved to be lucrative for the funeral industry. For example, until legally contested, funeral directors were able to claim that sealed caskets would prevent the deceased from decaying. That type of sales approach is believed to have had a powerful appeal to those who had difficulty confronting the reality of death and wished instead to think of their relatives in everlasting sleep.

In a larger context, the rising commercialism throughout society after World War II was echoed in the funeral industry. Although the kind of services, the types of caskets, and market approaches were at times deplored by some sectors of the public, the funeral industry gained a foothold in the market in ways that perpetuated its definitions of the appropriate way of handling the deceased. While the sector of the public that did not condone their practices or wished for greater choice remained relatively unorganized, the funeral industry became quite organized in its efforts to have its interests written into law and reflected in the everyday practices of the funeral ritual.

Clearly, funeral directors could not have successfully survived without the cooperation of the public. In certain intangible ways, funeral directors have filled a social gap in society that in previous times had been filled by members of the extended family or community. They may sometimes undertake subtle tasks, such as keeping family conflict at a minimum and creating a "dignified" atmosphere. Moreover, the funeral director may assume a posture of professional expertise at a critical time when no other authority is available to the bereaved.

Finally, I should note more recent developments in handling and disposing of the dead. While dominant social historical trends gave birth to the conventional funeral, the social response to it has in turn fostered the development of alternatives and innovations to conventional funeral and burial arrangements. Such alternatives as cremation or memorial services without the body present are social responses to elaborate rituals. While these truncated rituals reduce ostentation and costs, they do not seem to ameliorate the more fundamental problems of disruption, grief, and succession caused by death any better than conventional practices.

The Status of the Funeral Director

Since the work of the funeral director is being examined in the context of death work, it becomes necessary to inquire about the nature of this work. What are its distinguishing characteristics? More importantly, to what extent is the funeral director's work "professional"? This question forms the focus of the following discussion.

In order to be classified as a profession, work must be of a complex nature and require highly specialized skills acquired through a lengthy training period to ensure that abstract knowledge will be applied appropriately to specific situations. Like those in other occupations who wish to upgrade and dignify their work, funeral directors attempt to put forth a view of themselves as professionals who provide personal services to their clientele (see Bowman 1959; Pine 1975). But the work of the funeral director may be cast in several different categories inclusive of an entrepreneurial business, a profession, a service occupation, a complex organization, or a commercial trade.

Greenwood (1966), Wilensky (1970), and Parsons (1953) have analyzed the distinguishing characteristics that separate professional work from the rest of the occupational world. Although *expertise* is commonly taken as a major prerequisite of professional work, only those types of expertise broadly based upon a theoretical body of abstract and comprehensive knowledge can be viewed as professional. In this sense, specific problems are solved in relation to the general body of theory possessed by the professional. Because of the need for comprehensive theoretical knowledge, lengthy formal training is necessary. In reference to this first and most significant criteria, funeral directors do not measure up. Their work does not rely upon a systematic basis of abstract theory, nor is it necessary to undertake lengthy training to achieve competence in the field. Moreover, much of their training ordinarily centers on the technical aspects of embalming, and despite their interest in interpersonal relationships, they do not receive professional training in human relations.

Possession of expertise based on theoretical knowledge legitimizes *professional authority* (see Greenwood 1966). Essentially, the professional is *granted* special authority, which means the license to dictate what the client needs. The professional's prerogative is directly linked to the assumption that the client's lack of expertise necessitates professional opinion about *what* the problem is and what course of action should be taken to solve the problem.

Presumably, the professional will take an objective stance toward the client and treat that client impartially. This objective stance is understood to be a spontaneous consequence of the heavy socialization into the system of norms and values shared by the professional group. Because of that socializing, it is assumed that social controls become internalized and will therefore serve the client's best interests rather than the professional's self-interest. This is especially significant since the client probably lacks expertise in these areas and may be unable to evaluate the performance of the professional.

In the sense that Greenwood discusses professional authority, clients have quite a different role than customers. Put succinctly, clients are *forced* to accept the opinions of the professional, whereas customers may bargain and shop for comparative values on the service or object they are seeking. (Despite this, more public information in a number of heretofore professional areas of work, such as medicine and law, has resulted in persons who were relegated to the client status moving toward the customer end of the continuum.) The fact that most people do not systematically shop for a funeral director is, I believe, more by default than acceptance of the funeral director as a professional who has the right to define the services they need. Further, since imminent death is a sensitive topic, family members usually do not wish to shop for funerals at that time even though the possibility of death has become likely. After all, investigating different funeral arrangements for invalids may be defined by others as symbolically equivalent to wishing them dead. Since many families do not or will not shop for funeral services, structural conditions exist for them to grant the funeral director a modicum of professional authority. This authority might otherwise not be possessed since much of the pertinent information could be easily mastered by anyone who took the time to learn it.

The funeral director, who simply is not comparable to other professionals in the realm of professional authority, is similar to business people who know their products and services well and can assist customers in making selections efficiently. Yet, because of the mystifications surrounding death, the public aversion to both death and funerals, and the vulnerability of the bereaved, the funeral director is in an intriguing position by which trade information can be stretched into professional authority. By presenting a calm, authoritative self to the bereaved and giving them the message that they will not have to concern themselves with details, the funeral director may from the beginning establish a degree of professional authority that should not or need not be questioned (cf. Pine 1975).

As far as the legitimation of professional authority, the community granting the profession specified powers and privileges must also be taken into account. The profession's control over the education of its recruits is approved by the community, as are the licensing procedures outlining the tasks to be performed. Hence, if members of an occupation are able to get their prerogatives written into the law, then they can maintain exclusive rights over the area in which they work. Again, the control exerted by funeral directors may be by default rather than active competition with other occupations with less expertise to offer. Further, the preplanning for funeral and burial arrangements that many upper-middle-class people now engage in constitutes a serious challenge to the claims for professional authority that funeral directors attempt to make. Because the customer can make major choices in this area, the funeral director has much less control over claims to unique expertise than those advanced by the physician or attorney.

Another important characteristic of a profession is internalization of a code of ethics, a consequence of lengthy socialization and life-long participation in the professional subculture. In this regard, the extent to which funeral directors have internalized a code of ethics that is shared by all members remains questionable. Although they may share an occupational culture, they clearly do not experience a lengthy training period in which moral values based on altruism are imparted. (Of course, the extent to which altruism has been internalized by members of other professions is also questionable.) However, much of the criticism of the funeral industry is intrinsically related to the issue of moral values. Bowman (1959), Mitford (1963), and Harmer (1963) explicitly argue that the funeral director is interested in profits. Pine (1975), in contrast, emphasizes such personal services as the counseling provided by many funeral directors, particularly those who operate homes without a highly complex, formal organization. But personal services themselves do not constitute sufficient grounds for categorizing the work of the funeral director as professional.

Pine (1975) rightly notes that funeral directors aspire to be "professional" in their work and particularly in the image they have in their communities. By claiming professional status, funeral directors claim prestige and simultaneously seek to minimize the stigma they experience for being death workers involved in "dirty work." But issue may be taken with Pine on his categorization of the funeral director as a professional since he bases it on the grounds that funeral directors hope to improve the public image of the occupation and that they have the knowledge of what to do after a death.

Importantly, the necessary expertise required to provide personal services appears to be limited. Pine's emphasis on the funeral director's strategic mode of self-presentation and impression management leads one to wonder if whatever professional identity the funeral director claims is not open to assessment. The *way* of being a professional would seem to become internalized into the social construction of self. If so, then the played professional roles by and large appear to be spontaneous to the experiencing self as well as to the audience. In short, professional demeanor would become taken for granted. Preoccupations of professionals would be directed toward the client's problems rather than toward their self-consciously managed impressions.

The emphasis on self-conscious impression management described by Pine appears to be a consequence of two concerns of the funeral director: (1) The definition of the situation put forth by the funeral director, though unspoken, is so fragile that it may easily be questioned; and (2) playing a "professional" role appears to instill confidence in the bereaved and allow the funeral director to proceed with arrangements efficiently and smoothly.

While funeral directors may not claim professional status in light of the analysis above, two unique dimensions of their role should be highlighted. First, funeral directors have the sole responsibility of disposing of the dead. No other occupational group is in serious competition with the funeral industry for this task, although the way in which it is done is subject to competition. Second, because of their unusual position, funeral directors may enter into an intense relationship with the bereaved during the critical period following the death.

Personal services that Mitford (1963) calls "grief therapy" and Pine (1975) refers to as "counseling" may be provided. It is at this point that funeral directors as death workers may fill a gap in the social structure. If the bereaved exist in a social world where intimates are not present for direct interactional support or, if present, do not permit the expression of grief, funeral directors may be the recipients of those feelings, whether or not they solicit them. While it is clear that many funeral directors attend to the feelings of the bereaved in a sympathetic, concerned, and attentive manner (see Hutchens 1976; Pine 1975), it is not clear what exactly constitutes "grief therapy." Perhaps as a trade term it allows funeral directors to assert that viewing the embalmed, cosmetically reconstructed, dead individual is therapeutic for the survivors. That issue will be taken up again. For the moment, consider the fact that claims to any therapeutic role would enhance the occupation's professional status.

If funeral directors were, in fact, independent professionals with all the prestige accorded those in professional roles, their jobs would be coveted. But that does not seem to be the case. *Forbes* reports that International Funeral Services Industries bought 102 funeral homes and 17 cemeteries in the United States and Canada when the sons of undertakers opted out of the business ("Consumer Resistance" 1977). (While their stock was hot in 1970, it has since plummetted due to slightly lower death rates and low-profit cremations.) In the future, independent funeral directors might have difficulty maintaining their entrepreneurial status if they become caught between rising expenses and increasing public demand for simple, low-cost funerals. If so, then an increase can be expected in franchises and volume business. At any rate, the trend toward franchised funerals and volume business certainly would seem to diminish the kinds of services upon which professional status is claimed.

A concern with professional image is expressed by Bereday (1977), who argues for upgrading the funeral industry by increasing the educational requirements for its members. He states that funeral directors have a high social and economic visibility in their respective communities but that their high status is not supported by an "appropriate" level of education. Bereday remarks that affluence achieved without education is suspect in today's society. Moreover, he chastizes funeral directors for their gaudy accouterments and occupational argot. To professionalize images of the industry, Bereday makes such recommendations as changing what he calls the "low-class connotation" of the funeral "home" or "parlor" to the funeral "center." Similarly, he recommends that funeral "directors" become funeral "counselors." To do so, he urges training in the understanding of grief, legal, and medical matters. Further, Bereday states, "Above all, there is an obligation to participate in family budgeting" (p. 61).

In summary, it may be argued that the professionalism of the funeral directors seems mostly to lie in the world of appearances. When an impression of being professional is created with similarities to both physicians and clergy, funeral directors gain greater authority and control over the situation. Warner (1977) points out that funeral directors borrow the ritual and sacred skills of the minister besides invoking quasi-religious symbols in language and setting. In addition, they attempt to give an impression of possessing the kind of technical expertise and competence that characterize the physician's role. Despite these impressions their claims for professional status cannot be substantiated.

Selecting Arrangements

The selection of arrangements by the bereaved represents a pivotal area of death work for funeral directors and a major purchase for most families (although less time and thought typically is given to it than for other major purchases). In this section, I will analyze the dilemmas facing family members and the interactional context in which funeral directors work.

Traditionally, when arrangements are selected by the bereaved, three central characteristics of their particular circumstances stand out: (1) the lack of investigation of the kinds of available arrangements and their costs, (2) the negative effect that the emotional reaction to loss has on business negotiations, and (3) the survivors' lack of firsthand experience with the particular funeral director.

All of these characteristics influence the ensuing interaction between funeral director and customer, but the first is particularly important since there is little or no room possible for *comparative shopping*. Without comparative shopping, customers have lost much of their potential bargaining power before they even begin. Perhaps an analogous though crude example would be buying a car from one dealer who has several models to offer without seeking out the comparative prices of other dealers. Once the body has been taken to the funeral home, customers have essentially lost most of their bargaining power.

Similarly, the family's failure to conduct prior investigations poses another typical condition in the social structuring of interaction between funeral director and customer. Conditions permit funeral directors to attempt to sell an arrangement according to their assessments of the family's ability to pay and of the social status of the deceased. (These assessments are based on the bereaved's appearance, contents of the obituary, and similar sources of information.) Accordingly, funeral directors construct an image of a "proper" funeral for the individual's status and may attempt to induce customers to realize their image rather than the customers'. Sometimes the views of the family are so vague that they readily accept the funeral director's definition of the situation. All this leads to another dilemma for the family: what for them is an extraordinary context for making decisions is to the funeral director a routine contractual event. With interactional advantages structured in favor of the funeral director, it is not surprising that some people think they have been taken while others are appreciative of the funeral director's advice.

The interactional dynamics become more apparent when a closer look is taken of the situation. Unquestionably, funeral directors have at their disposal the relevant information about which agreements are to be made. When the family's knowledge of this situation is vague, they depend upon the funeral director for information.

The funeral director's control over the situation is of course increased when the survivors are experiencing deep feelings of grief, since they are unlikely to scrutinize what is happening. Besides, survivors who have had little experience with death sometimes wish to avoid the situation and leave decisions largely to the funeral director. Conversely, a fear of being too easily led into more elaborate arrangements than necessary is precisely the reason why some of the newly bereaved request that a less-involved friend, relative, or clergy person be present when the arrangements are made. Bowman (1959) finds that funeral directors are sometimes reluctant to have members of the Protestant clergy accompany their parishioners into the selection rooms since these ministers tend to emphasize economy in funeral arrangements.

Part of the problem for the funeral director is to negotiate arrangements that will actually be paid for. With that end in mind, some funeral directors occasionally attempt to dissuade the newly bereaved from their original choices or work out an "easy" pay plan to make monthly payments over an extended period of time.

While funeral directors must extract specific information from their clientele, their clientele also need information from them, information not easily extracted. Still, information control is not always simply a problem of extracting too little from an unwilling informant. In the case of the funeral director, as with other workers like the physician or auto mechanic, customers are often mystified and remain fundamentally uninformed when provided with a barrage of technical jargon to explain relatively simple problems. Hence, giving too much information can be an effective way to get customers to abdicate any control they anticipated having.

Information control also takes into account the strategic revealing of alternatives to the customer. Since the selection room is set up so that differences in caskets are obvious, customers are allowed to choose by themselves, frequently without the presence of the funeral director. Cheaper caskets often look so unappealing that a prospective buyer is led to make a more expensive choice than planned. Some of the cheaper caskets, for example, are lined with green plastic resembling the kind of life-size trash bag county officials use to wrap a corpse before transit. Of course, caskets may be done away with in most states when cremation is done locally. All that is necessary is a body-size cardboard box. Even with this information, a relative may find it disconcerting to dispose of the deceased in a mere box. And if the relative has doubts about the propriety of doing so, those doubts may be tacitly or explicitly fostered by the funeral director. One local funeral director made the following qualification after informing my class of the less expensive option: "Anybody who really cared about their relative wouldn't want him in a cardboard box. It just isn't dignified. It doesn't show the proper respect that you'd want to show for someone close."

Funeral directors' control is more pervasive than simply information; they control the entire situation. A sense of this control may be imparted and understood through their use of touch. Such control may be communicated even when the funeral directors are not attempting to use touch strategically. For example, when a male funeral director offers his arm to a widow to escort her into his office or gives a distressed widower a consoling pat on the shoulder, not only concern is shown but also the authority of someone capable of being in charge of the situation.

In any case, the initial encounter between the bereaved and funeral directors is likely to be skillfully managed by funeral directors who strategically attempt to maximize their objectives. Again, they are not solely monetary but may include keeping work routine and efficient through selection of a funeral ritual that can readily fit into their repertoire. Thus, some of the suggestions made to the relative by funeral directors may directly result from their interest in the *kind* of work to be done and *how* it is to be done. Funeral directors are likely to have several standard arrangements in which they have developed a sense of pride. Sometimes funeral directors' sense of "professionalism" is unpleasantly challenged if the family chooses much more unusual arrangements; generally, however, greater flexibility is more possible now than in the past.

Similar to functionaries in other institutional systems, some funeral directors are beginning to encourage innovative arrangements, some including the participation of their clientele. One mode of participation involves the bereaved in standard funerary practices, such as assisting the funeral director in the tasks of removing and preparing the body. Another mode of participation consists of individualized adaptations in the arrangements to reflect the lives of the bereaved. Hardy (1976) advocates accommodating the wishes of the bereaved and, in particular, involving the grieving peers of a young individual in active physical expression of their sentiments through singing, serving as pallbearers, or filling the grave.

However well-intentioned the individual funeral director may be, other widespread practices undoubtedly contribute to a measure of negative public feeling toward funeral directors. Questionable ethics or forms of coercion arise under certain conditions, such as when funeral directors believe the family will not question their authority on the matter at hand. Poor people, the inarticulate, or strangers, as well as those who are consumed by grief may become targets for this. Also, ethics may be subjugated to expedience. It is often easier and quicker to perform an ethically questionable act, like embalming the deceased *before* arrangements are selected by the family, than to take the time to do things in proper sequence. (Families may elect to pay for such unrequested services even when they are unwanted.) Coercion is more likely to be evident when funeral directors become committed to a course of action, often for what appears to them to be very good reasons. For example, the funeral director who had recently conducted a highly elaborate funeral for an elderly husband attempts to push the relatives to make comparable funeral arrangements for the newly deceased wife since he (correctly) feels that the survivors do not fully appreciate her wishes.

The funeral director's knowledge of the bereaved's feelings may also play a significant role in the negotiation of arrangements. Guilt feelings on the part of survivors are commonly believed to be manipulated by funeral directors, although there are no empirical studies to clarify the extent to which this occurs. The fact that some survivors feel guilty about their past relationships with the deceased may result in funeral directors becoming moral entrepreneurs if they evaluate whether the bereaved should atone for prior actions. For example, a funeral director who played the role of moral entrepreneur justified his stance in the following way to me:

> Ordinarily, I encourage people to purchase the kind of funeral which is well within their means, but if they let their mother rot and die in a nursing home then, I just say to myself, "let them just go ahead and spend, spend, spend, and I'll help them do it."

Whatever specific concerns are elicited by the death and funeral preferences, all participants are under time pressures to complete the arrangements. Ordinarily, the pressure of time works in favor of the funeral director since the survivors usually do not have the opportunity to obtain further information. Even when survivors hope to follow the wishes of the deceased, they may not have a clear conception of what the deceased or other relatives would have wanted. Usually, without that information in mind, the relatives are juggling views of what is appropriate, what is desirable for the deceased, and what choices they would prefer. Clever funeral directors sense this dilemma and may turn it to their advantage. For example, it is not uncommon to hear people say that they really did not know exactly what an elderly relative wanted. By not wishing to impose personal preferences upon the situation, the survivor sometimes ends up with much greater expenses than anticipated.

In the bargaining situation funeral directors, if given an opportunity, will push for an open casket viewing. There are several reasons why funeral directors feel this is the best method of handling the ritual. First, they believe in the importance of seeing the dead person as dead. They contend that in this way the reality of death cannot be overlooked and assume, moreover, that the constructed image of the deceased constitutes a "real" and appropriate confrontation with death. Second, the open casket funeral permits funeral directors to show their expertise in "restoration," an area that "substantiates" claims for professional status. Third, the open casket funeral gives funeral directors the opportunity to maximize the possibility of making the funeral an elaborate, expensive one.

Restoration is an important area of death work in the funeral home because of its relationship to subsequent services. How highly the restoration process is valued by the funeral directors themselves depends upon the kind of organization in which they work (cf. Pine 1975). Funeral directors at establishments in need of repeated business from the families served attend to the restoration more carefully. They need good evaluations of their work in order to maintain their reputations. Conversely, "volume" houses stress efficiency over the quality of the restoration. (Since funeral directors cannot control the volume of their work by altering death rates, their reputations among members of the community become their main means of attracting clientele, and a reputation is in turn believed to rest on the quality of restoration.)

The relative importance of the restoration is related to cultural variables, which brings us to another theme. In this discussion we have not yet taken into account the strong cultural traditions supporting the selection of lavish funeral arrangements. Many customers are not only satisfied with their expensive funeral selections but actively seek them out. In a materialistic society where personal value tends to be measured in monetary terms, it stands to reason that the poor as well as the affluent may desire elaborate funeral rituals. They may view them as personal statements of social and symbolic value, especially when they have gone unrecognized during life. When these views are reinforced by a shared culture that places a high value on display, sociability, and pageantry after a death, they may serve as a means of mitigating impoverished conditions in this world for the expected rewards of the "next."

In any event, subcultural values among the poor sometimes strongly support expensive funeral and burial rituals. A case in point is described by Mathias (1974), who argues that the characteristics of the Italian-American funeral in South Philadelphia reveal the persistence of cultural traditions of village life in Southern Italy. But she contends that the funeral pattern is one which the immigrant peasants borrowed from the landowners, although Italians generally had the habit of spending much of their earnings on rituals. In Mathias's tracing of the historical development of the contemporary Italian funeral, she discovers that the force behind it was *social competition* among the immigrants for goods and honor rather than the dominant folk religion of earlier peasant years. Competition existed not only following the death but also for years through the tending of the grave by family members who visited weekly and constantly compared their plots with those of others. The shift from folk religion to social competition brought about a correspondingly greater emphasis on the body and thus gave rise to further expansion of the funeral and burial rites. Now the Italian funeral is characterized by an emphasis on "proper," that is, lavish, display to validate social status. Because showy floral displays, cosmetic restoration, new clothes, bronze caskets, "perpetual care" graves, and the like are considered proper symbols of respect and social status, it is common for the funeral cost to range from 33-100 percent of the family's annual income.

Conjectures about the influence of cultural values among dominant groups are made by Pine and Phillips (1970), who suggest that funeral expenditures become a means of expressing sentiments about the deceased. They argue that because social and ceremonial arrangements for coping with death are diminished in today's world, funeral expenditures reflect both proper concern for the individual who died and the "standards of decency" in the community. While this position could be taken as a justification for existing practices, it should be noted that a more fundamental expression may underlie funeral expenditures—a statement of the identity of the bereaved. Conceivably, then, the cultural value most fundamentally at issue is the proper role and demeanor of the bereaved, not the deceased.

Finally, a word needs to be said about the role of culture in selecting a funeral director. While many survivors simply request the name of a funeral home from hospital staff, who generally refer on the basis of location or on a rotating basis using all local establishments, others choose a funeral director from their own cultural group. Hence, a black funeral director serves the black community; an Italian funeral director serves the Italian section, and so forth. A culturally specialized funeral director is in a unique position to perpetuate the funeral tradition of the specific community through the selection process. In short, under these conditions the choice of the type of funeral made by the bereaved is shaped by the original selection of the funeral director.

The Funeral Ritual

Historically, funerals have provided an important rite of transition for members of the intimate group and have constituted the last rite of passage for the deceased. The questionable symbolic significance of contemporary funeral practices in making a meaningful transition is an issue being raised by critics of the funeral industry. Whether or not the constructed ritual is meaningful to those who attend, the construction of the ritual is quite clearly a crucial element in the death work of the funeral director.

In order to get a sense of the possible meanings of the funeral ritual, I will take a closer look at both the ceremonial aspects of the funeral ritual and its social construction. Traditionally, the open casket with one or two formal viewings and subsequent religious service has been the funeral of choice in contemporary America. Funeral directors espouse the position that it is *necessary* to view the dead person before grieving can begin. While seeing the person as dead can be of immeasurable assistance to intimates confronting the reality of this death, there is no reason why the only place that can occur is at a formal viewing after restoration has been effected by the funeral director. For example, quiet leave-takings may be made either at the hospital or the funeral home before the ceremonies begin. Perhaps the more unexpected or incomprehensible the death is to the bereaved, the more symbolic significance the open viewing has. To illustrate, upon the accidental death of a close friend whose parents arranged for a closed-casket funeral, a young woman said to me, "I wanted that casket open; I wouldn't believe that she was dead unless I saw her dead." Similar comments were made about Vietnam soldiers sent home in closed caskets.

Some funeral directors, like Howard C. Raether (1971), see the trend of moving away from the viewing as indicative of "death-denying" attitudes among Americans. But, curiously, Raether and many other funeral directors do not believe that the deceased must appear in the state they were in while dying. Instead, they feel that the viewing may give the impression of the dead person at an earlier time through "restoration" of the deceased to a stage before the disease or injury had taken its toll. The central thrust of their work is to present a scenario in which the deceased appears to be at peace. Raether provides the underlying assumption behind the controversial "memory picture" of the corpse when he claims that cosmetic restoration "gives the bereaved an acceptable image to recall," rather than a death-denying image of life (1971, p. 141). Presumably, the funeral director is able to restore the deceased to the point where the image provided is one that reflects what the person *was* rather than reflecting an artificially contrived image. In that image, a bias towards youth may be discerned, since much of the restoration effort may be made to lessen the effects of aging as well as disease. For example, the following undertaker explained:

> I always want faces to keep a nice tight look, the beautiful youthful appearance that is so important. In our everyday work we do extra things in filling out a face, in giving it that certain look, that the average commercial embalmer won't bother with in the restoration arts (Rader 1975, p. 106).

Another funeral director linked the removal of the effects of aging with giving the family and the public a better image of death. When questioned about the service he performed, he proclaimed:

> What is our service? We give people a better impression of death, especially if the body is deteriorating. When we finish with them they do have a life-like appearance, they do seem to be about twenty or thirty years younger, the embalming fluids seem to put the albumin back in the skin. Formaldehyde. Firms things up when they are deteriorating, just like clockwork (Rader 1975, p. 106).

While the effect of the viewing has not been thoroughly researched, several studies support the funeral directors' assumption concerning the importance of it. Fulton (1976) reports that of 565 newly widowed respondents, those who had had a traditional funeral with the viewing and had involved friends and relatives in these events described fewer adjustment problems than those who did not. In contrast, those respondents who did not have a viewing or who had planned an immediate disposal of the body reported greater hostility, increased use of alcohol and drugs, and increased anxiety. Though no information is provided on whether similar differences could have been found independent of the death, the findings are provocative. Hutchens (1976), a funeral director who researched families his firm had served found that the majority of the 63 respondents (out of 100 questionnaires sent) held favorable attitudes toward the open casket viewing. In any event, whether the embalmer's art produces an acceptable image for the bereaved constitutes a key difference of opinion among those who subscribe to traditional funeral practices and those who do not.

Undoubtedly, viewings serve some significant functions. First, they dramatize the type of events that are happening. Second, they provide an opportunity for others to demonstrate their bonds with both the deceased and the bereaved. Third, they provide an opportunity to make direct farewells to the deceased and to acknowledge their significance to the living.

Because of the ceremonial nature of funeral rites, they are particularly suitable subjects for a dramaturgical analysis, whether or not participants subjectively view their involvements as performances. In the next few pages, I will use a dramaturgical approach to highlight aspects of these rites.

As Turner and Edgley (1975) reveal, the funeral director directs a staged "performance" in which the corpse ultimately becomes a major, albeit silent, star. The performance is preceded by exacting, often painstaking preparation of the body, while the scenes conventionally include the viewing, funeral service, procession, and burial rites. For the moment, we will be concerned primarily with the actual funeral service. According to Turner and Edgley, the funeral director exerts control over the mood of the scene by using music, which simultaneously introduces events and sets the emotional ambience for them. Turner and Edgley identify the plot of the scene as the story of the deceased's life and his or her personal attributes. The intimates lend support to the ongoing scene through the "authenticity" of their grief performances. A specific performance may be judged by criteria either upholding stoicism or expressivity. The audience judges not only the performance of the bereaved but also the entire scene.

Because, for many, the funeral has become something of an appropriate formality rather than an integral part of their existence, it is essentially a directed ritual—managed by a functionary who ordinarily has only a limited and brief relationship with the survivors. Since the funeral is a managed formality, most survivors accept and play passive roles assigned by the funeral director. In that sense, the bereaved may come to rely on the funeral director to help them through the performance. In turn, the funeral director encourages appropriate behavior for this performance and scene. Pine states that the funeral allows the bereaved to put on a "death-appropriate mask"; so men may have tears in their eyes, women may be disheveled, and so forth. Pine contends that the funeral performs useful social functions primarily by providing a setting where actors can express their grief in these ways.

In any case, work goes more smoothly for funeral directors when the bereaved play their roles within the framework of experience that they offer them. If the bereaved are recalcitrant about playing these roles, then the tempo and shape of the ritual may become distorted from funeral directors' points of view. But the bereaved ordinarily accept the guidance of funeral directors, who ceremoniously usher and seat the family in the front of the room where they are expected to be. Part of the drama of the funeral comes from ritual positioning of the participants. Funeral directors are also careful to maintain the proper atmosphere by making sure that doors are closed noiselessly and that the proper demeanor permeates the scene.

During the actual ritual, funeral directors are overseers who continually check all details while blending into the scene, while, in contrast, the clergy are major performers. Because the minister, priest, or rabbi provides a crucial dimension to the funeral ritual, funeral directors, when given the choice, tend to procure members of the clergy who play their roles "well." As one funeral director confided,

> We have a few men who we like to call. They say things well and at the right time and seem to give comfort to the family. Every once in a while, you get someone who says the wrong things and does a clumsy job. So when the family asks us to bring someone in, we make sure it is someone who will do the kind of job we like.

As Warner (1977) explains, the clergy have a delicate task since the way they handle the scene sets the tone for shared symbolic meanings to emerge. Warner (1977, p. 373) argues that Protestant ministers, as compared to Catholic priests, possess an "anemic liturgical apparatus and devitalized spiritual imagery" that reduces spiritual power since they must use verbal symbols without visual drama and must appeal to the audience on rational grounds rather than emotional belief.

Part of the delicate task of the clergy is to express a firm belief in immortality in general while asserting that this particular dead individual is a suitable candidate for it. And from the funeral director's point of view, a necessary function of the clergy is to validate the significance of the ongoing scene. Turner and Edgley (1975) point out that the minister may seriously undermine the meanings the funeral director is trying to construct by overemphasizing the supernatural aspects of the event. They argue that the minister may construct a counter-reality that "the body is a shell and the 'soul' has departed," which may result in questions about the ritual and the amount of money spent on it (1975, p. 386).

The reality of the scene may also be undermined by the character of the eulogy. When it is general and impersonal, the entire scene may appear incongruous to the audience who knew the deceased. The eulogy then becomes a standard speech, resembling a form letter, to be given to all (Hetzler 1976).

In contrast, the scene may be made real by individualizing the eulogy in order to genuinely reflect the life of the deceased. The moral attributes and past actions of the deceased are brought up for display and review to audiences that probably know potentially discrediting information that could cast doubt on their qualifications for "everlasting life." Hence, the clergy must construct the transformation between the persons known in the past to the now sacred dead (see Warner 1977). As the moral drama unfolds, themes affirming the deceased's respectability are supported even as previously negative traits are reconstructed as positive. Despite this reconstruction, a function of the eulogy is to remind funeral audiences that their lives, too, will ultimately be subject to similar public evaluation (see Turner and Edgley 1975).

The drama continues as the ritual scenes are constructed. The closing of the casket and its subsequent lowering into the grave are likely to elicit acute grief from the most intimate and support from others in the scene. Each ritual scene presumably underscores the fact that this person has died. Viewing, funeral, procession, and burial all become scenes wherein performances are played out. Yet whether the drama is "real" or remains mere theatrics depends on the perspective of the observer.

Social Meanings of Death Rituals

In the foregoing sections, the work of the funeral director was emphasized since it constitutes an important part of death work; however, any analysis of funeral work leads to the question: What meanings are attributed to the rituals surrounding death? To answer this question, we will need to examine the purposes funeral and burial rites serve.

From the perspective of Durkheimian functionalism (1955), ritual behavior is a duty imposed by the group. Through the rites, collective sentiments are renewed, moral unity reaffirmed, and cohesion re-established. In this way, the mourners are protected and preserved. Moreover, the rites serve to reintegrate the group, so a feeling of order may be imparted to the bereaved. These rites simultaneously define and dramatize the separation of the living from the dead by marking the end of the dead person's life.

Do death rites accomplish these purposes? Compared with traditional cultures in which the lengthy funeral rites paved the way for the new status of the bereaved, I believe that contemporary practices do little more than ceremonially announce the death and the corresponding changed status of the survivors. Since no guidelines are constructed for the future statuses of the bereaved, any grief that is experienced later by that person becomes a private burden for which neither the funeral industry nor the community takes responsibility.

Irion (1976) argues that the conception of the funeral is valid, but it has become distorted in ways that negate some of its major purposes because illusions of life are often constructed instead of the reality of death. In addition, for many, death rites themselves become an illusion since they are not a part of the context of everyday life. Paradoxically, individualized rituals and simplified services are also without context since they lack a powerful symbolic imagery and the force of tradition. As such, these new adaptations lose much potential for providing sources of social integration.

However, even in their present form, funeral and burial practices reaffirm social and symbolic values placed upon the institution of the family. The family is viewed as the social unit with which the funeral is largely concerned in both monetary and social senses. Yet sometimes the deceased's real ties are with friends rather than next-of-kin, although friends are usually not permitted to play a role in planning the funeral or participating in rites. As a consequence, they may feel that the rituals are not suitable for the particular person or occasion. More importantly, others usually take into account only the family's loss and *its* wishes concerning how last farewells to the deceased are to be made. Subsequently, the friends, for whom this death is most symbolically significant and most disruptive of everyday life, may not be given much emotional and social support during the loss. For example, after the accidental death of her lover, a young lesbian wished to be included in the funeral plans. However, her lover's parents were horrified to think that their daughter could have been a homosexual. Consequently, they not only refused to include the woman in the plans but also requested that she not attend the rites.

Turning to the wider meanings of funeral rites, what other views might we discover? For some, the commercialized funeral of today stands as perfect testimony to an alienated society supported by the everyday actions of alienated human beings who passively and unquestioningly perform their expected tasks. Hence, from this viewpoint, death rites symbolically reflect the alienated consciousness of the bereaved, who embrace the reified symbols of the funeral industry. They perceive dignity as being purchasable in the form of a specially designed casket, social worth as demonstrated in a large formal viewing, and status as established by interment in a mausoleum. Such symbols are often particularly compelling to those who are powerless and impoverished.

The culmination of an alienated funeral and burial setting can be witnessed at Forest Lawn, which is something of a planned community of the dead that has become a quasi-religious tourist attraction comparable to Disneyland (see Jacobs 1971). Such enterprises are above all lucrative. They are founded on the profit motive and perpetuated by individuals whose world view supports having their "glimpse of death tempered by the fantasies of the planners" (Harmer 1971). Still, it is clear that some who seek out the services of these establishments believe that they have demonstrated well their regard for the deceased (besides living up to their own self-conceptions by choosing an "appropriate" course of action). Consequently, any analysis of the social meanings of death must also examine the subjective beliefs of participants.

SUMMARY AND IMPLICATIONS

In this chapter, I have outlined the ways in which individuals in diverse settings manage death work. Workers attempt to manage the amount of intrusion death may cause. Routine ways of handling death typically result in keeping it contained so that it neither disrupts their work nor their thoughts. Although the new death workers neither hide death nor separate themselves from it, they, too, may be predicted to develop routine ways of handling their death work, albeit perhaps of a radically different order than that of conventional workers. Already, indications of a routinization of death are apparent in those who demand their patients to confront their deaths in specified ways or actually die according to prescription.

Whatever the specific character of the routinization of death work, control over it depends on acceptance or lack of scrutiny by the consumers. In most circumstances, the consumers or clients of death workers are apt to be immersed in their own concerns. Hence, they are unlikely to challenge the routinization of death during the time they are actually using the services. Also, when the consumers seek services as isolated individuals, they are less likely to challenge the forms of routinization encountered than when sources are organized for consumer groups.

In the course of their tasks, workers develop strategies to assist them in routinizing death. A common strategy is to separate the dying and dead from the living so that death remains hidden and its effects are minimized. An underlying assumption of those who devise strategies to minimize the effects of death is that confrontation with death is potentially disruptive. Consequently, workers devise strategies that make it routine, including (1) the separation of the physical setting of death work from other parts of the organization or community, (2) separation of workers who commonly handle the dying and dead from other workers, and (3) the removal of those who are dying or dead from ordinary settings. Two other means of minimizing the effects of death on the world of work are (1) the development of *self-protection* strategies to control interaction and (2) claims of *professional status*.

In the case of funeral directors, claims for professional status are not supported when their work is compared to a sociological model of professional work. Their expertise is limited and does not require the application of abstract theoretical knowledge. Similarly, professional authority is not justified due to the limited expertise. Yet, funeral directors perform a service for which no other occupational group competes. In that sense, they perform a function within the society despite their current lack of professional status.

Like other functionaries, the funeral director takes over tasks once performed by the family and the community. Because death is less frequent in the lives of many, they look to the funeral director for advice in making arrangements and playing their roles during the rituals. The ritual itself is designed to permit displays of grief. Managing the scenario demands attention to details in order that an appropriate impression is given and the bereaved feel that they have shown the proper respect for the dead.

Before concluding, I will add a few thoughts about the implications of the timing and pacing of work. In the preceding analysis, the concerns of both funeral directors and coroner's deputies for conducting their work *efficiently* are readily discernible. Due to the nature of work, these concerns tend to be felt by most death workers. Thus, the combination of the *organization* of work and the *volume* of it may keep the worker's eye more on deadlines than death. Surely, the new death workers hold some of the same concerns about organizing their work to time and pace it efficiently and manageably. One wonders, then, to what extent dying and death will become an object of work, albeit in a different form, to them as well as to more traditional death workers.

To conclude, I have emphasized in this chapter the routine character of death work in ordinary settings. For the most part, the deaths which these workers deal with are ordinary deaths from typical causes such as illness and accident. But these are not the only kinds of deaths or the only kinds of settings. In the next chapter, I turn to the routinization of extraordinary deaths, which often take place in extraordinary settings. As I will demonstrate, routinization of extraordinary death is a problematic issue for those who impose it on others.

REFERENCES

Anderson, Barbara (1977). Hospice of Sonoma County. Oral presentation, Santa Rosa, California, November 16.

Aries, Philippe (1975). Forbidden death. In Edwin S. Shneidman (ed.), *Death: Current Perspectives*. Palo Alto, Calif.: Mayfield.

Baird, Jonathan (1975). The funeral industry in Boston. In Edwin S. Shneidman (ed.), *Death: Current Perspectives*. Palo Alto, Calif.: Mayfield.

Bereday, George (1977). Educational upgrading of workers in bereavement services. *Advances in Thanatology* 4:56-71.

Bowman, LeRoy (1959). *The American Funeral*. Washington, D.C.: Public Affairs Press.

Calkins, Kathy (1970). Time: perspectives, marking and styles of usage. *Social Problems* 17:487-501.

Charmaz, Kathy Calkins (1975). The coroner's strategies for announcing death. *Urban Life* 4:296-316.

Consumer resistance (1977). *Forbes* 120 (November 15):144.

Durkheim, Emile (1955). *The Elementary Forms of Religious Life*. Glencoe, Ill.: Free Press. (First published in 1915.)

Fulton, Robert (1976). The traditional funeral and contemporary society. In Vanderlyn R. Pine, Austin H. Kutscher, David Peretz, Robert C. Slater, Robert DeBellis, Robert J. Volk, and Daniel J. Cherico (eds.), *Acute Grief and the Funeral.* Springfield, Ill.: Charles C. Thomas.

Goffman, Erving (1959). *The Presentation of Self in Everyday Life.* Garden City, N.Y.: Doubleday.

_____ (1972). *Strategic Interaction.* New York: Ballantine.

Gorer, Geoffrey (1965). *Death, Grief and Mourning.* Garden City, N.Y.: Doubleday.

Greenwood, Ernest (1966). The elements of professionalization. In Howard M. Vollmer and Donald L. Mills (eds.), *Professionalization.* Englewood Cliffs, N.J.: Prentice-Hall.

Gubrium, Jaber (1975). *Living and Dying in Murray Manor.* New York: Springer.

Hardy, William G., Jr. (1976). The adaptive funeral. In Vanderlyn R. Pine, Austin H. Kutscher, David Peretz, Robert C. Slater, Robert DeBellis, Robert J. Volk, and Daniel J. Cherico (eds.), *Acute Grief and the Funeral.* Springfield, Ill.: Charles C. Thomas.

Harmer, Ruth M. (1963). *The High Cost of Dying.* New York: Collier.

_____ (1971). Funerals, fantasy and flight. *Omega* 2:128-54.

Hetzler, Florence M. (1976). In a hospital room—and after. In Vanderlyn R. Pine, Austin H. Kutscher, David Peretz, Robert C. Slater, Robert DeBellis, Robert J. Volk, and Daniel J. Cherico (eds.), *Acute Grief and the Funeral.* Springfield, Ill.: Charles C. Thomas.

Holden, Constance (1976). Hospices: for the dying, relief from pain and fear. *Science* 193:389-91.

Hutchens, Gene S. (1976). Grief therapy. In Vanderlyn R. Pine, Austin H. Kutscher, David Peretz, Robert C. Slater, Robert DeBellis, Robert J. Volk, and Daniel J. Cherico (eds.), *Acute Grief and the Funeral.* Springfield, Ill.: Charles C. Thomas.

Irion, Paul (1976). The funeral and the Bereaved. In Vanderlyn R. Pine, Austin H. Kutscher, David Peretz, Robert C. Slater, Robert DeBellis, Robert J. Volk, and Daniel J. Cherico (eds.), *Acute Grief and the Funeral.* Springfield, Ill.: Charles C. Thomas.

Jacobs, Paul (1971). The most cheerful graveyard in the world. In Charles Muscatine and Marlene Griffith (eds.), *The Borzoi College Reader.* New York: Knopf.

Kron, Joan (1977). Designing a better place to die. In Howard D. Schwartz and Cary S. Kart (eds.), *Dominant Issues in Medical Sociology.* Reading, Mass.: Addison-Wesley.

Marshall, Victor (1975). Organizational features of terminal status passage in residential facilities for the aged. *Urban Life* 4:349-68.

Mathias, Elizabeth (1974). The Italian-American funeral: persistence through change. *Western Folklore* 33:35-50.

Mitford, Jessica (1963). *The American Way of Death.* New York: Simon and Schuster.

Parsons, Talcott (1953). *The Social System.* Glencoe, Ill.: Free Press.

Pine, Vanderlyn (1975). *Caretaker of the Dead.* New York: Irvington Publishers.

_____, and Derek L. Phillips (1970). The cost of dying: a sociological analysis of funeral expenditures. *Social Problems* 17:405-17.

Rader, Dotson (1975). Five undertakers. *Esquire*, February 1975, pp. 102-108.

Raether, Howard C. (1971). The place of the funeral director in contemporary America. *Omega* 2:136-49.

Remarque, Erich Maria (1929). *All Quiet on the Western Front.* Boston: Little, Brown.

Saunders, Cecily (1977). Dying they live: St. Christopher's Hospice. In Herman Feifel (ed.), *New Meanings of Death*. New York: McGraw-Hill.

Schwartz, Howard (1974). First impressions. Unpublished manuscript, University of California, Berkeley.

Stoddard, Sandol (1978). *The Hospice Movement*. Briarcliff Manor: N.Y.: Stein and Day.

Sudnow, David (1967). *Passing On*. Englewood Cliffs, N.J.: Prentice-Hall.

Turner, Ronny E., and Charles Edgley (1975). Death as theatre: a dramaturgical analysis of the American funeral. *Sociology and Social Research* 60:377-92.

Warner, W. Lloyd (1977). The city of the dead. In Robert Fulton (ed.), *Death and Identity*. Philadelphia: Charles Press.

Wilensky, Harold (1970). The professionalization of everyone? In Oscar Grusky and George A. Miller (eds.), *The Sociology of Organizations*. New York: Free Press.

CHAPTER SEVEN

THE ROUTINIZATION OF EXTRAORDINARY DEATH

Although death work is ordinarily thought of as linked to conventional settings like the funeral home, it also is a fundamental activity in extraordinary circumstances such as combat and state executions. In these circumstances, death is directly and explicitly *imposed* upon others, and at that, the work itself is *constituted* by death instead of simply resulting from the fact that people ultimately die. Because the work involved generates deaths, one might assume that profound questions about the nature and meaning of death would be raised by participants; however, this does not seem to be the case. Rather, death in extraordinary circumstances tends to be treated as a routine affair that is made comprehensible and acceptable through the unquestioned acceptance of mundane justifications.

A short analysis of murder is included in this chapter. Despite the fact that murder is not always a "job," it shares the fundamental characteristics of imposing death and being extraordinary. More importantly perhaps, murder is presented here as a constructed action, that is, an event that emerges through interaction rather than as, for example, the outcome of a "sick" personality or an uncontrolled impulse. As a constructed action, murder has decided similarities to capital punishment and war since all are mechanized, constructed actions designed to produce death.

In this chapter, then, I shall focus upon the *construction* of *action* leading to extraordinary death, which becomes treated, however momentarily, as a *routine event*. First, I analyze murder. Second, I discuss capital punishment, and third, I raise the problematic dimensions of the routinization of death in war.

MURDER

Social definitions of murder typically refer to the sudden violent act of one individual that causes another's death, usually as the culmination of a face-to-face encounter. More subtle forms of institutionalized violence are not, for the most part, defined as murder although they may result in deaths. Therefore, such death-producing social practices resulting in malnutrition in the elderly, predictable accidents, inequitable distribution of medical care, and even capital punishment are typically not defined as murder (cf. Kastenbaum and Aisenberg 1972; Vernon 1970).

Before delving into an analysis of interaction, some brief observations should be made regarding the relationship between murder and society. From a structural-functionalist perspective, homicide might serve as an important societal valve for releasing societal tensions. Homicide, like other forms of deviant behavior, serves two important functions. First, murderers themselves might be seen as frustrated individuals who are unable to realize their aspirations since society does not permit all of its members to realize the goals it sets forth for them. Second, deviant acts serve to clarify and reaffirm the shared norms and values of members of that society. By reducing the number of individuals who compete for scarce opportunities and by simultaneously reaffirming the righteousness of shared norms, homicide may serve to perpetuate an equilibrium within society by maintaining the balance of already existing institutions. Consequently, a certain amount of homicide may be a *normal*, that is to say, typical, condition for a society.

From a Marxist perspective, murder may also be produced by the society through the internal contradictions of the economic system. But instead of assuming that homicide might be a necessary, albeit unpleasant, form of deviance as set forth in a functionalist view, the Marxist theorist would assume that deviance of this type reflects at least two significant characteristics of capitalistic societies: *scarce, inequitably distributed resources*, and the *dehumanization of the self* and *others* as a result of alienation.

By maintaining conditions where personalized violence is institutionalized in lower class members' interpersonal relationships, conflict is intensified between individuals whose objective interests in society are similar. Hence, from a Marxist perspective, the kind of personalized violence found in typical murder cases would be predicted to be *contained*; that is, for the most part, it would be limited to the lower classes and found in the geographic areas in which they live. For example, in the past, when violent crime in the South was perpetrated by one black against another, little official scrutiny was given to those cases as long as the crimes were contained within the black community.

Turning to the analysis of interaction, four key dimensions need to be considered when murder is analyzed as a type of constructed action. These include (1) the *structure* of the situation, (2) the type of *relationship* held between the victim and murderer, (3) the *self-image* of the murderer, and (4) the *interpretation* of the actions of the victim. Each will be discussed below.

The structure of the encounter forms the social backdrop for the ensuing interaction. Informal, relatively unstructured situations more regularly form the backdrop of violent encounters than formal, structured situations. As Luckenbill (1977) finds, sociable situations like drinking or "partying" provide circumstances in which actors have considerable latitude in their behavior. In turn, that latitude in an unstructured situation permits the possibility of a hostile encounter resulting in murder.

The type of relationship that exists between the victim and murderer enters into the unfolding events. When the relationship is, for example, one of long-standing hostility, the possibility of violence may be built into the immediate encounter sooner than in encounters experienced in other relationships. The *intensity* of the relationship and its *immediate* meaning for the actor's self-image become highly significant. While these dimensions are obviously significant between couples, they also sometimes shape the character of a relationship between strangers.

Two aspects of murderers' self-images that affect the situation are their *characteristic personal responses* and the *specific identification of self* given in the event. First, as Athens (1977) reports, based on dominant characteristics, three types of self-images are found among offenders of violent crimes: violent, incipient violent and nonviolent self-images. Athens distinguishes the violent from the incipient violent on the basis of action. While the incipient violent threaten others and are verbally abusive, the violent readily resort to actual force. Second, the specific identification of self given in the event refers to the actor's interpretation of the meaning and intent of the other. When actors interpret the meaning and intent of the other as aimed to demean or degrade them, negative views of self reinforced by others contribute to the rising intensity of the situation.

The interpretations made by the actor shape the subsequent development of the violent act. They typically rest on three sources of provocation that are sometimes combined: *self-defense, frustration* by the other, or *malicious intent* by the other (cf. Athens 1977). When interpretations necessitating self-defense are made, the actor (correctly or incorrectly) perceives a gesture as indicating actual, impending physical attack. *Thwarted expectations* may lead to violence when the actor is frustrated by the other. Frustration of the actor's intentions commonly occurs when a woman refuses sexual favors or when a child fails to comply with parental orders (cf. Kastenbaum and Aisenberg 1972). Malicious intent of the other constitutes a direct, serious insult to the self-image of the actor in the situation. In this case, malicious intent frequently is interpreted by these actors as a definite attempt to frustrate them. Athens provides this example of an offender who describes his response to his wife's announcement over the phone that she was filing for divorce:

> When I did get home three hours later, she was in bed asleep. I woke her
> up and told her to get up, that I wanted to talk. I told her if she stopped
> with the divorce, that I would promise to act better and . . . but she

wouldn't buy any of it. I got angrier and angrier. Then she came out and said, "Look, please do me this favor and give me a divorce." At that moment I felt cold hatred for her inside me. I told myself that I better leave before I exploded on her, but then I decided the hell with it, and I looked at her straight in the face and said, "Well X you better start thinking about those poor kids of ours." She said, "I don't care about them; I just want a divorce."

My hate for her exploded then, and I said "You dirty, no-good bitch" and started pounding her in the face with my fist. She put her arms up and covered her face, so I ran and got my rifle and pointed it at her. I said, "Bitch, you better change your mind fast or I'm going to kill you." She looked up and said [in] a smart-ass way, "Go ahead then, shoot me." I got so mad and felt so much hatred for her, that I just started shooting her again and again . . . (1977, p. 66).

As suggested in the example, victims, however unwittingly, often contribute to the conditions leading to their demise. The logical extension of these conditions results in what are known as victim-precipitated murders. Wolfgang (1967) shows that provocation by husbands is a frequent source of murders by wives who act in self-defense. Because this type of murder is a product of interaction, it sometimes is unclear initially who will assume dominance and what the outcome of the encounter will be. In that case, the identities of murderer and victim are not always given in the encounter. Rather, they emerge from the encounter as the situation is negotiated by the disputing parties.

In any case, socially constructed definitions of provocation in combination with subsequent interpretation tend to result in a sudden *escalation* of the hostility of the encounter. When provocation is defined, the nature of the previous transaction becomes transformed into a different order of event, at least for the actor. In many cases, retaliation consists of a verbal challenge to save face. When, as in the example above, the victim dares the actor to either escalate the encounter into violence or back down, actor and victim form a *tacit* agreement to define their situation as one in which violence is a suitable mode of behavior (cf. Luckenbill 1977). In other cases, in which the actor possesses a violent self-image, the victim may be killed at the point when provocation is first defined.

By examining the self-image of the actor, murders that otherwise seem inexplicable become somewhat comprehensible. The murder of a popular schoolteacher by a total stranger may prove to be a case in point (see Pogash 1979). During a wait in line for a horror film, the teacher and his companions amused themselves with jokes as they observed other moviegoers' imitations of the fantastic costumes and painted faces of the characters in the film they were to see. Known for his outrageous sense of humor and ebullient spirits, the teacher's companions initially expressed no surprise when he moved up and down the line asking for a doctor. They thought he had simply pulled the best prank of the evening. But he had been stabbed in the back. A suspect with a lengthy police record, including incidents of "assault with a deadly weapon," was readily identified. The homicide inspector believed the attack was triggered by a disparaging remark about the shabby clothes worn by the suspect. Since the remark was made by someone standing next to the teacher, the inspector proposed that the suspect erroneously attributed it to the teacher. If the inspector's conjectures were true and the suspect possessed a violent self-image, a disparaging remark would then be sufficient provocation for violence. If so, the death may be placed in an understandable context.

The relationship between murderer and victim, however fleeting, is not the only cause of escalating violence. Another source, the *audience*, merits attention. Luckenbill found that audiences tended to actively encourage the use of violence or remain neutral, but did not intervene in the transaction. With the advocacy of the audience, or the interpretation of their advocacy, the actor may come to define the situation as one in which violence is *imperative*; otherwise, too much loss of face is at stake. In short, at this point in the encounter, the actor becomes committed to a violent course of action. Similarly, the victim may also define the confrontation as a battle in which the course is set for violence. When the participants share a mutual understanding that the event is decidedly violent, the course of the transaction takes on a determinant pattern.

Athens (1977) concludes that actors commit violent acts only after they construct *violent interpretations* of their situations. Although Athens did not pursue all the permutations of the dimensions discussed above, his data shows some striking connections between self-image and type of interpretation of provocation. According to his data, those who hold violent self-images invariably respond with violence to any of the sources of provocation, while those with incipient violent self-images respond to interpretations of necessary self-defense and the combined provocation of frustration by the other with malicious intent. In contrast, those with nonviolent self-images responded only to interpretations calling for self-defense.

Through the course of events, some interesting features of the interaction develop. Not only the nature of the event but also the *identity* of the other person becomes transformed when the parties are known to each other. Often, the victim is transformed from being a "significant other" in the life of the actor into something less than human. Then, any previous negative connotations the actor held about murder no longer apply; this act is not linked with conventional definitions of killing. Further, during these episodes, the actor is apt to be so engulfed in the moment that rational calculation of future consequences becomes absurd.

Essentially, as actors concentrate on the implications of the encounter for their self-images during the experience, other meanings of the act are unlikely to be entertained. Implicitly, at least from their interpretations of the encounter, these actors' humanity and sense of valued self come to rest at that moment upon asserting dominance over or destroying the antagonist, and either intention may culminate in murder.

If the actors had little in the way of conventional grounds for developing a positive self-image, then they may respond more violently. Violence may also be elicited when the victim questions some facet of the actor's self previously viewed as positive. Or for that matter, violence may be elicited when an aspect of self that had caused the actor profound private doubts is brought up for public display. In any event, it is likely that the victim raises an issue of central concern, such as sexual capability or cowardice, to the actor. Sometimes the issue may be of such a magnitude that all other creditable aspects of the actor's self are interpreted as resting upon it. Furthermore, someone with a negative or violent self-image has much less to lose than others by engaging in violence (cf. Kastenbaum and Aisenberg 1972).

To conclude, through evaluation of self and interpretation of the situation, the actor redefines physical violence, conventionally defined as extremely extraordinary. If, while redefining, the actor focuses most strongly on definitions of self as a *personal possession* superseding other concerns, then conditions are set for the victim's death to become routinized, despite later, rapid redefinition of the act as an atrocity. At the moment the encounter culminates in the victim's immobilization by a blow or wound, the actor has routinized an extraordinary way of imposing death.

CAPITAL PUNISHMENT

Capital punishment is institutionalized ritual murder inflicted by the state upon the condemned. The use of capital punishment is, then, a sanctioned type of routinized death work, an extraordinary death transformed into a bureaucratic ritual. Hence, the routinization of death becomes part of the working apparatus of the judicial system of the state.

Capital punishment reflects the larger society in which it exists. Since it is a form of violent death, it is apt to be found in societies where forms of violence are institutionalized. Thus, whether capital punishment is used, or is an issue in a society, depends upon its social structure and the values and beliefs justifying that social structure. Since capital punishment is related to the overall use of coercion by those who control the society, it can be expected that the incidence of death by capital punishment will increase when political domination is maintained by force to suppress dissent or opposition.

Any examination of capital punishment as a kind of work calls for an analysis of the underlying, supporting values on which that work is based. Consequently, the following discussion will include arguments that support and oppose capital punishment.

The major argument in support of capital punishment is *deterrence*. Since capital punishment is believed to be a rational means of deterring criminal acts, its presumed value lies in holding potential criminals in check. Proponents of capital punishment who agree that it is an ineffective deterrent now argue that the reason for its ineffectiveness is that death sentences are given sparingly and that many reviews or appeals are made. Thus some proponents of the death penalty are essentially arguing for more widespread and immediate use of it in order that it might become an effective deterrent to violent crime. Another strong argument is that capital punishment is just (Van Den Haag 1972). The argument goes that since retribution is a form of justice, capital punishment itself is just. Proponents of this position also argue that the problem has not been with the death penalty, per se, but with the *distribution* of that penalty, since, they argue, whether it is invoked depends on other variables than having committed the act. In particular, proponents like Van Den Haag assume that the distributive process, the trial, will be fairer when all participants recognize that life is actually at stake, since they will then take these trials more seriously. This position presupposes that the accepted "facts" of a given case stand by themselves. But when jurists hold views based on racist or class-biased premises, whether or not those premises are recognized as such, they will be predisposed to accept negative "evidence" as fact, as for example, when it is wielded against a black man.

The argument for just punishment is often buttressed with supporting rationales about the value of life. First, the rationale is put forward that life within the society must be given *protection* in the event the offender escapes or is released. Second, the rationale is offered that keeping the death penalty demonstrates the *value* of *life* since murder devalues human existence. The assumption here is that human life is sacred and anyone who violates it must pay in kind.

The last main argument for capital punishment is based on *economic expediency*. Retentionists sometimes claim that the costs incurred by the state in imposing the death penalty are less than those of rehabilitation and services for the prisoner with a life sentence. But counter-arguments from abolitionists indicate that the expense of appeals resulting in stays of execution are far more costly. The costs of being held in maximum security until the execution date alone are more than the costs of life imprisonment (McGee 1972).

Persons who wish to have the death penalty permanently abolished base their arguments on counterpoints to the rationales provided above. Since deterrence of crime is one of the most oft-cited reasons for reinstituting the death penalty, abolitionists have engaged in detailed research indicating that the death penalty does not particularly deter violent crime. There is no increase in murders or violent crimes in those states without a death penalty than there is in those with one (Glaser and Zeigler 1974). In any event, since those who might have been deterred do not come under public scrutiny, deterrence itself cannot be measured. If, however, capital punishment actually served as a deterrent to violent crime, then increases in homicide rates could be predicted after capital punishment had been abolished, but no corroborating evidence of this is available.

The position that capital punishment is not a deterrent is dramatically illustrated by Clinton Duffy, a former San Quentin warden. He describes a deputy sheriff who had brought prisoners to San Quentin for years, including some who were condemned to die (1971). Later, that deputy methodically killed his wife. Similarly, Duffy relates the story of a prisoner who helped to build the gas chamber, a source of much interest and conversation within the compound. That prisoner was later released and became involved in a family conflict during which he killed two relatives and a friend.

In the first case described by Duffy, the murder was premeditated and planned with care. However, as discussed in the previous section, many murders occur without much forethought; they are constructed during interaction. If deterrence is not an effective inhibitor in planned murders, it does not stand to reason that it would be effective in those crimes in which the act is constructed during a short interval of time as, for example, when the murderer is in a rage.

According to some abolitionists, the death penalty may in fact give rise to crime since some individuals are willing to risk death. Some even seem to relish the media notoriety they gain by requesting the death penalty. In the abolitionist view, the publicity and notoriety given to those who are willing to risk death spur others into committing the same kind of crime. The kind of crime committed acquires symbolic appeal that sometimes results in others viewing successful completion of the act as a mark of achievement and source of self-identification. Illustrations of this point may be found in cases of aircraft hijackings and political kidnappings.

The symbolic appeal of capital punishment leading to murders is elucidated by Graves (1956), who discovered that more homicides occurred on the weekends directly following Friday executions in California than on other weekends. This finding naturally raises questions about the effectiveness of capital punishment as a deterrent.

In contrast to the retentionists, abolitionists argue that capital punishment symbolizes a lack of regard for human life. The tacit lesson of capital punishment is that violence is accepted and affirmed; violence itself is of a higher priority than maintenance of life. Hence, in this point of view, capital punishment is based upon *vengeance*, rather than retribution, as some retentionists claim. In the larger sense, no amount of state executions can compensate for the loss of the first victim. The use of the death penalty symbolizes the power of the state and, when used extensively, it symbolizes the intolerance of the state for challenges to its interests. Furthermore, the use of capital punishment symbolizes that it is more expedient to eliminate offenders than to attempt to rehabilitate them. At this point, one can discern somewhat different assumptions held by abolitionists and retentionists about human nature and flexibility. Those who argue for retention see human nature as fixed and stable, since they doubt the possibility of successful rehabilitation once criminal behavior has been established. The abolitionist argument, in contrast, supports the concept of resocialization through rehabilitation. They view human nature as changeable.

Perhaps the most important argument against capital punishment is that the wrong person may be executed, and if the execution proceeds swiftly after sentencing, no possibility exists for correcting the error. Cases of mistaken identification, withheld evidence, or confessions by others point to the kinds of situations in which the innocence of the condemned is later discovered (see Ehrmann 1972). In other situations, questions have arisen as to whether accused individuals clearly understood the implications of what they signed or admitted (Ehrmann 1972). Similarly, a prosecutor may intimidate poorly educated defendants into pleading guilty to crimes that they did not commit by threatening that the death penalty may later be invoked. In addition, prisoners are sometimes reluctant to appeal when they receive life sentences for fear of drawing the death penalty on the appeal (Greenberg and Himmelstein 1972).

At any rate, receiving the death penalty causes great psychological stress for the convicted. Having one's date of execution postponed numerous times may in itself constitute "cruel and unusual punishment" since the prisoner is forced to confront the imposition of death numerous times.

No analysis of capital punishment in the United States is complete without a discussion of its relationship to racial discrimination. Wolfgang's studies (1967, 1974), as well as Garfinkel's classic study (1967), point to the fact that there has been systematic discrimination against blacks in the imposition of the death penalty. More severe punishment has been meted out to those black offenders convicted of crimes against white victims than in reverse cases. According to Wolfgang (1974), discriminatory practices are most evident when death sentences have been given out for rape. His detailed research, spanning a twenty-year period in seven Southern states, indicates that in rape cases involving white women, black defendants were 18 times more likely to receive the death penalty than when the racial status of defendant and victim were of any other combination. Given the compulsion to punish the black defendant, the chance of errors in identification is higher in these cases than in others. If this is so, innocent men have paid with their lives for crimes they did not commit.

Surely, the powerlessness of the accused blacks and the severity of their sentences must have had a symbolic effect on the consciousness of black people. One wonders if the relative frequency with which death has been imposed upon them by the working armamentarium of the state has affected their symbolic image of death. On a more political level, Bowers (1974) proposes that the death penalty may have served as an instrument of minority group oppression to perpetuate the subjugation of blacks. He argues that the distribution of sentencing of blacks for raping white victims suggests that capital punishment has been used as a means of protecting the white majority by maintaining a caste system.

These arguments suggest that the use of capital punishment reflects historical and economic conditions. Significantly, capital punishment has consequences other than simple retribution and deterrence since it may serve extra-legal objectives. Thus, as Bowers (1974) proposes, capital punishment may serve as a means of minority oppression and majority protection and repression during times of economic hardship or political instability. Because the execution rate peaked during the economic and political crises of the 30's, some weight is carried by Bower's position. Hence, capital punishment may become a form of systematic death work that reflects the socioeconomic conditions of the society at a given time.

How capital punishment is handled as a form of death work within a society is not only related to more general forms of death work in that society, but also sheds light on symbolic meanings of death held by the collective. J. Lofland (1975, 1977) argues that the industrial revolution gave rise to different strategies to deal with life and death exemplified by changes in ways of managing state executions. He points out that the state execution has changed from an *open*, public event to one that is *"concealed"* and made highly routinized, similar to other conventional rituals surrounding death.

By making systematic comparisons of the dramaturgy of historical state executions (circa 1700) with modern ones (circa 1950), J. Lofland clarifies key differences in values about death held in societies in which death is treated openly as opposed to ones in which it is hidden. Historically, instances of capital punishment were public spectacles replete with festivities and pageantry approaching those of a celebration. The condemned and the executioner took on public identities that were held up for scrutiny and evaluation as they played out their respective roles. While the "work" of the condemned was to provide entertainment for the audience with whom they usually shared a lively discourse, the work of the executioner was viewed as an act to be closely observed by the masses. Cooper (1974) notes that the executioner was a public celebrity who was abhorred or admired but who was still an institutionalized figure to be judged for his skill and general demeanor. The public character of the executioner's self then stands in stark contrast to the anonymous, minor bureaucratic role the executioner (who works only "part-time at piece rates") now possesses, a role entirely interchangeable with others having similar skills (J. Lofland 1977).

As J. Lofland portrays so well, the staging of the modern execution ritual differs markedly from those of earlier times. Since virtually no role is provided for public participation, there is no visiting by the curious or elite, no portrayal of unique personal identities, no lengthy dying process, and no prolonged disposal of the corpse.

While in earlier times, the condemned had the latitude to be themselves even as they were being executed, today the condemned typically have a single identity and play a single role—one conferred upon them by the bureaucratic apparatus. They are molded into objects that simply fulfill their bureaucratic obligation, to die without raising a fuss. The one recently condemned man with a unique public identity, Gary Gilmore, won it only because he proclaimed that he should be allowed to have his execution, an uncharacteristic stance for those who receive the death penalty.

Under ordinary circumstances, the role of the condemned is strikingly similar to that of the dying patient. And as J. Lofland suggests, the kind of death work characterized by the concealment involved in implementing the death penalty is evident in both the care of the dying patient and the preparation of the deceased for disposal.

In sum, on the institutional level of analysis, capital punishment may be viewed as a type of death work imposed by the society as a means of social control. Yet on the interactional level of analysis, capital punishment may be viewed as a type of "job," which replicates other private ritual tasks performed by bureaucratic functionaries in an anonymous, impersonal, but efficient, manner.

THE ROUTINIZATION OF DEATH IN WAR

Any examination of death work must include war since war is in essence death work writ large. Producing death is an obvious objective of work in the military during periods of armed conflict. Since the number of losses inflicted upon the enemy becomes the criterion of relative strength and success, perfecting the ways in which killing can be accomplished expediently, massively, and with minimal losses to one's side is a major objective. Consequently, creating death becomes a routinized activity for those involved, though many who do so play what seems to them to be such a small role that they may feel uninvolved in the killing even if they actually facilitate it through their everyday actions.

War shares some properties with capital punishment since it typically is condoned or *advocated* by members of society and is *legitimized* by its leaders. In contrast to capital punishment, the executions obviously are conducted on a massive scale, often with relatively few face-to-face encounters between executioner and victim. This impersonal, usually detached, characteristic of much of contemporary warfare contrasts it with many civilian murders in which the victim is known to the killer. In the most impersonal, detached circumstances, the extent of killing will not even be known since there is no contact at all with the victims. Deaths as a result of bombing missions exemplify this type of separation between killer and victim. But in war, different arenas of conflict develop, and thus somewhat varied kinds of killing emerge despite the fact that central underlying patterns characterizing death in war may be discerned.

Whatever else it may be, warfare is a type of institutionalized murder (Kastenbaum and Aisenberg 1972). Although typically defined in more ennobled terms, war may also be seen as a type of collective murder in which systematic killing of those people defined as "the opposition" is a primary objective and a major characteristic of what actually occurs. By virtue of the social legitimacy given to it, killing in war takes on a moral dimension in contrast to murder. As Toynbee points out, "The fundamental postulate of the institution of war is that, in war, 'killing is no murder' " (1968, p. 145).

Cultural Values and the Routinization of Death

When we compare the mutilation and devastation brought about by war to death under peaceful conditions, death in war is unequivocally extraordinary. However, within the context of war, highly atypical deaths become fairly routine. The raping and killing of the women of a captive territory, or the sudden, complete and horrifying transformation of a living human being into a corpse through instant mutilation are relatively infrequent events in civilian life, but become ordinary modes of dying in wartime.*

Given the extraordinary nature of dying in war and the peculiar character of work in war, a process of *routinization* develops whereby the strange is made familiar and explainable. Both the individual soldier and the people within the society contribute to that process of routinization. The following interrelated questions need to be examined in order to understand how the process of routinization is constructed: How is war accepted by a people? How do ordinary boys and young men become "soldiers"? Why do soldiers come to accept their tasks?

In order to answer these questions, the crucial role that ideology and language play in defining experience must first be examined. Clearly, ideologies founded in cultural values help to cloak the unpleasant fact that war is death work. Our everyday conventions and ways of using language help us to protect ourselves from directly confronting this reality. The language used to describe killing in war dilutes its impact, fosters its routinization, and creates distance between ourselves and death. In these ways, social meanings of death in war may be constructed such that the production of massive death becomes minimized. Similarly, our use of language serves to protect us from confronting death in the more immediate context of face-to-face interaction. To show how incongruous a direct description of action in war is with our taken-for-granted conceptions of an appropriate verbal account, imagine, for example, the discomfort and embarrassment that would be caused in a social group if when asked what he did for a living, a young man replied, "I kill." Or consider the outrage of the public if a key official were to admit to instigating foreign "uprisings" while knowing that civilians would be slaughtered. Because they are typically framed in language and meaning that make sense to us, the actions remain unquestioned and acceptable. We ignore or forget that verbal statements may mask an active involvement in causing the deaths of others.

* The following discussion is devoted to an analysis of modern combat. Because men have traditionally been the combatants in our society, the discussion uses male pronouns.

Cultural values are fundamentally at issue when the process of routinization is analyzed. Rather than representing a reversal of prior symbolic meanings, killing in war becomes routinized when certain preexisting values are intensified and others are minimized. Similarly, the acceptance of the people within society follows a corresponding theme. The specific core of values at stake may differ during different sociohistorical conditions, although some continuities may be discovered as, for example, when a people believe that its entire way of life is being threatened by an enemy.

The values implicitly supporting war may ultimately become the source of assumptions upon which a specific war is later based. Hence, during times of national crises such values can be drawn upon to justify the entry into or the existence of war. For example, ethnocentric values like patriotism, a belief in democracy, the belief in the "correctness" of the actions of leaders, and beliefs in cultural and political superiority all serve to justify actions taken in war. Furthermore, when preparation for war (characterized by the term "defense" instead of "offense") becomes a standard practice and war itself is a common prediction for the future, then the grounds are set for numbers of people to view it as inevitable. Consequently, extraordinary death through war may be assumed to be part of routine existence even before it has developed. When war has been institutionalized into the life of a society, the fabric of ordinary existence has largely been accommodated to it. As a result, "peaceful" historical eras seem inherently unstable. Expectations are of course facilitated by the steady flow of periodic episodes of small violent conflicts between representatives of conflicting nations. When represented as "crises," they could erupt into full-scale war. Frequently, members of the society perceive their potential parts in armed conflict or war as "heroic." Thus, the role of the hero and one's opportunity to play it are held within commonsense interpretations of behavior during war. Moreover, the mythology of the hero is a compelling theme in American culture that is deeply rooted in the consciousness of its citizens. Correspondingly, it is commonly assumed that the arena of war provides circumstances wherein one's role as a hero may be played out. Naturally, recruitment during wartime by the armed services appeals to the psychology of becoming a hero as well as to social values supporting patriotism and duty.

Lifton's (1973) comments about the mythology of the hero as warrior are instructive. He argues that the underlying symbolism indicates the need for killing to bring about regeneration with the objective of reestablishing or transcending the present order of things. Consequently, in this symbolic image, killing is believed to become the *means* through which existence is perpetuated or improved. But Lifton implies that warrior heroes reflect the social and power relationships within their societies. He argues that the "socialized warrior" emerges who acts in the interests of those in power. Since the socialized warrior tends to submit to blind obedience, he is easily corruptible. In this view, then, the socialized warrior is an unreflective automaton of death, whose killing simply represents the concrete arm of the state. Hence, the massacre of civilians exemplifies the kind of mass murder possible under conditions when socialized warriors pursue their images of heroism.

Images of Death Work

What does death work mean to those expected to do it? What symbolic images are held of it? At least three images of death work may be discerned: (1) a *calling*, (2) a *job*, and (3) *slavery*. The symbolic meanings supporting each image of work gives them definition and provides a basis for action. Although each image arises out of certain circumstances, sometimes the same individual will sequentially define his experience in relation to each of the categories as idealism wanes.

For those who subscribe to the values and goals of their society, death work in war is a *calling* of the highest order. In this image, the work of inflicting death tends to be merged with the highest social and religious values held by persons within that society, as killing becomes a sacred ritual and dying is an heroic sacrifice. Toynbee's term "nationalistic fanaticism" (1968, p. 148) applies to the world view of the soldier who believes killing to be a sacred calling. Further, Lifton's concept of the socialized warrior (1973) points to the fact that the unexamined pursuit of death work as a calling not only increases the power of the state but also leads to atrocities. Quite clearly, killing as a calling has powerful rhetorical value for the professional soldier. It also has a powerful appeal to the populace and serves as a ready rationale to justify past actions and future commitments of the state.

Although the professional soldier may be only dimly aware of it, the work of war can become so routinized that the core of his personal identity becomes immersed in it. Or other types of experience may be so limited or seem so far in the past that the soldier may come to feel that he knows and comprehends only his present experience of combat. Under these conditions, the world of the past and future appears to be both ambiguous and absurd in the mind of the soldier. Glimpses of this dilemma are provided by Paul in Remarque's *All Quiet on the Western Front.*

> *What do they expect of us if a time ever comes when the war is over? Through the years our business has been killing;—it was our first calling in life. Our knowledge of life is limited to death. What will happen afterwards? And what shall come of us? (p. 266-67)* *

While some see their tasks as a calling, others see them as *necessary work.* The war may be defined as necessary work of the society to be undertaken by

---

* Excerpt from *All Quiet on the Western Front*, by Erich Maria Remarque. "Im Westen Nichts Neues" copyright 1928 by Ullstein, A.G.; Copyright Renewed 1956 by Erich Maria Remarque. "All Quiet on the Western Front" copyright 1929, 1930 by Little, Brown and Company; Copyright renewed 1957, 1958 by Erich Maria Remarque. All Rights Reserved.

its youth as their *"job."* It is still not uncommon for a Vietnam veteran to say something like, "We went to Vietnam to do a job, so I wanted to do the best job of it I could." Doing the job is then defined as one's mandatory contribution to society. For many of those who participate in combat, doing the job is, at least initially, more than just fulfilling a societal expectation; it also provides an opportunity for self-validation in the male role. By being capable of doing the job, one demonstrates the prerequisite traits of aggressiveness, decisiveness, activeness—in short—"masculinity," on which the "job" is presumed to be predicated (cf. Lifton 1973). For many, particularly in the Vietnam war, the job was to be tackled and completed in order that more ordinary work and existence might be subsequently pursued. These and like views are typically based on assumptions, however implicit, of *practicality* and *expedience*. The job of doing death work may be construed as dirty, disgusting, odious, or whatever, but above all, necessary. To the extent that it is viewed as necessary, other alternatives are unlikely to be entertained, and the course of action is laid out.

In contrast to the view of death work in war as a job to be done, the third image of *slavery* symbolizes the *forced* character of the work. By viewing the work as slavery, the fundamental element of *choice* is eliminated from consciousness, and the social actor is absolved from questioning personal actions and values. The image of forced, but temporary, enslavement is held by those who are disillusioned with their nation's cause or feel betrayed by the powerful, whose interests they now represent. Others, who never possessed much commitment to the cause or the powerful, share this image. Thus, in Vietnam it was not uncommon for these men to acknowledge that they accepted their draft notices because they did not want to go to prison (Boyle 1972).

When soldiers view their work as enslavement, they sometimes turn their hostility against their officers rather than against the enemy. Such actions are particularly likely as the soldier's image of his work changes through disillusionment or betrayal. Additional sources of disillusionment and betrayal include wide acceptance of atrocities, rape, annihilation of civilians, and rampant profiteering, all of which may belie the recruit's conception of the "clean" war he had assumed his officers and predecessors were carrying out. When obvious gaps between expectations and actual experience are discerned, the individual will create new or different categories to capture the shifting experience. Sometimes these will be reflected by a different image of death work.

Before concluding this discussion, I should note the emotional "thrill" that killing gives some individuals despite any particular image of death work they may hold. Whether openly stated or tacitly alluded, killing gives some men a sense of power, mastery, and satisfaction. While this response might be more easily rationalized when killing is viewed as a calling, it could lead to increased repressed guilt or uncontrolled destructiveness when one of the other images of death work is held, since there is less commitment to abstract ideals. In any case, images of death work provide contextual properties that give shape to the actions that are played out.

Socialization to Death Work

In order to handle death work with routinized efficiency, one must be methodically socialized into the proper performance of one's role. As noted, some continuity with previously held values, such as conceptions of the masculine role based on aggressiveness, is discernible. When the military experience remains largely consistent with previously held values, the young recruit's present experience will remain unquestioned. Then, structural conditions exist for the new recruit to be a "good" soldier with consequent identification as a "hero" as he becomes a socialized warrior.

In a more traditional analysis, Teicher (1965) implies that the "good" soldier takes his country's enemies as his own, but this occurs only when his socialization process is successful. Of course, its success is heavily contingent upon the extent to which only one definition of the war, that professed by the military, is available to the new recruit.

For the military to function properly, it must have an effective force for handling death work well. Problems of discontent, disobedience, and inefficiency are avoided when the socialization process is thorough. When it is not, the soldier may not identify with his unit. This, in turn, can lead to lessened efficiency and can perhaps impair the safety of the group as a whole. Consequently, concerted efforts are made to instill in the recruits instantaneous, automatic obedience to orders.

During the socialization of the new recruit, aspects of his prior identity are stripped away from him in order that a new controllable identity can ultimately be created to serve the purposes of the military organization (cf. Goffman 1961). Through the intensive program in boot camp, the recruit's thoughts as well as actions are reformed to coincide with those of military officials (cf. Lifton 1969). Particularly, those aspects of self that center on reflectiveness, sensitivity, and human concerns are subjugated to discipline, routine, and toughness. As Eisenhart (1977) explains, rewards are given only for outbursts of violence and savage endurance.

By turning a naive teenager into a systematic killer without his questioning that transition, the socialization process of the recruit shows how effectively transformations in both personal identities and subjective realities can be accomplished without the full awareness of the experiencing person. Changes may not even be noted, although over time the recruits' actions may take quite a different course than he may have anticipated.

One marker of this transformation was the "rabbit lesson" given to marines just before leaving for Vietnam (see Eisenhart 1977; Lifton 1973). While the sergeant lectures to the new marines on escape and survival in the jungle, he fondles a live rabbit while he talks. After their attention has become focused on the rabbit, the sergeant breaks the rabbit's neck, disembowels it and throws the entrails out on the audience. One former marine recounts the lesson the following way:

What was so striking was how dispassionately *he did it. One minute it was this pretty, cuddly rabbit you'd want as a pet. The next it was a carcass and all the while, he just kept talking in a matter-of-fact way. The message was clear: do anything you felt you had to, to survive (White 1974, p. 4).*

Part of the socialization of the recruit consists of mastering the new language of systematized death with its obscure meanings. Euphemisms of military terminology cloak the essential intent, that of destruction and murder. For example, "dispatching the enemy," "mopping up operations," or "flushing out the enemy" essentially mean annihilating any human resistance, but this meaning is obscured by jargon, and symbolically, it becomes much easier not to deal with it at all. Not surprisingly, one may discover some men who have participated in heavy combat have not seriously confronted their own deaths or questioned the meaning of their actions.

In the socialization of the new recruit, the myth of the hero is blended with the conditioned, automatic physical response. The emphasis on sexuality and aggression is symbolically intensified through the new recruit's training with a gun. The gun becomes an extension of his body, and he "proves" himself, so to speak, by his ability to use it. Prior self-doubts that the recruit may have had about being a "sissy" or a "coward" become allayed when he can demonstrate his ability and readiness to kill (cf. Eisenhart 1977; Lifton 1973). As values fostering aggressiveness and sexuality are melded into *the* source of personal identity, the new recruit becomes motivated to meet the expectations. Since the recruit's identity is on the line, the fact that affirmation and validation are earned through killing becomes almost incidental to his need to possess a valued identity. Subsequently, the recruit is socialized to conduct his death work without questioning it.

Death work is made easier when the enemy is believed to be racially inferior. Hence, a heavy indoctrination of racist beliefs often takes place during basic training. When one set of opponents views members of the other as less than human because of their racial characteristics, it becomes easier to relegate them symbolically to a category of being undeserving of human concern. By viewing the enemy as less than human, they are more easily perceived as essentially dangerous obstacles that must be removed from the scene if one is to survive. Differences in language can have a similar effect, although those differences alone are not as strong as when the opposition also evidences racial and cultural differences. Under these conditions, killing human beings may not be subjectively defined by the socialized warrior as anything more symbolically significant than slaughtering animals for market.

Whatever the differences imputed to the enemy, the enemy becomes objectified and is viewed through categories causing it to be kept distinct and separate from oneself. Even when the soldier's immediate experience belies his earlier socialization, the shift in definition of reality may only be temporary. The following episode and its aftermath described by Remarque illustrate the point as the hero realizes that the man he killed is much like himself.

> But you were only an idea to me before, an abstraction that lived in my mind and called forth its appropriate response. It was that abstraction I stabbed. But, now for the first time, I see you are a man like me. (p. 226)*

But guilt may be quelled and anguish may cease when one's comrades provide reassurance that the killing was necessary for survival of one's self, unit, and country. In addition, when faced with the immediate reality of another firefight, one's earlier empathy for the enemy may be redefined as incomprehensible (cf. Remarque 1929).

The kind of training the new recruit receives sets into motion the conditions under which he adapts to the deaths of those around him without, paradoxically, confronting the possibility of his own death or even his own vulnerability. Perhaps a response predicated upon the subjective denial of death is a goal toward which the military aims. Some veterans express a type of conviction in their invulnerability. That sense of being invulnerable becomes, ironically, intensified as the soldier experiences death around him. A developing callousness toward death after repeated exposures to it is illustrated by the following veteran's description of his response to his second exposure to combat death.

> . . . Perhaps I am luckier than most. I don't really think it can happen to me. . . .
>
> These recapitulations of my perception of death—death of others and death of self—announced a mutation in my personality. I was becoming impervious to the death of my fellow soldiers, and, in addition, I was negating the possibility of my own possible demise (Baruch 1975, p. 94).

Some veterans who have felt that they were invulnerable propose that their conviction gave them added strength in combat situations. They feel it helped them to diminish their fear, allowing them to focus more acutely on external conditions during critical moments rather than on internal feelings. Although training instructs the soldier to expect the unexpected, to adapt quickly to survive and dominate, and to exclude other responses, even a seasoned warrior may have occasional glimpses of his imminent vulnerability,

* Excerpt from *All Quiet on the Western Front* by Erich Maria Remarque. "Im Westen Nichts Neues" copyright 1928 by Ullstein, A.G.; Copyright Renewed 1956 by Erich Maria Remarque. "All Quiet on the Western Front" copyright 1929, 1930 by Little, Brown and Company; Copyright renewed 1957, 1958 by Erich Maria Remarque. All Rights Reserved.

particularly when he learns that not even mere survival is guaranteed by aggressive behavior. Because the Vietnam war was not a territorial war, aggressive behavior was often especially costly because of booby traps and ambushes. As a result, some men felt a heightened awareness of impending mortality. Consider this comment by White:

> My room-mate, who was a medic in Vietnam, and I have discussed the curious feeling of suddenly becoming acutely aware of your own vulnerability. I felt it while walking down the trail [a situation in which he knew that each step he took might be his last], and he felt it when, quite unexpectedly, he stumbled upon an enemy weapons cache. The feeling is that you are not alone; that you are ultimately vulnerable and that mere circumstance may dictate your safety (1974, p. 6).

At those times, the soldier may come closest to confronting his mortality, however quickly he discounts the feeling when the moment of danger is past.

Distancing death from the self is a means of handling extraordinary circumstances. Similarly, potential meanings of the deaths of others are minimized and kept distant from the core of the self. This has interesting implications for the participants' feelings of guilt. When distancing is complete, little guilt is likely to be experienced about causing death. As one Navy bomber who was on the coast of Vietnam said to me, "I never thought much about killing, we were just bombing the hell out of *targets*, not knowing if we hit anyone or not." In other situations, attacking civilians and escalating the bombing were justified as expediting the end of the war. These justifications served as a means of distancing the amount and kind of deaths incurred.

The techniques of war contribute to the psychological distancing of combatants. As technical efficiency "improves" through the use of automated technology, like sensors, radar, computerized pinpointing, and automatic fire missions, greater psychological distance occurs between one's actions and the cause of death (cf. Eisenhart 1977.)

The implications of this distance are threefold. First, the realization of self as a hero becomes highly problematic if one is never quite sure which or whose actions resulted in death and destruction. Second, the distance between one's self and the dead corpses becomes so great that corpses simply become part of the estimated body count when it can be determined at all. Third, the symbolic reality of war may become so distant from the self that the individual may be able to ignore his work in it. Instead, the war becomes a series of exercises, missions, or electronic games, however absurd they seem.

Two major conditions served to perpetuate the psychological distancing between actual actions and death in the Vietnam war. First, the war was not a territorial war and, second, the enemy could not be easily separated from the general population. Further, the social construction of a meaningful war was made difficult in part because of those two conditions and the resultant ambiguity of the situation. Consequently, all Vietnamese became suspect as potential Viet Cong and, therefore, at least implicitly, deserving of death. These views are strengthened by slogans like, "The only good gook is a dead gook," with the parallel assumption that all Vietnamese are "gooks." With this set of beliefs, the peasants are transformed into a dangerous enemy. Having a dangerous enemy is a necessary condition of making war meaningful to the participants, particularly to those pursuing the myth of the hero. The symbolic definition of a dangerous enemy is reinforced when escalations in terms of personnel, planes, and armaments are made since this gives weight to the assertions of policymakers that the enemy is treacherous and cannot be destroyed by current methods.

Shared definitions of a dangerous enemy constitute a major justification for the war. But when one looks beyond the justifications, a more significant issue arises, that of the concept of war itself. In this society, the emphasis is placed on believing in the *justifications* offered for a given war, rather than on questioning the entire concept of war and its institutionalization into our moral and economic systems. Thus, many persons compared the Vietnam war to World War II as an unjust war as opposed to a just one. That is an indication of the greater emphasis on assessing the *type* of war that the society is engaged in, rather than assessing war as an issue in itself.

When members of a society have little firsthand knowledge or experience in the arena of warfare and all such information is processed through official channels of propaganda, they are more likely to accept than to question the justifications given for that war. Further, the more consistent the information is about the nature of the conflict, the more easily a citizenry, far removed from the actual conflict, will accept it.

Routinization of the kind of death experienced in such wars is also facilitated by the *distance* that the members of a society have from the combat zone. By not experiencing actual combat, the reality of massive death is unlikely to be impressed upon the populace. Under these conditions, the populace is likely to believe in the justifications offered by their leaders for the existence of that particular war. In short, not only are new recruits socialized to accept their role in war, but so is the populace.

SUMMARY AND IMPLICATIONS

By looking at murder, capital punishment, and war as forms of death work, we can see similarities in seemingly diverse phenomena. Murder is not usually conceived of as "work." However, when it becomes either *methodical* or *repeated*, its similarities to death work become more visible. At that, beyond the job of being a "hit man," others sometimes take on a "career" as a "murderer" and may subsequently attain celebrity status through the media.

A fundamental similarity in all three ways of imposing death is the *routinization* of *extraordinary* death. By virtue of the fact that these deaths are *intentionally imposed* upon individuals, they are usually beyond the realm of ordinary American expectation and experience. These extraordinary events are made *routine*, in part through justifications that make the action appear understandable, plausible, legitimate, or even commendable. The *legitimacy* of the imposition of death is assumed with capital punishment and war since both represent the "legitimized" functions of the state. However, the legitimacy of murder through direct violence is problematic. In that sense, the murderer is faced with a difficult problem. While justifications for capital punishment and war are provided by the society, murderers are left largely on their own devices to construct sensible accounts to explain and justify their actions. In this sense, then, the situation of the murderer, when compared with executioners and soldiers, points to the problematic nature of constructing a reality acceptable to self and others when it is not already socially supported.

Quite clearly, murderers with violent self-images readily legitimize a response of violence when they attribute malicious intentions to another individual. The incipient violent, in contrast, are verbally abusive, and the nonviolent resort to violence only in self-defense. Because murder is the product of an interaction process, it may not be initially apparent who will dominate the situation through force. When victims provoke actors by daring them to escalate the encounter into violence or back down, they form a tacit agreement to define the encounter as a violent one. That agreement is likely to be fostered by the audience, who tend to press opponents into escalating the encounter. Most importantly, murderers concentrate on the implications of the encounter for their self-images while inflicting death upon their victims.

Since capital punishment is a form of violence, it is likely to be found in societies where violence is institutionalized. Capital punishment is a ritualized type of death work legitimized by the state. Those who support capital punishment claim that it is a rational means of deterring criminal acts. Proponents of capital punishment often claim that the death penalty itself is just but the distribution of it has not always been just in American society. In contrast, those who argue against it claim that research indicates it is not a deterrent, and if it is, that deterrence cannot be measured. From this perspective, capital punishment is based on vengeance rather than retribution. Furthermore, the wrong person may be executed. Because a disproportionate number of blacks have been given the death penalty, there is ample reason to believe that it has not been distributed equitably.

The way in which capital punishment is now handled as death work reflects changing cultural traditions. The ritual of the state execution has shifted from an open event complete with festivities and individualized roles to a concealed, bureaucratic ritual where participation is limited to a few functionaries who play interchangeable roles.

Since war is death work writ large, creating death becomes a routinized activity for the combatants. By invoking ideological reasons, war becomes justified and legitimized. Everyday conventions and language help conceal the reality of death in war. For the combatant, some preexisting values centering on beliefs about masculinity, heroism, and patriotism are intensified while others are minimized. Killing becomes the means through which existence is perpetuated or improved. Three images of death work in war may be discerned. First, the image of a calling is based on merged social and religious beliefs where killing becomes a sacred ritual and dying, a heroic sacrifice. Second, the image of a job is rooted in beliefs that the work is necessary as the only practical expedient solution to the situation. Third, the image of slavery assumes a forced character of the work that absolves the issue of choice.

By being resocialized into the role of the combat soldier, aspects of the new recruit's prior identity are stripped away, and a new, controllable self is reconstructed in the form of a mechanized aggressor. Part of the resocialization process involves developing an objectified definition of the enemy in order that any human identification with them will be avoided. Through psychological distancing, the soldier forgets that the objects of his work are human beings. In this way, killing in war becomes an automatic, routinized response that is justified by the soldier and legitimized by the state.

But let's look further into relationships between justifications and the routinization of death. Possibly, the argument presented in this chapter has wider applicability circumstances other than those involving these forms of extraordinary death. For instance, some conjectures may be offered about an analogous routinization of consciousness in the public concerning the mushrooming proliferation of weapons capable of massive annihilation. This unprecedented production of weapons has not been seriously questioned by members of society. Why? Conceivably, the public has been socialized into accepting the escalation of war preparations as necessary. Surely, pervasive support of a set of justifications results in their becoming routine. Even daily reminders in the media of the awesome potential of arms does not seem to cut through the social support for them. I propose that, coupled with accounts of potential threats and crises elsewhere, the media serve in the routinization process. In essence, what I am suggesting is that members of society have routinized, and therefore explained the "correctness" of, pursuing a path that fosters the production of massive numbers of extraordinary deaths.

In this chapter, I have analyzed the routinized features of extraordinary deaths in relation to death work. But not all extraordinary deaths may be viewed as work. Notable among those that are analytically separate is suicide. While not work, suicide is an extraordinary form of death. Because of its extraordinary character, suicide similarly poses the problem of legitimacy of the action to self and others. As I will discuss in the next chapter, suicidal individuals also attempt to legitimize their acts by invoking justifications from shared cultural themes. In a similar way then, they also make an extraordinary way of dying "sensible."

REFERENCES

Athens, Lonnie A. (1977). Violent crime: a symbolic interactionist study. *Symbolic Interaction* 1:56-70.

Baruch, Joel (1975). Combat death. In Edwin S. Shneidman (ed.), *Death: Current Perspectives*. Palo Alto, Calif.: Mayfield.

Bowers, William J. (1974). *Executions in America*. Lexington, Mass.: Lexington Books.

Boyle, Richard (1972). *Flower of the Dragon*. San Francisco: Ramparts Press.

Cooper, David D. (1974). *The Lesson of the Scaffold*. Athens: Ohio University Press, 1974.

Duffy, Clinton (1971). An evening with Clinton Duffy. In Stephen Levine (ed.), *Death Row: An Affirmation of Life*. New York: Ballantine Books.

Ehrmann, Sara R. (1972). For whom the chair waits. In James A. McCafferty (ed.), *Capital Punishment*. Chicago: Aldine.

Eisenhart, R. Wayne (1977). Flower of the dragon: an example of applied humanistic psychology. *Journal of Humanistic Psychology* 17:3-24.

Eshelman, Byron (1971). Death row chaplain. In Stephen Levine (ed.), *Death Row: An Affirmation of Life*. New York: Ballantine Books.

Garfinkel, Harold (1967). Inter and intra-racial homicides. In Marvin E. Wolfgang (ed.), *Studies in Homicide*. New York: Harper and Row.

Glaser, Daniel, and Max S. Ziegler (1974). Use of the death penalty v. outrage at murder. *Crime and Delinquency* 20:333-38.

Goffman, Erving (1961). *Asylums*. Garden City, N.Y.: Doubleday, Anchor Books.

Graves, William F. (1956). A doctor looks at capital punishment. *Medical Arts and Sciences* 10:137-141.

Greenberg, Jack, and Jack Himmelstein (1972). Varieties of attack on the death penalty. In James A. McCafferty (ed.), *Capital Punishment*. Chicago: Aldine.

Kastenbaum, Robert, and Ruth Aisenberg (1972). *The Psychology of Death*. New York: Springer.

Lifton, Robert Jay (1969). Thought reform: psychological steps in death and rebirth. In Alfred R. Lindesmith and Anselm L. Strauss (eds.), *Readings in Social Psychology*. New York: Holt, Rinehart and Winston.

_____ (1973). *Home from the War*. New York: Simon and Schuster.

Lofland, John (1975). Open and concealed dramaturgic strategies: the case of the state execution. *Urban Life* 4:272-95.

_____ (1977). The dramaturgy of state executions. In Horace Bleackley and John Lofland, *State Executions Viewed Historically and Sociologically*. Montclair, N.J.: Patterson Smith.

Luckenbill, David F. (1977). Criminal homicide as a situated transaction. *Social Problems* 25:176-86.

McGee, Richard A. (1972). Capital punishment as seen by a correctional administrator. In James A. McCafferty (ed.), *Capital Punishment*. Chicago: Aldine.

Pogash, Carol (1979). A real killing intrudes on filmgoers' fantasies. *San Francisco Examiner*, January 14, 1979.

Remarque, Erich Maria (1929). *All Quiet on the Western Front*. Boston: Little, Brown.

Teicher, Joseph D. (1965). "Combat fatigue" or death anxiety neurosis. In Robert Fulton (ed.), *Death and Identity*. New York: Wiley.

Toynbee, Arnold (1968). Death in war. In Arnold Toynbee, A. Keith Man, Ninian Smart, John Hinton, Simon Yudkin, Eric Rhode, Rosalind Heywood, and H. H. Price, *Man's Concern with Death*. New York: McGraw-Hill.

Van Den Haag, Ernest (1972). On deterrence and the death penalty. In James A. McCafferty (ed.), *Capital Punishment*. Chicago: Aldine.

Vernon, Glenn (1970). *The Sociology of Death*. New York: Ronald Press.

White, Bill (1974). Sudden death. Unpublished manuscript, California State College, Sonoma.

Wolfgang, Marvin (1967a). A sociological analysis of criminal homicide. In Marvin Wolfgang (ed.), *Studies in Homicide*. New York: Harper and Row.

_____ (1967b). Victim-precipitated criminal homicide. In Marvin Wolfgang (ed.), *Studies in Homicide*. New York: Harper and Row.

_____ (1974). Racial discrimination in the death sentence for rape. In William J. Bowers, *Executions in America*. Lexington, Mass.: Lexington Books.

_____, and Franco Ferracuti (1967). Subculture of violence—a socio-psychological theory. In Marvin Wolfgang (ed.), *Studies in Homicide*. New York: Harper and Row.

CHAPTER EIGHT

THE SOCIAL CONTEXT OF SUICIDE

The study of suicide has been dominated by perspectives that primarily stress the psychological structure and motivations of the suicidal individual. In contrast, I intend to discuss suicide from a perspective that *situates* that individual in the *social context*. With that in mind, four specific objectives underlie the discussion in this chapter: (1) to raise central issues about suicide by looking at traditional perspectives, (2) to use traditional perspectives as a source of comparison with the perspective outlined below, (3) to propose that individuals draw upon and adapt wider social values to lend meaning to their suicidal experiences as well as their own motivations, (4) to depict the suicidal person's on-going construction of reality through interaction. By emphasizing the latter two objectives, I hope that some balance might be given to earlier treatments of the topic. Throughout the discussion, earlier ideas will be presented and analyzed. Specifically, major sections will be presented on (1) *perspectives* on *suicide*, (2) the *relationship* of *suicide* to social structural *values*, (3) *suicidal processes*, (4) the *effects* of *suicide* on *survivors*, and (5) *implications* of the analysis for *suicide prevention.*

PERSPECTIVES ON SUICIDE

What do people think about suicide? When is a death a suicide? Why do people commit suicide? These are some of the questions addressed in this section. These seemingly straightforward questions raise many forms of ambiguity and speculation that enshroud suicide. First, in this section, I will provide a *statement of position*. Second, I will introduce *definitions of suicide* in relation to actual situations and preconceived images. Third, I will

233

present the perspective of *suicide preventionists*. Fourth, I will outline traditional *theoretical perspectives*, and finally, I will comment on *studying suicide*.

Statement of Position

Because the position presented throughout the chapter differs radically from traditional views of suicide, I spell it out in some detail, thus allowing readers to juxtapose their own assumptions and ideas about suicide with those presented.

In keeping with central ideas of symbolic interactionism, I assume from the beginning that suicidal persons construct *meanings* of suicide, including their *private motivations* for committing it. But my argument goes one step further: I propose that suicidal persons construct their meanings of suicide and motivations for committing it out of collective values upon which the social structure rests. That is, *what* constitutes suicide and *why* it happens at all are both understood through the meanings conferred on it by various persons. Hence, meanings of suicide arise out of what people *think, feel,* and *do* about it rather than what is simply given in the act. And, to reiterate, I propose that what people think, feel, and do about acts defined as suicide are intertwined with larger social values and meanings. For example, because a man is ashamed of a relative who committed suicide, he wishes to hide it. But that shame and wish for secrecy is not due to any inherent nature of the act; it is rather that the survivor shares collective sentiments and values that suicide is shameful. Thus, the survivor *confers* meaning on the act, thereby making it shameful.

Taking the emphasis on values one step further, note that social values change over time. If so, then, the values making suicide a possibility change during specific historical periods, and they are also linked to concrete relationships with specific groups. In short, I contend that suicide is multidimensional, besides being intimately linked with sociohistorical processes. Further, the specific cultural milieu fundamental to the American experience fosters the development of certain types of interpretations of events that make suicide comprehensible as a "logical" outcome of events or "solution," as it may be called. Social structural values therefore play a crucial role in the ways the suicidal process is constructed and experienced by individuals. In turn, individual instances of suicide are related to and reflect the specific type of social structure we live in and the dominant ideologies that support it. For example, an unemployed machinist is full of self-pity because life has dealt him a "bad deal" and he subsequently "isn't making it." His depression and subsequent suicide attempt are understandable to others since shared views are held about what it means to be unemployed, depressed, and unsuccessful. Our very understanding of the situation reflects shared ideologies about what it means to live in this society.

The point to be underscored is that any general theory of suicide would need to take into account ideological stances founded in social values and the myriad of ways in which they affect meanings in everyday life.

Given these premises, suicide must be viewed as more than just a phenomenon that affects those with personal adjustment problems, such as those who are seen as "mentally ill." If we can assume instead that life is a struggle fraught with problems in the first place, the psychological theories that lay primary causation for suicide in the individual's psyche cannot be wholly accepted. I believe that suicide is produced by a *combination* of factors. Although some individuals systematically experience life situations that undermine their sense of self-esteem, their hope and their ability to cope with crises, the underlying *causes* of their responses stem from the social structure. Further, the social structure fosters subtle psychological responses in individuals. Responses then reflect social experience and are not an inherent part of the person's nature. To illustrate, due to the social structuring of her immediate situation, a woman who is chronically ill becomes very isolated. As she becomes more isolated, she becomes more agitated and depressed about the uncertain prognosis of her illness and her increasing deterioration. She becomes so consumed with herself that she overburdens others (like her doctor) with her concerns and fails to respond "appropriately" during the course of encounters with them. Since her physician views her inappropriate interaction and later, suicidal thoughts as certain indicators of an underlying psychopathology that had been "there" all along, he fails to see that her seemingly bizarre behavior is constructed in the face of her current dilemmas (cf. Charmaz 1973).

As this example indicates, my position differs from that found in much of the literature on suicide. In that literature, analyses of suicide tend to *separate* suicidal individuals from the context of their experiences. With that separation comes the separation of these *individuals' interpretations* of reality from the actual situations constituting those realities. Analysts of suicide usually fail to realize that the suicidal individual's interpretation is crucial for understanding the situation. Moreover, this individual's interpretations may be wholly ignored by those around him or her. Instead, others may give greater weight to "intrapsychic processes" without taking into account the individual's ongoing experience. For example, others may focus on the individual's depression without giving much attention to the social sources of that depression. This separation of the subjective meaning of suicide from the more general context of social values is a major shortcoming of much of contemporary thinking about suicide. Ordinarily, suicide is taken to say something basic about only the individuals who commit it and perhaps their immediate social relationships, but not something basic about the *society* in which it takes place.

The premise that one must look to the nature of social structure to understand the occurrences of and even the private reasons for suicide is not new; these themes may be discerned in Durkheim (1951) and Masaryk (1970) and are implied in M. Farber (1968). Durkheim emphasizes the social integration of the individual into the society, Masaryk attempts to connect suicide with the historical development of European civilization, and M. Farber suggests that alienation produced by the social structure is of crucial importance for fostering the development of suicide. In contrast to those who emphasize social structural variables, Douglas (1967) stresses the conscious individual's construction of meaningful action through the means of suicide. I suggest that these two contrasting sociological approaches are connected. What is new about this argument is the proposal that structural values are played out in the individual's consciousness.

Suicide must be made sense of, become *understandable* and *accountable* to members of society. Thus members draw upon the larger cultural context to make sense of suicide in their lives. Commonsense understandings that are fabricated out of the larger cultural meanings give shape to what is known as suicide. Practitioners, suicides, attempters, relatives, officials, and social scientists must be able to make sense of suicidal actions. Suicide often seems incomprehensible if it cannot be fit into a context of plausible meanings.

Although culture provides a framework through which suicide becomes identified, known, and understood, individual members of that culture *interpret* those cultural meanings in their own way. What everybody "knows" about suicide directly reflects cultural values about it. The commonly derived assumptions about the nature of suicide, what gives rise to it, and how survivors make sense of it tend to be rooted in the larger cultural matrix, although all may be taken for granted. Similarly, what given persons "know" about suicide is shaped by their immediate group associations, the members of which develop meanings about events and things. In some cases, such group affiliation may give rise to highly specific and articulated views of suicide. For example, suicide prevention volunteers will develop a shared set of assumptions about the nature of suicide, what conditions foster it, and so forth. Members of other groups may lead to other, perhaps less explicit but no less meaningful, views of suicide. Although the extent to which the values of the group mirror, reflect, intensify, or draw upon wider cultural values is ultimately an *empirical* question, I suspect that varied interpretations of these core values in relation to suicide may be seen in many subgroups and the different layers of the social strata. It stands to reason that within a particular group or social class, the accounts making suicide comprehensible may rest on specific dimensions of the core values. For example, "revenge" suicide might be found to characterize certain elements of the population, whereas suicides conducted with the idea of death as a "transition" into another world might be found more prevalent in other groups.

Perhaps most individuals take on views of their respective groups on matters like suicide as they are subjects about which everyone "knows" but not everyone comes close to observing or even acknowledging. The wider culture, as well as specific groups, not only provides terms to understand suicide but also definitions of motives for it. In turn, both become part of commonsense understandings about the nature of suicide. Hence, a language is provided in everyday life in which the motives for suicide become taken for granted by members of society. To the extent that individuals take these commonsense motives as adequate rationales for suicide, or essentially take them as given, they are unlikely to transcend them or to go beyond what is readily available.

Through experiencing a suicidal crisis oneself or by being closely associated with someone else who is experiencing such a crisis, participants may question former definitions of what suicide was all about and subsequently construct new meanings. Clearly, then, the meaning of suicide is also *emergent* in character.

Definitions and Images of Suicide

Beyond the moral and ethical questions it raises, suicide tends to be an inherently problematic issue for officials such as police and coroners besides social scientists. Defining a death as a suicide sometimes leaves sticky questions unanswered. In this section, I suggest the kinds of questions that arise when a definition of suicide is made. By definition, I mean here the category that is applied by persons whose job it is to "ascertain" that a given death is an actual suicide. Next, I outline major images that professionals and lay persons hold of suicide. These images are rooted in *preconceived ideas* about the intentions of the suicidal individual. Though there is no sure way of checking intentions once the individual is dead, these images provide powerful commonsense explanations for *why* a suicide occurs.

How are definitions established so that a particular death is in fact classifiable as a suicide? Douglas (1967) points out that definitions of suicide include different emphases on the *intentions* of the suicidal person, the *act* itself, and the *knowledge* of the actor. Quite clearly, the intentions of the actor are of real import for determining whether a death will be categorized as suicide. I will elaborate on this issue below; for the present, consider the difference between those instances when persons *intend* to die by committing an act and those instances when persons *initiate* an act directly followed by their deaths. Do both situations constitute genuine "suicide"? Or is one equivocable? In order to make the issue more concrete, an example will help. A woman who took an overdose of sleeping pills—more than the lethal amount—but is discovered accidentally and lives. A teenage boy partook of drugs and drink at a party, the combination of which can be lethal, and dies. Although some analysts might say that heavy drinking in combination with drugs itself shows self-destructive tendencies, was his death an accident or a suicide? Was the boy actually *aware* of what he took and hence aware of the danger? If investigators can find no clues that are commonly taken to suggest any intention of suicide, then the death becomes difficult to categorize as suicide. In the case of one teenage musician, all indications are that he was unaware of the lethal combination that he took at a party. Previously, his exposure to drugs was limited—nothing stronger than marijuana—until shortly before attending the party. There, a large amount of pure heroin was made available by a drug dealer who told the guests it was cocaine. Since many of them did not know the difference, they were unable to discern what they were snorting. The teenage musician was believed to be among this group. A few individuals were aware of the difference, but they did not choose to inform the others, who continued to drink alcohol and snort the drug. The individuals who knew what they were taking somehow discounted the risks, at least for themselves, until it was too late. Several people were seriously ill, and the one teenage musician died.

The ambiguous character of these examples shows the difficulties that arise when ascertaining whether a death is a real suicide. Sometimes, people are wholly unaware of the risk of death to which they subject themselves. Other times, participants are at least dimly aware of the potentially self-destructive aspects of their behavior. Still others are fully cognizant of both the risk involved and the potentially self-destructive aspects of their actions, but they feel assured that others will intervene. By committing their suicidal "gestures," they communicate symbolically with others and, if the planned intervention takes place, they live. But even the most carefully thought out plans sometimes go wrong. If so, then the intended suicidal gesture, meant only to communicate feelings like despair, anger, or estrangement, becomes a suicidal "accident." Litman *et al.* (1970) described such a case. A man who was estranged from his wife planned a suicidal gesture that he apparently expected to fail. While she was out with another man, he parked in front of her house and took an overdose of barbituates. The note he pinned to his chest indicated that he expected her to find him upon their return later in the evening. But in the dense fog, his wife did not notice his presence, and he died.

Another word of caution is necessary about the awareness of individuals who commit a seemingly suicidal act. Although they may be aware of the general risk of death involved, the potential destructiveness of the act may not necessarily be viewed by "suicidal" persons as applicable to self. As noted in the preceding chapter, cultural emphases on heroism, strength, and bravado, which are most observable in masculinity myths, may foster illusions about invincibility. For example, a young man who occasionally mainlined heroin thought that his strong body was able to handle large dosages. He claimed that he was able to take dosages of drugs that overcame more ordinary others. After building an amazing tolerance to the drug, he surprised his friends by overdosing.

In the discussion above, I stressed the nature of the act and the knowledge of the person. As I observed, it becomes even more complex when *intentions* are examined. Commonsense understandings lead one to think that suicide is an act of self-annihilation. That is, the killing of the self is intended to be a complete and final act. Yet, as will become clear throughout the chapter, *total* annihilation of the self remains another ambiguous and problematic issue. There is good reason to believe that many suicides wish to change only part of themselves or transform their situations as they now *exist*. Sometimes, a suicidal person wishes to live in a new or different way and thus wishes to kill the self living in the present way. Suicidal persons may also believe that by committing suicide they will experience the transition necessary to live in another way, as a result of reincarnation, rebirth, or even revenge. In short, the wish to die may be *ambivalent*.

Kubie (1969) argues that it is a mistake to assume that every act that can be defined as self-destructive has the objective of death. He claims that some mental patients who are released before they are "ready" will perform desperate self-destructive acts to justify returning to the hospital. He also argues that the distance that people now have from death contributes to their lack of awareness of the mortal implications of their self-destructive acts.

If definitions of suicide are ambiguous, images of suicide must be correspondingly ambiguous and contradictory since images provide sources for definitions. The literature on suicide seems to confirm the contradictory nature of these images. Essentially, different writers have different images of what suicide is. Their images tend to reflect commonsense images of suicide held by members of society. Important assumptions about images of suicide indicate social values, particular conceptions of death, the intentions of the actor, and the degree of rationality attributed to the actor. An exploration of images of suicide opens up some of the major issues that will be addressed throughout the chapter.

The image of suicide as a *gamble* with death is emphasized by Stengel (1969) and Lester and Lester (1971). Suicidal persons may not care whether they live or die. By taking the risk of forcing the possibility of death, suicidal individuals may force a confrontation with their future. For example, by gambling with death, someone may attempt to force a lover to reassess the relationship. Although it is desperate, the gamble with death is made to control the outcome of a relationship. In this way, a gamble with death may also be a gamble with life.

Since what is being risked may be symbolically or expressly communicated, the image of suicide as a gamble coincides with the image of suicide as a *means of communication*. What is communicated may vary considerably. Some images of suicide are based upon the assumption that the suicide's personality traits (with notable emphasis on his or her "weaknesses," such as cowardice) are communicated in the suicidal act. Other images of suicide emphasize the communication of feelings, such as *revenge, pain, helplessness,* and *despair*.

Similarly, suicide can also be viewed as a *dialogue* with the person's significant others. The nature of the dialogue can differ according to the analyst of suicide. For the preventionist, suicide is a *cry for help*, while for the more phenomenologically oriented analyst (see Hillman 1964) the symbolic dialogue may rest on a desire for *transformation* of self and situation. Both the image of the cry for help and the image of transformation assume that *change* is of greatest significance, although the former image legitimizes intervention by outsiders. However, the two images differ on the issue of rationality. As I examine later in greater detail, the image of the cry for help corresponds with the view that the suicide has a *mistaken* or *irrational* view of death. In contrast, the image of transformation acknowledges that death may be *chosen.*

Underlying most images of suicide are the issue of *ambivalence* and the question of *rationality.* Ambivalence toward life and death may echo the ambivalence the person may feel toward self and others. When the suicidal experience is characterized by ambivalence, these persons typically feel pushed and pulled by forces they do not understand and cannot control. For example, a respected member of the community was discovered to have sporadic, secret homosexual encounters with strangers. His wife (who felt that she was to blame for his homosexual urges) described his distraught behavior. Although he was full of remorse for the mortification the family felt, she thought he was extremely ambivalent about his own worth. Besides feeling that he had no control over his urges, which he, like his family, saw as wholly unacceptable, he felt he now had no control over his life since his "problem" had become more public. He hung himself in his garage.

Whether the suicidal person's views are rational raises an important theme in most images of suicide. The question is, does suicide represent a rational choice or is it produced by unconscious, irrational motivations? This question has long been discussed by suicidologists and laypersons alike. Children and adolescents, particularly, have been assumed to become suicidal due to irrational thinking or impulsive acts. However, Jacob's (1971) study of adolescent suicide systematically refutes this assumption. Jacobs concludes from his data that adolescent suicide, when studied phenomenologically, can be taken only as a conscious, rational choice.

The rationality of suicide is illustrated by Peck and Wold (1977), who describe a young girl they saw in therapy. Her suicide attempt was preceded by a long list of behavior problems and family conflicts, particularly with her stepmother. Both the girl and her stepmother initially had similar accounts of the causes of her unhappiness. Most of her friends were going to attend another high school, and she knew very few people where she would be going. The therapist requested that the father also attend the sessions, but he did not come. At one point the therapist asked the girl what her father would think about a particular issue. Her response was to burst into tears as she disclosed that her father was terminally ill. (At first the stepmother was angry that the family secret had been revealed.) The therapist interpreted the girl's suicidal and depressive behavior as her way of dealing with her grief over her impending loss and her fright about being abandoned when she had such a tenuous relationship with her stepmother. When viewed in the context of her experience, the girl's suicidal thoughts and actions appear to be rational.

The rationality of the suicidal experience must then be examined from *inside* the situation in the context of the immediate experience of the actor. But because that context may be precluded from the scrutiny of any observer, particularly a professional one, suicide appears to outsiders to take on irrational properties. A thorough analysis of these situations might demonstrate how what seems to be an impulsive, spontaneous act is constructed systematically out of the logic of the person's experience and immediate situation. In a word, what seems to be illogical and irrational reflects the logic of an experience that is outside the realm of the conventional reality of agents of social control and even intimates, but not of the actor who has chosen self-destruction.

Theoretical Perspectives on Suicide

Theoretical perspectives have both reflected and influenced the popular images of suicide that are discussed above. For example, issues of irrational and unconscious motivations reflect the psychoanalytic tradition, and issues of choice reflect existentialist concerns. In this section, I introduce four major approaches that include some traditional notices about suicide. They include *psychoanalytic, existential, Hillman's subjectivist,* and *Durkheim's sociological* perspectives. In addition, I have added some comments on the civil libertarian perspective to the discussion on Hillman, since it coincides with Hillman's focus on choice. All of the perspectives can be used later as sources of comparison with the symbolic interactionist perspective that is elaborated throughout the chapter.

Psychoanalytic perspective Consistent with the general psychoanalytic framework, the psychoanalytic view of suicide emphasizes *unconscious motivation* and *repression.* In Freud's view, the self-hatred seen in depression originates in repressed anger toward someone else. Because the person cannot consciously acknowledge that anger, it becomes turned *inward* upon the self. Freud's analysis emphasizes the loss of the other through some means. The person had and has a strong identification with the lost other but is unable to transfer and attach that identification to new intimates. Consequently, the person feels a good deal of *ambivalence,* that is, mixed feelings of love and hate, with his or her strong feelings of identification and resentment over the loss.

Hendin (1957) attempts to clarify the relationship with the other by emphasizing the dependency adaptation in depression. He argues that the kind of identification the person has with the lost other is fundamentally dependent. Since that dependency is frustrated, and feelings toward the other are characterized by ambivalence, the person's rage becomes turned inward. Whether the repressed aggression results in suicide depends on the strength of these feelings. As Rushing (1968) points out, in the psychoanalytic view, suicide is a form of *"murder."* When self-murder occurs, the lost love object incorporated into the self is also killed.

Relationships between murder and suicide have been elaborated upon by Menninger (1938). He argues that suicide involves "the wish to kill, the wish to be killed, and the wish to die." Menninger also postulates that suicides are immature individuals who are fixated at earlier stages of development. Further, he emphasizes an exaggerated response to frustration and implies that the person is submissive and dependent in order to fulfill desires. Hendin (1968) claims that suicidal persons have always been problem children who were spoiled, complacent, and oversensitive. According to him, their feelings are easily hurt and they are poor losers.

A sociological commentary on depictions of the suicidal personality would take into account the fact that such characterizations are *reconstructions* made after the person has been defined as a "case" with a serious problem. Because suicidal patients tend to pose difficult dilemmas for treatment specialists, who often feel a sense of failure with them, quite possibly these dilemmas and the stigma of suicide shade the characterizations that are made.

In a somewhat different vein, Kilpatrick (1968) argues that hopelessness and alienation lead to the conditions of accumulated self-contempt which then results in suicide. She argues that psychosomatic diseases may replace or alternate with suicidal impulses. But she also emphasizes that suicide occurs only in severely neurotic individuals.

To summarize the psychoanalytic view of suicide, the unconscious motivations that are believed to underlie behavior give rise to uncontrolled impulses. Yet the source of those impulses is thought to emanate from unresolved issues from earlier stages of development. In the psychoanalytic view, feelings the actor does not understand give rise to what is assumed to be an irrational act.

An existentialist perspective An existential view of suicide would take into account the significance of the confrontation with death characteristic of the suicidal experience. Because existentialists stress the crucial importance of the confrontation with death for taking moral responsibility over one's life, the idea of death through suicide takes on different dimensions than in the public. From an existentialist view, it is conceivable that the confrontation with death during a suicidal crisis may cause suicidal individuals to sense their *aloneness* and *personal responsibility* for their experience. Moreover, the *choice of death* may be fully akin to the *choice of life*, both the result of reflection.

Death through suicide or other means is not the enemy that it is in other perspectives. Rather, leading an unexamined life without moral fortitude is a more important issue to existentialists. To the extent, however, that existentialists see both life and death as lacking inherent meaning, there is no absolute meaning, per se, in the suicidal experience: whatever is made of the experience would be conferred by the actor. Hence, meaning of the suicidal experience could be constructed only by the individual.

Camus (1955) raises the issue of suicide when he argues that suicide provides the only serious philosophical question. Camus's question is based on his premise that human life is devoid of meaning so one must ask if suicide is not the appropriate response to life? For Camus, life is *absurd* and death is the most obvious of all absurdities. According to his reasoning, the realization that life is meaningless and life and death are both absurd does not leave a person in a suicidal crisis. He assumes that life will be lived better if it has no intrinsic meaning. Presumably, living existentially means *authentic acting* while being continually aware of the absurd conditions of human experience. That awareness leads one to continue to challenge the nature of one's world. By doing so, suicidal persons maintain their integrity as they attempt to control their fates. Consequently, Camus's answer to his philosophical question is negative. And, in the last analysis, his approach underscores the existentialist stance that the person ultimately faces life and death alone.

Hillman's subjectivist perspective Hillman, a noted Jungian psychologist, provides a therapeutic approach to suicide. With its existential and phenomenological overtones, Hillman's approach to treatment of suicide (1964) takes a subjectivist perspective. Essentially, Hillman attempts to look inside the suicidal person's reality. Since he is a therapist, Hillman's concern includes the quality of the suicidal experience and the therapist's understanding of it from the actor's point of view, instead of from preconceived or objectivistic notions.

Because he takes issue with traditional approaches to suicide, his book, *Suicide and the Soul*, is an important contribution whether or not one agrees with his thesis. Consistent with psychoanalytic imagery, Hillman contends that suicidal persons typically have little understanding of their actions. Further, he also assumes that death is within us although we consciously try to separate ourselves from it. Thus, he claims that ordinary persons are not in touch with death though it is a part of their being. Consequently, death may seem to "overtake" individuals as if it emerged from external pressures that control them.

For Hillman, death through suicide is not nearly so important as the life of the soul. By soul, he means, essence, mind, or spirit. The death experience, according to him, may be necessary in order to preserve the life of the soul. Hillman's position fundamentally rests on his view that the subjective reality of the suicidal individual has first priority for those who study or work with suicides.

By taking the radical position that death can be *chosen*, Hillman also assumes that suicidal behavior is meaningful. But its meanings may be best understood by getting *inside* the experience of the suicidal individual. Thus Hillman acknowledges that the problems confronting the suicidal person look and feel unique despite the proclivity of social scientists and practitioners to judge and categorize suicide according to external criteria believed to be objective. In fact, he makes a cogent argument that the objectivist position of judging suicide from the outside only limits understanding of it.

Hillman contends that suicidal persons are attempting to live out their mythic fantasy through the death experience. But, he warns, individuals who understand their myths are rare; this is why death seems to take these persons by surprise. Yet, according to Hillman (1964), the impulse to die may not be anti-life, it may be a demand for a fuller life, one that permits the expression of individuality.

Hillman's view, as well as the existentialist view, of suicide fits nicely with those who hold a civil libertarian position. Szasz (1971), a foremost spokesman of that position, espouses the view that one's life is one's *property*. If so, then suicide becomes a *choice* the individual can make about what to do with it. Ultimately, then, what one does with one's life is one's responsibility, not the responsibility of the state or the psychiatric establishment.

Szasz clearly attributes a degree of *rationality* to the suicidal person, something neither suicide preventionists nor psychiatric observers usually define. Szasz insightfully notes that the suicidal person's wish to die is typically and erroneously redefined by practitioners into a representation of deep-seated irrationality. Further, through the process of redefinition, the suicidal person's human value becomes reduced, and his or her symbolic world is undermined or invalidated. Szasz emphasizes that the person's aspiration to die is radically invalidated as personal autonomy and individual choice are extinguished by the preventionist. To dramatize his point, Szasz (1971, p. 14) contends that suicidologists turn Patrick Henry's dictum, "Give me liberty or give me death," on its head. Szasz states, in effect, that it is transformed into *"Give him* commitment, *give him* electroshock, *give him* lifelong slavery, *but do not let him choose death"* [emphasis his].

Both Hillman and Szasz believe that choosing to die is a basic human *right*. While I am sympathetic to their intent to encourage conceptions of individualism to develop along the lines of civil liberties, another view might put their position into perspective. If, as many contend, the character of human existence is fundamentally alienating in contemporary society, then the right to commit suicide should logically be a human choice. But the positions taken by Hillman and Szasz seem to reflect the conditions of modern society, what *is*, rather than what could *be* in the future.

In some ways in contemporary society, suicide typically represents a statement of individualism. But I believe that when it is viewed politically, ordinary suicide is a fundamentally *conservative* action. Because in the context of our cultural meanings suicide reaffirms individualism, it does not result in any serious challenge to the ongoing social order. Possibly, the energy turned inward to the self could be redirected toward constructing a more humane social order. If so, then a greater potential for social change might develop. Although the last comments may seem whimsical, they point to the fact that ordinarily suicide may be an isolated, individualistic protest against present conditions. If this protest could be in some way changed into collective action, perhaps at least some of the social conditions could be alleviated that give rise to suicide becoming a viable choice. Like Patrick Henry's choice of liberty *or* death, the quest for death of one could be transformed into the quest for liberty for many.

Durkheim's sociological perspective Emile Durkheim's nineteenth century study of suicide (1951, originally published 1897), widely acclaimed the classical sociological statement on the subject, attempted to demonstrate that even such private and seemingly individualistic acts as suicide are ultimately determined by social forces (despite the psychological predisposition to it possessed by some individuals). In order to validate his argument, Durkheim claims that certain regularities are apparent in the social suicide rates. It was the regularity in the rates that he sought to explain rather than the etiology of suicide in the individual. For Durkheim, these rates constituted "social facts." They are those facts that are general throughout a society and exercise constraints over its members. Because social facts are *general*, their explanation was said to reside in the *society* and not the individual.

Durkheim accounted for the regularities in suicide rates through social explanations. He found that societies in which Catholicism was the dominant religion had lower rates than those in which Protestantism was institutionalized; married persons suffered suicide less than unmarried; widowers had higher rates than widows; and so forth. His major argument rested on what he considered to be the key differences between values that Catholic and Protestant denominations imparted to their members rather than their prohibitions against suicide since he viewed these prohibitions as equally stringent. Basically, he saw that Protestantism gave rise to individualism due to its emphasis on free inquiry. In contrast, Catholicism gives greater regulation and provides a powerful source of social integration to its constituencies. Stated simplistically, Durkheim's thesis emphasizes that the more integrated the individual is into social institutions, the lower will be the rates of certain types of suicide. Social integration rests upon sharing a set of values, beliefs, and norms that govern behavior. By possessing roles linking persons to their group affiliations, those persons are integrated into society as a whole and, further, are constrained in their behavior. For example, the traditional marital role simultaneously provides regulation of behavior through the expectations and obligations inherent in it, and it links the person to the wider society.

A major problem with Durkheim's analysis is that he failed to take into account how human beings construct the official rates upon which he relied so heavily. For example, officials in a Catholic society might be less inclined to categorize a given death as "suicide," since the person could not be buried in hallowed ground, a great stigma. Further, when a close look is taken at Durkheim's analysis, it may be discerned that he simply took commonsense conceptions of his day as the explanation of his data (see Douglas 1967). Nevertheless, social integration is Durkheim's key variable (although his use of integration is not wholly distinguished from his emphasis on regulation).

In his analysis, Durkheim developed three types of suicide: *egoistic*, *altruistic*, and *anomic*. These types of suicide are related to his conception of social integration. Egoistic suicide occurs when the person is inadequately integrated into the society. The ego affirms its own autonomy but cannot cope with the conflicting pressures to which it is subjected. The person can no longer find a basis for existence. Since the person's frame of reference primarily revolves around self-concern, there is no social authority to which allegiance is held. Durkheim's prototype of an individual given to this type of suicide is the intellectual, who is less likely to be linked to society in conventional ways than others.

The second type of suicide, *altruistic*, occurs when the individual is overly integrated into the society. The ego is not the individual's property, as it were, but stands in service to the group. The self is not individualized; it is blended into the fabric of society. If death is expected by the group, then the individual unquestioningly and willingly dies. The Kamikaze pilot of World War II is an exemplar of altruistic suicide. Under these circumstances, the socialization which these persons receive in society prepares them to accept the group's objectives even at cost of their lives.

The third type of suicide, *anomic*, is perhaps the one for which Durkheim is most famous. This type results from the *lack* of *regulation* of the individual. The causes of anomic suicide arise from political and economic crises causing the individual to no longer feel the moderating effect of collective existence. The norms governing his or her existence no longer control the individual's passions. Poverty, per se, does not give rise to anomic suicide; rather, it is elicited by sudden reversals due to changes in the larger economic or political sphere. A crash of the stockmarket is the classic situation where previously experienced regulation is no longer felt. The businessman who commits suicide after a crash is the prototypical individual in anomic suicide.

Durkheim's analysis has itself become a prototype of social scientific research and, until recently, it has been uncritically accepted. Douglas (1967) argues that Durkheim's argument shifts and changes as he bends the data to fit his preconceived theory. Consequently, Durkheim logically "proved" things that should be subjected to empirical tests. Perhaps most importantly, Durkheim's theory of suicide rests on an uncritical acceptance of the suicide rates of specific populations of people. Because these rates share all the general problems inherent in survey research and all the specific ones arising from studying suicide, Durkheim's theory must be taken as a preliminary set of ideas instead of the definitive sociological work on suicide.

Suicide Preventionist Perspective

The perspective of the suicide preventionist must be explored since it has dominated much thinking and research about suicide. This perspective shares domain assumptions with other helping professions and occupations in which a quasi-therapeutic stance is taken. Concepts of death as well as the nature of suicide are held within this perspective. In the discussion below, I will explicate these issues by paying particular attention to the views of Shneidman, a leading suicidologist.

Shneidman (1970) emphasizes analyzing suicide from outside the experience. Accordingly, he has classified the *role* people play in their death. Three of his major categories are *intentioned, subintentioned* and *unintentioned* death. Suicide is believed to figure heavily with the first two and often must be distinguished from the third. By intentioned death he refers to cases in which a *direct role* is played by individuals in their demise. He contends that people seek or initiate death. He also contends that some ignore the fact that termination necessarily involves a cessation of experience. Others, according to Shneidman, gamble intentionally with death, but all play a direct role in their death. It is this group of persons with whom suicide preventionists may have the most contact.

The next group, subintentional death, is extremely important for Shneidman's framework. In subintentional death (see Shneidman 1970, p. 18), suicidal individuals' actions in producing their deaths are believed to be much less directly ascertainable. Instead, these actions are seen as *indirect* or are not consciously perceived by the actor. From this perspective, persons who play a subintentional role may not directly confront their desire for death. If they had internalized the taboo against suicide, confronting their desire to die might be shocking to their self-images. Clearly, these people do not take very good care of themselves. Basically, according to Shneidman, they do not wish to live. In cases of subintentioned death, it is assumed, for example, that ulcer patients continue to drink, older persons do not eat, cardiacs continue to smoke, and drivers are on the road while drunk.

The death of a rock star who took drugs and alcohol simultaneously might be viewed as a subintentioned death by some, although it was officially judged an accident. Combined use of drugs and alcohol was common in his world and apparently he had taken them together many times before his death. The coroner ruled out suicide since all indications were that after drinking beer the musician had taken heroin to get high but during a recent incarceration had lost his tolerance (see "Sid Vicious Dies of Drug Overdose" 1979). But those who accept the category of subintentioned death would question the coroner's ruling. This musician had attempted suicide three months before when he was free on bail. Also, he had been charged with the killing of his former girl friend, a crime to which he initially had allegedly confessed. Obviously, once the musician is dead, he cannot be interviewed.

Thus, his case nicely illustrates that ultimately whether such categories as subintentioned death are accepted is a matter of perspective.

For the suicide preventionist, the carelessness of individuals, like the musician above, is seen as clearly self-destructive, but in other cases it is believed to remain more covert. Psychosomatic diseases, for example, are sometimes believed to indicate subintentioned suicidal feelings. Shneidman notes that the newly bereaved person may behave in ways that suggest subintentioned death. The hastening of death in the newly bereaved has been clarified by Parkes's discussion of the broken heart (1975). The vulnerability to death of the recently bereaved appears to be well documented since these individuals have a much higher death rate. Nevertheless, when one ascribes subintentioned wishes to someone, one is assuming that an objective observer may view that individual's experience more accurately than he or she who lives it.

But to return to the perspective of the suicide preventionist, many potential suicides are seen as *illogical*. Shneidman and Mandelkorn (1970) state that the suicide stumbles into death while gasping for life. Thus, they emphasize the ambivalent stance that the suicide has toward living and dying.

It is in this sense that suicide preventionists see death as the *enemy*. They take the position that the person loses sight of what death is: an *absence* of experience. Consequently, one cannot be a spectator to it. It is this, they contend, that suicides lose touch with.

Shneidman and Mandelkorn (1970) state that at best one can only *fantasize* what it would be like to be dead, as imagining what one's funeral will be like. Such fantasizing, they propose, may cause the final step into suicide since it contributes to the person's denial of death. In Shneidman's view (1973), to believe that one can experience or observe one's death is *denial*. Shneidman implies that in order to commit suicide at all, one must deny the reality of death. He says that when one is about to put a bullet through one's head, one is denying death. He also remarks that if suicidal persons could write a logical suicide note, they would not have to commit suicide. Here, Shneidman suggests that impaired logic characterizes many of the notes, and if the persons were able to think logically, they would not be impelled to commit suicide.

In a word, suicidologists argue that logic of the suicide is a *specious logic*. They particularly take issue with romanticized, externalized images of death promoted in the media and cultural folklore. These images may show death to be passive, peaceful, and comforting. Or they may show death to be heroic in the case of men or altruistic in the case of women. In keeping with stereotypical sex roles, themes of men dying in defense of their beliefs and women dying in demonstration of their love are common cultural images. According to suicidologists, such images are highly seductive; they lead us away from the "reality" of death, which is to them an absence of consciousness (see Shneidman 1973).

The romanticization of death, according to this view, makes one more vulnerable to suicide. In this phenomenological critique of suicide prevention, Hoeller (1973) points out an underlying assumption of suicidologists: to entertain thoughts of suicide is to flirt with the enemy. Life is seen as a precious possession not to be tampered with. Underlying the suicidologist's concern about suicide comes the crucial question: Do any of our lives have value at all? Life *must* have value according to this perspective. Essentially, suicides are viewed as having taken leave of their senses, however temporarily. From the logic of suicide prevention, it then becomes the *right* and *obligation* of the preventionist to intervene until the person has gotten in touch with the "reality" of death.

The basic assumption of a suicide preventionist is that every suicide is *a cry for help*. That cry for help is seen as a cry for life. The suicidal person is seen as basically *ambivalent*, wishing both to die and be "saved." Suicidologists find that those feelings are typically communicated to others before the actual suicide attempt, although indications of suicidal intentions may be ignored. At times, such communications may be intentionally given to persons who will react in an overtly hostile manner. This may be used as one means of validating the growing belief that suicide is the "only way out."

The view that most suicides are a cry for help *legitimizes* the stance that suicide preventionists take. Although Shneidman and other suicidologists themselves show considerable sensitivity to their clients and an awareness of the complex issues involved in the wish to die, other suicide preventionists may apply their perspective more concretely and without the sensitivity of their progenitors. Instead, their views of suicide often strikingly resemble commonsense views of suicide. They may invoke a set of rules on how to handle the suicidal person (cf. Sachs 1967), and these rules frequently reflect the stigmatized identity conferred in the wider society.

In effect, suicide preventionists become agents of *social control*. When the preventionist mentality is taken to its logical extension, all the armamentarium of society may be invoked against a person's wish to die. In a sense, the first objective of the preventionist perspective is social—to preserve lives in the community. Those preventionists who are sought out by the suicidal person in situations such as crisis centers or switchboards view the person's initial seeking of help as legitimizing the actions they subsequently take to preserve life. But, in any case, preservation may occur without regard for the *quality* of existence. Hillman (1964, p. 35) reveals that preventionists parallel the medical paradigm when he says, "Promoting life has come to mean prolonging life," in that they, too, opt for length over quality of life in their pro-life stance.

Szasz (1971) challenges the ethics of preventionists and psychiatrists who treat suicidal persons with his strong civil libertarian position. He claims that these practitioners employ the most vile methods to accomplish their objectives. An example of the kind of method to which he refers is the practice of keeping callers, who wished to remain anonymous, on the phone until their locations can be discovered and the police can intervene.. Even more reprehensible to Szasz is the practice of incarcerating suicide attempters in psychiatric institutions. He sees this as a form of punishment that may paradoxically increase these patients' desire for suicide.

Szasz (1971) contends that the hidden motive of the psychiatric preventionist is to gain control over the patient's life so that any self-doubts the preventionist has about the value of his or her own existence will be quelled before they arise. Although some of the practices invoked in the name of "help" are ethically questionable, the motives of the helpers are unlikely to be wholly self-oriented. Whatever else, the perspective of preventionists is significant since it has not only shaped the views of others but has also contributed to the structuring of suicidal crises.

Studying Suicide

Since suicide is one of the most problematic areas to research, the dilemmas and problems it poses should be mentioned. Presumably, the function of any social scientific method is to enable the investigator to make closer, more systematic observations of the phenomenon being studied. By making systematic observations, it is anticipated that the investigator may separate commonsense beliefs about suicide from those views derived from the research. The purposes of the research, then, are (1) to ascertain or clarify what the phenomenon is and how it develops, (2) to isolate the social conditions that foster its emergence, (3) to distinguish it from other closely related phenomena, (4) to identify the properties that uniquely constitute it, and (5) to demonstrate when and why they change. Yet, it must be acknowledged that any method of doing research is itself based upon certain assumptions and values. In this sense, an allegedly "objective" picture of what is "true" must be seen in direct relation to the methods used to study the phenomenon. Fundamentally, the methods that are chosen to research a given phenomenon structure the observations that are then made. Moreover, the researcher's values do not stand in isolation to the problem. Values underlie the choices made of problems to be studied, methods to be used, and analyses developed during the research. Because of the nature of the suicidal act, conducting first-hand observations becomes difficult, to say the least.

From Durkheim's work to the present, much research on suicide has depended upon analyses of vital statistics, although they have not been gathered for the specific purposes of research. Assumptions are then made that official statistics actually represent the actions being studied. Further, as Douglas (1971) notes, it is tacitly assumed that all persons, including the officials who construct and impute the categories to specific actions, share universal categories and meanings about suicide. More important, however, is the fact that statistics on suicide are usually systematically biased in specific ways. As noted, the most fundamental issue, the identification of a death as a bona fide suicide, is itself problematic.

In his analysis of the events preceding death in the twelve cases he studied in depth, Wallace (1973) notes the questionable nature of the label "suicide" given by officials to four of them. He questions the quality of medical examination given and the politics of identifying suicide. Because they are political appointees, Wallace questions the quality of the work of medical examiners and coroners. He remains convinced that one man whose health was deteriorating rapidly did not intentionally commit suicide. In another case, Wallace suggests that the man could not likely have drowned in his bath. In another instance, labeling a prison death "suicide" probably was far more expedient than assuming it was due to accident, negligence, or murder, since those categories not only would call for more investigation but might also elicit public scrutiny of the institution involved. Wallace challenges the fourth allegation of suicide in the following way:

> "Acute depression while walking the MBTA (train) tracks" is the fourth of these findings that many question. Unless he can communicate with the dead, the coroner had no basis to judge the psychological state of the deceased (1973, p. 214).

In the above examples, it appears that the examiners chose to judge the deaths as suicide when they may not have been that. More commonly, however, deaths likely to be suicides are shunted into another category, such as that of accident. Douglas (1971) found that coroner's officials relied almost exclusively on their *commonsense definitions* of what suicide is (most were unaware of legal rules governing their activities and investigations). Moreover, it is clear that coroner's departments differ widely in the sophistication of their methods, the thoroughness of their investigations, and so on. In many counties, the decision of whether to pursue an autopsy by a medical examiner is determined by nonmedical coroner's deputies, who also employ commonsense reasoning in their determinations (see Charmaz 1976). Furthermore, the statistics constructed by a particular agency may reflect such varied dimensions as the reporting procedures, conceptions of what stands as a "good" job, and justifications for financial support for the services provided by that department besides the degree of technical expertise of the medical examiner.

The ways in which decisions are made to categorize a death as suicide rest in part on the investigator's *judgment* of the deceased's intentions. Family members may systematically distort the picture they give of the person's prior situation to avoid the designation of suicide on the death certificate. Like the social scientific researcher, the official who investigates the suicide necessarily attempts to *reconstruct* the past of the deceased in order that clues as to his or her intentions might be gleaned. Whatever clues are gleaned, they are combined with the present knowledge of the death. Besides, whoever recalls earlier events does so selectively as he or she reconstruct the past. As images of the deceased's life are reconstructed, the investigator makes commonsense judgments as to whether self-destructive intentions seem to be plausible in this particular case.

Physicians may also try to keep their assessments of suicide as the actual cause of death from becoming public information. When the suicide is a prominent member of the community or the physician feels that categorizing the death as a suicide may be harmful to the family, other categories may be invoked. For example, family may pressure the physician to alter what seem to be the facts in order that they may keep their suspicions a secret.

Perhaps, on a more general basis, there is good reason to suspect that systematic biases occur in rural areas, resulting in low suicide rates (see Charmaz 1976; Douglas 1967). Due to the less specialized services available in rural areas, investigations are less apt to be as technically precise and efficient as in urban areas. For example, autopsies are less routinely given, sophisti-cated techniques leading to clues are less available, different investigative procedures are invoked, and the medical examiners themselves often are moonlighting practitioners from other fields who have no special expertise in pathology.

Douglas (1967) argues that the most important source of error in official statistics has been the same error made in theoretical treatments of suicide: the erroneous assumption that suicidal actions have *unidimensional* or *universal* meaning in Western society. For example, if a death is categorized by an official as a suicide in New York City, and a similar death occurs in Gilroy, California, one would assume the latter would be categorized as suicide as well. But that is often not the case. The situation then becomes more complex when suicide rates are studied comparatively to make assessments about the relative stability of social institutions. To illustrate the dilemma, consider the following question: how can an investigator be sure that divorced persons are less linked to the social structure through studying their higher than average suicide rates in a certain city if the rates themselves are compiled on ambiguous data? Could it not be the case that more frequent placement of divorced persons who die somewhat mysteriously into the category of suicide repre-sents our commonsense rather than empirically tested understandings of what their lives are like? That is, a commonsense view of divorced persons is that they are lonely and alienated. Hence, if that view is held, it becomes much easier to believe that a specific divorced person who dies could have been led to suicide out of loneliness and despair without checking further. Yet, those who categorize a death as a suicide presume that the category itself possesses objective properties that would be agreed upon by everyone.

As suggested above, the problem of studying suicide becomes even more apparent when specific groups are examined. Because suicide rates are given so much credence for the construction of comparative data on different groups, many commonsense beliefs are built about those groups statistically described as the most affected. For example, Sweden is commonly believed to have among the highest suicide rate in the world; however, those statistics must be viewed in light of contemporary culture in Swedish society. Rudestam (1975) argues that the materialistic and secular culture born out of the Protestant Ethic in Sweden has led to accurate statistics. His argument is buttressed by the fact that others have reported that Sweden's unpredicted death rates as a whole are comparable to those of other Western societies (see Farberow 1975). Hence, what might be classified as an accident in the United States might be a suicide in Sweden. Thus, the higher official rates do *not* reflect a higher frequency of suicide, but instead represent different *norms* of classifying deaths.

Cultural influences on American statistics might be an issue in the high suicide rates of American Indians. Webb and Willard (1975) cast doubt on whether the presumption of high suicide rates in this group is in fact the case. They argue that the uncritical acceptance of statistical surveys without knowledge of Indian cultures perpetuates questionable assumptions about the nature of suicide in Indian life. They propose that suicide among Indians has been viewed ethnocentrically by those who mistakenly view Indian cultures as disturbed forms of European-American culture. Interestingly, Webb and Willard point out that most research on American Indian suicide has been done either to justify establishing a suicide prevention program or to evaluate an already existing one. Thus, the objectives of the research might distort the findings. As Webb and Willard suggest, what suicide is and the significance of it must be situated squarely in the specific culture of the various Indian groups.

Some final comments need to be said about an often made major distinction between *attempted* and *committed* suicide. This distinction has frequently illuminated psychological studies since some researchers claim that very real differences may be discerned between those who attempt suicide and those who commit it. While the suicide attempt or gesture sometimes is a means of communication about oneself and one's situation, including interpersonal relations, there is no particular reason to believe the difference is qualitative. As suggested above, an element of indeterminacy occurs with the suicide attempt. To illustrate, Alvarez (1971) contends that Sylvia Plath's successful suicide was in part a cry for help since she had left a note requesting that her doctor be called. Similarly, Lester and Lester (1971) report a case of a woman who was angry with her husband and wished to "teach him a lesson." She took a large number of sleeping pills at 4:30 p.m., one-half hour before the time he daily arrived home from work. But, by chance, since he was involved in a traffic accident that day, no one came to the house until 9:00 p.m. In the interim, the woman died. Lester and Lester point out that the intent of her action was clearly aimed to be symbolic rather than actual suicide.

Then, too, whether the outcome of a suicidal act is lethal depends on the technique used and the technical proficiency of medical institutions and their supporting services (see Douglas 1967). Consequently, whether suicide is actually committed is only *partially dependent* on the actor's intention. As Douglas emphasizes, seemingly absurd aspects of the situation may, in the last analysis, give shape not only to how it is defined but also whether it becomes a bona fide suicide.

VALUES, SOCIAL STRUCTURE, AND SUICIDE

Because in the past suicide has been so thoroughly conceived of as an individual problem, it is necessary to place it in a social structural context. In order to do that, we must look more closely at the ways experiences of suicide reflect and dramatize more widely held *values*. In this section, I will first examine dominant social structural values in relation to suicide. These values are, I propose, built on the residues of the Protestant Ethic with its underlying emphasis on *individualism*. I will follow that examination with a theoretical . discussion that links alienation fostered by the social structure with suicide.

Social Structural Values and Suicide

I have argued throughout this book that neither the Protestant Ethic nor the mode of individualism it spawned is dead. But both are perhaps revealed in different and more complex ways in contemporary culture than in previous eras. While cultural diversity no doubt results in multiple meanings of suicide, I will be concerned with dominant values and the pervasive ways in which they give shape and meaning to the suicidal act.

To begin, a reappraisal of our contemporary concept of individualism is in order. Of particular importance in relation to suicide are those fundamental values derived from individualism, including *individual achievement*, *personal responsibility*, and *personal control* of one's self and one's world. The Protestant Ethic fosters a negative view of human nature with its tendency to view acts and individuals as unworthy. When this view is turned inward, it may lead to profound distrust and dislike of self. The inner loneliness and lack of social connectedness, consequences of internalizing such values, further perpetuates and reaffirms individualism. Hence, perhaps most basically, this set of values and beliefs lend themselves to the type of isolation and despair often characteristic of suicide. In addition, *fragmented* social relationships frequently experienced also reaffirm individualism. In our industrial society, the weight of carving out an existence is typically believed to be left to the individual. Consequently, some persons, even those who live in proximity to others, may come to view even their most intimate relationships as characterized by *emotional anonymity* and a *lack of personal disclosure*.

Individualism has many ramifications. One of the most obvious and most familiar is the success and failure theme so pervasive in Western society. Success and failure go beyond the narrow boundaries of achievement; they constitute basic themes on which *selves* are made and judged. Since the weight of making a success of oneself and one's life is presumably the responsibility of the individual in this society, even those who realize that the hard-work theme is a myth may experience self-blame and guilt for what they subjectively define to be their "failures."

What constitutes "failure" needs further examination. Little more than a decade ago, imputations of individual failure seemed to be readily made according to life's vicissitudes. Thus, an inability to compete in the job market or to sustain a crumbling marriage then might have been socially and personally defined as failure. Our social structure now seems to permit a much greater range of explanations for such events.

Despite the current latitude for behavior and lifestyle, I believe that themes of failure still are pervasive, but they crop up in perhaps more subtle ways. What is more significant is that the failures are *subjectively defined*. These definitions arise from meanings the experiencing individual has constructed within the social fabric of personal existence. Although blame and guilt are often themes—either internalized as self-blame or projected onto others—they do not always figure in themes of failure. For example, after a kidney patient's transplant fails, his condition worsens. After discouraging rounds with dialysis between two transplant attempts, he comes to regard his *life*, as well as his efforts to struggle against his illness, as an ultimate failure. He is financially and psychologically devastated by the spiraling and seemingly uncontrollable problems spurred by his physical condition but he does not blame either himself or his doctors for his present circumstance. Another kidney patient quietly commits suicide by pulling his shunt out. Because of his conceptions of his role as the breadwinner he can not tolerate becoming such a financial "liability" as he called himself. Rather than further impoverishing his family, he elects to die.

Similar themes emerge when individualism is analyzed in relation to success. An individual may make personal sacrifices to achieve a modicum of success, yet finds when that point is reached, that results are not what have been expected. At this time, that person may feel that his or her expectations have been betrayed; they turned out to be hollow. Betrayal of hopes and desires may cause the person to reassess his or her life and the relative value of it.

For example, the myth of the "golden years" is predicated on a tranquil, comfortable retirement and is rooted in conceptions of "successful aging." But after years of planning and saving, a woman of 68 discovers that they are neither tranquil nor comfortable. Her husband's illness followed by rampant inflation wiped out much of their savings; his death subsequently wiped out her tranquility. She feels overcome by loneliness and her struggles to maintain her existence. Though she begins to wonder if life is worth living after all, she blames only herself for not dealing with her situation more "successfully."

In the examples above, those involved did not question their individual responsibility for handling their situations as best they could. In these kinds of circumstances, success and failure tend to be measured in terms of the intentions, actions, and products of individuals. The society is not blamed for its reluctance to provide comprehensive medical care. The community is not blamed for its lack of social resources. And the extended family is not blamed for its inability to sustain a member in crisis (although individual members might be). More likely, the actor experiences a *stress overload* that is diffused only among a few others, if anyone. And if blame is placed anywhere, it is apt to be placed squarely on oneself.

The tendency to blame oneself when events take a negative turn is of course consistent with the Protestant Ethic. First, the emphasis on the individual inhibits looking further for causal explanations of events. Second, the Protestant Ethic fosters in individuals the development of anxiety and self-accountability. While I certainly am not positing self-blame as any general explanation for human behavior (as many explanations may be and are plausible), I do contend that self-blame figures heavily in certain types of suicide.

Self-blame may not be offered as the first explanation for difficulties or misfortunes. Indeed, it may be defined only after several different, sometimes isolated events have occurred. Most notably, self-blame emerges in conjunction with definitions of personal failure or remorse. Jacobs (1971) provides us with an example of a suicide note in which blame is directed inward to the self. By taking the blame for earlier events, this individual seems to seek atonement through suicide. The first few sentences of the note read:

My Dearest Ones:

When you get this it will be all over for me on earth but just the beginning of my punishment for what I have done to you all. I am truly sorry, if you can believe that (Jacobs 1971, p. 100).

More directly in keeping with traditional views derived from the values of the Protestant Ethic are subjectively defined *personal failures* to fulfill goals and realize plans. Themes revolving around personal failure appear to constitute major concern among people who commit suicide. A failure to achieve goals sometimes is interpreted by these persons (as well as those around them) as an indication of a lack of personal adjustment or psychological integration. In that way, the failure to achieve goals becomes directly joined with the failure to be a *valued person*. Also, in keeping with the logic of the Protestant Ethic, the self is intertwined with actions in the external world that give symbolic significance. As the failure to achieve those goals becomes merged with personal identity, the person may become fearful of attempting new alternatives since they, too, carry the risk of failure. In this sense, failure may provide the person with a new view of himself or herself, or it may confirm earlier secret doubts. A heavy sense of personal failure is likely to be heightened when the person is acutely aware of the fact that significant others are also conscious of it. To the extent that they take this failure as a *symbolic marker* of who the person "really" is, their definitions subtly influence the suicidal process. Nonetheless, when the person integrates all those definitions of failure into the self, suicide becomes a plausible line of action. Suicide may then become a means of *symbolic atonement* for the accumulated failures of the self. The following suicide note reported by Jacobs suggests the symbolic significance of definitions of failure.

To my family and friends:

I'm sorry it has to be this way. For some reason, I have set unattainable goals for myself. It hurts to live and life is full of so many disappointments and troubles. What I would really like to say is that I can't face up to problems the way I should. Society is always judging you and telling you what to do. My problem I think is that I have always thought only of Bill [himself]. Everything I have done hasn't satisfied me. Why this is, I cannot tell you. It is a very funny feeling that I get inside when I sit down to do something. Maybe like what I write or do won't be accepted by society. Competition is another thing I hate. Maybe I expected too much out of life. Please don't cry or feel badly. I know what I am doing and why I am doing it. I guess I never really found out what love or responsibility was.

> *Bill*

I might also add that I had in recent years no great desire to continue living. Saying goodbye to all of you who I was close to would only make things harder for me. Believe me I tried to cope with my problems, but I couldn't (1971, p. 88).

A relationship between control and failure has been noted above in passing. Now we need to ask more generally in which ways control is a problematic issue in the development of suicide? I believe it has several dimensions of special significance to an analysis of suicide: including the themes of (1) control over personal reality, (2) "losing control" of oneself, and (3) taking control of oneself through suicidal action. Clearly, in regard to the first theme, some people experience only a tenuous hold on their personal realities. One consequence of that tenuousness is taking refuge in external routines provided in everyday life. Another is to attempt to exert control over others. In that way, one's power is displayed to oneself and others. Further, control over others makes one's world more predictable. Threatening suicide may be used as a means to exert control over someone else and to form expectations of the future. Not surprisingly, an occasional individual makes the threat good.

But the attempt to control others is not always perceived as ending with death. The suicidal person may feel that the ultimate way to control the other is through the expected guilt and remorse achieved by dying. That guilt may then be heightened when blame for the suicide is laid squarely on the other. Thus, a suicide note may read, "You got what you always wanted now."

To turn to related issues, a lack of control over one's life is linked broadly to *achievement* for some persons. When unable to take control over their personal realities, in ways that they had assumed, hoped, wished, or planned, individuals may not be able to achieve or realize their dreams and aspirations. Achievement must, in this context, be seen in its most *general* sense. What an individual may have wished to achieve may have been broadly construed, such as a type of self, type of existence, or a subjectively defined sense of well-being. Consider what happens if the avenues to realize that kind of existence or self are closed to the actor. That person may define his or her situation as one in which he or she has very little control. If this definition is simultaneously buttressed by external social pressures to become another kind of person who more readily fits into ongoing social reality, few options to do otherwise may be perceived. Further, to the extent that prior hopes and dreams differ markedly from what is now experienced, the actor may begin to feel hopeless.

The second dimension of control in relation to suicide is the theme of "losing control." Perhaps because the cultural emphasis on self-control is so prevalent, feelings of losing control over one's self and subjective world appear to be particularly significant with suicide. In this case, that individual is likely to have accepted a psychiatric paradigm in which "loss of control" is defined and then taken as an indicator of mental illness. Even if suicidal persons do not define their actions as indicating loss of control, others surrounding them often do. In that way, their experiences are *invalidated*, which may heighten the suicidal crisis. Simultaneously, the original definition of the persons as lacking control is reaffirmed and even magnified. Similarly, suicidal persons may later accept the definitions of others and redefine their experience as a loss of control, total breakdown, and so forth, despite the fact that during the experience they maintained that it made sense. For example, a woman who had once been suicidal reflected on how differently she perceived her experience then as opposed to now. She said: "I thought I knew what I was doing. It all made sense then. Now I see that I was absolutely crazy. My mother thought I was crazy. My sister thought I was crazy. But I thought I was on top of everything—they were right all along."

Loss of control in this sense is often literally intensified with the use of alcohol and drugs. Not uncommonly, the person greatly increases intake of either or both in the months preceding the suicide. In addition, the attempt often coincides with use of alcohol.

The third dimension of control refers to using suicide as a means of taking control over one's self. The underlying meaning of suicide in this instance is clearly not self-destruction: it is *self-affirmation*. However, using suicide as a means to attain self-affirmation may be most plausible under those conditions when the individual feels subjectively powerless and without other alternatives. This type of suicidal process might then be found with people in situations in which there are objective, external constraints, such as prisons. Also, in the face of a world wherein self-determination is systematically denied them, some individuals use suicide as a means to assert their refusal to be controlled. In their own way, they develop versions of the cultural themes of independence and self-control. By this point in the suicidal process, these individuals may feel suicide is the only meaningful event over which they can take control. This type of meaning of suicide is apt to emerge under two conditions. First, this meaning may develop when the individuals define their situations as characterized by a *systematic denial of rights* ordinarily accorded to others of similar statuses. For example, a young professor's major source of self-worth was derived from his work. After initially supporting him, his colleagues no longer valued his work and sought to terminate him. He felt strongly that they did so in ways which systematically denied him of his rights and the respect due to an equal. Others who were associated with him saw this as contributing to his later suicide.

Second, and perhaps more commonly, *powerlessness* contributes to the conditions in which suicide becomes a possibility. In a society in which power is highly valued, a sense of powerlessness over one's circumstances may lead to a sense of futility. When individuals feel they exist involuntarily only under the domination of others and they feel that the conditions of their domination cannot be altered, suicide may emerge as a choice. How powerlessness is experienced may be a major variable in determining who commits suicide. Quite possibly, those who were socialized to expect greater autonomy have the most difficulty in accepting their subjectively defined powerlessness. For example, a newly quadriplegic male patient was neither accustomed to the extreme physical limitation he now experienced nor was he acclimated to usual ward regimentation. He began to feel increasingly powerless in the face of the constraints that both imposed upon him. From his perspective, his powerlessness was affirmed daily in his new physical dependency. Over time, he became increasingly despondent and began to hint of suicide.

Powerlessness may then lead to hopelessness and, when experienced over time, to feelings of helplessness. If this occurs, the self-esteem of the person is likely to be diminished as well. Low self-esteem tends to perpetuate dependency on others. Kobler and Stotland (1964) have found that persons with low self-esteem often depend on others for direction and are responsive to their expectations. The self-perpetuating cycle of powerlessness, low self-esteem, hopelessness, and helplessness sometimes is seen in hospitalized mental patients identified as suicide risks. By experiencing the relatively concrete limits of action imposed by staff, suicidal mental patients may feel the very tangible evidence of their powerlessness. Although the same process may be witnessed in the larger society, it tends to be more elusive and less direct. By being subjected to surveillance to prevent their suicides, their powerlessness may be dramatically symbolized to institutionalized patients. Paradoxically, then, the kinds of measures used for "treatment" of the suicidal problem may perpetuate the social conditions fostering its development.

Alienation and Suicide

The preceding discussion suggests that *alienation* is an issue in many cases of suicide. Alienation may be defined as a state of consciousness resulting from a concrete relationship between human beings and their products. It is predicated on powerlessness and characterized by estrangement. When experiencing alienation, individuals become separated from their creative *products*, from *others* and from *self*. Since alienation arises in situations where the actor is powerless, it is a psychological response to a social structure founded on *domination*. For Marx, alienation is a direct human consequence of social relationships rooted in economic existence (see Fromm 1962). Although the concept of alienation is most often used in conjunction with exploited labor, it has broader implications. Since suicidal persons' lives are often characterized by the kind of estrangement and powerlessness reminiscent of alienated labor, the concept appears to fit their situations.

According to Marx, the conditions of human labor and, more generally, human existence in a capitalistic society, prevent the realization of human potential and creativity (see Fromm 1962). Instead, the distorted selves that are created under capitalism tend to be narrowly defined and readily replaceable selves that are saleable in the marketplace. Since the marketplace is competitive, some selves don't measure up to "standards." In any case, individuals tend to remain isolated and fragmented, estranged from each other as well as themselves. Importantly, from this perspective, it can be predicted that such a social order should give rise to a large number of human casualties, some of whom become suicides.

Alienation, then, results in a *loss of self* or a *lack of self-realization*. Because individuals may not be wholly aware of their alienation, they may experience feelings of frustration, worthlessness, dependency, and powerlessness without connecting their feelings to the social structure. Rather, these feelings are apt to be intensified by the individuals' tacit acceptance that they reflect who they are and what they may become. When persons make such assessments, feelings of hopelessness follow. As we shall see in the next section, that hopelessness may begin the spiral downward into suicide.

M. Farber (1968) proposes that there is much overlap between alienated and suicidal states of being. Because he implies that suicide is an interactive process between the individual and society, he emphasizes social structural changes as the means of achieving suicide prevention. M. Farber's argument rests on the assumption that the source of our suicides is fundamentally due to our social structure and culture. He finds that certain types of stress in everyday life increase vulnerability to suicide. According to him, people who need nurturance, love, and help from others because they are impaired are seeking it from others who are similarly impaired, and thus are not able to give it. This line of thought parallels the Marxian conception of alienation. By remaining isolated from others, our genuine human needs are not met and autonomy is not gained. Since individuals lack control over their lives and their fates, dependency is fostered and yet *cooperation remains limited*. Both Farber and Marx view the social structuring of human relationships as crucial for both the kinds of selves that develop in society and the nature of fundamental human concerns.

M. Farber proposes that both alienation and suicide will be reduced if (1) sources of hope are introduced into the society, and (2) social institutions are restructured to foster a sense of competence in individuals. But the nature of that hope and the kinds of competences fostered must be more diverse than ordinarily occur under current conditions. The sense of competence to which M. Farber refers essentially means that individuals subjectively feel that they have the internal resources to cope with the demands of living. In effect, this conception places the responsibility for handling life on the individual. Nonetheless, M. Farber recognizes the importance of structuring society so that individual potential may be more developed. If the person could experience greater control over everyday experience, then the internal resources that Farber defines as necessary for reducing suicide would logically develop.

From a Marxist point of view, restructuring the society and building the internal resources of individuals are part of the same dialectical process. In that sense, then, restructuring society reduces alienation, and this in turn fosters the increased involvement of the individual.

In this section, I have drawn relationships between social values and suicide. Because these values foster conditions leading to alienation of the individual, they are important to consider when studying suicide in contemporary American society. But an analysis of values is not sufficient to explain suicide since they do not answer the question: How does the suicidal process develop in interaction? I will now turn to this question.

SUICIDAL PROCESSES

Most fundamentally, a suicidal crisis is a crisis of the *self* and its meaning. I presented some general thoughts in the last section about *why* the crisis occurs. Now I address *how* it occurs and *what* it means to the experiencing self. In this section, processes that constitute a suicidal experience are illuminated. Although I do not propose to trace all paths to suicide, I intend to tap fundamental elements of suicidal processes. Initially, I explore general conditions leading to *social constructions* of *suicide*, followed by an analysis of what Alvarez (1971) calls "the *closed world*" of suicide." I address the *responses of medical staff* to show how they, too, contribute to the suicidal processes. Last, I offer some brief theoretical comments on the relationships between *suicide* and the *self*.

Social Constructions of Suicide

From the symbolic interactionist point of view, suicide is an emergent process *constructed* through interaction. Hence, structural variables are not in and of themselves enough to explain suicide. For example, an important social and symbolic loss may contribute to conditions fostering suicide, but the loss alone may not constitute the sufficient conditions for suicidal actions. In any case, social structural and situationally structured variables must be examined from the standpoint of how they are *subjectively experienced, acted upon*, and become a *source of interaction* with others. Although structural variables may help to identify groups of people who are perhaps more likely candidates for suicide, they cannot be used to determine among whom it will occur.

Hopelessness seems to be a key factor in many suicides. Hopelessness is often related to losses of various kinds, such as the loss of an intimate, a reputation, or life chances. An objective loss and its subjective realization may be gradually experienced although they are more noticeable when the loss is sudden and definitive as in a broken relationship. In contrast, when selves are destroyed slowly, losses may occur imperceptibly.

Also, when a major transition in life does not fulfill the individual's expectations or wishes, hopelessness sometimes develops. Afterwards, the person may not be able to return to the former role and identity that gave substance to his or her life. For example, a man is promoted to a prestigious managerial role in his organization. He finds he had little anticipation of the stress experienced in his new position but feels trapped, since there no longer is any possibility of returning to his previous one.

At this juncture, I should emphasize that the issue of hope is fundamentally tied to the issue of *meaning* in life. Hope is maintained as long as someone feels life has meaning and value. In this sense, hope is maintained if persons have symbolic images of what they live for. Yet to the extent that individuals live for something that is taken for granted, they may maintain hope without being explicitly aware of it. When that hope is questioned and becomes problematic, a drift into hopelessness may begin. For example, a man who had a stroke assumed that he would have a full recovery of the use of his arm and leg. As his expectations and hopes were questioned, first by the physician and then by himself through experience, he began to feel hopeless as he saw himself as a helpless burden.

To a significant degree, hopelessness is frequently intertwined with feelings of helplessness and a lack of control over objective experience. The despair that hopelessness generates tends to undermine previously valued aspects of self. Similarly, the value of central activities becomes undermined, although they were previously a source of self-confidence. The activities become removed or separated from subjective experience. Hence, they assume increasingly less value to the person even when they are still competently, though mechanically, performed. To illustrate: if persons who once took much pride in their job performances redefine their jobs as meaningless, then they can no longer base positive self-images on it.

The feelings of hopelessness and helplessness resulting in suicidal actions gradually evolve and cause individuals to *reinterpret* or *evaluate* their experiences. Jacobs (1971), in his research on adolescent suicide, addresses the ways in which a major personal problem can lead to a lack of hope. Jacobs argues that the individual must be faced with an *unexpected, intolerable,* and *unsolvable* problem. The unexpected nature of the problem may perhaps be more characteristic of the adolescent suicide described by Jacobs than adult suicide. The unexpected nature of the problem may set the social conditions in motion under which suicide becomes a possibility to someone—even persons who have not given indications of suicidal intent to others or to themselves. Hence, the unexpected problem may lead to what becomes the unexpected suicide. In contrast, other suicides result from lengthy reviews of personal situations, during which the nature of the problem becomes known and may even be expected to worsen. (For example, if the problem is defined as a devastating terminal illness, the person expects the situation to become worse.) In that sense, the problem is not unexpected, and perhaps even *spiraling consequences* of it may be anticipated, although they are also likely to be viewed as unsolvable. As Douglas (1967) remarks, sudden great personal loss may lead to the imputation of suicidal actions or communications to an individual even before that individual has communicated those ideas to others. But if Jacobs's analysis of the process is accurate, the pivotal issue would be the extent to which the suffered loss is subjectively believed to create unsolvable problems.

Still, one might ask what other general conditions foster the development of unsolvable problems. I find that *social isolation* underlies the process of defining a problem as unsolvable. Social isolation results in individuals becoming separated from ordinary worlds of everyday life. These worlds are, perhaps, meaningless since they cannot or do not share them. As social worlds become diminished and constricted, isolated individuals attribute much meaning to those few persons with whom they are involved. Consequently, they often "over-burden" these others with their painful problems. As a result, others may begin to back off despite their symbolic significance to the isolated. Further, an isolated suicidal person who does not pursue new relationships sometimes tries to keep another symbolically alive in fantasy after the relationship is presumably severed, as occurs in a broken love relationship. To the extent that this person attempts to live in the past and retrieve a lost relationship, social isolation is apt to be increased. If all attempts to retrieve the lost relationship fail, the "unsolvable" problem may be defined and suicide may then become a possibility.

The link between social isolation and the actor's definition of suicide as a "reasonable" course of action is further illuminated by Jacobs (1971). In this connection, as we shall see, he emphasizes (1) the importance of *legitimizing* one's suicidal actions, since suicide itself is a violation of social trust, and (2) the development of the suicidal person's *blamelessness* for the overwhelming problem.

Jacobs assumes that most people, including those who later commit suicide, have internalized values viewing suicide as irrational and/or immoral.

Hence, Jacobs analyzes the process of transforming an "irrational," proscribed act into a "reasonable" choice. According to Jacobs, *increased social isolation* contributes to the transformation process making suicide a reasonable course of action. Following Durkheim's logic, social isolation would loosen the social constraints that ordinarily serve both to integrate persons into society and to regulate their everyday lives. When the usual constraints linking them to the ordinary ways of thinking, acting, and feeling become loosened, former constraints over behavior are no longer believed to apply to current circumstances. Subsequently, these persons become able to violate society's trust in them as members who will uphold commonly shared values and norms, specifically those against suicide. Although Jacobs treats trust violation as if actors explicitly think about it, it seems more plausible that this transition is apt to occur on an implicit level. Nevertheless, the shift in *self-identification* is significant for the development of the suicidal process.

Jacobs's explanation of the transformation of self-identification revolves on the definitions of the problem experienced by the suicidal persons. The unsolvable nature of the problem figures here. Even though, according to Jacobs, the original problem was unexpected, these persons come to view it as symbolic of their entire biographies, rather than representing isolated misfortunes. In the light of their new misfortunes, suicidal persons may come to reconstruct the past in negative terms as they link their new misfortunes to it. Jacobs stresses that they see the previously unexpected, now unresolvable problem as something they expect will make the future at least as intolerable as the present.

The view of an intolerable future combines with a growing sense of blamelessness for the problem. Justifications for the impending suicide attempt are constructed with the belief that everything possible was done to resolve the problem, but such resolution was not forthcoming. Because the problems have become so intolerable and unresolvable, death becomes viewed as a solution, and suicide is seen as the "only way out" (Jacobs 1971). Hence, Jacobs argues that suicides feel essentially blameless for their deaths because they did not want the suicide to materialize. Feelings of self blame may, however, be experienced about the original *cause* of their situations.

At this point, suicidal persons become resolute in their commitment to suicide as *the* course of action (Miller 1967). In the suicide notes, Jacobs finds that suicides beg the forgiveness of other persons while reasoning that suicide is the only solution. By this time, suicidal persons have created their own logic as interpretations are made. Not only is the forbidden act made legitimate, but they are exonerated for it. Invoking this self-created logic, these individuals feel that they did all that was humanly possible to alleviate the problem. In short, by this time, these suicidal persons have entered the "closed world of suicide" (Alvarez 1971).

A Closed World of Suicide

One's reasoning takes on new dimensions in the closed world wherein suicide becomes the only sensible action. Subjective reality is characterized by a *shrinking into the self*. As suicidal persons retreat from the world and the world withdraws from them, they become increasingly immersed in self. Hence, the self becomes *separated* from ordinary everyday worlds, and the suicidal person's perspective becomes different than that of others. Phenomenologically, then, the person has become encapsulated in a qualitatively different reality (cf. Charmaz 1977; J. Lofland 1969).

Sylvia Plath's metaphor of the bell jar (1975) captures the essence of the closed world. The closed world of the suicidal person is similar to being trapped in a tight, airless cage, where one is caught in one's stagnant breath while totally separated from the rest of the world. When reality has seemingly closed in, the event of the suicide attempt seems to be impulsive even to the individual who makes that attempt. Yet that person may be tacitly aware of actions contributing to the possibility of suicide. Thus, Alvarez describes how he had been stashing sleeping pills: "I had been collecting the things obsessionally, like Green Stamps, from doctors on both sides of the Atlantic. Weeks before I left America, I had stopped taking the things and had begun hoarding them in preparation for the time I knew was coming" (1971, p. 264).

While suicidal individuals may feel that others cannot comprehend the nature of their experience, subjective meanings of suicide also may not be very well articulated by them (Douglas 1967). Thus, as Douglas notes, suicidal individuals may not seem to understand what they did or why they did it. The lack of clarity they feel then contributes to their feelings of losing control (Douglas 1967). If persons cannot determine what something means, they cannot control it. It seems to take hold of the self. In this way, individuals may begin to feel consumed by suicidal thoughts.

In looking back at his suicidal experience, Alvarez (1971) acknowledges the lack of clarity that he felt at the time. He describes the combined feeling of losing clarity and control in the following manner:

> I inhabited a closed concentrated world, airless and without exits. I doubt
> if any of this was noticeable socially; I was simply more tense, more
> nervous than usual, and I drank more. But underneath I was going a bit
> mad. I had entered the closed world of suicide, and my life was being
> lived for me by forces I couldn't control (1971, p. 259).

The construction of the process of becoming consumed by suicidal thoughts may then elude individuals, who live in their closed world. Explicit awareness of subjective experience may not necessarily change the course of events. Instead, awareness of the difference between subjective experience and the experience of others may cause these persons to feel further alienated from others and their shared world of everyday life. Yet the separate reality of the suicidal experience may have positive consequences for them. As Hillman (1964) emphasizes, a suicidal crisis may provide freedom from the usual view of things. In this sense, the new perspectives gained through the experience may liberate the self from ordinary constraints of everyday life in order that a transformation of self becomes possible.

But from the perspective of someone living in a closed world incomprehensible to others, personal problems seem insurmountable. The combination of the unsharable experience and insurmountable problems then makes suicide a reasonable solution in the mind of the person who attempts it.

Jacobs's emphasis on the attempts of potential suicides to exonerate themselves from blame for the problems raises some issues. Although some of the notes provided by him corroborate that point, an analysis of other suicide notes would not necessarily lead to the conclusion that exoneration of blame for the problems, and subsequently for the suicide, is desired by the person. Some suicide notes seem to show the suicides taking *direct responsibility* for their problems and fates. The suicidal action then becomes a way of atoning for failure to solve the problems. Rather than externalizing the problems, these suicidal persons may have *internalized* all the blame, guilt, and accountability for the problems. This in itself may become the reason for the suicide. The following two notes in *Clues to Suicide* (Farberow and Shneidman 1957) illustrate this theme:

> *Dear Mary, I'm sorry for all the trouble I've caused you. I guess I can't say any more. I love you forever and give Tom my love. I guess I've disgraced myself and John. I hope it doesn't reflect on you (p. 204).*

> *Mary Darling. It's all my fault. I've thought this over a million times and this seems to be the only way I can settle all the trouble I have caused you and others. This is only a sample of how sorry I am. This should cancel all.*

> *Bill (p. 206)*

If the notes can be taken as rational statements of direct meaning as Jacobs suggests, it follows that the self-blame theme must also be accounted for to understand suicidal processes. From a more psychiatric perspective, one might question whether the suicidal individual intended to make the other person feel even more guilt by accepting the blame in such a dramatic way. In that sense, demonstrating acceptance of blame through committing suicide could constitute an extreme case of revenge suicide. Yet it cannot be assumed that such notes necessarily represent underlying hostile motivations. Hence the actual intent behind the note may ultimately be assessed only in relation to the person's biography.

Although many who commit or attempt to commit suicide may be socially isolated individuals, others are not. Some persons, like Alvarez (1971), carry on the normal round of activities that constitute their everyday worlds although they may view their roles as increasingly meaningless. When this occurs, these persons are likely to feel increasing distance from others in their everyday world. Consequently, the concept of "social isolation" does not fully account for the kind of experience some potential suicides have. Instead, *emotional isolation* more fully describes the feelings and experiences of potential suicides who are around others but are without meaningful sharing, reciprocity, or mutual cooperation. Thus, felt intimacy markedly diminishes. Conditions under which emotional isolation develops includes (1) the aftermath of open hostilities or (2) growing awareness of deep-seated antagonisms or different values.

Insight into cases in which emotional distance characterized the marital relationship is provided by Wallace (1973). He found that in these instances the husbands who committed suicide had died socially before they died physically. Despite the emotional distance, these wives stayed with their husbands. They also experienced some of the social isolation their husbands experienced as they lost friends, neighbors, relatives, and their financial and emotional resources. Wallace reports that extreme emotional distance was noted with several women who continued to live with their husbands. One woman's comment was: "He had done too much and my heart was hard like a rock" (Wallace 1973, p. 80). Another woman stated that she had been more or less on her own for as long as two years (Wallace 1973).

Emotional isolation also underlies the conditions under which suicide becomes both a reasonable and acceptable "solution." When the person experiences emotional isolation from others, it becomes easier to justify making suicide an option. By the time suicidal individuals are sufficiently distanced from others so that the act of suicide makes sense to them, the thoughts and feelings of those who will be most affected become secondary at best.

Emotional isolation is often buttressed by social isolation between participants in the scenario. In other words, relationships may be further strained by changes leading to greater social and emotional isolation of the participants. For example, a man experienced substantial losses of self when his chronic illness necessitated his wife taking on the additional role of breadwinner as well as greater household duties. He resented her for being able to work and taking over responsibilities on which he had previously based his self-image. In turn, she resented his resentment and the way he responded to his illness. With the added burdens and obligations she now had, she was unable to give him much time, and he spent increasing amounts of time alone. He became emotionally and socially isolated simultaneously.

Intensification of emotional isolation occurs whenever the person is extended a real or symbolic invitation to die. Jourard (1971) states that the invitation to die may be explicitly given or it may originate as an unconscious wish in someone's mind. In either case, to the extent that whoever extends the invitation is symbolically significant in the life of the person, the direct or hidden message will be understood.

Implications of an invitation to die become more visible when actual situations are examined. For example, when recounting the circumstances surrounding her husband's suicide, a young wife avowed that her intentions and actions were causative factors in his death. Essentially, she believed that she had killed him. Her description of events indicates that she had given him an invitation to die. She said:

I really believed that I killed Phil. Here in this book (diary) I state (laughs nervously) that Phil must die, it must be done. A few months before he died, and from then on, things just started collecting and uh, I suppose I did drive him a bit nutty, uh, just through being myself and he couldn't accept it (Wallace 1973, p. 143).

In the situation of persons moving into a suicidal crisis, the invitation to die may actually be meant as an invitation to change, to transform a suffering self. But those in crisis may interpret that invitation as one that is total and encompasses the whole of their beings.

Jourard (1971) maintains that the invitation to die may be vigorously declined when given openly in good faith. But a covert invitation or one conveyed through indifference is more difficult to oppose. Moreover, if the message is given repeatedly, then persons who receive it are likely to suffer serious damage to their self-images. When negative views of self are repeatedly given by someone who has the power to define the *essence* of the self, then the invitation to die cannot be denied or perhaps even refuted. As Jourard implies, under these conditions, the self becomes annihilated and replaced by one that is alien. Thus, the invitation to die may further whatever feelings of self-estrangement the person experienced besides the growing emotional distance from the other person.

Unfortunately, those who are exceptionally needful of the support of others (as people who are moving into a suicidal crisis are likely to be) are more apt to receive invitations to die. Hence, they are more apt to be susceptible to the invitation when it is given. If Kobler and Stotland (1964) have correctly hypothesized that suicidal people seek more guidance from others and are more responsive to it when given, then the invitation to die becomes all the more symbolically significant. Under these conditions, such an invitation may greatly exacerbate and intensify a precipitating crisis. Quite clearly, an invitation to die validates whatever feelings of frustration, worthlessness, and hopelessness the person may have had independently of the encounter.

A consequence of the invitation to die is the increased emotional and social isolation of suicidal individuals. At a time when they are already vulnerable, the invitation to die may strikingly reveal to suicidal persons how *alone* they are in the world. These individuals may feel they have lost whatever status of personhood others had bestowed upon them in the past. That feeling is likely to develop out of the content of human relationships. As someone becomes more needful, others may attempt to take on the responsibility of interacting with this individual in crisis, but if it is sustained, they are likely to back off. Although the drama of crisis has a certain amount of appeal in this society, sustained crisis tends to be seen as an unwelcome burden. In addition, when defined as a burden, anger is likely to be expressed toward someone who is seen as causing the crisis.

In this sense, suicidal crises with these characteristics tend to be inherently hierarchical in this society. When persons are needful and seek fulfillment of those needs from others, they usually develop a relationship wherein the other person has greater power, control, and autonomy. Help and concern tend to be bestowed by the powerful person. Those who feel the need for such help may place themselves in a subordinate position in order to receive it. Both parties involved may feel that any help given is at the discretion of the helper. Thus, issues of whether persons really deserve help may arise. Of course, those who need it may not feel they are really deserving of it. Because their self-images have already been diminished, these persons may feel that any help or concern given is not a right but a privilege, a widely shared assumption in this society. Those who are defined as having extraordinary needs become viewed as persons somewhat undeserving of the privilege of help. Since the needs are extraordinary, and thus disrupt the ongoing lives of others, these needs are likely to be seen as excessive.

Responses of Medical Staff

In the discussion above, I have emphasized the role of intimates in the construction of the crisis. But what part do medical staff play? How do they respond to the suicidal individual?

Welu's systematic observations (1973) of reactions of emergency room staff to those who attempt suicide shed some light on these issues. He claims that harsher modes of treatment are frequently used than the patient's actual medical condition indicates after self-inflicted injuries are diagnosed as not being life-threatening. Initial responses of concern rapidly shift to responses of annoyance and irritation. Not infrequently, medical staff are highly resentful of suicide attempters who take up their time in a busy emergency room. To illustrate, a patient who refused to take the treatment was told, "If you don't take it I'll have to force it down you; I don't have time to waste on you" (Welu 1973, p. 105). Welu also found hostility and disdain exhibited toward patients for their ineffectual attempts. Thus, comments like, "He should have put the gun to his head and done a good job," were not uncommon (Welu 1973, p. 105).

Interestingly, Welu discovered that the response of nursing staff members differed from that of physicians in intensity and type. Nurses had fewer negative remarks than physicians except when the patient was notably un-cooperative during the treatment procedures. According to Welu, 50 percent of the suicide attempters received positive responses from nurses, compared to only 10 percent positive responses from physicians. Similarly, 5 percent of the suicide attempters received hostile or punitive responses from nurses, while 30 percent of them received hostile or punitive responses from physicians. The remainder in each category were treated with indifference.

The implications of Welu's research are at least as important as the findings. As I noted earlier, from the standpoint of suicide prevention, in-different and hostile responses to suicidal patients who are already socially isolated, psychologically powerless, and emotionally distraught may sym-bolically reaffirm their doubts about self-worth and the relative value of living. Further, this type of response may symbolize to suicide attempters the lack of recognition of their uniqueness as human beings in a mass society. In short, an inhumane response from medical functionaries may perpetuate the suicidal process.

Suicide and the Self

The foregoing analysis shows how a suicidal crisis is steeped in symbolic inter-actions as intentions are communicated by various participants. Although the self of the suicidal person may be more fragile than ordinarily experienced in everyday life, that person is often open to the suggestions and implied meanings of others, regardless of the content of those meanings. Conse-quently, I propose that the boundaries of the self become much more *permeable* during the suicidal crisis. Who the person is and may become are open to *redefinition* and change. Indeed, the suicidal crisis may be a way of transforming the self. Hillman (1964, p. 74) states it simply when he says, "The suicide is the urge for hasty transformation." What constitutes that transfor-mation may depend largely on the responses of others and how these responses are interpreted by the suicidal person. When persons are open to change, they are open to the validation by others that there is hope of becoming different kinds of selves and hope of experiencing different kinds of existences.

Hillman's overall perspective on suicide (1964) has some parallels with my analysis. In *Suicide and the Soul*, he argues that the confrontation with death through suicide constitutes an attempt at radical change. Part of the radical change that suicide provides is a severing of suicidal persons' identification with the form of existence they had. By changing those identifications, these persons attempt to realize another way of being. By emphasizing transforma-tion and their desire for a radical change in being, Hillman implies that they wish to define themselves in new ways. They attempt to do this, Hillman states, by releasing the self from the commitments, networks, and structures from which it had been imbedded. And for Hillman, in order for this trans-formation to take place at all, the death crisis must be experienced.

In describing their attempts at transformation through suicide, some suicide attempters corroborate Hillman's argument. They describe the feeling of release from their former selves that they gained in the suicide act. Hence, they experience a resolution of their earlier crisis through their confrontation with death. Litman (1970) describes an unemployed artist whose depression worsened. His psychological problem, according to Litman, centered on his feeling of guilt, worthlessness, and lack of acceptance of his current dependent and low status. Although his detailed plans to shoot himself in the brain were executed, he was shocked to find himself alive. After his hospitalization, he became a gardener, shed his former identity as an artist, and felt reborn. Similarly, a young man described his suicide attempt to me in the following way:

> After I cut my wrists, I could feel all the tension stored up in me evaporate. I felt a tremendous release. All that was dragging me down no longer mattered. It was a resolution; I had made the transition. Now it no longer mattered if I lived or died—I knew I was reborn.

In this case, the individual experienced a radical change of self through the suicidal crisis. If this occurs, a new perspective on reality is gained through the suicidal crisis.

EFFECTS OF SUICIDE ON SURVIVORS

Suicide leaves its mark on the survivors; in some cases it constitutes a lifelong burden that gives rise to feelings of self-doubt and continued questioning as to the "real" reasons behind it. The negative effects of suicide upon intimates derive from two sources: *social* and *self*. Those who are apt to feel them most are intimates such as spouse, parent, lover, or child, whose lives are closely intertwined and whose identities are directly linked with the suicide. In more impersonal and transient circumstances, such as a casual roommate relationship, social stigma and self-blame are less likely to be felt so deeply by participants. Under these circumstances, any blame and responsibility for the suicide becomes much more diffuse and more easily rationalized than when lives are intertwined.

Since blame and responsibility are felt and often questioned, suicide results in a stigma for close survivors. For example, Cain and Fast (1972) found a repeated theme of blaming the survivor's spouse by the community, neighbors, family, and particularly, in-laws. They found that the survivor of suicide was left with almost no social support. Instead, these survivors were avoided by the very persons who would have been sources of support in other circumstances, such as death by accident. Gossip and rumor tend to heighten the stigma of the survivor and the subsequent shame that stigma fosters. Even if survivors know they did not "drive them to it," they are apt to be left with no means of imparting that message to others. In essence, survivors remain "guilty" of the charge of causing suicide.

In particularly sticky situations, questions of responsibility and guilt are even more direct. The survivors may be suspected of murder by police or coroners until their investigations are completed. But even without direct accusation of guilt, the suggested meanings of others may be abundantly clear. Paradoxically then, the survivors are likely to receive the least social validation of self at precisely the time they need it most.

Occasionally, the social response to suicide can set in motion a chain of destructive events that culminates in the closest survivors becoming damaged persons. First, being ostracized and stigmatized by others fosters the development of shame and questioning of one's self and one's motives. Second, the events that preceded the suicide are likely to raise questions in the minds of the survivors as to whether they had done the "correct" thing. Subsequently, the combination of the suicide itself and the responses of others to it forms the conditions under which earlier events and one's role in them become defined as *problematic*. Third, the lack of social support has the effect of simultaneously heightening guilt and turning inward whatever grief might otherwise be expressed. Fourth, because of the taboo nature of the topic and the evident social response to the suicide, the survivors may take the cue and attempt to minimize its effects by avoiding it, hiding it, and hiding 'themselves. This sets up the conditions for the suicide to become particularly destructive to any children in the home. Surviving spouses abandoned by other adults to experience grief alone may in turn do the same thing to their children. Hence, the process of mourning might seem both *distorted* and *aborted* while those involved attempt to figure out ways of making sense of their situation.

Whatever else, a recurrent theme is typically found in these survivors: guilt because they did not *rescue* the suicides from their "impulses." The emphasis on guilt and rescuing looms large in American society, in part because of a narrow range of interpretations made of the suicidal action. Like other situations that affect the individual but speak to larger social issues, suicide is defined primarily as the upshot of "personal problems" affecting the deceased. The fact that suicide may reflect more general issues concerning the quality of life in this society tends to be ignored. Since the emphasis is on "personal problems," the possible role of the survivor becomes understood as the key to understand suicide.

In this vein, Henslin's argument (1972) focuses squarely on the problematic features that the wider cultural interpretation of suicide caused by "personal problems" makes for the survivor. He correctly points out that events and relationships do not have any natural or intrinsic meaning. Despite this, meanings are conferred upon them that tend to be taken as objective and true.

Because of the cultural emphasis on the deceased's personal problems, survivors are left to question their roles in those problems. Consequently, survivors may be motivated to account for the act in ways that minimize their participation in the process. Henslin found that some interviewees treated the suicide as an *external event* completely beyond the control of anyone, least of all themselves. In that way, they construct an account that vindicates them of guilt.

In contrast, a number of psychoanalytically oriented case histories and research reports, Arthur (1972), Cain and Fast (1972), Tooley (1972), indicate that children may be less able than adults to construct accounts for themselves and others to relieve themselves from guilt. Cain and Fast's studies (1972a, 1972b) especially show the intense guilt felt by 45 disturbed children who were seen in the child guidance center in which they worked. Cain and Fast found that these children had multiple sources of their feelings of guilt. First, previously held hostile feelings about the parent are assumed by the child to cause the parent's death. Second, feelings of guilt and responsibility are present since the child had long been blamed for the parent's depression or despair. Third, the other parent had given the child the responsibility of keeping the suicidal parent intact or reporting any strange behavior by that parent. Fourth, specific incidents such as a fight with the suicidal parent or some type of "misbehavior" immediately preceding the suicide later is interpreted by the child as causing the suicide.

Despite disclaimers from adults, including therapists, the children may insist that they provoked the parent into suicide or were ultimately responsible for it. Quite clearly, the suicide of a parent may evoke feelings of worthlessness, abandonment, and rejection in the children. The children may feel rejected and worthless in their reasoning that the parent did not find them worthy of living for or loving. From a psychoanalytic view, the damage of self-esteem may be irreparable unless therapeutic measures are taken. In this view, the behavioral consequences of a damaged sense of self-esteem are believed to take varied forms, such as angry outbursts, destructive behavior, or even over-achievement in order to disprove the dead parent's "judgment" of worthlessness.

The difficulties of the child are magnified if a "family myth" is created about the parent's death (Warren 1972, p. 114). The myth becomes a form of doublethink negating the reality known by the child, who may even have witnessed it. For example, the child whose father shot himself may be told that it was a hunting accident. Or the one who found his mother in the car with the motor running may be told it was a heart attack. Although Cain and Fast found that children who were given distorted messages or direct lies may learn to distrust the surviving parent, they were more apt to *distrust themselves* and their own interpretations of reality.

Identification with the deceased parent appears to be more of an issue with teenagers and adults than young children. As Cain and Fast (1972) observe, numerous cases have been recorded wherein the adult child commits suicide in a similar or an identical way to the parent. Identification in the suicidal act may lead some persons to the conviction that they will inevitably share the fate of their parent, as if this fate were externally imposed upon them.

Whether the traumatic experience of suicide of a parent seriously damages a child may depend upon the quality and quantity of social support afforded the child (Sandler 1967). As Dorpat (1972) suggests, the emotionally crippling aspects of parental suicide seem more likely to emerge when open communication about the deceased or the mode of dying is *forbidden* and grief is *repressed*. Further, the suicide can become a self-fulfilling prophecy for the child's fear of abandonment and rejection. If the surviving parents are consumed by guilt, grief, and additional obligations, the children's growing belief in their own worthlessness may be validated. But if the children are nurtured, supported, and made to feel symbolically significant in the life of the surviving parent and other caring adults, less damage need be done. In summary, then, a lack of direct disclosure and openness in the face of death and grief can be expected to have pervasive negative consequences on those who are directly involved.

SUMMARY AND IMPLICATIONS

The significance of the social context in which suicide occurs is demonstrated in two ways. First, suicidal individuals draw upon social structural values to understand, construct, and justify their feelings and actions. Second, relationships with others contribute to the process leading to suicide. Other perspectives typically emphasize the suicidal person's psychological state. The psychoanalytic perspective, for example, emphasizes repressed anger toward another, which is unacceptable to self. That unconscious anger is believed to be transformed into self-destructiveness. An existentialist position, in contrast, emphasizes the reflections of the individual. Existentialists would find no meaning in suicide, per se, but demand that one be continually aware of the absurd conditions of human existence.

Whether the individual should be able to choose death underlies much debate about suicide. Szasz and Hillman not only assumed that death may be chosen, but that the suicidal experience is meaningful. In contrast, suicide preventionists assume that the potential suicide is illogical and loses sight of what they take as the real meaning of death, the end of experience. Thus, they believe that to choose death is to lose sight of what death is, and intervention becomes a moral responsibility.

Durkheim's early sociological study of suicide rates was the first serious challenge to individualistic theories of suicide. He argued that the real causes of suicide had to be explained in social structural variables since he viewed the regularities in the suicide rates as social facts. Durkheim's three types of suicide, egoistic, altruistic, and anomic, are related to his conception of social integration. Egoistic suicide reflects the person's inadequate integration into society. Altruistic suicide reflects such a great degree of integration that the self is not individualized. Anomic suicide results from a lack of regulation; the individuals are left without norms to govern their existence. Although Durkheim's study stands as a challenge to psychologistic theories of suicide, he took for granted that the source of his data, the suicide rates, represented objective facts. But statistics on suicide are systematically biased in certain ways since even the most basic issue, the determination of a given death as a suicide, is sometimes problematic.

Though questions may be raised about the validity of Durkheim's empirical findings, social structure needs to be taken into account when the causes of suicide are sought. Dominant social values revealed in the Protestant Ethic, such as beliefs in individualism, independence, and achievement, are related to the suicidal process. Such values afford individuals measures of self-worth. When subjective evaluations of self-worth do not measure up to preconceived standards and expectations, individuals are apt to view themselves as failures, a view often accompanied by feelings of self-blame. Definitions of failure are related to feelings of a loss of control. Losing control of self and over personal reality are common themes among the suicidal. With such losses comes a loss of self of the suicidal individual.

Loss of self is intensified during the suicidal process. Untenable situations become defined as unsolvable problems by the suicidal individual. Over time, the person becomes increasingly separated from others, often concretely by social isolation, sometimes phenomenologically through emotional isolation. In either case, the suicidal person comes to live in a separate reality. The prohibitions against suicide loosen as the problems increase. The individual begins to see them as hopeless, and suicide becomes defined as the only solution. As isolation intensifies, the responses of others may constitute an invitation to die. By negating suicidal individuals or invalidating their experience, the invitation to die is given. Because the suicidal person's self-image is already undermined, such an invitation may take on much greater meaning. Negative views of self are often reaffirmed by both intimates and medical practitioners who treat suicide attempters. At the very time the individual's self is open to redefinition by others, rejection is a common response.

Suicide also affects the selves of the survivors. Left without support from others, the survivor may be unable to counteract tacit and explicit accusations of contributing to the suicide. The accusations do not simply come from others; often, they are made by self. Children, particularly, are likely to feel that they are responsible for a parent's death since they are less able than adults to construct accounts that absolve them from guilt.

At this point one might ask: What are the implications of this analysis for suicide preventionists?

By and large, the traditional viewpoint of the suicide preventionist is one made from the *outside*; it is an external view that takes into account different concerns and priorities than the suicidal person possesses. But when emphasizing the *content* of experience, people take a different stance toward it than when they analyze it wholly by its external characteristics. This may reveal one of the major problems with suicide prevention. Because it ordinarily is a stopgap measure, usually given under emergency conditions, the subjective experience of the suicidal person may remain unrecognized and essentially unshared while the preventionist attempts to use whatever tools or constraints are readily at hand to prevent the suicide.

Yet by not recognizing, sharing, or validating the experience that the suicidal person is having, the suicide preventionist may unwittingly perpetuate that person's suicidal desires. Unfortunately, much of what is called suicide prevention may negate the self of suicidal persons and the authenticity of their experience. If this occurs, suicidal persons are apt to feel even more lonely and alienated from others than before seeking help. As in other bureaucratic rituals, these individuals may be subjected to a number of demeaning practices, and their personal value may be called even more into question. All this may happen at a time when their feeling of self-esteem is most vulnerable.

Part of the negative response to the suicidal person may be due to the stigma attached to suicide. Although that stigma has been commonly understood and assumed to exist, even among preventionists and medical specialists, it has not been well researched.

Clearly, the stigma conferred upon suicide attempters through the responses of others may have devastating effects on the self-images of those who are open to the definition of others. Yet the suicidal process might be turned around if different strategies were invoked. Here, important cues may be taken from Hillman (1964). Paradoxically, when the analyst has one foot in the experience and one foot outside of it, as Hillman suggests, the sharing of that experience alone may be sufficient to bring the person through the suicidal crisis without any active prevention by the other person.

If the boundaries of the self are more permeable during the suicidal crisis, validation of the experience reflecting the self may provide a source of hope. In that way, the closed world of suicide opens up and possibilities for other ways of being may be discerned by the suicidal person. Further, through sharing the suicidal crisis, suicidal persons may be able to clarify to themselves the nature and development of their feelings. By gaining a perspective on those feelings, they may begin to feel that they are gaining control over their experience. In addition, through the realization that the other person is attempting to understand their experience, rather than placing constraints upon it, a measure of trust is built up. This may link otherwise isolated persons to social reality. Moreover, when concern is given freely without strings or conditions, suicidal individuals may begin to feel they have some value in the world.

Suicidal crises, like other crises, cut through the usual routines of daily activities. To give suicidal persons the kind of concern to which I have been referring is not easily fit into the structure of ordinary life. This constitutes a reason why potential suicides are isolated in their crisis. If they communicate a need for help to others, those others may feel they have neither the time nor the expertise to give it. Because the implications of responsibility loom so heavily with the potential suicide, others may steadily back out. Nonetheless, it is conceivable that this kind of concern could be given by those who are most significant to the suicidal person. And if it is given, then perhaps the processes leading to suicide will be reversed.

In this chapter, my analysis centered on the isolation of the individual undergoing a crisis of meaning—of self and existence. That crisis is characterized by immersion within a reality separate from others. Isolation within a separate reality is not unique to the suicidal. Those experiencing intense grief have a remarkably similar experience. Also similar is the effect of social values on the bereaved. In the next chapter, I describe the context and experience of intense grief.

REFERENCES

Alvarez, A. (1971). *The Savage God.* New York: Bantam Books.

Arthur, Bettie (1972). Parent suicide: a family affair. In Albert C. Cain (ed.), *Survivors of Suicide.* Springfield, Ill.: Charles C Thomas.

Atkinson, Maxwell (1975). Some cultural aspects of suicide in Britain. In Norman L. Gaberow (ed.), *Suicide in Different Cultures.* Baltimore: University Park Press.

Bakan, David (1969). Suicide and immortality. In Edwin S. Shneidman (ed.), *On the Nature of Suicide.* San Francisco: Jossey-Bass.

Cain, Albert C., and Irene Fast (1972a). Children's disturbed reactions to parent suicide: distortions of guilt, communication, and identification. In Albert C. Cain (ed.), *Survivors of Suicide.* Springfield, Ill.: Charles C Thomas.

_____ (1972b). The legacy of suicide: observations on the pathogenic impact of suicide upon marital partners. In Albert C. Cain (ed.), *Survivors of Suicide.* Springfield, Ill.: Charles C Thomas.

Camus, Albert (1955). *The Myth of Sisyphus and Other Essays.* New York: Random House, Vintage Books.

Charmaz, Kathy (1973). Time and identity: the shaping of selves of the chronically ill. Ph.D. dissertation, University of California, San Francisco.

_____ (1976). The coroner's strategies of announcing death. In Lyn Lofland (ed.), *Toward a Sociology of Death and Dying.* Beverly Hills, Calif.: Sage Publications.

Choron, Jacques (1969). Mortality and death. In Edwin S. Shneidman (ed.), *On the Nature of Suicide.* San Francisco: Jossey-Bass.

_____ (1972). *Suicide.* New York: Charles Scribner's Sons.

Dorpat, T. L. (1972). Psychological effects of parental suicide on surviving children. In Albert C. Cain (ed.), *Survivors of Suicide.* Springfield, Ill.: Charles C Thomas.

Douglas, Jack D. (1967). *The Social Meanings of Suicide.* Princeton, N.J.: Princeton University Press.

_____ (1969). The absurd in suicide. In Edwin S. Shneidman (ed.), *On the Nature of Suicide.* San Francisco: Jossey-Bass.

_____ (1971). *American Social Order: Social Rules in a Pluralistic Society.* New York: Free Press.

Durkheim, Emile (1951). *Suicide: A Study in Sociology*. New York: Free Press. (First published in 1897.)

Farber, Leslie H. (1969). The phenomenology of suicide. In Edwin S. Shneidman (ed.), *On the Nature of Suicide*. San Francisco: Jossey-Bass.

Farber, Maurice L. (1968). *Theory of Suicide*. New York: Funk and Wagnalls.

Farberow, Norman L. (1975). Cultural history of suicide. In Norman L. Farberow (ed.), *Suicide in Different Cultures*. Baltimore: University Park Press.

_____, Richard Kalish, and David K. Reynolds (1975). A cross-ethnic study of suicide attitudes and expectations in the United States. In Norman L. Farberow (ed.), *Suicide in Different Cultures*. Baltimore: University Park Press.

_____, Robert E. Litman, and Edwin S. Shneidman (1961). The suicide prevention center. In Norman L. Farberow and Edwin S. Shneidman (eds.), *The Cry for Help*. New York: McGraw-Hill.

_____, and Edwin S. Shneidman, eds. (1957). *Clues to Suicide*. New York: McGraw-Hill.

Fromm, Erich (1962). *Marx's Concept of Man*. New York: Frederick Ungar.

Hendin, Herbert (1957). Suicide: psychoanalytic point of view. In Norman L. Farberow and Edwin S. Shneidman (eds.), *Clues to Suicide*. New York: McGraw-Hill.

_____ (1968). The psychodynamics of suicide. In Jack P. Gibbs (ed.), *Suicide*. New York: Harper and Row.

_____ (1969). *Black Suicide*. New York: Basic Books.

Henslin, James N. (1972). Strategies of adjustment: an ethnomethodological approach to the study of guilt and suicide. In Albert C. Cain (ed.), *Survivors of Suicide*. Springfield, Ill.: Charles C Thomas.

Hillman, James (1964). *Suicide and the Soul*. New York: Harper and Row.

Hoeller, Keith (1973). Phenomenological foundations for the study of suicide. *Omega* 4:195-208.

Jacobs, Jerry (1971). *Adolescent Suicide*. New York: Wiley.

Jourard, Sidney M. (1971). The invitation to die. In *The Transparent Self*. New York: D. Van Nostrand.

Kilpatrick, Elizabeth (1968). A psychoanalytic understanding of suicide. In Jack P. Gibbs (ed.), *Suicide*. New York: Harper and Row.

Kobler, Arthur L., and Ezra Stotland (1964). *The End of Hope*. Glencoe, Ill.: Free Press.

Kubie, Lawrence (1969). A complex process. In Edwin S. Shneidman (ed.), *On the Nature of Suicide*. San Francisco: Jossey-Bass.

Lester, David (1972). *Why People Kill Themselves*. Springfield, Ill.: Charles C Thomas.

_____, and Gene Lester (1971). *Suicide—The Gamble with Death*. Englewood Cliffs, N.J.: Prentice-Hall.

Litman, Robert E. (1970). Suicide as acting out. In Norman L. Farberow, Robert E. Litman, and Edwin S. Shneidman (eds.), *The Psychology of Suicide*. New York: Science House.

_____, Theodore Curphey, Edwin S. Shneidman, Norman L. Farberow, and Paul Tabachnick (1970). The psychological autopsy of equivocal deaths. In Norman L. Farberow, Robert E. Litman, and Edwin S. Shneidman (eds.), *The Psychology of Suicide*. New York: Science House.

Lofland, John (1969). *Deviance and Identity.* Englewood Cliffs, N.J.: Prentice-Hall.

Maris, Ronald W. (1969). *Social Forces in Urban Suicide.* Homewood, Ill.: Dorsey Press.

Masaryk, Thomas G. (1970). *Suicide and the Meaning of Civilization.* Chicago: University of Chicago Press.

Menninger, Karl (1938). *Man Against Himself.* New York: Harcourt Brace and World.

Miller, Dorothy (1969). Suicidal careers. Ph.D. dissertation, University of California, Berkeley.

Parkes, Colin Murray (1975). The broken heart. In Edwin S. Shneidman (ed.), *Death: Current Perspectives.* Palo Alto, Calif.: Mayfield.

Peck, Michael L., and Carl I. Wold (1977). The suicidal patient: adolescent suicide. In Sandra Galdieri Wilcox and Marilyn Sutton (eds.), *Understanding Death and Dying.* Port Washington, N.Y.: Alfred Publishing Co.

Plath, Sylvia (1975). *The Bell Jar.* New York: Bantam Books.

Rudestam, Kjell Erik (1975). Suicide in Sweden and the United States. In Norman L. Farberow (ed.), *Suicide in Different Cultures.* Baltimore: University Park Press.

Rushing, William A. (1968). Individual behavior and suicide. In Jack P. Gibbs (ed.), *Suicide.* New York: Harper and Row.

Sachs, Harvey (1967). The search for help: no one to turn to. In Edwin S. Shneidman (ed.), *Essays in Self-Destruction.* New York: Science House.

Sandler, Joseph (1967). Trauma, strain and development. In Sidney S. Furst (ed.), *Psychic Trauma.* New York: Basic Books.

Shneidman, Edwin S. (1970). Orientations toward death. In Norman L. Farberow, Robert E. Litman, and Edwin S. Shneidman (eds.), *The Psychology of Suicide.* New York: Science House.

_____ (1973). Death, the enemy, Tape 19, produced by *Psychology Today.* Del Mar, Calif.: Ziff-Davis.

_____, and Philip Mandelkorn (1970). How to prevent suicide. In Norman L. Farberow, Robert E. Litman, and Edwin S. Shneidman (eds.), *The Psychology of Suicide.* New York: Science House.

Stengel, Erwin (1969). A matter of communication. In Edwin S. Shneidman (ed.), *On the Nature of Suicide.* San Francisco: Jossey-Bass.

Szasz, Thomas S. (1971). The ethics of suicide. *Antioch Review* 31:7-17.

Taylor, Steve (1978). Suicide and the renewal of life. *Sociological Review* 26:373-90.

Tooley, Kay (1972). The meaning of maternal suicide as reflected in the treatment of a late adolescent girl. In Albert C. Cain (ed.), *Survivors of Suicide.* Springfield, Ill.: Charles C Thomas.

Wallace, Samuel E. (1973). *After Suicide.* New York: Wiley.

Warren, Max (1972). Some psychological sequelae of parental suicide in surviving children. In Albert C. Cain (ed.), *Survivors of Suicide.* Springfield, Ill.: Charles C Thomas.

Webb, John P., and William Willard (1975). Six American Indian patterns of suicide. In Norman L. Farberow (ed.), *Suicide in Different Cultures.* Baltimore: University Park Press.

Welu, Thomas C. (1973). Psychological reactions of emergency room staff to suicide attempters. *Omega* 3:103-109.

CHAPTER NINE

THE SOCIAL PSYCHOLOGY OF GRIEF AND MOURNING

What is grief? How is mourning experienced by members of society? How does grief affect different people? These are some of the questions I will attempt to answer in this chapter. I will emphasize grief due to loss of persons who were intimates of the bereaved for sustained periods. First, I will attempt to describe the nature of grief as many persons now know it. Second, I will explore the relationship between grief and culture, followed by a detailed picture of how the process of grieving affects the self. A fundamental assumption in the discussion is that in our culture, the crisis of loss of the other results in *loss of the self*. Last, I will discuss the special problems that widows and widowers share.

THE NATURE OF GRIEF

Grief, bereavement, and mourning are related terms used in relation to surviving the death of a significant other person, often of a close family member. For clarification, I have provided the following initial definitions. Grief is the subjective, emotional response to the death of the significant other. Bereavement is the status conferred upon someone when this person dies. Mourning is the process through which grief is faced and ultimately resolved or altered over time.

Surely death is a universal experience that demands of survivors some awareness and accommodation to its reality. But that awareness and accommodation may take varied forms. Most analyses of grief and mourning take for granted that it is a singular type of response that is part of the universal human condition. Yet as Volkart and Michael (1977) point out, the extent to which loss is subjectively felt and expressed differs widely among cultural groups who experience death under different social conditions. They argue that the view of death as an inevitable loss of life is a peculiarly Western notion. Moreover, in some cultures, Volkart and Michael find that death "represents a gain for the deceased and improvement in his prospects and status and that mourning for his loss is inappropriate" (p. 197).

They suggest that it is a *cultural definition* that makes death a loss and grief prescriptive. Thus, culture-bound *grief expectations* develop that have two significant dimensions. First, the survivor "should" feel grief for the "loss" of the deceased. Second, the "felt" grief should be expressed and "worked out" in order to preserve the mental health of the survivor.

Taking Volkart and Michael's argument one step further, I argue that culture does not simply give rise to the patterned ways of handling grief, but instead implies that the subjective interpretation of cultural meaning in conjunction with the backlog of personal experiences of the bereaved give rise to the very *feelings* that are defined as "grief."

For a starting point, we can take the feeling of loss, suffering due to shock, disbelief, numbness, anger, despair, guilt, and disorganization as some of the signs of the loss the person may be feeling in this culture at this historical point during the initial reaction to death (cf. Glick, Weiss, and Parkes 1974). Specific shape and expression of these feelings emerge from the individual's past and present experience.

When are feelings of loss heightened? This occurs when one's life and *self* are imbedded in the activities, events, and person that are gone. Or the loss may be that of freedom, physical function, social status, or reputation. The experience of loss encompasses more than physical death of a loved one; it may be a *symbolic* death of ourselves when we lose significance in the lives and thoughts of others. Consequently, some valued part of oneself may be lost, and perhaps an entire identity that one valued and predicated one's self-image upon may be gone.

In this culture, selves tend to be situated in relatively few intense, stable relationships. In contrast, Volkart and Michael (1977) report that people in some other cultures have multiple relationships, which result in the self being situated in a wider network. They suggest that we in American society not only become dependent upon a few significant others for shared role relationships, but that we become dependent on their specific personalities as well. In that way, the death of a significant other constitutes a loss not easily replaced.

In our society, loss and grief seem to be responses to life's transitions when those transitions are characterized by *finality* and *lack of choice*, which affects our lives and our self-images. It is one thing to end a marriage or a job on one's terms through one's choices, and quite another to end the marriage through death and the job through termination. When a choice is made, it typically results because the person foresees new alternatives. In some instances, such as ending a "bad" relationship or leaving a tension-filled job, the choice may be made because of the negative experiences associated with the past—one may wish to again recapture a self "uncontaminated" by one's current associations. For example, a woman may wish to be her "own person" again in the way that she saw herself before marriage. Hence, she may choose to end the marriage relationship.

Finality then makes for a reappraisal of one's circumstances, if not also of one's self. Often, the life of the other person or the aspect of life that constituted the loss had become immersed with the bereaved's taken-for-granted being. Consequently, even those who made choices and forced the shape of events may experience some feelings of loss and disorganization since their everyday lives were at least in part due to the event, relationship, or person that is now gone. Finality necessitates certain readjustments even when a good deal of choice existed about the direction of action to take. For example, a woman remarked to me: "It was my idea to end the relationship, but at the time I had no idea of how secure I actually was. I didn't realize how much of my life was invested in the years spent in my marriage."

In any case, the experience of loss is related to *personal identity*. The extent of loss depends upon how immersed the identity of the bereaved is in the circumstances within which the loss is felt. But since we are not always aware of how loss affects us, many losses that we experience become rationalized and justified without much overt feeling. The loss of grandparents, older persons, or those with whom we had no sustaining intimacy might not be viewed as very critical if they do not cause immediate losses to our self-images and our subjective worlds. We may ignore the pangs of regret or pain that the loss might suggest. If so, we are very likely also to *negate* the feelings of loss of others who are affected by crisis or death. The denial of legitimate grief for an older person is a case in point—even Simone de Beauvoir (1973) shared the common assumption that grief for an elderly parent by a woman over 50 was "neurotic."

Sorrow tends to be understood in terms of contrasts—it is more deeply felt if compared to joy, such as the joy of earlier days or the comfort of emotional security. In a society where emotional security and feelings of well-being are highly prized, it logically follows that fear is often a component of sorrow—fear that the prior sense of well-being or state of affairs will not be regained in some way.

When sorrow is felt, the experiencing person feels that nothing will ease his or her pain. The void in oneself and one's world that is created by loss may be characterized by incompleteness, separation, hopelessness, and a profound sense of disorganization. When sources of personal identity are limited, the bereaved person feels that no similar identity as that shared with the deceased will develop or can be constructed in the future. Hence, the pathos of loss may strike more deeply. For example, if to lose the other means a set of shared understandings about the world, a way of life, and a valued identity, then depression and fear may be extreme. Then, the death reflects not only death of the other but, in a very real sense, death of the *self*.

The clinical view of grief, with which I take issue, treats it as if it were a *disease process*. The disease imagery includes notions that grief is something one is afflicted with, something inside the person that must be gotten rid of. The feeling of loss is given negative connotations—it is something that should not be there, something that should not be experienced beyond a certain point. Experiencing sorrow, particularly beyond the initial few weeks when friends and relatives allow for it, becomes something to be hidden, like symptoms of a disease one does not wish others to know one has.

That there is something wrong with sorrow is implied by Howard Becker (1969), who called sorrow the emotion of "weakness," rooted in the wish for security and at that, an appeal for help. The grief, however, that gives rise to this "weakness" points dramatically to human need for communion and inter-dependence. Since that type of interdependence is antithetical to American cultural ideals rooted in Puritanism, it is not surprising that Becker castigates it. Correspondingly, it can be anticipated that the dominant theories in psychiatry and psychology echo the prevailing cultural ideals. Since Becker, in his clinical point of view, assumes that grief elicits the underlying weakness of the person, the logical extension of his concept is that grief is something to conquer, to overcome. Still, this type of reasoning which assumes that grief elicits an underlying weakness is a cause of personal concern to some newly bereaved individuals, especially widows, who become fearful that they might totally "fall apart" or become "too dependent" upon others. In essence, grief in this society is marked by the *vulnerability* of the person who experiences it.

The definition of grief as a disease is somewhat enhanced by observations of increased morbidity and mortality of survivors (Frederick 1977; Parkes 1972). Because grieving survivors often suffer a great deal of stress, they are especially vulnerable to disease and death (Frederick 1971; Rees and Lutkins 1967; Parkes 1972). The potential physiological effects of grief cannot be denied or underestimated. Although these physiological effects result in disease, grief itself cannot be categorized as a disease. Rather, the physio-logical effects may be intensified due to the ways in which grief is *socially defined* and *structured*. In short, I am suggesting here that institutionalized patterns that force survivors to handle intense grief independently give rise to high disease and death rates among them. Furthermore, as I will indicate throughout the chapter, more recent studies recognize that the cultural view of grief as a disease to be "worked out" and "gotten over" does not reflect the actual experiences of many bereaved. For them, life is never the same, grief is never wholly "resolved," and they never quite recapture the selves they had been before the loss (see Glick, Weiss, and Parkes 1974; Parkes 1972; Wallace 1973).

CULTURAL CONTEXT OF GRIEF

In any culture, we can discern norms for the role of the bereaved and discover expectations about how grief is to be expressed. Deep-seated cultural themes are played out and reaffirmed in the grief process in highly taken-for-granted ways. What is ordinarily taken to be an individualistic and personal response to the loss must also be viewed in the context of the culture in which the person exists.

Strong relationships between grief and the Protestant Ethic can still be discerned in many sectors of our society. Although other trends are discernible in handling grief, such as the expressiveness of portions of the black community, the Protestant Ethic has been a dominant influence in our culture. Unlike Rosenblatt, Walsh, and Jackson (1977), who use indicators of religious behavior to conclude that the Protestant Ethic is no longer a significant force affecting grief, I believe that taken-for-granted views reflecting deeply instilled values of the Protestant Ethic remain. In my view, these values are long divorced from religious behavior. Thus, I maintain that the Protestant Ethic has had a significant ideological impact on our customs concerning grief. In keeping with the heavy emphasis on individualism, self-reliance, independence, and hard work, grief becomes something to be handled alone by the bereaved person. That is, the problem of grief becomes a problem only for the significant others of the deceased—it is not a problem for the larger community or even the kinship network. To handle grief, one must rely on one's self. Like disease, if grief is something inside of the bereaved, then it is logically their personal problem, and they must ultimately rely on themselves to "work it out" and resolve it. Because survivors have been left to their own devices for handling grief and have found it a painful experience, I argue that a need has been created for counselors, therapists, and self-help groups to help people contend with grief.

However, for the most part the structure of social relationships contributes to conditions wherein grief is primarily experienced by those who are most intimate with the newly deceased. Since so much weight is placed upon the nuclear family relationship, grief tends to be most experienced in relation to that unit, and the expression of it may be most readily apparent within the unit. But, paradoxically, the small *size* of the unit fosters the emphasis on self-reliance and handling grief independently. Consider Lynn Caine's comment on needing someone to talk to in her grief:

> *Who was there? Not only could I not talk about my grief, I had no one to talk to.*

> *Family? I couldn't. The nuclear family is too small for talking. Our intimate world is so concentrated that when a member dies, our world contracts—sometimes to just one person (1974, p. 140).*

Even if support is given, the small size of the nuclear family unit does not necessarily mean that family members will become more unified in shared grief. The actual circumstances may appear to the bereaved as demanding quite the opposite response. When, for example, a parent dies, the surviving parent may be overwhelmed by the additional roles placed upon him or her and the felt need of being strong "for the children," who are also experiencing grief. Thus, during the very time when feelings "should" emerge and be confronted, grief is suppressed while the newly bereaved struggles with new responsibilities and also takes on the burden of the emotional responses of others. The upshot is that the structure of the nuclear family can result in the suppression of grief of the newly bereaved even when that bereaved person may have held philosophical views that supported the notion of the immediate expression of feeling.

Since many Americans do not have a sustained community of friends and relatives available to them, the structure of mourning becomes individualistic. Participation in such a community would, I believe, provide ritual meanings and, likely, more intimate support to the bereaved. Most significantly, community participation would provide continuity in the life of the bereaved in ways that might diminish the disorganization of self that occurs with grief. In this sense, the *location* of life and death assumes significance. And as Goody (1974) and Vinovskis (1978) argue, historical changes fostering the growth of individualism with the concomitant loss of community fundamentally affect the experience of grief.

Perhaps most importantly, many Americans have internalized the view that grief is a *private* affair that should not be displayed in public. Beyond the truncated set of rituals accompanying the funeral, little public acknowledgment of loss is made. Expression of grief appears to be rigidly controlled in most cultures—whether emotional display is demanded or prohibited—and Americans usually feel it inappropriate to give way to feelings in the presence of others. The tendency to keep grief private is logically consistent with the way illness is treated in this society. As I argued in Chapter 3, illness is ordinarily defined as a private affair. Not only are details of the patient's condition kept confidential, but details of the bereaved's condition are also to be kept private.

Hence, the tendency to keep grief suppressed and private is not an isolated psychological response. It is usually part of a larger social process in which grief is the final conclusion of events. And, as noted, it is certainly related to widely held values concerning what we are and how we appear to others. Still, the relationship of grief to illness cannot be understated. Given the dominant cultural emphasis on stoicism, on handling things alone, and making the "best" of the situation, both the terminally ill person and the family member are apt to have been well socialized into treating their situation as private. Despite the current quasi-psychiatric trend toward expressing anger about such situations as death, a myriad of emotional feeling may be experienced and yet remain largely ignored and unexplored. When those involved do such a good "job" of repressing their emotional responses, the responses remain unidentified. It is not surprising, then, that when death actually occurs, some survivors may not seem to express much depth of feeling or disclose personal concerns. Their socialization has been too effective for that.

The stoicism and individualism displayed in the grieving process are also important because they become the yardstick upon which the bereaved's self-worth is measured. Being "strong" is highly valued in this society. When people manage grief with equanimity, without unburdening the depth of it to others, those individuals are permitted to see themselves as "strong." To break down in tears or show anxiety publicly may be taken as a sign of weakness, particularly when continued over time.

From the discussion above, one might argue that this stance toward grief symbolizes the fragmentation and atomization of everyday existence since the burden of grief is placed on the individual. But ways of handling grief may not all be characterized by individualism. There are strong indications, for example, that values emphasizing social support and expression of loss are fostered by some subcultural groups and ethnic minorities. Masamba and Kalish (1976) point out that emotional catharsis is a major component of the funeral service in the Black church. Further, in subcultural groups where extended kinship networks are readily available to the bereaved, the individual is apt to be provided with continuing support and assistance. If the bereaved person had previously maintained close ties through sustained face-to-face interaction with relatives, these relatives can provide the social circumstances wherein grief can be expressed. For example, Kalish and Reynolds (1976) describe Mexican-Americans as not only having a familistic culture but also as permitting the free expression of grief. In summary, then, the structure of family and cultural existence gives shape to the circumstance in which grief is known, felt, and expressed.

THE SITUATIONAL CONTEXT OF GRIEF

It becomes clear that an analysis of grief cannot be separated from the context in which it is experienced and expressed. Part of this context is situational since the situation lends shape to ongoing events. The moments surrounding death and loss affect how it is understood and handled. Therefore, the consequences of a given situation must be examined to understand more fully the grief experienced by survivors. At least three major variables influence the type of grief felt by the survivor: (1) whether *death expectations* were held, (2) the *intensity* of *involvement* of survivor and deceased, and (3) the *structure* of *relationships*. These variables influence the extent to which the survivor will feel guilty about the death. In this secton, I will discuss anticipatory grief and analyze death expectations. I will then comment on the structure of relationships and conclude by discussing the intensity of involvement in conjunction with these other topics.

Anticipatory Grief

The kind of grief that friends and families experience is directly related to the way in which the person dies and the amount of involvement the deceased recently had in the lives of the survivors. Anticipatory grief is defined as that grief which occurs *before* loss takes place. As implied by the discussion of Kübler-Ross's stages of dying, the concept of anticipatory grief is extremely significant for the dying person; however, I am going to concentrate here on the implications of it for the survivors.

Anticipatory grief is believed to be evinced when the kind of emotional reactions ordinarily seen after death in survivors are observed before death. Some observers (Gerber 1974; Fulton and Fulton 1971) believe that anticipatory grief is a form of *emotional preparation* that reduces the intensity of grief after death. They assume that emotional preparation takes place and that it subsequently reduces the intensity of grief.

Anticipatory grief presumably prepares or *socializes* persons into the experience of loss. The preparation is social and psychological as well as emotional since, presumably, these individuals imagine themselves without the dying person. At this time, those who are closest to the dying person may begin to construct social ties and symbolic meanings that leave the dying person behind. When dying persons are permanently separated from the everyday existence of those with whom they had been closest, experiencing anticipatory grief may have the consequence of severing emotional ties before biological death occurs. In more extreme instances of this severing, patients die symbolically and socially before their actual deaths. In perhaps more ordinary cases, the bereaved are spent of emotion by the time the death occurs and have begun to take over the duties and obligations that coincide with their new roles. In any case, anticipatory grief means that a prior intimate relationship shared with the dying person has been essentially *resolved* or ended.

Practitioners sometimes believe that such resolution should be encouraged. In one case, Goldfogel (1972) provides a history of a 52-year-old woman whose 6-year-old son was dying of leukemia. Since her husband had died five months before, she was overwhelmed by her son's dying. Initially, she expressed hope for a recovery and openly acknowledged her avoidance of questions about his prognosis. Her hopes waned when he was placed in an oxygen tent, as it represented a symbol of death to her because her husband had died in one. As her son visibly deteriorated, she began to verbalize thoughts that she wished his suffering to end. She felt then that she was pronouncing him dead. After sending his clothes home she felt guilty because she thought doing so symbolized giving up. The boy's agonizing near death one day as he pleaded for fluids even resulted in the nurse feeling helpless and angry that he did not die. Although in this case the mother's grief was not completely over, her socialization into his illness resigned her to his impending demise. Other parents occasionally abandon the child when they begin to give up hope.

Psychiatric observers tend to think that the anticipatory grief process is a positive one that can eliminate or minimize later problems for the bereaved. Still, in order to ascertain whether or not it is positive, one must examine the subjective experience and symbolic meanings of those who are close to the dying process. Surely, anticipatory grief is difficult to measure and what is called anticipatory grief by an outside observer may represent an emotional disengagement or sometimes callousness, which is socially engendered rather than simply being a psychological process of adjustment to loss.

Anticipatory grief has been described by Fulton and Fulton (1971) as a psychological phenomenon with social consequences. I prefer to view anticipatory grief as a social phenomenon with psychological consequences since, from my view, the causes of anticipatory grief are fundamentally *social*. The social structuring of relationships shapes the conditions in which the behavior labeled anticipatory grief develops. In a society in which personal relationships are easily fragmented and made problematic, where intimacy itself is often treated as a negotiable commodity and individualism leads both to expediency and self-sufficiency, it logically follows that loss may be seemingly "accepted" so that indifference increasingly earmarks the stance the survivors take toward the dying patient. No doubt the concept of anticipatory grief is descriptive and accurate for some who before the death identify the loved individual as "gone"; experience their grief; are socialized into new roles, views, and actions; and come to some resolution about their personal identities. Yet I maintain that in other cases to which the label "anticipatory grief" might be applied, the dying held only a *marginal position* in the social and symbolic lives of their survivors before their terminal stages of life, even if they are close to the survivors in the kinship network.

The marginal position of the dying person becomes apparent when the issue of *intimacy* is explored. This raises the question of how and from whose point of view intimacy is defined. While the relatives may be close in the kinship network, they may not be equally intimate. For example, an aged mother's "closest" relative and "intimate" is her adult daughter. But from her point of view, the daughter's intimates consist of her husband and children. This qualification is significant since systematic investigations of the grief of widows (Ball 1976-77; Glick, Weiss, and Parkes 1974) reveal that anticipatory grief was not evidenced even when death was expected. However, these data do not specify exactly how long death expectations were held or whether the dying were able to function and be known as they had been in the past. It is conceivable that anticipatory grief is identifiable under conditions when the dying individual experiences substantial irreversible changes in mental functioning over months or years, and the family is acutely aware of them. Suggestive of this are Dorothy Paulay's remarks about her shift in stance toward her husband when she began to see him as dying. She said:

> I lost hope for my husband's recovery, then redirected it to rebuilding our family life. I redistributed my time and my energy and started to cope at last with the reality of Jean's illness. I continued to care for him,

to arrange satisfactions to fill his limited life, but my hopes and goals were directed in rebuilding my own life . . . (1977-78, p. 178).

Despite whatever subjective experiences contribute to feeling and action, others may judge the individual on different grounds. Fulton and Fulton (1971) insightfully note that the expectation of "normal" grief is held not only by the average person but also by medical practitioners. Consequently, staff may become highly critical and disdainful of families who do not exhibit the signs of "normal" grief. When staff become the surrogate family for the patient, they are more likely to show the signs of "normal" grief than are actual family members. As this occurs, staff may attempt to make relatives feel guilty about their lack of emotion, or they may feel quite angry with them and impute feelings of callousness to them. Such imputations may elicit a sense of shame or guilt from the relatives, if they do not already have these feelings. Perhaps the relatives' guilt for their lack of involvement perpetuates that lack of involvement. For example, a professional woman feels guilty about not visiting her mother more frequently at the nursing home. With her 12-hour days at the office and her social commitments, she finds the 18-mile trip to the nursing home inconvenient. But she feels guilty about her infrequent visits and the reproachful glances from staff. Her guilt becomes self-perpetuating. She feels guilty for not going more often, then expects to be *made* to feel guilty and so delays further and then feels even more guilty for her delay.

This discussion points to an ambiguous issue: It is very difficult to know when responses are based upon anticipatory grief and when they more accurately reflect a situation in which whatever loss might have been experienced is redefined in other ways that systematically reduce any emotional investment the survivor had in the dying person. In a society where so many persons are constantly projecting themselves into the future, rather than fully experiencing the present, it seems likely that those who cannot share the future may get left behind in the thoughts and plans of others.

Death Expectations and Grief

Whether death is expected is commonly thought to shape the grief process. Although death expectations affect how grief is experienced, someone's response to grief may be intense even if incipient death was believed to be certain. Knowing that death is impending may result in specific actions such as making final farewells, resolving the relationship, or doing whatever is felt to be necessary. For example, the son of an alcoholic father remarked, "Me and my father never talked for a long time. Then I heard the man had cancer—we talked" (Calkins 1972, p. 26). Sometimes, participants will intuitively form death expectations that result in their taking such actions. If, however, death expectations had existed and the survivor chose not to act but felt that some action was necessary, then that survivor is apt to feel guilty in the face of loss. As I will explore later, survivors often experience problems with grief despite their death expectations.

The *absence* of death expectations is commonly thought to present a more problematic situation for the survivor. Sudden death causes initial intense problems in the *realization* that the death has actually occurred. That realization remains problematic when the bereaved does not see the deceased at the hospital, coroner's office, or funeral rites.

Under most circumstances, sudden death contributes to the difficulties of the survivor even when that death conceivably "makes sense," as with a job-related death in a high-risk occupation. For example, the survivors of a combat victim knew that death in war might occur, but his actual death still elicits a certain amount of shock. When one is not part of the dying process of an intimate, accepting that death as real becomes more difficult even if the reason for the death "makes sense." Accidents, suicides, and war victims fall into this category. One can understand the accident; one understood the person's feelings before the suicide; one expects death in war. However, one's full realization of the death in everyday reality takes time, even when the death is understandable. The following reflections of a young woman about the death of her lover reveal the ways that the intimate attempts to forestall the possibility of the understandable death:

> *October, four years ago, I was alone in Mexico City, waiting to be joined by J. when I got news that war had broken out in his country. I knew he wouldn't be coming. I knew that he was, by then, in a tank, somewhere in combat. The only thing that I remember about the five days that passed before I learned of his death, was praying. I talked to God incessantly, "Please make him O.K. Please make it be over. Please make him safe." I prayed without stopping, certain that God recognized J's goodness and believing that the power of my love was a moving force. I believed that I could, through God, keep him from harm.*

> *Once I believed that he was dead, I had to come face-to-face with the "reality" of life, or really, what was the reality of death. The single most difficult and devastating thing that I have had to learn in life is that I cannot insulate those that I love from harm with my love. It seems so glaringly naive, pathetically unrealistic, crazy even, but somehow, without even knowing it, I had believed that I could.*

One might suspect that these statements were made by someone who had not previously encountered death. But that is not the case. She had witnessed both death and loss many times before, including several friends who had died of heroin overdoses and one who was shot only a few feet away from her. These earlier deaths were even more unexpected. While trying to forestall J's death she came to feel that she had, in a sense, experienced his death.

Quite possibly, full realization of sudden death is more difficult as the survivor has less of a context in which to place it and therefore make it understandable. Hence, sudden death becomes even more inexplicable when due to some extraordinary event such as choking on a piece of meat or being murdered by a stranger. The more bizarre the cause of death is to the relatives, the greater the amount of difficulty they will have in making sense of it. For example, months after her brother was shot in a barroom altercation by an off-duty policeman, a woman could still not make any sense of his death—it remained inexplicable to her. She was not handled "well" by either the police or coroner's departments, as she was informed that her brother was dead when he was actually in the last stages of dying. Consequently, she missed saying her last farewells to him. She was told to report to the coroner's office before his corpse arrived from the hospital! The bureaucratic ineptness with which she was treated added to her sense of the unreal, incomprehensible nature of her brother's death and the events that surrounded it. If for no other more humane reason, it is bureaucratically expedient for functionaries to manage survivors of such incidents so that they are less apt to question the official definition of the situation or raise a fuss. Families who are not handled well are apt to cause further disruptions, as this woman did. She was raising questions and protesting the official definitions a year after the actual event.

Sudden death leaves the survivor without preparation, without anticipation. Since many people do not deal with death openly, they are unlikely to discuss it or make plans that take into account that possibility. Consequently, relatives may be socially and financially overwhelmed by problems the death generates. For example, a widow may find herself living in a home with mortgage payments that are more than her reduced monthly income can accommodate comfortably. But on a more fundamental level, the survivors are left the task of *integrating the loss* and its impact into their sense of self and everyday life. When the other person's life is intertwined with the survivor's, sudden death is apt to become all the more painful.

The quality of interaction previously held with the deceased affects the character of experienced grief—a dimension of particular importance with sudden death. Since most people do not live their relationships as if they are fragile and may be suddenly ended, survivors often engage in much ruminating about how things would have been "different" if their shared life could be relived. In this instance, a survivor may regret having lived as if there would always have been a future for the relationship.

Similarly, any previous death expectations for the dying affect the quality of the grieving experience. While some relatives who expect imminent death attempt to resolve their relationships with the dying, or at least give the situation its "due," those who did not attend to the dying person are apt to experience conflict or guilt in their grief. Basically, if survivors feel strongly that the deceased knew his or her value in the relationship, that belief will strengthen the survivors. But if some estrangement had been felt, or previously been made obvious, the conditions are formed for personal guilt to be experienced. Hence, both funeral directors and family members sometimes report that the greatest expression of grief is shown by the relative who had systematically rejected the person before death. Surely public and private knowledge of a previous lack of interest in the deceased's welfare may add to whatever feelings of guilt are experienced by the survivor.

It is commonly believed that expectations of certain death assumed with specific terminal diseases provide the survivors with psychological armor for handling their grief. This is not necessarily the case. Instead, grief following the death of someone known to be terminal often constitutes a personal crisis in the life of the most intimate survivor. Three conditions affect the quality of the grief experience: (1) the prior *structure of care*, (2) the *response of others*, and (3) the *implications of emotions* elicited by a lengthy dying process.

The prior structure of care appears to affect the experience of grief in two striking ways. First, immersion in the care of the dying person often results in *separation* and *insulation* from direct confrontation with death. Despite "certain" death expectations, grief later becomes a crisis when the dying person and his or her care were *the* integrating dimension of everyday life of the caretaker. Care of the dying gave the caretaker meaning and purpose to life. Second, lengthy terminal care provided by an institution usually symbolizes impending death. Under these circumstances, intimates ordinarily have *reorganized* their lives without the dying person. Thus, as I explained earlier, social death may occur before biological death and anticipatory grief could take place.

Possibly, immersion in care and reorganization without the dying person represent two extremes in a continuum of the effect of the prior structure of care. All kinds of gradations exist between. Thus, an intimate who willingly provided loving care to a dying person for several months still experienced shock and disbelief when that person was hospitalized and died shortly thereafter. In an earlier research project, for example, I talked with a woman who described the care her sister had given their aged mother as consuming her sister's life. The sister experienced a severe response to grief. Even though the mother's death had been anticipated, and brief hospitalization had preceded it, the involved daughter had not been fully aware of the mother's rapidly deteriorating condition (Calkins 1972).

By being immersed in the daily problems of caretaking, the relative does not fully realize that death is impending. With the added significance of the intimacy of the relationship, maintaining the dying person became a taken-for-granted but imperative task to the relative. Under these conditions, when the relatives' minds are consumed with the exigencies of everyday activities, the impact of the actual death is apt to be great. This is especially the case when the dying person and the relative have been systematically isolated from others.

Most importantly, *social isolation* prior to the death forms a condition under which grief is intensified. The role that illness plays in the construction of that social isolation has been largely overlooked. The social isolation that follows death has been acknowledged; however, often that isolation is simply a continuation of what had been set into motion long before. In my research (Calkins 1972), I found that the working-class women who so willingly gave care to their aged mothers were lonely and experienced a gap in their lives which the relationship with their mothers filled. Since many working-class families use their kinship network as the source of social ties in the ways that middle-class persons use friendships, it stands to reason that the aged mothers would continue to share intense relationships with their adult daughters.

In these cases, as well as with widows whose lives had revolved around their husbands, the grief experienced after the parent's death was intense. Clearly, the subjective experience of grief defies what might seem to be a logical response from outside of that experience. That is why the parameters of grief must be examined within the context of the actual experience.

The structure of care and the subsequent amount and type of involvement are related to the response of others. Often, families back off from the care of a relative, such as an aged parent. Hence, if one person takes on the care, he or she tends to be forced to handle it independently. Then, after the death occurs, relatives may also expect this survivor to handle grief independently. A paradox sometimes occurs here. Since the less-involved (or, more likely, uninvolved) relatives have more distance from the situation, they are apt to see the signs of deterioration more clearly than the person who is actually doing the caretaking (see Calkins 1972). But due to the clarity of their perceptions, they may mistakenly think that the involved relative also has an accurate expectation of death. Hence, they see the involved relative's later shock or disbelief as inappropriate.

Because of this sort of rationale, those closest to the bereaved may not permit the bereaved their experience of grief. Hence, the expression of grief becomes defined as *illegitimate*. Family and friends attempt to force a truncated grieving process on the newly bereaved. The pressure to repress grief is illustrated by this comment made by an impatient adult daughter of her newly widowed mother: "She should accept it—after all she has watched him die for two years" (Calkins 1972, p. 34). In contrast, when the death had not been anticipated, those surrounding the bereaved person are more likely to define the bereaved's feelings of grief as legitimate, at least immediately following the death, even when they do not wish to be exposed to those feelings. Clearly, in the first situation above, the bereaved may become isolated in their grief, even during the first days and weeks after the death. That isolation shapes their experience and in a real sense may sensitize them to new views of self and their place in the world. Furthermore, the isolation and inhibition of expression of feeling actually tend to prolong the grief process.

Now, by turning directly to the emotional implications of a lengthy dying process, I will illuminate the consequences for experiencing grief. During this discussion, I will focus on anger, relief, and guilt.

Many people who experience the loss of an intimate are aware of anger about their situations. They feel angry with the deceased person for leaving, and often feel angry about the added burdens that the death means. They feel angry about the disruption of everyday life and their personal worlds. In addition, they feel angry about the toll that caretaking and the dying process has taken on them. In addition, if while the person was dying, resentment about the *situation* became manifested as resentment toward the *other*, then as we have seen, involved relatives who voiced their despair and invited the other to die are likely to experience remorse while grieving.

What, specifically, are the effects of these earlier resentments on grief? Obviously, the relatives may feel *relief, anger,* or *guilt.* Relief has several major dimensions. First, relief is frequently felt in consideration that the deceased's suffering is over. Many persons now acknowledge feeling relief for that reason. Second, relief is felt due to the ending of the uncertainty. Third, and most important for this discussion, relief is felt because the death means the end of an ordeal and beginning of more "normal" activities.

Anger toward the deceased and relief about the death are not always thought to be positive or respectable feelings. What happens when they are believed to be wholly negative? According to the psychoanalytic view, these feelings are turned inward against the self and take the form of *depression* and *guilt.* Certainly the above situations are not the exclusive causes of guilt, but they surely contribute to it.

Guilt is a pervasive theme in any analysis of grief. Sometimes guilt has an objective basis, such as when a small child is killed because a parent was inattentive. Or guilt may be manifested because the bereaved had rejected the deceased before death occurred. More often, perhaps, guilt arises out of subjective definitions of events that outsiders would easily discount. For example, a wife might feel guilty for having encouraged her husband, who was a cardiac, to follow his prescribed exercise regimen if he succumbed while following it. In any case, guilt elicits ruminations about the past and self-blame for the role one played in it. In his reflections about failing to seek medical consultation early for his long-deceased wife, Robert Anderson discloses:

> I made the discovery of the very small lump in my wife's breast. I had no idea what it was. I said nothing until a solicitation from the Cancer Society listed the warning signals of cancer. For years after, I cursed my own ignorance and the negligence of all the doctors who had never taught my wife breast self-examination. For years, with hot flashes of anger and guilt, I went over and over those weeks of delay. Why didn't I mention even in passing the small lump in her breast? My brother is a doctor; why didn't I check with him? A simple phone call. For years I rewrote com-

*pulsively that scene in my head, playing it differently—I mention the
lump to my wife; we go to the doctor; we are in time, and my wife is
alive (1974, p. 74).*

Guilt and subsequent intense or prolonged grief are also likely to develop in
situations in which the bereaved's feelings about the deceased are *conflicted*.

In summary, the *type* and *intensity* of prior involvement tend to crucially
affect the way in which grief is experienced. And as I discuss next, involvements are imbedded in a structure of relationships that crucially affect the
grieving process.

The Structure of Relationships

The impact of death is most clearly seen in the ways in which it affects intimate
relationships. With the fragmentation of families, geographical as well as
social mobility, and increased numbers of single persons, significant intimate
bonds are often found outside of the kinship network. But custom and law do
not acknowledge this significance. Hence, coroner's deputies are occasionally
forced to turn a woman out of a home shared with her recently deceased lover.
To date, little research has been conducted on the special problems that grief
and death pose for survivors who are intimates but not kin. Much of what
follows emphasizes the nuclear family since that is what has been attended to
in the literature.

When the nuclear family is an *isolated* unit in the social structure, the
death of one of its members is typically very disruptive for the others.
Although the point in the life cycle of the deceased is important to consider for
how grief is defined, similar attention must be given to the bereaved. In that
vein, I will offer some comments on the special issues that are raised by
addressing the life cycle.

The effects of loss of a parent upon a child have been largely unexplored
except by those from the psychoanalytic tradition. From that perspective, the
trauma of loss of the parent in childhood can be devastating for the development of the child. The child in our society often suffers grief privately, as the
surviving parent does. Widows often try to "spare" their children the pain of
grief so they try to cope in what they perceive to be "normal" ways, that may
mystify children who are aware of what has happened. By attempting to hide
their feelings and distract their children from the reality of death, these widows
may perpetuate anxiety and unresolved grief in their children. In that way,
grief is repressed in the child, and from the psychoanalytic perspective, the
child's psychological development is arrested or retarded from that point.
Similarly, from this perspective, the child may look for qualities of the lost
parent, especially when the parent is of the opposite sex, in marriage. Despite
the dismal predictions one might make from this perspective about the future
of bereaved children, Bendiksen and Fulton (1977) find that there are fewer

behavioral disorders among them than among those whose parents are divorced.

Nevertheless, the psychoanalytic perspective is valuable for understanding the child's behavior immediately following the death, since in this perspective there is much emphasis on discovering the latent or hidden meanings of explicit behavior. Since children communicate with action often more than words, the surviving parent needs to attempt to discern the symbolic meaning of the action, especially when the child makes no verbal reference to the dead parent. If the parent attempts to make feelings explicit, then the child will have some reassurance that it is permissible to verbally express thoughts or feelings. Granted, the stage for such expression is ordinarily built before the death; however, even at this point, airing feelings helps to alleviate later problems. Just as the parent may experience disbelief over the death, it may be initially incomprehensible to a child. In such a situation, it seems advisable to permit the child time to adapt to the loss while acknowledging its reality. Furman (1970) gave the example of the 6-year-old boy whose mother had died. Prior to her death the child showed an interest in school; afterwards his interest diminished and was marked by the fact that he no longer brought papers home. The boy's older brother explained the reason by saying that bringing the papers home would make him too sad since there was no mother present to show them to. By making the meaning of the boy's action explicit, the family was able to handle it.

The same issues arise with children as discussed in relation to suicides, though they may not be as pronounced. To reiterate, first, children often feel guilty when a parent dies if they have resented the parent. Second, children may have felt anger toward the parent if the parent's illness had encroached upon their routine activities and forced more responsibility on them than peers had. Third, children may silently question whether resentment toward the parent had anything to do with the death. Fourth, children are apt to feel anger toward the deceased parent for abandoning them. In any event, a sensitive parent who can make such issues explicit contributes to the children's making a more positive adaptation to grief and loss.

In our society, loss of a child is believed to be the most difficult. The resulting grief strains the nuclear family, often to the breaking point. Grief-stricken parents are sometimes unable to offer each other much comfort. If one parent is blamed for the death, or feels self-blame, deep rifts are apt to occur between the couple.

Since many of the particular issues facing the middle-aged person's death of a spouse are raised in the section on widowhood, I will not cover them in this section, but I will remark on the aged. Initial research on the meaning of loss to older persons is ambiguous and inconclusive (see Parkes 1972, Lopata 1973). For example, Ball's study (1976-77) indicates that older widows accept loss more rapidly than younger ones. Yet the death of a spouse in old age is often the most significant of a *series* of losses, including health, home, and social status. What grief means to older persons who experience multiple losses remains to be discovered. Still, what grief is to the bereaved is meaningful only when viewed in relation to the structure of that individual's bonds with others.

THE EXPERIENCE OF GRIEF

Grief is conventionally viewed as a process that consists of facing the reality of loss and reintegrating one's life and one's self-image without the person who died. In this section, I will offer a theoretical discussion of the effect of grief on the self. The crucial issue of grief is the *loss of self* that occurs when a valued relationship ends. For the most part, that issue has been minimized in the literature, which places greater emphasis on "successful" resolution of grief. I will follow this discussion with a description of the subjective experience of grief, divided into a three-phase process: *transition, realization,* and *reintegration.* Again, the phases will be related to their significance for the self.

Grief and the Self

In our culture, grief over death of an intimate shakes the foundations on which the self is *constructed* and *known.* The meanings through which the self had been known are dramatically changed by the death. Also, the self is situated in a *structure* of relationships in which the deceased intimate had played a central role. Since roles are usually *reciprocal,* the one on which the self had been largely predicated may no longer be possible. One cannot view oneself as a "wife" without a husband or as a "parent" without a child. Consequently, the death causes a fundamental loss of meaning and structure. Marris (1974) succinctly states, "The fundamental crisis of bereavement arises, not from the loss of others, but the loss of self."

Underlying the "resolution" of grief is the commonly held notion that the bereaved must gradually *relinquish* the symbols and actions that represent significant dimensions of the prior shared relationship. For example, the widow must cease to assume that her husband is still the head of the household. Most importantly, relinquishing symbols and actions means relinquishing parts of oneself. When, for example, widows talk about "falling apart" or "coming unglued," they hint at the lack of integration they feel their selves and their lives now have.

As Marris notes, the purposes that gave life meaning have been knocked asunder. To the extent that those purposes were shared purposes or assumed a shared existence, loss is viewed as causing one's life to become abruptly meaningless. Marris (1974) argues that in order to reconstruct meaning, the bereaved must reestablish continuity with the past without the deceased. For Marris, symbolic meanings must be detached from the previously shared relationship, which are then recreated independently of it.

The loss of self experienced through loss of the shared relationship is frequently a dimension of self unknown to any but the deceased. Without the other, that dimension of one's self no longer exists. To the extent that this often very private dimension of self defines the total self, such a loss becomes devastating. For example, a young woman discloses her feeling about the death of her lover:

> For me, it was as though a "part" of me had been discovered or uncovered through him, through our unique relationship, and that was a "me" that I would never want to be with anyone else, ever again. It was as though I consciously allowed that part of me to die. In fact, in a way, I willed that part of me dead.

One way in which some bereaved maintain continuity is through their identification with the deceased (explored more fully below). Rather than attempting to maintain their former roles with the deceased, they consciously or unconsciously attempt to *become* the deceased. This is often seen in widows whose thoughts and actions seem to reflect the perspectives held by their husbands (see Parkes 1972).

In order to alter the loss that grief causes, the self must change. The self and grief are simultaneously transformed as new meanings are developed and a new structure of life is constructed. Initially, activities are often a distraction but may later take on meaning in their own right. For example, a widow uses her job first as a means of escape from her grief, but later she develops new interests in it that she finds rewarding. As new activities and new intimates are developed to which the self becomes committed, greater investment of self is made in the symbols of one's present and future activities. Under these conditions, images of the prior relationship are apt to be left in the past.

But not every bereaved person easily makes the transformation of self and grief. Maintaining grief consistently over time necessitates that the self remain essentially the *same*. Remaining in the same social world and maintaining the same world view are preconditions for the self to remain the same. Surely, one's status in life greatly affects one's life chances for "successful" adaptations to grief. To the extent that few opportunities are subjectively perceived or objectively exist for one to construct a new reality that is separate from the one shared with the deceased, it is unlikely that changes in self would occur as rapidly. Instead, the self may remain invested or immersed in the relationship with the deceased. The kinds of self-identification the bereaved person made prior to the death are contingent upon keeping the memory of the deceased person alive, which may be seen for years after the actual death. Thus, widows particularly sometimes link their identities to their deceased husbands long after the immediate circumstances following their deaths.

The Grieving Process

Changes in the self occur as grief is experienced. These changes can be seen in the process of grieving, which may be divided into three general phases: *transi-*

tion, realization, and *reintegration.* These terms reflect my view of grief as a normal process and death as a normal event. Although I believe grief is normal, I do not see it as having a "natural," or *singular* course. Rather, the grieving process may take varied directions of which I suggest the major ones in our culture below. (I will emphasize widows in this discussion only because most research on grief has been conducted with them.)

Transition In the first stages of grief, the bereaved person may feel that the world has become *unreal.* Similarly, a curious disjointedness of self is often experienced, as shock and disbelief are initial responses to the news of death. The self that the bereaved is presenting to the world seems totally divorced from the self that they experience. In addition, the unreal character of death and the events surrounding it, sometimes exemplified by the funeral ritual, cast a dream or nightmarish quality on the bereaveds' subjective experience. Perhaps, due to the distinctions often made in this society between public performances and private meanings, bereaved persons may play out a role that they define as "expected" and "proper." Consequently, when the impact of the death would seem to be the greatest, the bereaved often, at least publicly, mask and hide feelings. Maintaining composure in that way, not "giving way to grief," tends to be rewarded as a dignified way of treating the situation. Widows, especially, may find themselves trying to retain their composure in order that they may administer to the grief and needs of others who may be less affected by the death. Despite whatever the rewards, the upshot of handling the situation as a public performance in this way is that grief may be delayed. One of the widows interviewed by Glick, Weiss, and Parkes made this comment:

> *It's like you're in shock. Through the whole thing I didn't cry. If I had I would have been better off, I think, because the next day, that night— when I was awake I could control myself—but as soon as I started dozing off something was taking over me, I don't know what, what it was, but I went through a loose spell (1974, p. 59).*

Ordinarily, considerable psychological and physical distress is experienced during the first few days after the death. The bereaved person may be struck by waves of emotion that culminate in weeping. This weeping is often touched off by something over which the bereaved feel they have no control. Glick, Weiss, and Parkes (1974) comment that at times the widows' crying and sadness seemed to be without content in view of their dazed conditions, but at other times the full awareness of their loss seems to result in deep grief for their husbands.

Part of the distress felt is distress for one's self and one's life due to the absence of the deceased. Women who have had no other identity than that provided by their spouses, for example, are especially likely to feel *lost* and *unprepared* for the future that confronts them. The world may be suddenly perceived as hostile rather than hospitable. Newly bereaved spouses may suddenly become aware of the amount of emotional, social, and economic dependency that they had experienced and that was abruptly severed. Hence, Parkes reports new widows feel anxious, restless, and panicky (1972, p. 33).

During this period of early bereavement, the survivor may have difficulty sleeping, eating, and functioning generally. In my view, institutionalized customs contribute to this difficulty. Friends and relatives may swarm around the newly bereaved at first and may not permit the bereaved person to do anything. Everyday routines are lifted out of the bereaved's hands; the funeral arrangements may be taken over by a relative who is much less emotionally involved but has "good business sense"; the family doctor may be called to "help" by prescribing tranquilizers for the days and sleeping pills for the nights so that the edge is taken off the survivor's grief. This tactic, of course, adds to the unreal feeling the bereaved may have about the unfolding scene around them. It also contributes heavily to causing a delayed grief reaction to occur later when there is no one who can and will genuinely help. Such tactics serve the latent function of letting everyone else get through a troublesome period without having to deal with the thoughts and feelings of the person most affected.

At this point, the bereaved exhibit mixed responses. While wishing to "get things done," they are easily distracted. While wishing to have support, they begin to withdraw. While resenting pity from others, they feel self-pity. Events and emotions feel strange and estrange the bereaved. The ordinary becomes extraordinary, but yet lacks definition. The bereaved's existence seems distorted, ambiguous, and unreal.

Since the newly bereaved's social worlds have been altered, if not completely shattered, they are disorganized, distractible, and confused. Parkes (1972) states that the stress of the situation may reach a point after which the individual's learning capacity diminishes and that individual may become overwhelmed by the confronting crisis. Surely, if the person has had little experience in handling crises of this magnitude, stress is apt to be increased.

During the initial period of bereavement, it is not unusual for the bereaved to be angry toward the dead person. The anger may be due to resentment for being overwhelmed by the situation and the necessity to carry on. Anger may be generated by the individual's feelings of helplessness and perhaps hopelessness. The person may feel helpless in the face of the crisis and in view of the burdens engendered by it. Often, resolution appears hopeless. These feelings are prone to be intensified in cases where the individual's life was wholly intertwined with the deceased.

Ordinarily, during the first few days following a death, if there is no other adult in the home with whom the grief may be shared, a member of the family or a close friend may insist upon staying with the newly bereaved. Widows, especially, are likely to be given this kind of "help." As Glick, Weiss, and Parkes note, the assistance is usually given by unattached females who have no competing responsibilities. Greater concern for the bereaved seems to be exhibited by others when the deceased is either a spouse or a child, as these losses are presumed to "merit" deeper grief. Much less concern is shown for persons whose aged parents die or persons of almost any age whose friends die. How concern is structured by others is a reflection of the much higher value placed on the nuclear family than on extended kinship networks or friendship circles.

Conventional sex roles may be observed in the aftermath of a death. Women in the family tend to provide emotional support and help with routine household tasks. Men may be called upon to assist with the funeral director or helping with other business arrangements. In some families, the same person provides these functions for various members of the family. For example, one uncle may become recognized for his ability to negotiate with the funeral director, so he either volunteers his assistance or is called upon to help when needed. While the distribution of tasks may reaffirm relationships, the newly bereaved may be viewed as incapable of handling the situation. Thus, the intentions and interpretations of actions are of special significance for the implicit messages that the bereaved receive about their new roles, social identities, and self-worth as the transition is socially constructed.

Realization From the early stages of grief that shock and disrupt the bereaved, the character of grief shifts as these persons begin their everyday lives without the deceased. In the phase of realization, the bereaved learn the *nature* and *extent* of their *losses*. Disbelief shifts to sadness and pain and perhaps despair. The reality of the situation encroaches upon the boundaries of the sense of self; the integrity of personal identity becomes problematic. With the realization of the death, the bereaved may define a loss of the sense of self that they had possessed in the past. Further, as the reality of the situation impinges on the survivors, there may be an attempt to become the dead person as a practical way to handle the everyday situations they confront.

The realization of loss through death may be so difficult a phenomenon to integrate into their consciousnesses that the bereaved may come to think they have gone mad. Under conditions where intimate social worlds are fragile and circumscribed to few persons, the loss of the intimate throws the bereaved into a social reality that, however temporarily, seems mad. If a sensible account of the world had been known and one's reality constructed only through the assumptions shared with the deceased person, then loss may make a previously orderly world chaotic and crazy. The rationality of this notwithstanding, because craziness, per se, is seen in American society to reside in the individual, the bereaved may come to view their preoccupations and obsessions with the lost intimate as signs of emotional instability.

After they have been left alone, the realization of loss sinks into the consciousness of the bereaved. This realization is buttressed by the course of events. The influx of friends and relatives tends to evaporate shortly after the funeral. No immediate new arrangements need to be made. Instead, one's emphasis shifts to more ordinary existence. Others are beginning to expect the newly bereaved to "adjust" and either get back into old routines or establish new ones. The bereaved may feel as alone in their grief as they have become socially. The reality of loss is now acutely experienced in one's everyday life. At this point, the bereaved are apt to have what Parkes calls (1972, p. 39) "*pangs*" of grief, characterized by episodic suffering, inability to handle the present event, a tendency to look back into the past and fervently miss the absent person. These pangs of grief are present from the first, but they are also experienced acutely when there are no longer so many distracting people and events to turn the bereaved's consciousness toward other things. If the deceased had shared the survivor's home and reality, then the structure of that person's everyday world alone will elicit pangs of grief. Seeing a picture, remembering a shared event, the conspicuous absence during meals—all may elicit a flood of tears, remorse, and sadness. The widowed may be acutely aware of their lack of companionship, affection, and sexual intimacy. Whatever the specific area or stimulus that gives rise to the feelings of loss, the pang of grief gives rise to the pain and suffering that the loss has incurred.

It is important to note that these episodes of grief are much more characteristic of the grief process than is the prolonged depression sometimes attributed to bereavement. Although at first they may be quite frequent and occur spontaneously, over time they become infrequent and occur when the survivors are specifically reminded of the deceased and their losses. The survivors are more susceptible to these pangs when they are alone with their memories. This is why holidays and anniversary dates of important events shared with the deceased become especially painful. Yet in any case wherein one suffers a loss and is left to live in the reality that had been previously shared, the pangs of grief are apt to emerge.

Parkes (1972) argues that the restlessness, ruminations, and loss of interest in people and things that ordinarily gave pleasure or demanded attention give rise to *pining* and *searching* for the lost loved one. Pining represents the subjective response to separation; searching may seem at face value to be irrational, although later the bereaved may be better able to accept their losses, in some measure because of this searching for the dead person as a part of their grieving process. Such searching may occur in two forms: (1) the bereaved may look back and attempt to remember every detail of events and persons that keeps the deceased alive in their memories, or (2) the bereaved may be haunted by the possibility of encountering the dead person again. As one of the widows Parkes interviewed stated: "Everywhere I go I am searching for him. In crowds, in church, in the supermarket. I keep on scanning the faces. People must think I'm odd" (1972, p. 47). In any case, the survivor is preoccupied with thoughts of the deceased. So preoccupied, survivors often ruminate about the events that led up to the death. Frequently, their thoughts lead to feelings of guilt and self-blame since they may feel that they could have controlled the situation and thus averted the death.

Searching and ruminating combine as a way in which the bereaved attempt to seek explanations for the death and why it happened to their loved ones. This seemingly excessive searching that some widows do for their husbands may perhaps be only a more exaggerated version of the kind of searching that newly bereaved persons generally engage in, particularly when the death was not anticipated.

Widows may frequent areas that are associated with their husbands when they are preoccupied with their loss. Possessions that were prized by the husband or were in some way particularly associated with him become adopted and treasured by the widow. Lynn Caine describes the feeling of comfort she received from wearing her husband's robe:

It smelled of Martin. I started wearing it. It dragged around my ankles, but I pulled the sash tight and felt comforted in it. I'd come home from work and get into that old robe every night. Then came a time when I would put it on on Friday nights and droop around the house in it all weekend (1974, p. 95).

Ironically, the bereaved may experience a stronger sense of identification with the dead person *after* the death than before. Perhaps this is due to the bereaved's concerted attempts to assess what the dead person would have wanted in a particular situation and then try to construct their actions to be congruent with that assessment. The deceased then remain a *symbolic source of reference*, or role model, who provide norms and values for the bereaved. Although the bereaved may not be entirely aware of how deeply such thoughts affect their consciousnesses, they are aware of their needs to take into account what the deceased would have thought, said, and done. In this way, the dead person lives on in the subjective experience of the survivor. Widows are subsequently able to make their husbands real to their growing children, and children are able to know and remember a dead parent.

Yet the felt identification may become an oppressive obsession for the living. A widow may come to realize that her existence has become wholly constructed by her need to keep her husband symbolically alive. Sometimes this may have adverse effects on both adult survivors and the children of the deceased. Adults may remain in the past while they actively attempt to shut out the present and the future. In their efforts to maintain their identification with the dead individual they may attempt to recreate continually that person's former world. This may be discerned in the survivor's attempts to retain the same social reality, as well as in the more concrete manifestations of preserving the same physical environment. Widows who are searching for their husbands may refuse to alter their living arrangements so that things are left the way he knew them. In one of my interviews with a woman who had been widowed for several months, she said:

Look at this house. I keep everything just the way he likes it. I know its crazy, but I still keep the furniture arranged so he could get around in his wheelchair. I feel like I'm waiting for him to come back from the hospital. That's probably why I can't bring myself to give away his clothes.

Spouses may reveal that they feel the presence of their lost partner in the shared familiar environment. To change the environment might precipitate a sense of further loss, or doing so might be seen as a threat to weakening the relationship still attempted to be shared with the deceased. Clearly, the identification the survivor has with the deceased, when it consumes the survivor's consciousness, may contribute heavily to a growing social and emotional isolation. Thus, with widows especially, an interactive process may be discerned when these strong bonds of identification are evidenced during bereavement. The widow withdraws from others and is unable to concentrate on more ordinary events, while society simultaneously withdraws from her. The withdrawal of the widow may be marked by a kind of apathy and disinterest in others. When so consumed by her loss, she lives in a separate world distinguished by her suffering and pain. When that pain is publicly revealed to others, they usually feel uncomfortable for any of these reasons: (1) embarrassment, (2) inability to offer comfort, or (3) remembrance of personal losses.

Family members as well as friends and acquaintances often experience distress over the way one member responds to the death. Student nurse Mary Jo Klepser described her mother's and sister's grief in the following way: "I hated my mother for crying. She cried everyday, everywhere we went, anyplace that my father had previously been. I was embarrassed and refused to go anyplace with her. Amy [her sister] just had snappy remarks for everyone" (1978, p. 421).

In the face of their emotions and isolation from others, a widow may seek solace by looking back at the relationship with her husband. Her identification with her deceased husband may be intensified by her newly changed social reality. As she becomes acutely aware of her altered social status, with the problems of having become a person who is socially stigmatized, she may resort to her imagined conversations with her husband as a source of solace and self-affirmation. When the self is not being affirmed in the present reality, it is a logical step for the person to resort to prior identities that were positively valued by others. Hence, the transition from the identity of wife to widow may be a painful one indeed. In her imagined and often carefully rehearsed dialogues with her deceased husband, the widow may recapture some of the aspects of the prior identity of wife, on which she, too, is apt to have placed a higher value than on that of widow. The survivor faces a world much more problematic than the one that had been known and shared before. The objective, very real issues that face survivors surely affect their subjective experience. The need for continuity, for integration of self, and for an understandable reality all contribute to her need to keep her husband alive.

Similarly, as a widow may idealize the lost husband with whom she identifies, children may have or be presented with an idealized image of a deceased parent. Identification with the deceased parent may be strong and reaffirmed by the surviving one. The deceased parent may be imposed upon the child as a model for the child to live up to.

When identification with the deceased consumes the survivor, suicide may be considered. In such situations, the survivor's identity is merged with or submerged in the deceased's prior identity. Although it is not unusual for bereaved lovers or spouses to have suicidal thoughts during the period when they are most devastated by the death, most move out of this phase. The presence of children or other pressing responsibilities act to form links to the outside world even when survivors' identification with the deceased is marked and they feel that "I might as well be dead."

If there are no other major links, such as job, children, and so forth, that tie the bereaved into the routines of everyday life, then they are apt to be more vulnerable to thoughts of suicide, particularly if death is seen as the way of reintegrating one's self through reunion with the deceased. So suicide may be subjectively defined as both the escape route from a disorganized world and the source of reintegration of identity.

Feeling the presence of the dead person is often a source of comfort to the bereaved. The lost persons may be recovered through the sensation of their presence, through dreams or visual images. Such images are ordinarily taken to be illusions or hallucination by professionals who see the bereaved in some context, but also, at times, by the bereaved themselves. During this time, they need reassurance that the intensity of their emotions is a natural response to loss. If others share the intensity of feeling that the bereaved feel, or are at least exposed to it, they may at least be able to move beyond their preoccupations.

Reintegration Reintegration represents the phase in which the bereaved has adapted to existence without the deceased. The changes in self and action that signify reintegration take several patterns. The most obvious of these patterns are those predicated upon identification with the deceased and those founded upon new forms of participation.

Reintegration through *identification* affords the bereaved a sense of continuity with the past even if that identification has resulted in a greatly changed self. For example, in order to maintain continuity with her past, a widow makes concerted attempts to make the kinds of decisions she thinks her dead husband would have wanted. As she does so, she finds that she is becoming more like him. By attempting to live out the symbols and actions of his world, she constructs a self that resembles his.

This kind of identification goes beyond simple replication of the ideas and actions of the deceased. Taken to its logical conclusion, the survivor internalizes the values, attitudes, and personal style of the deceased. Marris (1974) implies that the identification becomes so well internalized that the husband's preferences and ideas become the widow's own. Over time, identification causes changes in expectations, obligations, and attitudes. Thus, reintegration for the bereaved results in personal change, sometimes of profound dimensions.

Similar changes may be observed when reintegration is founded upon new forms of social participation. In contrast to reintegration based on identification, much less attempt is made by the bereaved to act the part formerly played by the deceased. The deceased is then much less of a symbolic role model. Rather, identification with the deceased is now only partial or wholly separate from symbolically significant activities and persons. Although the deceased may still be highly valued and held in esteem by survivors, they have begun to act as individuals independent of the prior relationship.

Reintegration under these circumstances takes the form of *redirecting* one's life. Generally, in our age-graded society, the life situation of a younger person is more favorable for redirecting life experiences than that of the older adult. The bereaved may choose new pursuits, such as work, education, or travel that might have been untenable or impossible while sharing a relationship with the deceased. Gradually the symbolic world and type of social experience known previously with the deceased person is left behind. If the survivor pursues such avenues for change, then the self may become so different that a lack of continuity is felt between the present and prior self.

As reintegration takes place, the self changes in ways that permit new meanings and purposes to develop. By being forced to face drastically altered circumstances, new aspects of self emerge as interaction ensues. Previously unrecognized strengths and talents may be tapped in the process to afford the bereaved with new sources of developing a sense of competence and self-esteem. Conceivably, as new experiences and personal actions are defined as positive by self and others, reintegration will be fostered. But due to the exigencies of the situation, it may be forced and occur so imperceptibly that it may be defined only long after having actually occurred.

In either pattern, however, symbolic markers sometimes pinpoint the time when the bereaved moves from the stage of realization to reintegration. A feeling of resolution of grief may be experienced in the aftermath of an episode of intense grief, such as uncontrollable weeping. One of Glick, Weiss, and Parkes's interviewees (1974) felt peaceful after such an episode. Another commented on the feeling of self-respect gained when she was able to handle a situation that had raised self-doubts.

Or specific events that transcend the individual may be taken as the symbolic marker identifying the change from realization to reintegration. For one man, an organizational crisis at work in which he played a pivitol role became a symbolic marker of the change. For a woman, her awareness of a particularly beautiful natural scene after months of withdrawal into herself marked her change. Most important about the change is the subjective realization of personal change. The bereaved are keenly aware that they have changed.

Reintegration is not simply a reentry or return to conventional social roles to anchor the survivor into the social structure. Instead, it constitutes a *reorganization* of the subjective self.

PROBLEMS OF WIDOWHOOD: AN ILLUSTRATION OF GRIEF AND BEREAVEMENT

The role of widow in American society is problematic for many women who experience it. On both the social psychological level of interaction and structural level of social role in the society, a widow's position in this society is a fragile, tentative one. The structure in which the widow's existence takes place gives shape to the quality of interaction and the social psychology of her everyday life. The role of widow cannot help but be colored by the fact that she is *female* and associated with *death*. Widows are sometimes believed to carry the stigma of death; they become visible symbolic reminders of disruption of life and one's inevitable end. That alone suffices for some to back off from former social relationships with the widow. Further, because of her association with death, others may feel very awkward about talking with her about her genuine concerns.

Structurally, the widow has a marginal status in society. Lopata (1973), who completed an important study of widows, emphasizes that the traditional role of wife is much more clearly known in this society. Yet the familiar norms and values supporting the role of wife are inadequate, or even entirely inappropriate, for the new role in which the widow finds herself. In a sense, widowhood itself is somewhat of a *transitional* status in our society in which a woman moves from the role of wife to single woman, albeit some women remain "widows" forever. And others become wives again before they subjectively experience themselves as single women.

In attempts to assess the kinds of conditions that cause problems for the widow's resolution of grief, three major areas have been viewed as significant: *anticipation* of *death*, the *structure* of *everyday life*, and *age*. Although anticipation of the husband's death has been found to be positively related to its acceptance, subjective awareness seems to be a better indicator than objective information about the husband's terminal illness. Interestingly, Sheskin and Wallace (1976) found in cases of suicide as well as natural death that widows who anticipated their husbands' demise were better able to view its actuality as real.

But being able to confront the *reality* of death is not the only dimension of grief. The *structure* of everyday life also contributes to whether the widow will have problems in handling her grief and reintegrating her life. When death is anticipated, the woman typically has been forced to take responsibilities before the death occurs. Yet, as Sheskin and Wallace note, taking responsibilities often consumes the woman's energies and serves to isolate her socially.

Age appears to be an important variable as to whether the widow suffers problems in adapting to her new status. Contrary to popular belief, initial research suggests that younger widows (although age levels are not well defined) experience greater problems than older widows (Ball 1976-77; Sheskin and Wallace 1976). Ball reports that widows under 46 who have little or no warning of their husbands' impending death constitute the most vulnerable candidates for a severe response to grief. Younger widows are much more likely to seek psychiatric help than older ones, who report increased physical symptoms that Ball (1976) insightfully notes may disguise the impact of grief. (Besides, psychiatric treatment may be more acceptable to younger women.)

In any case, regardless of outcome, becoming a widow is a critical life transition that results in severe emotional distress. From her extensive contact and research on bereaved spouses, Silverman (1975) reports that the widowed, in general, develop serious psychological problems when they cannot give up their marital role. Speaking broadly, if the widow had embraced the dominant ideology supporting the traditionally circumscribed view of what it is to be a wife, then widowhood is apt to be more problematic for her than someone who has additional sources of self-identification. That is, if she had been a housewife, and her identity had been primarily bestowed upon her by her husband and his status, and she had been emotionally, socially, and financially dependent upon him, then problems of constructing a life as a widow might be expected. Lopata's data show that the widow who places primary emphasis on motherhood, or who has had interests and friends of her own before the death of her husband, may find that some problems often experienced in the transition from wife to widow are diminished.

I contend that the situation of widows, in general, reflects the social values imposed upon women in a sexist society. More specifically, the problems incurred by, and psychological damage done to, women by treating them as children is dramatically symbolized by the plight of many widows in this society today. She may be ignorant about her financial situation, inadequately prepared for meeting her social and economic needs, and unable to cope with her emotions. All the usual problems and burdens of widowhood become intensified if she had been a "child" during her marriage and now is bereft of the former protection, guidance, and nurturance that had been so readily available to her. As one woman of 62 who had always been her husband's "little girl" said to me,

> Was I unprepared! I wasn't able to do anything for myself. I didn't even know how much George made in a year. I had done a little housekeeping and spent most of my other time going to fashion shows, shopping, and that kind of thing. I grew up more in the next two years than I had in the first sixty.

The void that the loss causes is heightened by *idealization* of the dead husband. Idealization is identified by researchers when the husband and marriage are portrayed in glowing terms without reference to or explicit denial of any problems in the relationship or irritation with habits of the deceased. Glick, Weiss, and Parkes provide this example of idealization:

> People talk about the dead and they say, "Oh he was a wonderful fellow." But in this case everything they said about him is truthful because he was great, he was a wonderful guy. He helped everybody. He would help anybody that he could. Sometimes I think he overdid it, you know, but let him do it because it always made him happy that he could help someone (1974, p. 144).

Some widows believe, perhaps in part through idealization, that no other relationship could possibly fill the void left by their husband's death. Widows who feel this way avoid expanding their social networks and may be very wary of becoming friendly with potential suitors. This stance is reinforced and perpetuated by the widow's children when they do not wish to see her remarry. Or friends and relatives may encourage her to remain engrossed in the memory of her husband as a way of showing her continued devotion to him.

A major problem for many widows is *loneliness*. The term loneliness implies that the experiencing person finds her relationship lacking in intensity, strength or quality, and frequency of contact. Similarly, Parkes (1972) implies that loneliness stems from deprivation of necessary psychological support. Loneliness of widows is fostered by both social structural and social psychological conditions. Widows tend to be structurally isolated and are also apt to feel psychologically abandoned due to their loss.

As Lopata (1973) discusses, the loneliness of widows takes at least several forms that vary with widows who experience differing biographical and social conditions of existence. Due to the intimacy shared with the husband and, often, the lack of other close relationships, the loss of the husband constitutes a tremendous void in the life of the widow. Lopata notes that those who have experienced intense relationships in the past, but who have not been able to recreate that same intensity, are likely to feel lonely. She also states that someone who is unable to modify her expectations of that level of intensity experiences increased loneliness. Perhaps, once a woman has experienced a sustained gratifying relationship on an intense level, it becomes part of her self-image and experience.

Some valuable cues as to the nature of their loneliness may be gained from Lopata's data, but her data raise more questions than provide answers to the issue, since it seems as if some widows she interviewed could not, or chose not to, disclose what their husbands meant to them in their private thoughts. However, hints of feeling emerged from those widows who stated that they wanted to love and be loved in ways that children and friends do not love one. That loneliness is magnified when someone feels she does not fit in, as suggested by Lopata's finding that many widows miss having a male companion.

But perhaps more significantly, Lopata's data indicate that the husband provides a basis for a way of life for the wife. His presence is particularly missed, since a way of life had been planned around him. Additionally, the *reciprocity* in the woman's everyday existence is lost. Finding others who will take over the responsibilities previously shouldered by the husband for the maintenance of home and lifestyle becomes problematic and may set in motion such other difficulties as competing with a daughter-in-law for a son's time for household tasks.

Clearly, the significance of Lopata's responses does not lie exclusively in the *problems* of widowhood but can instead be placed in a critique of American society in general and women's roles in it in particular. While Lopata does not deal with either of these issues, they are fundamental to what it means to be a widow in this society. Essentially, Lopata's analysis takes for granted the social context in which widowhood exists. In that sense, her analysis focuses on the individual's response to a problematic situation in which the situation itself (crisis in a fragmented society) is largely taken for granted. Consequently, by focusing on the individual, Lopata emphasizes the adjustment, or lack of it, of the individual to the established social structure. Lopata makes many insightful comments about the situations that widows confront. However, she places most of the responsibility for handling those situations on the widows rather than addressing the cultural values and social policies that give rise to her observations. Lopata seems to give most credence to those women who handle their situations independently according to values consistent with the Protestant Ethos, while she directly criticizes those who do not have personal resources to attract others. Though the focus of her criticism is directed to those widows who, from her perspective, have little to offer socially, Lopata's criticism may be transformed into a larger criticism of our society. What kind of *social structure* fosters conditions in which women are either so undeveloped or reduced in their human qualities that they have little to give others? Some clue is given in other responses in Lopata's data. For some women, it appears that the main property of the marriage was simply its continuity and the structure that it gave everyday existence. For them, whatever intimacy was derived from their situations seems to have developed from the propinquity structured by the situation.

One of the major problems of widowhood, and a strength of Lopata's study for noting it, is *downward mobility*. The husband's death frequently signals a transition into notably worsened economic conditions for his wife. Even widows who had previously experienced affluence may suffer serious financial problems and subsequently have to drastically alter their life-styles. It is not uncommon for a woman to know virtually nothing about the possible benefits for which she is eligible, or about the family's finances. Middle-class widows occasionally are shocked when they rudely discover that no plans had been made for the loss of the breadwinner. Often, widows find that the jobs for which they are qualified do not pay sufficiently to maintain the life-style that the family had previously shared. Older widows may face special problems when their husbands die, since their incomes may not only be drastically reduced but they may also be unemployable. Widows of late middle age may discover that they are too old to work and too young to collect survivors' benefits from social security. Yet they may be left with high mortgage payments, children to educate, no medical coverage, and virtually no income. One 55-year-old widow recounted some of the events following her husband's death three years before:

> After twenty-seven years of marriage we had what I thought was a comfortable life, nice house, two cars and only one more child to put through college. Then my husband died. He had some life insurance, mortgage insurance and some savings, but it didn't add up to enough to take care of me and send my son to school. Not very long after his death, I was having trouble making mortgage payments and I couldn't seem to get a job. A financial advisor at the bank told me to sell my house. I told him, "Sure it's gone up in value but rents these days are more than the payments, and a two bedroom apartment just isn't enough room for both me and my son. Besides I'd use up the money in a couple of years." So I tried harder to get a job; I practiced my typing, which was never great, took a bookkeeping class and pounded doors looking. I didn't get anything and I resented that. Yes I resented it; I had worked hard all my life, been a good wife and raised four good kids; then I couldn't even get a job when I needed one.

This particular widow eventually found a position. Although it meant that she had to economize in ways that she never imagined in her marriage, she was able to keep her home and some semblance of her former life.

Most important to note is the gradual downward mobility that coincides with aging. It occurs over time as the widow attempts to live on a fixed income and manage her needs independently, while living in an economy in which inflation is increasing (Butler 1975; Tissue 1970). Over time, the aged widow has to restrict her spending more stringently in order to maintain an existence independent of her children. Downward mobility leads to a more constricted life style since the woman can no longer afford the same kinds of activities as her friends. As friends and neighbors move out of her immediate locale, she can neither maintain the relationships nor can she replace them. As her neighborhood changes, she may find that she has little in common with the newcomers, which ultimately serves to increase her isolation. Consequently, she may reject the few possibilities that she has for social relationships.

Lopata found that uneducated women in her Chicago study were more isolated than women with an education. She also found that religious background and ethnicity correlated with widows' scores on a friendship scale. According to her findings, Protestant women were more likely to realize high or medium levels of friendship than were either Catholics or Jews. Since Jewish women were disproportionately low scorers, Lopata suggested that there might be some cultural sanction concerning forming friendships. Women of German and Norwegian extraction scored high on the friendship scale, but women of Polish or Russian descent were low scorers. Black women scored at both extremes. Those who had been divorced or widowed previously scored higher on the friendship scale than those who had only one partner. Older widows in Lopata's study identified as friends only those who shared the same ethnicity, religion, and marital status. If the widow had not been involved in friendship networks during her marriage, it was unlikely that she would become involved with them as a widow; friendship may not be very meaningful to some persons. In working-class families, the extended family often plays a role similar to that of friends in middle-class families, since visiting, mutual help, and support are given within the confines of the family network, although they may not be extended to others beyond it.

A major concern of many widows who have children remaining in the home is how they will manage to raise them as a single parent with reduced finances. Avoiding being overly solicitous with the children seems to be a fairly common concern of widows (see Lopata 1973; Glick, Weiss, and Parkes, 1974). They feel unsure of themselves when dealing with external crises and internal struggles with the children. For example, the widow's authority with a teenager may be held in question by her child, since she is now without the actual or symbolic validation of this authority as provided by the father. Also, the widow's authority in dealing with her children may be brought into question by her own family. Further, the widow may find that her relatives now feel free to question her actions and undermine her autonomy. Thus, she may be subjected to conflicting pressures to become independent in some areas of her life and to remain or become dependent in others.

It should be emphasized that the problems confronting younger widows (less than 50 years old), may be of a qualitatively different character than those who are older. Whether children are grown and independent contributes to this difference. If the widow has children to support and consequently feels compelled to seek work, she may identify significantly different kinds of concerns than do widows who do not have dependent children. Or, correspondingly, those widows who feel forced to seek employment for self-maintenance face different kinds of issues than those who do not or cannot work.

Forced independence characterizes the situation of widows who must make the shift from wife to single woman. A widow may actively seek independence, not so much for herself as for her children. Thus, the pressure to remain responsible for the children may be the impetus propelling the younger widow to seek new alternatives in her life. A major consequence of forced independence is the transformation of the widow to another kind of person than she previously was. Hence, these widows often comment on how they would not have chosen the path they took, but that they had changed after their husbands' death. Some widows remark that they come to like and value their new independence once they become accustomed to it. Perhaps the most positive outcome occurs when the widow recognizes the changes she has made and has no regrets about making them. Such changes may be represented in qualities that are sought in a new marriage partner, one whose life and outlook are compatible with the changes she has made. As one widow said to me, "Although I was happy in my first marriage, I am a different person now, so I am looking for different things in a mate."

Not much attention has been given to the situation of the widower confronting the loss of his wife. There may be some specific reasons for this that reflect other issues and widely held cultural values. First, since there are fewer widowers than widows, due to the lower life expectancy of men, there aren't as many of them to be concerned about. Further, widowers do not bear the stigma of death commonly attributed to widows. Whereas widows are treated as closely associated with death, widowers tend to be treated much like divorced men. Consequently, it is not uncommon for a widower to be welcomed into old and new social circles; whereas a woman in the same circumstances may be systematically excluded from both. Treas and Van Helst (1976) find that the marriage rates of older Americans reflect this. Men over 65 are six times more likely to marry than their female counterparts, although the difference in the relative populations of men and women is much smaller. Further, with each five-year interval, the probability of an older woman marrying rapidly declines.

In general, the relative differences in the social treatment of widows and widowers are likely to be due to differential cultural values on gender. By and large, males are more valued than females in this society and, thus the treatment of the widow may reflect her doubly devalued position, of being female and mateless, not to mention the fact that she is also likely to be old and without valued skills beyond those of a housewife. In the practical world of experience, the widow may find herself in a most disadvantageous position. However, the widower with children to care for, especially one with a limited income, may have similar overwhelming problems in managing his situation. If either his relatives or his deceased wife's relatives are in the locale where he lives, they are likely candidates for helping out with the care. Even with help, the widower may find his added responsibilities overwhelming, and like the widow with children, he may find the mere mechanics of everyday life so time consuming that he also becomes socially isolated from other adults during his nonworking hours.

One major aspect of the difference between widows and widowers may be related to the cultural emphasis on stoicism, especially for men, in the face of personal crisis. Unlike widows, widowers show few outward symbols of their grief (Glick, Weiss, and Parkes 1974, p. 272). With such an emphasis, the widower may not receive even emotional support during the initial days and weeks after his wife's death. This premise is corroborated by Glick, Weiss, and Parkes (1974, p. 268), who found in their study of widowers that others viewed them as needing help with household and parental obligations, but left them to handle their feelings alone. Several cultural themes conceivably contribute to this perception. Not only do cultural expectations exist that men "should" show greater control over their feelings, but many men have internalized beliefs about remaining independent, and therefore aloof, from others.

Glimpses of stoicism may be seen in extreme situations as revealed in specific cases, such as the professor who finishes his lecture despite the fact that he is notified of his wife's suicide earlier that day, or the physician who finishes his round of appointments even though his wife has just succumbed. In such cases the widower is apt to view grief as a weakness that would be revealed by even acknowledging the event. Consequently, loss and grief are reaffirmed as *private* rather than *public* events.

Since superficial sociability does not reveal the character of one's inner world, emotional distance and independence can be maintained despite congenial relationships. That distance may be exhibited during the time of bereavement when a widower gives indications to others as well as himself that he does not need or should not be consoled by others. With the cultural emphasis on male stoicism comes a greater reluctance to break the walls of silence that are customarily built in everyday interaction. Hence, others may define breaking into the widower's inner feelings of loss as much more of an *intrusion* than they would for a female counterpart. In this way, the widower may suffer perhaps even more *emotional isolation* than the widow, although he may not be as isolated socially as she is (Glick, Weiss, and Parkes 1974). If so, then during the intense period of grief, widowers might be found to experience more somatic complaints than do widows, who may have more avenues for emotional expression, particularly at that time in their lives.

The importance of emotional isolation may be discovered through the widower's adaptation to his new status as a single person. If a widower remains emotionally isolated and does not have other supportive persons who will explore his feelings of loss and sorrow with him, it stands to reason that, despite social activity and social acceptance, newly bereaved widowers will not show any more significant "recovery" rates than widows. Although widowers were less apt than widows to describe themselves as depressed or unhappy at the end of the first year of bereavement, Glick, Weiss, and Parkes (1974) found that they did report considerably greater feelings of distress than did non-bereaved men.

Given the fact that men have more economic and social options in the world than women, it is not surprising to find that their responses to loss are considerably different than those of women. Since they are more likely to be tied to their other usual roles, such as work, they are more likely to remain integrated in prior social worlds than the widow. In contrast, the widow who has been a housewife for a number of years is unlikely to get a job that challenges her in the same way that a life-long career or occupation consumes the interest of the widower. But Glick, Weiss, and Parkes's data indicate that widowers are aware of and concerned about the lower level of functioning that they experience on the job after their wives' deaths. Interestingly, these widowers tended to handle that problem by seeking remarriage, which would not only help them personally but would recreate a stable home if there were children to be cared for.

The difference in male and female sex roles shows strikingly in the reactions to the impact of loss that Glick, Weiss, and Parkes found in the small sample of widowers they studied. The women in their study seem to have had the *totality* of their lives and social worlds destroyed by the death of their husbands. In contrast, the widowers appear to have the *organization* of their home lives seriously altered. While the widows often described their loss in terms of the symbolic imagery of *abandonment,* men tended to view their loss in terms of having lost a *part* of themselves. Perhaps a major difference in the imagery used by these respondents points to a contrast in how the self is affected by the loss. It would seem that the selves of the men were left damaged, but the possibility existed for adjustment to the altered state of affairs; whereas the women whose selves may have been submerged in their husbands felt a more total loss that irrevocably altered the kind of self they could claim. In short, the imagery used suggests to me the plausibility that from the beginning the widowers were dealing with a qualitatively different experience of loss than the widows.

SUMMARY AND IMPLICATIONS

In American culture, the experience of intense grief generally results in loss of self of the bereaved. What grief is, how it is felt, and what is to be done about it are all culturally defined. Loss and grief are responses to personal transitions when these transitions are characterized by finality and lack of choice, although overt responses of grief to transitions other than death of an intimate are often not seen as "legitimate" by self or other. Grief is commonly given negative connotations, as it is viewed as a disease process inside the afflicted person to be gotten out and rid of.

Common norms for handling the distress elicited by grief are related to the underlying values of the Protestant Ethic. Hence, grief becomes something to be handled as a personal problem to be "worked out" and resolved alone. The typical structure of everyday relationships contributes to isolation in grief. The nuclear family is often too small to afford support to all of its members. When families are isolated in their communities, little support is widely available unless there are formal organizations developed specifically to serve the bereaved. Repression rather than expression of grief is more apt to be encouraged by others when the bereaved is in face-to-face contact with them. However, in contrast to the individualistic way of handling grief in the dominant culture, values emphasizing social support and expression of loss are encouraged in both Black and Mexican-American cultures.

The situational context of grief also affects how it is experienced. Whether death expectations were held appears to be an important variable in the quality of the survivor's grief. When death expectations are held long in advance of biological death, the survivor may experience anticipatory grief and thus be socialized to the fact of death. As a result, the survivor's grieving is thought to be finished before death occurs. Anticipatory grief can be an authentic response only when the prior relationship with the dying is resolved and essentially ended. When the dying no longer share a significant role in the intimate worlds of the survivor, anticipatory grief may be a more frequent response. However, others who expect a display of "normal" grief may foster feelings of guilt in the survivor who does not or no longer grieves.

The absence of death expectations causes an initial intense problem of realization of the death for the survivor. It may also leave the survivor with deep regrets for earlier feelings and actions toward the deceased. Although the absence of death expectations poses problems for the survivor, the presence of them does not necessarily ease the situation for the most involved. The quality of the grief experience is affected by: (1) the prior structure of care, (2) the response of others, and (3) the implications of emotions elicited by a lengthy dying process. Immersion in care often paradoxically leads to separation and insulation from direct confrontation with death. Social isolation of the survivor before the death tends to intensify felt grief. Intense grief is experienced when the relationship was a significant one imbedded in continual interaction. Despite this, others may not permit the survivor to express deep feelings of grief when *they* had long expected the death.

For some, the dying process is so arduous and stressful that anger about the situation becomes transformed to anger toward the dying. Such anger gives rise to feelings of guilt after the death occurs, particularly if it caused rifts between the survivor and the dying. Guilt may then arise in response to the prior actions of the survivor. Hence, a common source of guilt is a failure to identify appropriately or act upon the symptoms of the deceased as they developed. But feelings of guilt and subsequent intense and prolonged grief are also apt to develop when the survivor's feelings about the deceased are ambivalent and conflicted.

Another important variable affecting the quality of grief concerns the prior structure of relationships. With the high values on youth and children, the death of a child is thought to evoke the most intense grief. The death of a parent commonly results in guilt in the children as they feel self-blame for the death and anger at the parent for abandonment.

Intense grief shakes the foundations of the self. Shared meanings and purposes are destroyed when held only with the deceased. In the first phase of grieving, *transition*, the survivors often feel the world has become unreal as they experience bizarre thoughts, feelings, and disbelief. The self as well as the personal world of the bereaved has become disorganized. In the second phase of grieving, *realization,* the bereaved learn the nature and extent of their losses. Disbelief shifts to sadness and sometimes despair. The reality of loss becomes apparent in the bereaveds' everyday activities. Pangs of intense grief are elicited by memories. The bereaved tend to experience both social and emotional isolation while they simultaneously withdraw from others. Because of a strong sense of identification with them the deceased become a symbolic source of reference for the bereaved. Suicidal thoughts are common, although pressing responsibilities such as children usually spur the bereaved to keep functioning. Emotional support from others also assists the bereaved to function and move into the next phase, *reintegration.* In this phase, the bereaved have adapted to existence without the deceased. Reintegration may be founded on identification with the deceased when the survivor develops a self that is much like that of the deceased. Or reintegration may be founded on new forms of social participation. The survivor's self changes in response to the new social worlds and actions confronting him or her. In either case, reintegration represents a reorganization of the subjective self. Nevertheless, not all selves change, since not all of the bereaved transform their grief. Some make concerted efforts to remain the same in order to keep the memory of their deceased intimate alive.

The role of the widow is problematic and tentative since there are few clear-cut norms for handling it. In addition, many women are wholly unprepared for the financial and social realities that face them. Loneliness is a significant problem for the widow since she is often deprived of psychological support and her husband gave meaning and structure to her life. The problems faced by widows, such as loneliness, psychological deprivation, and financial devastation, reflect larger issues of the experience of crisis in a fragmented society in general and the problem of women's roles within it in particular. However, the weight of these problems is often left to the widows themselves.

As a result of social realities, bereavement seems to be a different kind of experience for the widow than the widower. The foundation of the widow's life seems to be destroyed; whereas, the organization of his home life is disrupted for the widower. But despite the greater disorganization confronting the widow, the widower may be even more emotionally isolated in his grief due to traditional sex role expectations of stoicism and self-control.

What are the implications of grief for the bereaved?

Intense grief makes for both a *problematic reality* and a *problematic self.* Death of the other means losing the shared reality that had been experienced in the relationship. For widows, the marriage relationship offered a certain amount of *insulation* from the realities of others and from the external world. Even when companionship and affection appear to have been limited, relationships provided continuity and structure in the lives of those who shared them. Some become committed as much to the *structure* of the *relationship* as to the other, and the self is situated within that structure, thereby providing insulation from the world. In conflicted relationships, the survivor may remain unaware of the extent to which the relationship, perhaps even the conflict, provide a form, a structure, and a way of being in the world.

Conceivably, the intense grief observed when relationships had been characterized by ambivalence represents something more than simply, or only, guilt. It might represent the grief over a self made *vulnerable* through loss of its structure. This type of grief parallels that experienced in response to the loss of a more stable relationship. In both situations, widows frequently allude to a bewildering feeling of literally not being themselves. By losing the other, the bereaved has experienced a form of symbolic death. A crucial dimension of self has been lost or negated.

The depth of that loss is often interpreted by the bereaved as being so profound that it is beyond words. Like intense romance, one's intense grief is felt to be like no other's. The bereaved feel that no one else could suffer such pain, despair, sorrow, remorse, or bewilderment. Such feelings make for immersion in self-pity, withdrawal, and sometimes a sense of superiority due to the burden of one's sufferings. A widow, particularly, may suffer further isolation when her feelings clash with a now problematic world. In that sense, the emergence of formal friendships offered by volunteer organizations of widows provides a promising means for aiding the widow to put her self and her situation into perspective so that her potential for living in the world is enhanced.

REFERENCES

Anderson, Robert (1974). Notes of a survivor. In Stanley B. Troup and William A. Greene (eds.), *The Patient, Death and the Family*. New York: Charles Scribner's Sons.

Ball, Justine (1977). Widow's grief: the impact of age and mode of death. *Omega* 7:307-33.

Becker, Howard (1969). The sorrow of bereavement. In Hendrik M. Ruitenbeek (ed.), *Death: Interpretations*. New York: Delta Books.

Bendiksen, Robert, and Robert Fulton (1977). Death and the child: an anterospective test of the childhood bereavement and later behavior disorder hypothesis. In Robert Fulton (ed.), *Death and Identity*. Philadelphia: Charles Press.

Butler, Robert (1975). *Why Survive?* New York: Harper and Row.

Caine, Lynne (1974). *Widow*. New York: Morrow.

Calkins, Kathy (1972). Shouldering a burden. *Omega* 3:23-36.

Charmaz, Kathy (1973). Time and identity: the shaping of selves of the chronically ill. Ph.D. dissertation, University of California, San Francisco.

de Beauvior, Simone (1973). *A Very Easy Death*. New York: Warner Paperbacks.

Frederick, Jerome F. (1971). Physiological reactions induced by grief. *Omega* 7:297-305.

_____ (1976-77). Grief as a disease process. *Omega* 2:71-75.

Fulton, Robert, and Julie Fulton (1971). A psychosocial aspect of terminal care: anticipatory grief. *Omega* 2:91-100.

Furman, Robert A. (1970). The child's reaction to death in the family. In Bernard Schoenberg, Arthur C. Carr, David Peretz, and Austin H. Kutscher (eds.), *Loss and Grief*. New York: Columbia University Press.

Gerber, Irvin (1974). Anticipatory bereavement. In Bernard Schoenberg, Arthur C. Carr, Austin Kutscher, David Peretz, and Ivan K. Goldberg (eds.), *Anticipatory Grief*. New York: Columbia University Press.

Glick, Ira O., Robert S. Weiss, and C. Murray Parkes (1974). *The First Year of Bereavement*. New York: Columbia University Press.

Goldfogel, Linda (1972). Working with the parent of a dying child. In Mary H. Browning and Edith P. Lewis (eds.), *The Dying Patient: A Nursing Perspective*. New York: The American Journal of Nursing Co.

Goody, Jack (1974). Death and the interpretation of culture: a bibliographic overview. In David E. Stannard (ed.), *Death in America*. Philadelphia: University of Pennsylvania Press.

Kalish, Richard A., and David K. Reynolds (1976). *Death and Ethnicity*. Los Angeles: University of Southern California Press.

Klepser, Mary Jo (1978). Grief, how long does it go on? *American Journal of Nursing* 78:420-22.

Lopata, Helena (1973). *Widowhood in an American City*. Cambridge, Mass.: Schenkman.

Marris, Peter (1974). *Loss and Change*. New York: Pantheon Books.

Masamba, Jean, and Richard Kalish (1976). Death and bereavement: the role of the Black church. *Omega* 7:23-24.

Parkes, C. Murray (1972). *Bereavement: Studies in Grief in Adult Life*. New York: Basic Books.

Paulay, Dorothy (1977-78). Slow death: one survivor's experience. *Omega* 8:173-79.

Rees, W. Dewi, and Sylvia G. Lutkins (1967). Mortality of bereavement. *British Medical Journal* 4:13-16.

Rosenblatt, Paul, R. Patricia Walsh, and Douglas A. Jackson (1977). *Grief and Mourning in a Cross-Cultural Perspective*. New Haven, Conn.: Human Relations Area File Press.

Sheskin, Arlene, and Samuel E. Wallace (1976). Differing bereavements: suicide, natural and accidental death. *Omega* 7:229-42.

Silverman, Phyllis Rolfe (1975). The widow to widow program: an experiment in preventive intervention. In Edwin S. Shneidman (ed.), *Death: Current Perspectives*. Palo Alto, Calif.: Mayfield.

Tissue, Thomas (1970). Downward mobility in old age. *Social Problems* 18:67-77.

Treas, Judith, and Anke Van Helst (1976). Marriage and remarriage rates among older Americans. *The Gerontologist* 16:132-36.

Vinovskis, Maris A. (1978). Angels' heads and weeping willows: death in early America. In Michael Gordon (ed.), *The American Family in Social Historical Perspective*. New York: St. Martin's Press.

Volkart, Edmund H., and Stanley T. Michael (1977). Bereavement and mental health. In Sandra Galdieri Wilcox and Marilyn Sutton (eds.), *Understanding Death and Dying*. Port Washington, N.Y.: Alfred Publishing Co.

Wallace, Samuel E. (1973). *After Suicide*. New York: Wiley.

Weiss, Robert S. (1973). *Loneliness: The Experience of Social and Emotional Isolation*. Cambridge, Mass.: MIT Press.

CHAPTER TEN

THE FUTURE OF DEATH

Death lies in the future for everyone. But the future of death takes shape in whatever collective meanings and practices are constructed by people around concrete instances of death as they engage in their everyday lives. Although present meanings and practices are being questioned, such as death as something to be feared and dying something to be hidden, the extent to which these questions challenge the foundations of the American stance toward death remains debatable. In the following pages, I raise questions about the future of death for the individual, but first I briefly review and put into perspective what has been covered in the preceding chapters.

IN RETROSPECT

What has the foregoing analysis shown death to be? In which ways are the situations of individuals who confront death and dying affected by wider social values? How does death affect the self-images of those directly confronting it? To answer these questions, first recall my argument that the problematic situations confronting those who face death symbolize less visible kinds of situations experienced under more ordinary conditions of existence. What happens with death and dying reflects what happens in everyday life. The kinds of issues faced do not reflect a difference in nature, but rather represent a difference in intensity and scope. Thus, issues concerning choice, disclosure, accountability, and control, which are discussed in detail in the preceding chapters, are all part of everyday life. Importantly, too, constructing a self is a problematic issue for many that is greatly intensified and more visible with those who face death. Not only do the dilemmas posed by death reflect those in everyday life, but a study of concrete instances of death and dying reveal much about the character and mood of contemporary American culture.

In a study of death and dying, the significance of culture is twofold. First, it gives rise to common meanings of ways to think, act, and feel in the face of death, some of which become concretized in powerful organizational forms. Second, culture provides the backdrop from which individuals interpret and construct their own meanings and actions. In taken-for-granted ways, individuals take into account wider social meanings and occasionally even transform them in their everyday interactions. Hence, those who face death in some way do not live in a social and psychological vacuum. Instead, their everyday worlds and modes of acting within them are made sensible by virtue of their taken-for-granted understandings derived from cultural values and social participation. The American understanding of death and dying as primarily psychological and personal issues is itself a view derived from shared values that are reaffirmed in actual circumstances.

Significantly, cultural values are related to the conceptions of death constructed by individuals. Whatever conceptions of death are held, they are apt to shape the individual's experience with it. Death conceptions and individual experience share a reciprocal relationship as each influences the other. Ordinarily, death conceptions shape experience. But when experience radically differs from earlier conceptions, changes in them can be expected. In this sense, such divergent individuals as dying patients, student physicians, and combat soldiers may be resocialized into new conceptions of death that make sense of their recent experiences.

In order for individuals to make sense of their experiences, both consciousness of the feelings raised and definition of them seem to be prerequisite: consciousness in the sense that the individual feels and knows, definition in the sense that what is felt and known is able to be articulated and understood. Otherwise, someone remains in a state of awareness but with ambiguity and often with great confusion about his or her experience. The surreal or unreal existence of the suicidal and bereaved, for example, constitute cases in point where consciousness is sometimes without clear definition. Further, to the extent that individuals define their responses as unique, they will be unable to identify and act upon whatever shared experience and collective origins their responses might otherwise reveal.

Perhaps what becomes most obvious in the study of death and dying is how willing others are to define reality and personal identity for the one confronting death. Such definitions are obviously supplied by the representatives of formal organizations such as medical practitioners or funeral directors. But they are also supplied by intimates. In the face of definitions of one's reality and self made at a time when they are most questioned, the dying, suicidal, and bereaved frequently find themselves accepting new and disturbing views of who they are and what lies ahead.

For many, maintaining a subjectively valued self while facing death remains highly problematic. Some may bargain for the social supports that symbolize a valued self. Others may use the situation to gain an acclaimed identity previously not accorded to them. Yet it is not uncommon for the self of the individual to be transformed. That transformation may result in the dying becoming wholly dissociated from their pasts. Or it may result in becoming objects for workers and others to redefine and mold in either conventional or more contemporary ways.

Thus, the selves of those confronting death are, in fundamental ways, shaped out of the social circumstances in which they exist. If continuity is to be maintained between their prior selves and present circumstances, special effort will need to be made, not only by those confronting death but also by concerned others. In short, the social nature of the self is dramatically revealed in the face of death.

THE FUTURE OF DEATH

What will be the shape of death in the future? Will it have new dimensions? Will dying be a qualitatively new process if radically different social conditions prevail? How might our conceptions of the nature of death and dying change in the future? To answer these questions, I will put into perspective some major ideas raised in the foregoing chapters. In that way, we can examine current trends in relation to their implications for the future. Consistent with the social psychological emphasis in this book, the following discussion focuses on the dying individual. For this individual, the future of death will reflect the character and meaning of death held in the wider society.

Arguments are already being made that the character and meaning of death are changing as it is increasingly brought into the public arena for discussion and scrutiny. Yet changes in attitudes may not necessarily indicate dramatic changes in the ways Americans view and manage death. The willingness to attend lectures, participate in seminars and workshops, or commune with the dying may indicate the emergence of new ideas and altered conceptions, although in some respects these new ideas are currently limited. For example, one must ask if participation in these new public death rituals leads to changed actions and beliefs when participants talk about death as the *core* of the ritual as contrasted with directly experiencing the dilemmas posed by death? Or do actions and beliefs change after dying is actually confronted? One must also ask to what extent such rituals feed public fascination with death without forcing any profound changes in values or challenging existing practices such as care of the dying? Finally, a question arises regarding the relative effect of these rituals on populations as a whole. To what extent do they affect people who have the power to alter current practices?

For that matter, does the death and dying movement challenge ongoing practices of care of the dying? The current emphasis on eliciting and confronting the feelings of the dying and others seems to me to be the tip of the iceberg. While clearly important, permitting the expression of feeling is only a small change, and I suspect it is permitted only in certain specialized environments wherein some practitioners feel equipped—if not compelled—to confront and deal with the feelings of particular dying patients or bereaved. As noted earlier, even this seemingly innocent and psychologically laudable enterprise raises some hidden issues. The potential intrusiveness of the death and dying movement in the lives of those confronting death is of course a major drawback of it. When feelings are sought out by overly zealous practitioners, they may be largely responsible for *creating*, rather than merely eliciting, the patient's "response." And to the extent that *expectations* are formed by practitioners as to what the patient should be thinking, feeling, and doing, moral questions arise. Basic among these is the question: What right does the practitioner have to teach the patient "how to die"? When this is the hidden agenda or explicit approach, then whatever private meanings held by the patient are likely to become subordinated to the ongoing program structured by practitioners. To have one's definitions of reality undermined and one's feelings questioned in these ways while dying may constitute a new form of professional dominance of questionable value.

In any case, the emphasis on confrontation of feelings ordinarily fits into the existing model of medical care. This approach is unlikely to challenge basic structural relationships that fundamentally shape how care and dying are organized. If anything, the approaches constitute a new frontier for developing the patient-practitioner relationship in much the same ways as it is organized in other sectors of medicine. What the new interest in dying does provide is a new *arena* for practitioners to try out their skills and sell their services. Hence, the emphasis on dying may, as is currently occurring, bring into existence several new forms of *specialization*. Although these new specializations may become more or less prevalent, they result in a further segmentation of *preexisting institutional structures* rather than the formulation of markedly new forms of social organization based on new conceptions of practice.

If the new interest in death takes hold in the form of developing relatively stable organizational structures, what basic purposes might these new structures serve? One conjecture is that practitioners within them will take the burden of dealing with the "unsalvageable" dying patient away from others who neither wish to deal with death nor who do not respond to medical intervention. Perhaps, at least in the initial stages of organization, psychosocial support to the dying and their intimates may be largely provided by volunteers who work under the supervision of practitioners. While the services to the patient and the medical institution might be mutually benefiting, one needs to ask in these situations who actually benefits? From the standpoint of organizational analysis, it seems that this type of organization simply fills an existing gap in medical care. Thus, such programs help to patch the existing problems within the institution of medicine without raising questions as to whether its fundamental nature ought to be changed.

Questions arise, too, about whether gradual changes in our handling of the dying, ostensibly in the interest of the patient's welfare, may have the unintended consequence of protecting medical domination and conventional beliefs about death. One such change might be the care of the dying person at home. Since more and more people are living with terminal illness for extended periods, it makes sense that they should wish to limit their hospitalizations and thus maximize their time in familiar surroundings with intimates. Hopefully, more physicians will encourage this practice and seek to devise ways to make it possible for a small family or an intimate to handle the care of the dying. Many patients will need special adjunctive services of an otherwise onerous nature for their relatives to handle but may nonetheless be provided at home by visiting practitioners of various types. Thus, patients are able to exert much greater control over their dying, practitioners and, most importantly, *self* than is possible in a hospital, while the costs of dying are likely to be considerably reduced.

Relinquishing the patient to die at home will, I predict, become a more accepted practice in the future. But, it appears to me that economic imperatives, rather than humanistic ones, may be primarily responsible for the shift. It seems probable that medical institutions will attempt to accommodate public pressures in the face of skyrocketing costs. Permitting patients to die at home would be one form of such accommodation. If the patient has someone who can give care, it may make good economic sense to encourage it. Besides, the high costs of care may come to far exceed what can be handled by insurance and relatives. If so, I suspect that home care of the dying will become legitimized as a viable practice despite the current dilemmas some consider it to pose in regard to shortening the life of a patient.

My argument essentially rests on predictions that the medical institution will sanction certain types of practices in the care of the dying, not because of their humanistic value so much as because these practices provide expedient solutions to pressing problems. Consistent with this argument is the view that changes in the care of the dying will be accepted by organized medicine as means of protecting their interests rather than fundamentally challenging them. It may then become feasible to condone or encourage practices outside of the usual realm of medical involvement that do not present a serious challenge to traditional medical prerogatives.

For death and dying to change in this society, a number of other changes must occur. Changes in the system of medical care must be foremost among them since dying is ordinarily dominated by the medical institution. Otherwise, the changes made in dying and death will remain limited and relatively superficial. There are structural limits to having a humane death in this society, and attitudinal changes will not have much impact unless they are buttressed with basic *structural changes* in the nature of care of the dying. In turn, changes in the medical care system both demand changes in the wider society and are caused by them. It seems unlikely that medical care, one of the last holdouts of the entrepreneurial dream and increasingly situated in corporate structures, will bring about its own fundamental changes.

How might change come about? My view takes into account both the subjectively defined motivations of the individual and external, observable conditions within the society. The two exist in a reciprocal relationship, and thus each is affected by the other. Surely, the awareness of individuals about the plight of the dying person, coupled with *concrete actions* about it, contributes to the construction of change.

But how does that kind of awareness and action come about? Death must be made real, immediate, and subjective. Hence, for any awareness to take the form of concern translated into action, death must be defined as a part of life. Further, if death is to change, so must views and practices toward aging. As argued throughout this book, attitudes toward the aged are related to attitudes toward death. Whether or not one believes the aged to be visible symbols of impending mortality, they are both avoided and excluded from the subjectively defined worlds of many Americans. Besides, the aged constitute a sizable proportion of those who die. An expanding of these worlds to include the aged would, in my opinion, coincide with a greater willingness to face death subjectively.

Actions tend to reflect deeply held value stances, although the person may remain unaware of them. How, then, do values change? The first level of change may come with the sometimes jarring awareness of what one's actions mean in relation to underlying values. That awareness is likely to stem from experiences that question the presuppositions one holds. Since experience is subjectively perceived, actions and events may be interpreted in divergent ways. Consequently, an event such as attending a workshop on death may affect participants in somewhat different ways. Yet talking about death is only one level of experience. Living with tangible dilemmas posed by it constitutes quite another. I contend that those subjectively defined interpretations that arise out of experiencing those dilemmas and reflecting upon them are most likely to result in a changed stance toward death. And a changed personal stance is strengthened when reaffirmed by the views of others.

Changes in personal experience occur in conjunction with changes in the wider society. It follows, then, that new interpretations will be prompted by changes in the society. The recent emergence of the *active dying* due to earlier detection of disease and improved technical maintenance constitutes one change. The increasingly high costs of medical care is another. Both force attention on the dilemmas posed by dying, if not also on death. Changes in the wider society are in turn affected by new ways of thinking about and handling death. Hence, the intentions of individuals and the circumstances founded in society exist in a dialectical relationship. This reciprocal influence holds even when the initial impetus for change is derived from technological modification of the disease process or demographic changes resulting in greater numbers of dying individuals.

Changes in the social organization of dying have met a responsive chord among a certain sector of the nursing profession, many of whom are concerned with nursing education. Their efforts have been joined by members of the clergy, other health-related workers, and consumers. But except for a few individuals, those who have the most power, the physicians, typically have neither envisioned ways of improving the social organization of the dying process nor offered programs to create fundamental departures from the traditional medical model of care. Were they to participate in a movement for constructing major transformations in the nature of care, the impetus for restructuring the care of the dying would be much greater.

Clearly, the kinds of changes being discussed would result in a shifting of values as well as a shifting of priorities. The values centering around individualism might shift slightly. One possible shift would be from the kind of individualism that demands stoicism and results in isolation to that which emphasizes the individual's right to shape and control his or her experience. If individuals had rights while dying, such changes as controlling physical care would be permitted to them. In concrete situations, the patient could then choose high dosages of medication for pain or choose to be without medication at the end in order to experience the final moments of dying. Or the patient could request human companionship, or reject it when it becomes intrusive. Such changes reflect a shift in values but retain an emphasis on the individual without forcing narrowly defined views upon the patient. The dying patient would become an active instead of passive participant.

Ultimately, the future of death may encompass a recognition of human rights and humane care. From my perspective, humane care cannot exist without the recognition and extension of the human rights of the dying and their intimates.

Whatever forms death and dying take in the future will, I contend, reflect the particular socio-historical conditions shaping the society as a whole. Similarly, the form given to dying, conceptions of death, and the experience of grief will all be constructed in ways that are uniquely consistent with American traditions. Some support for that supposition is already given by the existence of the current "death with dignity" trend.

As the economic and social pressures grow to change the social structure of dying, what it is understood to be will also change. Thus, the reality of death is ultimately a social construction given an "objective" character through thought and action. Because the reality of death is a social construction, it is subject to changes as human beings transform their social conditions and are transformed by them. In conclusion, the beliefs, values, norms, and practices constituting the reality of death are constructions of interacting persons who shape both society and history. Thus, the nature of their emerging thoughts and actions will give shape to death in the future.

NAME INDEX

SUBJECT INDEX